LES
PARISIENNES

Also by Anne Sebba

That Woman: The Life of Wallis Simpson, Duchess of Windsor

LES PARISIENNES

How the Women of Paris Lived, Loved,
and Died Under Nazi Occupation

ANNE SEBBA

St. Martin's Press 〽 New York

www.stmartins.com

Library of Congress Cataloging-in-Publication Data

Names: Sebba, Anne, author.
Title: Les Parisiennes : how the women of Paris lived, loved, and died under
    Nazi occupation / Anne Sebba.
Description: First U.S. edition. | New York : St. Martin's Press, 2016. | "First
    published in Great Britain by Weidenfeld & Nicolson"—Title page verso. |
    Includes bibliographical references and index.
Identifiers: LCCN 2016020685| ISBN 9781250048592 (hardcover) | ISBN
    9781466849563 (e-book)
Subjects: LCSH: Women—France—Paris—History—20th century.
    | Women—France—Paris—Biography. | Paris (France)—
    History—1940–1944. | France—History—German occupation, 1940–
    1945. | Paris (France)—Biography. | Paris (France)—Social conditions—
    20th century. | Paris (France)—Politics and government—20th century.
    | World War, 1939–1945—Social aspects—France—Paris. | World
    War, 1939–1945—Influence. | BISAC: HISTORY / Europe / France. |
    BIOGRAPHY & AUTOBIOGRAPHY / Cultural Heritage.
Classification: LCC HQ1620.P2 S43 2016 | DDC 305.40944/361—dc23
LC record available at https://lccn.loc.gov/2016020685

Our books may be purchased in bulk for promotional, educational, or business use. Please contact your local bookseller or the Macmillan Corporate and Premium Sales Department at 1-800-221-7945, extension 5442, or by e-mail at MacmillanSpecialMarkets@macmillan.com.

First published in Great Britain by Weidenfeld & Nicolson, an imprint of The Orion Publishing Group Ltd, an Hachette UK company

First U.S. Edition: October 2016

10 9 8 7 6 5 4 3 2 1

For Thomas, Isabella, Sophia and Charlotte

'The last of the human freedoms – to choose one's attitude in any given set of circumstances, to choose one's own way. And there were always choices to make. Every day, every hour, offered the opportunity to make a decision, a decision which determined whether you would or would not submit to those powers which threatened to rob you of your very self, your inner freedom . . .'

Viktor Frankl, *Man's Search for Meaning*

INGRID BERGMAN/ILSA: 'Well, Rick, we'll always have Paris. Do you remember Paris?'

HUMPHREY BOGART/RICK: 'I remember every detail. You wore blue; the Germans wore grey.'

Casablanca

'One of the peculiarities of the present war is the exclusively danger-ously feminine role it imposes on women. Is it because of the total occupation of our territory, the omnipresence of an alien and virile multitude, that women are assuming the externals of gamines and the manners of pupils? I incriminate none of her ulterior motives, well knowing that she never exposes the best of herself. But the scarcity of her hair, the indiscretion of her curls, the inadequately long skirt open to both the wind and the casual glance, all these are errors in which French charm has committed too many provocations.'

Colette, *Paris from My Window*

'Définer Arlette? Elle est jusqu'au bout des doigts une Parisienne. Elle en a le charme, l'œil coquin, le velouté dans les manières en y ajoutant une nonchalance héritée probablement d'une aïeule, une de ces belles femmes qu'aimait à peindre Winterhalter.'

Pierre Combescot , Preface to *Une Vie pas comme une autre*

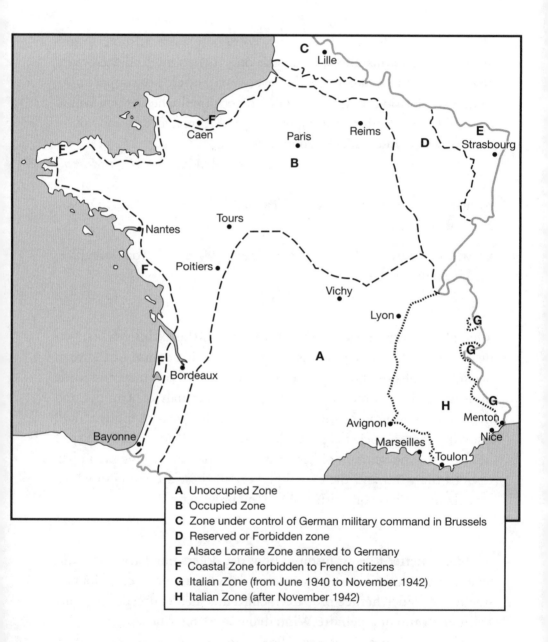

A Unoccupied Zone
B Occupied Zone
C Zone under control of German military command in Brussels
D Reserved or Forbidden zone
E Alsace Lorraine Zone annexed to Germany
F Coastal Zone forbidden to French citizens
G Italian Zone (from June 1940 to November 1942)
H Italian Zone (after November 1942)

CONTENTS

Prologue

Les Parisiennes

Paris, mid-July 2015, and the city is swelteringly hot. By 19 July, thunder is in the air. I am sitting on a temporary stage, waiting for the rain, enraptured by an unremarkable woman in her late eighties telling a most remarkable story. Annette Krajcer is one of the few surviving victims of the most notorious round-up in French twentieth-century history. In July 1942, when she was twelve, she and her mother and sister were arrested by French police and taken in buses to a Paris sports stadium, the Vélodrome d'Hiver, along with 13,000 others, including more than 4,000 children. After three days of being held in disgusting conditions with almost nothing to eat or drink and with totally inadequate sanitary facilities, they were crammed into cattle cars and taken to another camp, Pithiviers, fifty miles south of the capital. This was just a little better as they slept on straw-filled bunks and were given some meagre rations. But two weeks later, the girls' mother was taken away and they never saw her again. Abandoned, they were now taken back to Paris, to a holding camp in the suburb of Drancy. Most of the children who returned with them on this occasion did not survive much longer as they were shipped to Auschwitz and gassed. But Annette and her sister Leah were, miraculously, saved. A cousin who worked as a secretary in the camp saw their names on a list and managed to organize their liberation. They spent the next three years in hiding, but at the end of the war they were reunited with their father, who had been a prisoner of war working on a German farm in the Ardennes.

Today Annette is recounting those events to an audience that is mostly elderly but includes Parisian dignitaries and journalists. Her story is especially distressing because the mention of lists is a reminder of how the Jewish community was itself forced to compile names and addresses of its own members. She cannot, she says, pass a day without thinking of the other 4,000 children who did not have such useful cousins.

Also telling a story that oppressive morning is Séverine Darcque, a thirty-three-year-old teacher who owes her existence to Pierrette Pauchard, a farmer's widow from Burgundy recently declared one of the Righteous Among Nations (the official term used by the state of Israel to describe non-Jews who risked their lives during the Holocaust to save Jews from extermination by the Nazis). Pierrette was among those French men and women who put their own lives in danger to help Jews survive, and Séverine's dramatic story shows how courageously many ordinary French people behaved. Pierrette saved at least five Jewish children who grew up alongside her own, one of whom was an abandoned eighteen-month-old baby named Colette Morgenbesser. Séverine is Colette's granddaughter but thinks of herself as a descendant of Pierrette too.

The stadium no longer exists, but this ceremony is now held annually on a nearby site in the shadow of the Eiffel Tower following President Jacques Chirac's groundbreaking 1995 speech when he officially recognized French culpability for the 1942 round-up. The Vichy government, then headed by Pierre Laval, agreed to help the Nazi occupiers by delivering up thousands of foreign Jews, and their children born in France who were therefore French. The number of those who lived through the events being commemorated diminishes each year, but some of their children now attend to honour their parents' memory. In less than an hour, the two women making formal addresses have revealed some of the myriad narratives which make up the complex patchwork of experiences in France during *les Années Noires*, the Dark Years. In different ways they have both shown that 'the past' is not yet 'the past' in France. Above all they demonstrate how harshly the burden of decision so often fell on women, usually mothers, and how murky was the range of choices.

Echoes of the past continually resonate in modern-day France, because what happened here during the 1940s has left scars of such depth that many have not yet healed. There is still a fear among some that touching the scars may reopen them. Nearly eighty years after the conflict ended, I am frequently warned as I plan interviews and research for this book to bear in mind that what to me is history is

still the highly sensitive present for many; some people may not talk
to me. Nowhere was this more evident than in today's Vichy, the
spa town which became government headquarters after the fall of
France in 1940. The hotel which housed Marshal Pétain and many
other government officials for four years now serves as the town's
Tourist Information Office, yet the young staff working there when
I visited were unable to confirm any details of life in the town in
the 1940s, a period about which they apparently knew nothing. My
request to see the plaque, located inside Vichy's opera house, which
declares that it was there that on 10 July 1940 the National Assembly
voted full governing powers to Field Marshal Philippe Pétain, thus
ending France's Third Republic, was turned down. Bizarrely, the
plaque states that eighty *députés*, elected members of the National
Assembly, or Parliament, voted to 'affirm their attachment to the
Republic, their love for freedom, and their faith in victory [over Ger-
many]', not that 569 members did *not* affirm their attachment to the
Third Republic. Indeed, they condemned it, thus paving the way for
the Vichy regime, which governed the defeated country during the
Occupation.

On one occasion in Paris I found myself caught up in a demonstration as thousands of French had chosen that day, Mother's Day in
France, to protest against the recent legalization of gay marriage. The
events, bizarre in a modern nation renowned for its tolerance, resonated in a strange way for me because *la Journée de la Mère* had been
a matter of national political importance for Vichy France. Pétain
used such occasions to bolster the moral and cultural conservatism
of his authoritarian regime, glorifying the family as an institution
in which the man was head and the woman occupied her place by
virtue of being a mother. France's low birth rate had been a concern
for many years and, ironically, one of many reasons for welcoming
thousands of foreign Jews to France in previous decades had been to
help counterbalance this. Under Pétain, lessons in housekeeping, in
which girls had to learn how to make simple clothes and undertake
laundry, bleaching, ironing, cookery, nutrition and other aspects of
domestic hygiene for one hour minimum per week, became obligatory in all lycées and colleges up to the age of eighteen. For while
the world war was being fought, France was attempting a national

revolution, creating a society that would turn its back on republican values. The demonstration that I witnessed was largely peaceful, with the police estimating that about 150,000 people took part. But for me it was clear evidence of the persistence of the past in present-day France. Even today there are significant welfare advantages for mothers of three or more children.

During the last few years, several people I tried to talk to about their memories, or of how their family survived, simply refused to answer my emails or phone calls. Almost all who did agree and who had lived through *les Années Noires* began by telling me, 'Ah, c'est très compliqué . . .' Very often, once we started speaking, it became clear that the choices they made during this decade had much to do with what happened to them or their parents during the previous conflict, the First World War, or the Guerre de Quatorze (War of 1914) as it is called here. Memories of that war were often 'cultivated' by the French, preserved artefacts became relics as photos of battlefields and devastated towns acquired almost holy status and there remained a deep-seated mistrust of their German neighbour. Naughty French children in the 1920s and 1930s were often reprimanded with the words, 'If you don't behave, the *Boche* [offensive slang meaning a German soldier] will come and take you.'

But then, as the second war progressed and Paris felt eerily empty with few French men to be seen and almost no cars, other factors came into play. Many women in Paris responded positively to German men, who were usually polite, often cultured, and sometimes offered the only source of food. A lot of the women, including intellectuals and resisters, played on their femininity to get what they wanted or needed, sometimes using sex, sometimes being used for sex, and at all times concerned with their appearances and with looking fashionable. Having family cutlery melted down in order to create a stylish bag or brooch, or buying leg paint to simulate stockings, occasionally took precedence over finding food.

I want to examine in these pages what factors weighed most heavily on women, causing them to respond in a particular way to the harsh and difficult circumstances in which they found themselves. M. R. D. Foot, historian of the SOE as well as soldier, was well aware of how many women, often young teenage girls, were heavily involved from the earliest days in helping men escape. 'Evaders often found that they had to trust themselves entirely to women,' Foot wrote; 'and without the courage and devotion of its couriers and safe-house keepers, nearly all of them women, no escape line could keep going at all.' Why did they choose to risk their young lives and their families? I will use the word choice – what choices they made – while recognizing that not all of them had a real choice as defined by anyone living through the war years. For women, choice often meant more than simply how to live their own lives but how to protect their children and sometimes their elderly parents too. One interview was almost abruptly terminated when I asked the noted playwright Jean-Claude Grumberg if he could understand how his mother had made what I considered the unimaginably brave choice to pay a *passeuse*, a woman who promised to take him and his slightly older brother to a place of greater safety in the south of France. As added protection, his mother was not allowed to know where the children were in case she was arrested and forced to reveal this information. Grumberg was silent at first and then stared at me disbelievingly.

'La choix, c'est contestable,' he replied eventually.

Anyone who used the word 'choice' in the context of the situation facing his mother could not have grasped the complexity of life for a Romanian-born Jewish woman in occupied Paris after 1942, a woman whose husband had been arrested, who could not speak fluent French, who was forbidden to move around freely or even, on a scorchingly hot day, to buy her Jewish children a drink in certain places at a certain time, and who was caring for a sick mother-in-law.

He repeated: 'Choice? How can you ask me about choice?' But I persisted, apologizing for any unintended offence, because choices, however heart-wrenching, were indeed made by women, especially by women.

Sacha Josipovici, born in Egypt and travelling, she hoped, also to a place of greater safety with her child on false papers, from Nice to La Bourboule in central France without her husband, had decided that if the train was stopped 'and I was asked to account for myself I would most probably, despite my papers, say that I was Jewish. I felt that even though it would mean leaving you [her three-year-old son] with strangers, it was something I would have to do. There aren't many moments like that in life but I felt that this was one of them.' In the event she did not have to make that choice. Other women, travelling on false papers, hid compromising documents in their children's bags. I have met those children and would not like to say the actions were without consequences.

'You were not given the choice,' insists Jeannie, Vicomtesse de Clarens who, as Jeannie Rousseau, began her opposition to the Germans as soon as war was declared. 'I don't even understand the question,' she says with a rare clarity when asked why she risked her life. 'It was a moral obligation to do what you are capable of doing. As a woman you could not join the army but you could use your brain. It was a must. How could you not do it?' Other women were brutally honest in admitting that there was a 'taste for danger that drove us on . . . but above all it was the joy, the thrill of feeling useful, the camaraderie of battle in which all our weapons were born of love'.

And of course there were constantly lesser choices that had to be made. Was it collaborating to buy food on the black market if your children were thin, ill and vitamin deficient? Was sending your children to a cousin with a farm in the countryside acceptable? Was it a choice to walk out of a café or a restaurant if German soldiers walked in, or was that deliberately courting danger given that behaving disrespectfully could have fatal consequences? Were those who made up lists and saved children of relatives before they saved the children of strangers culpable? Or should one blame only those who forced them to create the lists in the first place?

I want the pages that follow to avoid black and white, good and evil, but instead to reveal constant moral ambiguity, like a kaleidoscope that can be turned in any number of ways to produce a different image. Such a multifaceted image is far from grey. Was everyone who remained in Paris, who carried on grinding the gears, pressing the buttons, stocking the shops and performing in theatres or nightclubs, in some way complicit in the German adventure of keeping Paris alive and alight? The unreal situation of 'occupation' is itself a perverting one, arguably more difficult morally than the predicament presented by war. Of course there are fewer casualties, but fear, shame, anger and the terrible feeling of powerlessness, together with the compulsion to do something and a complex and often heady mixture of hate and perhaps self-interest – not to speak of individual love affairs – confuse any straightforward response. I want to explore, with as little hindsight or judgement as I can muster – after all, we British did not suffer occupation so what right have any of us to judge? What were the possibilities? Here is one absolute: I think I would go to any lengths to save my children. A handful of women went to extraordinary lengths to save other people's children. But these are extremes and not all situations in the pages that follow are extremes offering absolute choices. The life that most of us engage in is a muddle, and that is what is so compelling for any writer or historian looking at France between 1939 and 1949, especially through the eyes of women. Turn the kaleidoscope one way and see women destroyed by the war; turn it the other and find women whose lives were enhanced with new meaning and fulfilment.

When I began this book a male historian suggested I spend hours in the subterranean Bibliothèque Nationale reading the diaries of men like Hervé Le Boterf and Jean Galtier-Boissière. But, important though these may be, I have tried to find an alternative, often quieter and frequently less well-known set of voices. I have relied on interviews with women who lived through the events, of necessity as children, as well as on diaries, letters, ration cards and memoirs of those no longer alive, both published and unpublished. I have watched intensely dramatic films, read hundreds of letters of denunciation, seen and touched hollow jewellery made with limited materials as well as cork or wooden-soled shoes, whose *clackety-clack* provided the soundtrack to the Occupation. Some voices weave in and out of the story, occasionally in different locations, others disappear entirely from the narrative either through death or because they leave France. It was always going to be hard finding women who admitted that they had worked for a German victory (although there are some) and so occasionally I have relied on a male account of a situation pertaining to women or used historical records of women who betrayed.

It has been exciting and rewarding to discover that women's influence and activities during these years were considerably greater than might be expected from the public roles they were allowed to play in society at that time. Before 1939 women in French society were often politically invisible, without a vote and needing permission from husbands or fathers to work or own property. Yet women were actively using weapons in the resistance, hosting evaders on the run, delivering false identity papers, at the same time as they were performing all the old familiar tasks of cooking, shopping and caring for their homes. Women were now in charge, looking after the elderly as well as the children, duties which often prevented their own escape, and sometimes they were holding down a job too. Shortages and lack of refrigeration forced women to queue, for an average of four hours a day, to gather enough to feed the family they were being encouraged to bring into the world. Some women resorted to collaborating and some were straightforwardly victims, but others were simply bystanders, caught in the crossfire, and it is their role that occasionally proved crucial.

One more thing: the word 'Parisienne' may summon up to many the image of a chic, slim woman who wears fashionably elegant clothes and is alluring to men. Undeniably, women in Paris used fashion to defy the occupier in a small way, perhaps by adopting culottes to ride bicycles when the fuel ran out or by making ceramic tricolore buttons. Yet this is not a book about fashion, even though fashion was important both to Parisiennes themselves and to the German occupiers. But, while admitting that the glamorous description fits some of the women in this book – women who wore designer suits while risking their lives to deliver vital information, women who believed that wearing an outrageously large hat was a form of resistance – I am giving it a wider meaning. Many typically Parisian women found themselves, through necessity, living or subsisting outside Paris, while others in this story, though remaining in the city, were not Parisiennes in the accepted use of the word. If I had been in any doubt about using the term to describe a woman not living in the city but imprisoned in a camp, wearing rags, with sores on her skin, scars from lashings and unwashed hair, I felt justified when I learned that, instead of eating the ounce or so of fat she was given daily, she massaged it into her hands after concluding that these needed preserving more than her stomach. That seemed to me the reasoning of a true Parisienne.

PART ONE

WAR

1939

PARIS ON THE EDGE

When the future looks uncertain some women get married, others get divorced, yet more buy jewels and hundreds go into hiding. Just a few, a very few, give such opulent balls that the world seems for a moment to have tilted on its axis.

On 1 July 1939 Elsie de Wolfe, an American-born interior decorator and failed actress, gave one of the grandest and most bizarre parties ever hosted by a private individual. Elsie, by then aged eighty-one and married for the previous thirteen years, much to everyone's surprise, to the retired British diplomat Sir Charles Mendl, had shown her mettle during the First World War when she had remained in Paris volunteering in a hospital and winning the Croix de guerre and the Légion d'honneur for her relief work with gas-burn cases. Now she nursed a passion for parties. Owner of the newly fabulous Villa Trianon, a Louis XV chateau in the grounds of the Palace of Versailles, Lady Mendl was the best-known American hostess in Europe. She had devoted the last thirty-five years of her life – both as Lady Mendl and long before when she was the close companion of the theatrical agent Elisabeth Marbury – to the villa's restoration and redecoration (it had been unlived in for many years). Giving lavish and original parties there was now her life's work. She had recently created a dance pavilion with a specially imported spring-loaded floor, and had installed glass walls so that the views to the gardens were unimpeded; she had also had the space wired for sound under the supervision of her friend Douglas Fairbanks.

Throughout the 1930s, Elsie had organized a succession of dinner dances, bals masqués, themed parties. She was credited with inventing murder-mystery parties and, occasionally, she gave small parties for about forty close friends. As she entered her ninth decade her energy seemed undimmed. She still worked at her diet as well as her daily exercises and was so well known for her handstands that Cole Porter immortalized her in his song 'Anything Goes'. As Wallis Simpson, her friend and admirer, said of her: 'She mixes people like a cocktail – and the result is sheer genius.'

For the previous year Elsie had been planning the most spectacular ball yet. Ever since the previous summer when she had thrown an extravagant circus ball featuring acrobats, she had determined that next time she would outdo herself by repeating the theme but with elephants as well as clowns, tightrope-walkers and jugglers. She may have been inspired by a visit to India, or perhaps she even remembered an occasion thirty years before when she had seen elephants walking sedately through Boston. Whatever the inspiration, she knew that the elephants would create an incomparable social buzz. However precarious the world situation, she was not going to abandon her plans for an unforgettable night of entertainment.

It was a balmy evening on 1 July 1939 when shortly after 9 p.m. the chauffeur-driven Mercedes and Rolls-Royces and numerous taxis began disgorging the 700 or so guests at the Boulevard Saint-Antoine entrance to the Petit Trianon. Although the men in their elegant white tie and tails may have felt the heat, most of the women, in outfits designed by Coco Chanel, Elsa Schiaparelli, Jeanne Lanvin and Lucien Lelong, needed cloaks or jackets before the party was over at dawn.

Elsie herself draped a long, shocking-pink cape over her shoulders. Beneath the cape she wore a magnificent ivory silk gown emblazoned with silver sequins and jewelled butterflies designed by her favourite couturier, Mainbocher, who was now basking in international fame as the designer of the pale blue wedding gown worn by Wallis Simpson for her marriage to the recently abdicated Duke of Windsor. It was Elsie who had effected the introduction to the couturier. Although she was small in stature Elsie cut a striking figure as a circus ringleader with a diamond and aquamarine Cartier tiara in her hair. Brandishing a whip 'as if to defy the fates', she walked bravely between the legs of the elephants before leading eight white ponies and dogs through their paces in a circus ring laid out on the lawn. In addition, she had hired a blind strolling accordion player, a Hawaiian guitarist who floated on a boat in the swimming pool and three orchestras in rotation playing in the dance pavilion. In one part of the gardens she had placed a champagne bar in a small circular tent with a striped roof set up around a fat tree trunk; not far away was a hot buffet which stayed open until 5 a.m., serving (unusually for Elsie who did not place much store by offering food to her guests) lamb chops, scrambled eggs, cakes and even more champagne.

In social terms, the surreal occasion was considered a triumph. Everyone talked about the magnificence of the gardens with their unusual topiary as much as they praised the originality of the entertainments – although some complained about the inevitable smell given off by the animals and about their need regularly to relieve themselves, a detail left out by *Vogue* and others in their coverage of the spectacular event. The magazines were no more interested in the guests – aristocrats, diplomats, dukes, duchesses, princesses, writers, designers and artists, many of whom will reappear in the following pages – describing the clothes they wore and the jewels adorning their gowns. One of the most beautiful was a stunning Brazilian woman, Aimée de Sotomayor, widely considered one of the most glamorous women of the twentieth century, whose smiling photograph from that night appeared in *Vogue* a month later. With gardenias strewn in her blonde hair, she was wearing one of the first dresses designed by the then little-known Christian Dior, albeit not yet under his own name label. Christian Dior himself was, according to Aimée, 'a little sad' not to have been invited. However, Aimée's style made a big impression on one of the other guests, the textile magnate Marcel Boussac. After the war, Boussac was to finance Christian Dior in creating his own label and design house.

Few among *le tout Paris* were concerned that night with what was going on in the rest of Europe because they believed that France would not be seriously affected, or at any rate not for long. Surely the seemingly impregnable Maginot Line, a series of concrete fortifications along the border with Germany, would protect the country? Throughout the spring and early summer the social season had continued as normal; in fact there was a sense of recklessness in the determination to celebrate which none in this high-society group considered excessive or out of place.

In April, Hélène Arpels, a former model born in Monte Carlo to

Russian parents now married to Louis Arpels, youngest of the brothers in the jewellery firm Van Cleef & Arpels, was photographed with friends at Longchamp races, all wearing stunning designer outfits. A month later Hélène was snapped at the supremely smart Hippodrome de Chantilly in a dress by Maggy Rouff, a designer intensely proud of her royal clientele, and a white hat by Reboux, the house that had created Wallis Simpson's wedding-day halo hat two years before.

Since the death in 1938 of Alfred Van Cleef, the family jewellery business had been run by his daughter Renée Puissant, a young widow. Renée had been briefly married to Emile Puissant, a racing driver, whom she met through her mother, Esther, his nurse during the First World War. When Emile was killed in a car crash in 1926, the administration of the firm passed to Renée.

Just as Parisian couture was flourishing, so was high art. That July, serious music-lovers travelled to Bayreuth, the town dedicated to the performance of Wagner operas, to admire the first French woman ever to sing Isolde there. Performing this role was considered a huge triumph for the Parisian-born Germaine Lubin, who seemed to have reached the pinnacle of her career. Wagnerian heroines were invariably German, and the French were proud of her achievement. Germaine Lubin had been educated at the Collège Sévigné, a well-known private girls' school in Paris founded in 1880, intending to train as a doctor like her father. But she was persuaded to study singing instead at the Paris Conservatoire where Gabriel Fauré, deeply impressed, encouraged her. Her fine voice as well as her statuesque beauty ensured an early success singing roles from operas by Strauss as well as by lesser-known French composers. But, since 1930, she had found a niche tackling most of the great Wagnerian roles including Sieglinde in *Die Walküre*, Elsa in *Lohengrin*, Brünnhilde in the *Ring* Cycle and Kundry in *Parsifal*, and it was for these that she was renowned.

Although married in 1913 to the French poet Paul Géraldy, with whom three years later she had a son, the marriage was not a success and came to an end in 1926. Lubin was always surrounded by a posse of male admirers, including Marshal Philippe Pétain, whom she first met in 1918 when he was at the height of his fame as the hero of Verdun. A soldier famous for his womanizing, he was immediately smitten and even proposed marriage to Lubin though she was not free.* Instead, the pair conducted a warm correspondence and remained friends until Pétain's death in 1951. But Lubin was always less popular with female colleagues such as the Australian soprano Marjorie Lawrence, another Wagnerian, who found the Parisienne arrogant and overrated.

'War between me and Lubin was on,' Lawrence wrote in her memoirs, describing a moment of upstaging when the pair took their bows at the end of a performance of *Lohengrin* in 1933, in which Lawrence sang the role of Ortrud. 'Lubin refused to shake my hand when I extended it to her and, being more practised than I in the tricks of the opera trade, she was able to edge herself in front of me and behave as if all the cheering was for her.'†

At Bayreuth, Lubin established friendships with several members of the Wagner family and was even complimented by Hitler himself (a photograph of the pair together would eventually seal her fate) when he told her she was the finest Isolde that he had heard. Lubin hoped to follow up her triumph by taking the role to the Metropolitan Opera in New York, having been recommended to the Met's management by the Norwegian soprano Kirsten Flagstad. However, she could not travel during the war and was never to sing in the United States.

Also at Bayreuth that month were two English sisters, Unity and Diana Mitford, there at the personal invitation of Hitler. As soon as they arrived the girls were presented with two bouquets, one from Herr Wagner, the composer's grandson, and one from the Mayor of Munich. On 2 August, the final day of the festival, Hitler invited them for lunch and Diana remembered him remarking that, as England seemed determined on war, it was now inevitable.

But an inability to face reality was not exclusively the preserve of

---

* Pétain was over sixty when he finally married, in 1920, Mme Eugénie Hardon, one of his mistresses, a divorcee who already had a child. Ironically, while Vichy prioritized raising the birthrate and protecting the family, he did not, as far as is known, father any children of his own.

† The rivalry ceased in 1941 after Lawrence tragically contracted polio and left Paris.

the fashionable and wealthy. The writer Colette may have been at the height of her fame in the late 1930s but she was famously indifferent to politics throughout her life. By 1935, aged sixty-two, despite being married to a Jewish journalist, Maurice Goudeket, she still did not wield her pen to warn of the dangers of Hitler's policies in Germany or of the failure of the Popular Front government and the rise of the far right in France. She was constantly writing – mostly novellas at this stage of her career – and also, in the first weeks of the war, giving broadcasts to Americans about the atmosphere in Paris which involved her travelling across the city in the early hours of the morning, often in a state of *déshabillée*. The two major pieces of journalism that stirred her in 1939 were both about unhinged murderers: one a toothless woman brothel-keeper in Morocco who tortured and killed her child prostitutes, believing that females had no value; the other, a man with many aliases who gruesomely murdered no fewer than five people, seemingly at random, for small amounts of money. The latter, Eugen Weidmann, was to become notorious as the last person guillotined in public in France, although the guillotine, that peculiarly French invention, would still be used during the war. Colette, appointed special reporter for *Paris-Soir* during the trial, devoted much time and thought to the brilliant investigative essay she wrote on Weidmann's spiritual capacity for truth. Why did she not find it equally interesting to study the rabble-rousing tyrant from Munich about to unleash mass murder? Was it because, in Colette's worldview, war and politics were the follies of men? The female self, struggling with the pain and ties of love, remained her natural subject until war affected her personally. Only then did she become engaged. Perhaps more remarkable, as the *New Yorker* correspondent Janet Flanner wrote at the time, was that in 1939, even as France stood on the brink of war with Germany, 'Weidmann's being a German was not considered an additional crime.'

Today, observing these events with the advantage of hindsight, one can only marvel at the blind sense of unreality shown by most of those that summer who were managing to live a carefree life dominated by concern about being seen in the latest fashionable hat. On the Champs-Elysées, where the expensive hotels were filled with American and English tourists and the pavement cafés were thriving, it was impossible not to notice the extraordinary confections that passed as hats merely because they sat on women's heads, creations both tiny and huge, decorated with feathers, flowers and jewels and worn with more than a touch of insouciance. 'The Parisian women,' according to Elsa Schiaparelli, 'as if feeling it was their last chance, were particularly chic.' Flanner had a slightly different perspective on the phenomenon. 'It has taken the threat of war to make the French loosen up and have a really swell and civilised good time,' she wrote.

There were exceptions, however. As the *New York Times* reported on its political pages, the circus ball had provided the setting for the second meeting that day between the French Foreign Minister, Georges Bonnet, and the German Ambassador in Paris, Count Johannes von Welczeck. The French minister had given warning that his country would not stand idly by, as it had over Czechoslovakia only a few months earlier, if Germany invaded Poland. Just two weeks after the ball, on 14 July, Paris celebrated the 150th anniversary of the storming of the Bastille and the French Revolution. How many of those who took part in the long-planned pageants, military parades and days of dancing in the streets saw the irony of festivities marking the birth of democracy and the end of tyranny in 1789? Clearly, the deeper significance of the date was not overlooked by everyone. The extent to which the legacy of the Revolution was accepted by the whole of France was about to be severely tested.

Thousands of Spanish republican refugees, who had fled over the border into France after the Battle of Catalonia, were only too aware that fascist tyranny, in the shape of General Franco, had not been beaten in their own country. Some 17,000 were now living in appalling conditions in a hastily constructed camp at Gurs in south-west France, one of the first of about fifty camps on French soil where non-native refugees were 'concentrated'. The internees had created an orchestra and constructed a sports field; on 14 July 1939 they arranged themselves in military formation in the field and gave a boisterous rendition of 'La Marseillaise'; they then took part in sports presentations and various choral and instrumental concerts. From the start, Gurs was overwhelmed by the numbers of internees sent there. In 1939, at the outbreak of war, it took in German prisoners of war and French nationals with suspect political views and later, after the

German defeat, Jews. Those held at Gurs were neither tortured nor beaten, but food was scarce and often inedible and conditions barely tolerable. There was no sanitation, no running water other than constant rain, no plumbing nor proper drainage as the buildings were unfinished, no one imagining that the situation would continue for long. There was a separate women's camp at Gurs* and initially the commander permitted some imprisoned women to rent a horse and cart and leave the camp to buy provisions.

Crane Brinton, a brilliant Harvard history professor whose particular expertise lay in the study of revolutions, wrote with great prescience in an essay published on 15 July 1939 that he saw much metaphorical rain ahead. As he contemplated the 150th anniversary of the storming and taking of the Bastille by the people of Paris, he predicted 'changes which, in pure logic, are quite antithetical to what the men of 1789 were striving for . . . Democracy is in for harder sledding than it had throughout most of the nineteenth century.'

On 1 September, two months after Elsie Mendl's surreal circus ball, Germany invaded Poland and democracy was indeed tested. General mobilization of all young men between the ages of eighteen and thirty-five was announced in France immediately, and on 3 September France and Britain declared themselves at war.

Several of those who had attended the circus ball fled the capital as soon as they could. The Duke and Duchess of Windsor swiftly made plans to leave Paris and return to England. But as no palace, castle or royal residence was put at their disposal by the British royal family they were forced to stay at the Sussex house of their loyal friend and the Duke's erstwhile best man 'Fruity' Metcalfe. Since it was clear that the British authorities were not going to provide them with a wartime home, like many others they soon returned to Paris and continued to live with uncertainty, watching and waiting. Many others among *le tout Paris*, finding themselves without servants, moved into the Ritz Hotel, where they were observed by the playwright Noël Coward, who remarked that September when he started

---

* For a while the artist Charlotte Salomon, the philosopher Hannah Arendt, and Dora Benjamin, sister of Walter, were all incarcerated here.

working in the city for the British government, 'Paris is beautifully "War gay". Nobody ever dresses and everybody collects at Maxim's.' Coward found himself a beautiful flat in the Place Vendôme, exactly opposite the Ritz, 'where they have the most well prepared air raid shelter'. The Ritz shelter, frequented by some of the best-dressed women in Paris, was soon famous for its fur rugs and Hermès sleeping bags. Gabrielle 'Coco' Chanel, the influential designer who, as soon as war broke out, closed her Rue Cambon boutique, thereby throwing hundreds of women out of work, declared that this was 'not a time for fashion' – a decision that seemed deeply unpatriotic. She then moved into a suite at the Ritz for the duration of the war. Although the Chanel perfume and jewellery business remained open, she was not the owner, a situation that she was to dispute after the war.

Soon Chanel, approaching sixty, was openly consorting with Baron Hans Günther von Dincklage, a tall, blond and handsome German officer in the Abwehr or German Military Intelligence, known as Spatz. Spatz had been previously married for fifteen years to Maximiliane von Schoenebeck (who was known as Catsy), the Jewish half-sister of the writer Sybille Bedford. Sybille later settled in England. But in 1935, as soon as the Nuremberg laws, the anti-Jewish statutes, came into force, Spatz quietly divorced Catsy while remaining on friendly terms with her, so that few people realized they had parted. It was several months later, after another affair, that he took up with Chanel. The hapless Catsy had been briefly interned in 1938 'pour espionnage', having been under surveillance for the previous two years partly because she was a German alien. Described by French military intelligence in 1939 as 'Baronne Dincklage', she was ordered in November to be interned again, as her presence in France apparently represented a danger, presumably owing to Dincklage's well-known Nazi connections. In the early 1930s, when the couple lived together at Sanary-sur-Mer, a resort to the west of Toulon stuffed with German refugees, rumours were rife about his espionage activities, but there is no evidence that Catsy, who was punished, was involved in them.

Elsie Mendl insisted on sitting out the rest of 1939 in Paris, even though her husband, Sir Charles, in spite of his protestations about having no religion, was keenly aware that in Nazi eyes he was Jewish and therefore in danger. One evening, Elsie invited Noël Coward to dine. Fellow guests included the Windsors, who were in fine defeatist form. The Duke held forth about the coming battle, insisting that 'the German spirit was very important because they are awfully dogged and capable of really surprising endurance in the face of practically anything, which is very important'. Not many in Paris in 1939 shared his views on German superiority.

While most of the German army was engaged in Poland, and as long as French soil had not yet been violated, many Parisians could close their eyes to the imminent dangers because they were convinced they would swiftly repel the Germans. For them, war seemed a distant event concerning other people. Hence this period soon came to be known in France as *la drôle de guerre* and in England as the 'phoney war'. The playwright and avant-garde artist Jean Cocteau was missing his lover, who had been mobilized and was serving at the front. So when one of his friends offered to drive him there, he accepted with alacrity, ignoring any risks, entranced by the prospect of a clandestine lovers' meeting.

The friend was Violette Morris, a lesbian former athlete who ran a car-parts store and therefore had access to transport. Yet Morris, an eccentric outsider with dangerous opinions, then living on a houseboat on the Seine with an actress lover, was not someone to tangle with. This convent-educated, former boxer and javelin-thrower had, in 1928, been refused a licence to participate in the forthcoming Olympics by the Fédération Française Sportive Féminine (FFSF – French Women's Athletic Federation) largely because of complaints about her overtly public lesbian lifestyle. With her cropped hair, Morris had been dressing as a man since 1919 and was a heavy smoker, considered unacceptable in female society at the time. Morris appealed against the ban, and, when she lost, had both her breasts removed, apparently so that she could sit more comfortably in a racing car. Although she was a talented athlete excelling in many sports and had served as a nurse on the Somme in the Great War, she increasingly felt an outcast from French society, declaring: 'We live in a country made rotten by money and scandals . . . governed by phrasemongers, schemers and cowards. This land of little people is not worthy of survival. One day, its decline will lead its people to the ranks of slavery but me, if I'm still here, I will not become a slave. Believe me, it's not in my temperament.'

At the end of 1935 Morris was approached by the Nazis and invited at the personal request of Hitler to visit Germany for the 1936 Berlin Olympics, where she was treated to much fanfare. She retained her links with the Nazis in disgust at her treatment by the French. Then, in 1937, she killed a man but escaped a murder charge on grounds of self-defence. For Cocteau, an artist who claimed to be apolitical, to be seen in the same car with such a person was risky indeed, just as it was for Morris to drive him there since neither of them had a pass for the front.

Clearly, French society of the 1930s could not accommodate Violette Morris, who, unable to perform in the international sporting competitions in which she excelled, soon found a place for herself among the seedy petty criminals and German admirers of the extreme right. Exactly what Morris subsequently did to help the Germans and whether her life of collaboration turned to treason is the subject of academic debate. But, as the phoney war came to an end, Violette Morris was one of those on the fringes who found a home as she edged closer to the Gestapo.

There were thousands of others in Paris that year, guests neither at the circus ball nor at any of the many other summer extravaganzas, neither concert- nor opera-goers, participants neither in the Bastille Day celebrations nor in outings to Deauville, the fashionable resort favoured by so many Parisians – just ordinary men and women for whom the insecurity of 1939 had turned into a nightmare long before 3 September. Some Parisiennes – those who had already had their lives turned upside down for the past few years – were not heedless of the current dangers. Miriam Sandzer, aged sixteen when she arrived in Paris in 1930 with her family from Poland, had been visiting the Préfecture de Police in Paris almost daily since 1936, trying to help refugees regularize their situation as they flooded in from Poland, Germany and other countries threatened by Hitler. Her father owned a lingerie factory in the 19th arrondissement and, above it, had founded a small synagogue. Miriam's job, in addition to

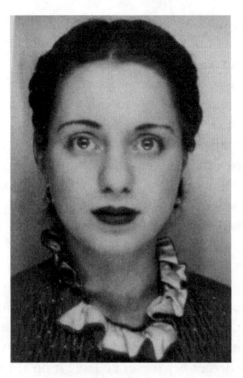

Miriam Sandzer in 1936, aged twenty-two, looking exotic and strong-willed

working long hours in the factory, was to try and arrange papers for the refugees, some of whom arrived with little more than a change of clothes, while others had jewellery to sell, but all were suffering from having nowhere to stay. Refugees could neither register in a hotel nor sleep rough because they risked interrogation from passing police-men asking randomly, 'Vos papiers, s'il vous plaît.' If a passport with a valid entry visa could not be produced, or if anything looked ques-tionable, the individual would be detained in a police station until deported. The Sandzer family, deeply involved in helping foreign Jews to settle and find accommodation, could be under no illusions about the gloom ahead. Sometimes they welcomed a refugee family sleeping on mattresses in their own spare room, or persuaded friends to do likewise, until temporary permits could be arranged and the exiles could legitimately stay in a hotel. When more accommodation was needed, M. Sandzer paid the next-door brothel-keeper to vacate his premises for a year so they could use his twenty-three rooms to house refugees. Miriam had got to know the Chef de Police rather well over recent months and was learning fast 'how corrupt these people were, how money talks in every language . . . with a bribe it was possible to extend their temporary permits until such time as they were able to secure an entry visa to an overseas destination'.

But the endless quest for life-saving papers was becoming harder all the time. As the stream of fugitives kept swelling, more and more tasks fell to Miriam, both in the factory and at the police station. Her elder brother, Jack, had left Paris to live with his wife and baby in Honfleur, her mother was occupied with Miriam's much younger brother, as well as with an elderly mother, and was cooking for large numbers of transient people, so Miriam not only became buyer for the business but also worked at cutting, sewing and designing the garments they produced. However, for the previous four years she had been engaged to Ben, the son of close family friends from Poland, who was now living in England. In 1939 Ben came to Paris and begged her to marry him and leave for London. 'But how could I leave my parents when a war was going to come? How could I just go?' she later wrote. In addition, having spent so much of her time organizing travel permits for others, she now found that her own were invalid. She could not travel as her Polish passport had expired and, in order for it to be valid for renewal, she required a red stamp which showed she had been to Poland in the last five years, which she had not. When she went to have it renewed it was confiscated. Marriage was her only hope of escape, but Ben, convinced from his London vantage point that there would be a long and devastating war ahead, had already volunteered in 1938 and now could not get enough leave for the two weeks necessary to fulfil the residency requirements in order to obtain a wedding licence in France. Like so many other young women in Paris, Miriam Sandzer was doubly trapped, both by her sense of duty to family and by the interminable complications of documentation.

Anyone who had been reading newspapers in the previous year would have been aware of the true situation – how at Munich in 1938 British Prime Minister Neville Chamberlain and French premier Edouard Daladier had avoided going to war over Czechoslovakia, insisting that by agreeing to Nazi demands they had achieved 'peace in our time'. Although half a million people had greeted Daladier euphorically at Le Bourget airport in the belief that war had been averted, others recognized that this was little more than a breathing space. In Britain it was not long before the infamous prime ministerial waving of a piece of paper at Croydon airport was revealed to be meaningless. *Kristallnacht* had, after all, started on a Parisian pretext: the shooting two days previously of a German diplomat, Ernst vom Rath, at the Embassy in Paris by a young Jewish teenager, Herschel Grynszpan. When on the night of 9–10 November 1938, thugs viciously attacked Jewish shops and businesses throughout Germany, not only were windows and store fronts shattered but with them any illusions which some still held that Hitler could be satisfied merely with the Sudetenland. It became increasingly difficult for Jewish or political refugees to escape from the Reich. On 15 March 1939 Hitler's forces invaded and occupied Czechoslovakia while France and Britain stood by. But the invasion of Poland, six months later, could not be tolerated. There was little to cheer about at the start of hostilities because memories of the Great War were still too raw.

Mobilization began immediately. The French government telephoned its chosen young men or sent private messengers to their homes, and posted notices announcing *Appel Immédiat*. There was general chaos and an oppressive worry as plans were suddenly made or changed without warning. The nineteen-year-old Jacqueline de La Rochebrochard, who hailed from a large family of old Breton nobility, had been planning her wedding to Lieutenant Joseph d'Alincourt for later that year. But, given only a few hours' notice of his departure for a post in eastern France, 'Without hesitation, we decided to marry at once. It was already late at night. We awakened the mayor. He agreed to officiate in the little town hall that also served as the village school. Early the next day our parish priest celebrated the wedding mass, and Joseph left immediately.'

The greatest emotion was seen at railway stations as men travelling to their regiments said goodbye to their mothers, fathers, wives and children. Station buffets now operated with self-service, a new phenomenon, as most waiters had been called up; there were also Red Cross workers doling out milk and dry bread to children, while Boy Scouts tried to help refugees with luggage. Although actual fighting still seemed distant to those in Paris, in reality there was nothing at all phoney about the next few months as far as Hitler and his generals were concerned; the Germans were training reservists and rushing equipment to the various fronts while the Nazi–Soviet Pact of August 1939, still being digested with horror by the Allies, as well as by many European communists, neutralized the possibility of Germany being attacked in the east.

Since 1933, when Hitler had come to power and introduced laws preventing Jews and others from leading normal lives, refugees from Germany, Austria and eastern Europe had been escaping in whatever way they could to find work or a home. Many trusted that in France at least, the first country in Europe to emancipate its Jewish population, they would find refuge. But alongside the longstanding revolutionary ideals and declarations of human rights which underpinned French philosophical thinking, the country had had a long history of anti-Semitism which had never entirely disappeared and which, from time to time, flared up angrily. The Dreyfus affair, which lasted approximately from 1894 to 1904, had left deep-rooted scars in France and, even though anti-Semitism subsided in the 1920s – partly because it was hard to accuse Jews of not being patriotic when so many had given their lives fighting for France in the First World War – it revived again in the 1930s. This time it was fuelled by the renewed influx of foreign Jews fleeing the Nazis, which came on top of the earlier wave of immigration of mostly poor Jews from the east escaping pogroms at the beginning of the century. In 1936 France had its first Jewish Prime Minister, Léon Blum, serving at the head of a Popular Front coalition. Blum introduced several important social reforms, including paid holidays for workers, and he was also (to an extent) a champion of women's rights. But although three women served in his cabinet, women in France still did not have the vote, nor the right to have a bank account in their own name. Blum's tenure in office was short-lived and he resigned in 1937, unable successfully to tackle the country's economic problems. The anti-Semitic far right, not afraid to brandish the slogan 'Better Hitler than Blum', was now able to win over elements of mainstream conservatives and socialists not previously associated with anti-Semitism, denouncing the alleged Jewish influence which, they argued, was not only pushing France into a war against Germany, against the country's best interests, but also allowing the country to become 'the dump bin of Europe'.

At the beginning of the war the number of Jews in France was approximately 330,000 compared with 150,000 in the interwar period. In Paris alone the number had risen from some 75,000 before 1914 to 150,000 in the 1930s. This increase fed the latent anti-Semitism in France and helped stimulate the growth of a right-wing fascist press. In addition to the Catholic and royalist *Action Française* of Charles Maurras (who led a movement of the same name), the three main journals were the weekly *Gringoire*, edited by Horace de Carbuccia, *Candide* and *Je suis partout*, the latter being the most openly anti-Semitic of all. By the end of 1936 the circulation of *Gringoire* had risen dramatically from 640,000 at the beginning of the year to 965,000. In February 1939, *Je suis partout*, where Robert Brasillach was editor in chief from 1937 to 1943, devoted an entire issue to an attack on Jewish doctors and medical students in France.

But there were inconsistencies. *Gringoire*, *Candide* and *Je suis partout* all prided themselves on the amount of space they devoted to literary criticism as well as political commentary. For example, alongside a diatribe against Léon Blum, *Gringoire* published the work of Irène Némirovsky, the Russian Jewish novelist who had become something of a darling of the right-wing press after her novel *David Golder*, the story of a greedy Jewish banker with an unfaithful wife and demanding daughter, had achieved enormous success in 1929 before being turned swiftly into a film. Brasillach, as well as the literary critic of *Gringoire*, greatly admired Némirovsky. Yet in 1938 Brasillach called for Jews from foreign countries to be considered 'as aliens and to place in opposition to their naturalization the most imposing of obstacles'.

In June 1939, when Irène revealed in an interview, 'How could I write such a thing? If I were to write *David Golder* now I would do it quite differently . . . The climate is quite changed!', she clearly understood that the establishment had not embraced her after all, that she was merely tolerated. Yet by 1939 she had been living in France for twenty years, ever since her family had fled Russia after the Revolution. French was her language of choice, the language which she had spoken since childhood, which she had studied at the Sorbonne and in which she now wrote. France was her country of choice. She wanted to be a French (not Russian nor Jewish) writer, writing about the French bourgeoisie. In 1926 she married a banker, Michel Epstein, a fellow Russian Jew whom she had met in France, and by 1939 the couple had two daughters, Denise, born in 1929, and Elisabeth, born in 1937, both French citizens by virtue of their birthplace. With her elegant clothes and fine seventh-floor apartment in the Avenue Constant Coquelin near Les Invalides, as well as a French nanny for the children, a maid and a cook, she was to all outward appearances a true Parisienne with a lifestyle largely paid for by her literary earnings. Yet Irène and her husband were actually foreigners who did not even apply for naturalization until 1938, even though Irène had been eligible since 1921, three years after the beginning of her stay in the country. Michel's formal request to the Service des Naturalisations de la Préfecture de Police was supported by letters from his employers, the Banque du Pays du Nord, as well as from some of Irène's impeccable literary admirers. Yet they heard nothing in response. In April 1939 they were asked to produce documents already submitted, yet by September, when they had still heard nothing, they were told that the delay was caused by 'circumstances' – that is, war. Their request had effectively been ignored, a rejection from which Irène suffered deeply. They were now stateless.

Earlier that year Némirovsky and her family had converted to Catholicism, with the baptism celebrated on 2 February in the old chapel of the Abbaye Sainte-Marie de Paris. It may not have been a deeply spiritual act but she had never identified herself as Jewish (she had been married in a synagogue, she maintained, purely to please Michel's father) and felt genuine affinity towards Christianity. Presumably Irène also saw the conversion, in a world climate of increasingly virulent anti-Semitism, as a protective measure for the whole family.

In August 1939, following the Nazi–Soviet Pact, Michel started to worry that he and his wife might be viewed not merely as stateless but, worse, as Russian and therefore as enemies of France. In addition, if he lost his job in Paris, they might need to rely solely on Irène's earnings for the entire family. He therefore wrote to her publishers asking for support and received a warm but useless letter in reply. The Epstein family then took their summer holiday in Hendaye, on the Basque coast, but in September, as soon as war was declared, Irène sent her daughters out of Paris to stay with the family of the nurse she had employed for the last ten years, Cécile Michaud, at Issy-l'Evêque, a small village some four hours to the south-east of Paris. During the first winter of the war, Irène came often to visit her daughters but did not move herself. There was, she felt, no need to leave Paris as yet.

That summer, when war was finally declared, many French families were on holiday or had children away at camp without their parents. It had been an especially hot summer and Claire Chevrillon, an English teacher at the Collège Sévigné, was in the mountains of the Drôme, at Valcroissant, helping direct a scout camp throughout August. The camp took a hundred little boys used to a suburban life in Paris and, by transplanting them into wild valleys and mountains for a month, tried to teach them to appreciate the beauty and dangers of nature. Claire, whose father André Chevrillon was one of the country's foremost literary critics and whose mother came from a well-to-do, assimilated Jewish family, understood immediately the significance of the announcement of general mobilization. Her family had been aware for months of the dangers of Nazi doctrines spreading across Europe. Now, as parents were furiously sending telegrams to request the immediate return of their children to Paris, Claire's fellow Director at the resort left immediately to become an army nurse. Claire single-handedly closed down the camp in twenty-four frantic hours before depositing the children with their relieved parents at the Gare de Lyon. 'This,' she remembered thinking, 'is the end of happy life.'

Throughout France, women were rapidly trying to digest what war would mean for them. To many people, it was immediately clear that it was women, even without the right to vote and, for married women, without the right to own or control their own property, who would be playing a pivotal role in the forthcoming drama. One of the arguments used to exclude women from participating in French elections was that their economic dependency would prevent them from making free choices. In the early twentieth century, with continuing battles between republicanism and the Catholic Church, it was further argued that the duties of mother and wife would be incompatible with exercising the right to vote. Only since 1938 had they been given the right to take on a job outside the home without their husband's or father's permission. There were already some mutterings that this might give them inflated ideas or, as one senator declared, 'If, because of the hostilities, a woman might be called upon to play a role outside her normal attributes she should be aware that this is only as an exceptional measure.' This was a vain and desperate wish, of course, on the old senator's part. Nonetheless the laws, first forbidding then encouraging married women to work, were deeply revealing of the conflicting attitude toward women in France. The ideal of the woman as wife and mother was permanently in tension with the need for, as well as desire of, women to work.

One area where it was acceptable for women to work and which changed little with the outbreak of war was entertainment. On 24 September the Comédie-Française – the first theatre in Paris to reopen following the declaration of war – staged a poetry matinée. The historic building itself, protected by a ten-foot-high wall of sandbags at the entrance, had been emptied of its great marble busts and other thespian treasures as well as half of its male personnel. Some of the company's actresses had also moved to the country, but enough actors remained to plan a continuing schedule, starting that autumn.

Right up until 1939, films were still being made in France, and Parisians flocked to the cinema to see the young woman hailed as the new Garbo, Corinne Luchaire. Luchaire had had a peripatetic childhood after her parents separated and she had gone with her mother to Germany where she made friends with several high-ranking Nazis. But she was not unfamiliar with Jews either, because her grandfather, the playwright Julien Luchaire, had married a Jewish woman as his third wife, and her father's sister, Ghita, was married to the Jewish philosopher Théodore Fraenkel. Nonetheless, both she and her sister had always wanted to act, and Corinne made her debut at the age of sixteen in a play written by her grandfather called *Altitude 3200*. At seventeen she starred in *Prison sans Barreaux*, and then, because she spoke fluent English, took the lead role when it was remade in English in 1938 as *Prison without Bars*. The following year saw her again starring in the first film version of the novel *The Postman Always Rings Twice*, which was called in French *Le Dernier Tournant* (The Last Bend). Corinne was emblematic of a generation of women who wanted to work and for whom becoming a film star was not only liberating but financially rewarding, and it did not require a professional qualification. It was a gratifying career path for any woman who enjoyed being admired by men, which soon meant being admired by Nazis.

Similarly, there was no shortage of young female dancers to perform at the cabarets and nightclubs that were flourishing as never before. Early in 1939, having been in Paris less than a year, a young South African girl auditioned as a dancer at a Montmartre cabaret. The twenty-one-year-old Sadie Rigal had left her father and five siblings behind in a Johannesburg boarding house, determined to make it on her own in Europe where she dreamed of joining the Ballets Russes. Sadie's father David had taken responsibility for bringing up the family when her mother, two years after Sadie's birth in 1917, was confined to a mental institution following the death of her youngest son in the flu pandemic. Life was tough for the Rigal family, but Sadie clearly had talent and, in exchange for generally 'helping out', a cousin who ran a small dance school agreed to give her free lessons. She started to win competitions, graduated to a more advanced teacher and, after performing one last solo in Cape Town, departed for Paris in 1938. Here she studied with Russian teachers, of whom there were many in Paris at the time, prior to the big interview that was her life's ambition.

Meanwhile, to make ends meet, she auditioned for the famous Bal Tabarin music hall at 36 Rue Victor Massé, just behind the Place Pigalle, which had opened in 1904 and become hugely successful. The Bal Tabarin floor show was one of the best known in Paris, with semi-naked girls cavorting in unusual positions, gracefully performing acrobatics and spinning around a cage, some hanging on with their teeth as others bent backwards. Man Ray, the surrealist photographer, made a famous series of images of the cabaret in 1936 in which the girls look like a fantastic human tree. When

Pierre Sandrini became Artistic Director as well as co-owner in 1928 he introduced ballet to the floor shows, with costumes designed by Erté, which transformed the performances into spectacular tableaux. There was a new show every year, each with a theme, such as *The Planets* or *The Symphony*, some of them inspired by historical figures such as Cleopatra and Mme de Pompadour.

In the summer of 1939 Sandrini, who was to be Sadie's saviour in the precarious years to come, encouraged her and a friend to go to London to audition for the Ballets Russes. Both were accepted but were then told to wait in Paris because the company was due to travel there in December. So they returned to the French capital but, once war broke out, found themselves stranded as the Ballets Russes never came. David Rigal scraped together enough money to offer his daughter a ticket home to South Africa, but she refused, embracing uncertainty and deciding to chance her luck in Paris.

The Bal Tabarin was never quite as famous as the Folies Bergère, which after 1918 became enshrined as something of a national monument. There were even wild claims that the magnificent breasts of the dancers were somehow symbolic of the best of France that had been fought for in the recent war. It was where thousands of men, seduced by the legend of 'Gay Paree' and Parisian debauchery, paid to watch increasing amounts of naked flesh revealed on stage amid increasingly sumptuous costumes and sets. Yet the Folies Bergère launched the careers not just of scantily clad dancers but of many stars including Maurice Chevalier, the singer and actress Mistinguett and the black jazz singer and dancer Josephine Baker. It was also where another talented young girl, born in Dublin with neither money nor parents that she knew of, learned how to dance and entertain.

Margaret Kelly, nicknamed Bluebell because of her penetrating blue eyes, spent only a few years with the Folies Bergère before creating her own group which she called the Bluebell Girls. She was still only twenty-two. This troupe was sometimes engaged to perform at the Folies Bergère and sometimes at the Paramount Cinema on the classier Boulevard des Capuchines, one of the largest and most ornate of the old-style picture palaces in Paris, still used as a cinema in the mornings, and with a very different atmosphere from the floor shows of Montmartre. Kelly quickly became a successful choreographer, impresario and administrator, taking her girls on tours of Europe and acquiring considerable fame in her own right. She had been close friends for some years with the Romanian-Jewish composer and pianist at the Folies Bergère Marcel Leibovici, and although all backstage romances were officially forbidden, in 1938 Marcel proposed. He was thirty-four and she twenty-six. But getting married was complicated as Bluebell would have lost her British citizenship if she married a Romanian. They resolved the problem eventually by getting the Romanian Embassy to supply documents saying that he was no longer a citizen of their country – in other words that he was stateless, a brave undertaking for him. But then there was the problem of his religion since Bluebell wanted a church wedding and Marcel, although not observant, was Jewish. So determined was she to have the Church's blessing that she petitioned the Archbishop of Paris, who referred her case to the Vatican. Marcel then had to promise in a formal interview with the Archbishop that he would raise any children of the union as Catholics. Finally, on 1 March 1939 they were married in a civil ceremony and, later, at the huge La Trinité church, they received a religious blessing. They also held a party at the Pavillon Henri IV Hôtel in Saint-Germain-en-Laye, a popular tourist destination just outside Paris, having chartered a bus to bring as many dancers as it would hold. There was no honeymoon and the next day was business as usual. In July 1939 their first child, Patrick, was born.

With so many couples getting married in 1939, several jewellers now benefited from the flourishing trade in engagement rings. At least if the husband was killed, the war widow would then be able to obtain some financial compensation. But in the chaotic frenzy of changing roles, moving home and worrying about relatives at risk, there were almost as many couples separating or getting divorced. Comtesse Lily Pastré, approaching fifty, was forced to begin a new life in 1939 as, at the end of the year, she finally agreed a divorce settlement with her husband, the enormously wealthy Comte Jean Pastré, whose infidelities had nearly destroyed her.

Lily was born Marie-Louise Double Saint-Lambert in 1891, daughter of a rich family with Russian antecedents on her maternal side, while her great-grandparents on her paternal side were hard-working entrepreneurs and co-founders of the Noilly Prat liqueur business. As heiress to the Noilly Prat Vermouth fortune, Lily was rich in her own right. Nonetheless, her childhood had not been one of luxury, and she had been brought up in an austere Catholic, authoritarian household. As a young girl she was tall, blonde and slim and a talented tennis-player. But the first great sadness in her life came when her elder brother, Maurice, was killed in 1916 during the Battle of the Somme. Two years later, partly to strengthen alliances between families of the haute bourgeoisie in Marseilles, she agreed to an arranged marriage with Comte Pastré. The couple had three children – Nadia, Nicole and Pierre – but as was normal in her circle, Lily was not expected to spend much time with her children, who were brought up by a nanny and an English governess. With few options, Lily made her life in the concert halls and opera houses of Paris and became deeply knowledgeable about avant-garde music, theatre and art. In 1939, aged forty-eight with three adult children, she moved out of Paris as the divorce settlement left her with the family chateau at Montredon near Marseilles. But she was shocked to find herself shunned as a divorcee by French provincial society, even though her husband was the adulterer. She had little idea of what to do with her life and, as the gossip from Paris about her husband's latest conquests reached her, she lost self-confidence, put on weight and started to drink. For Lily, the war was in some ways to be her salvation.

Noor Inayat Khan, an Indian princess, living with her family in the wealthy suburb of Suresnes in 1939, was also recovering from the break-up of a longstanding affair and recognized that war was going to put an end to her fledgling career as a children's writer. Noor was born in Moscow in 1914 to an Indian father who was a distinguished Sufi teacher and direct descendant of Tipu Sultan, the eighteenth-century Muslim ruler of Mysore, and an American mother, Ora Baker. The family lived first in London before settling in Paris, in a large house named Fazal Manzil in Suresnes, where Noor studied harp and piano for several years, culminating in a period at the Paris Conservatoire under Nadia Boulanger. This was followed by a course in child psychology at the Sorbonne. Noor was often described by her friends and teachers as quiet and dreamy, but she was also both talented and clever. By her mid-twenties it was clear she was suffering deep emotional turmoil, was often in tears for no discernible reason and seemed close to a complete breakdown, most probably because for the last six years she had been involved in an intense relationship with a Turkish Jewish pianist known as Goldberg (his first name was never used), who lived in Paris with his mother.

Noor and Goldberg had first met and fallen in love while both were students at the Ecole Normale de Musique, and for a while he was accepted into the Khan household of Fazal Manzil and even given the name Huzoor Nawaz. But Noor's family were not happy about the relationship, believing the class divide was insurmountable. Goldberg came from an impoverished working-class family – his mother worked in a laundry – who could hardly afford to pay his fees, while Noor was a noble princess. They believed her attraction to him stemmed partly from her sympathy for his deprived background and fear that if she left him he might try and end his life.

By the summer of 1938 she had passed exams which qualified her to teach child psychology, but the Khan family did not expect its women to take on professional, paid jobs. Instead she was establishing herself as an author and poet, contributing regular children's stories, based on ancient Indian and Greek legends, to the Sunday *Figaro*. In addition, some of her stories were broadcast on Radio-Paris's 'Children's Hour' and won her excellent reviews at a time when stories of Babar, the elephant created by Jean de Brunhoff, and his queen, Céleste, were standard fare in every Parisian nursery. She often worked on her writing alone, in her room at night, but by the middle of 1939 she appeared to be happier and was contemplating ending the relationship with Goldberg and going to Calcutta to accept the proposal of another man, a wealthy Dutch Sufi aristocrat called Peter Yohannes, whose advances she had previously rejected. However, lacking the money for the fare to Calcutta, she put the trip to one side and continued to work on stories for newspapers as well as on her first book, *Twenty Jataka Tales*, which was published that summer in England. In the wake of her success she developed plans for a children's newspaper and began collecting material for that. For Noor, the announcement of war ended her radio and newspaper work almost immediately as paper shortages loomed and stories about fairies and mythic creatures of the forest seemed inappropriate. The journalist with whom she had been working on the children's newspaper backed out, telling her it would be impossible to go ahead at such a time when all that anyone wanted to read was hard news.

Throughout September the atmosphere in Paris was a panicky one as impoverished refugees were flooding in, soldiers drafted out and families, unable to decide whether to remain in the capital or travel to the coast, criss-crossed the country trying to find a place of relative safety. Most private cars were requisitioned and from now on travel, other than by train or bicycle, was difficult or impossible. Claire Chevrillon, the English teacher, and a social worker friend now began escorting women and children out of Paris into the country to save them from possible bombing attacks. To appear more professional and inspire confidence, Claire wore her scout uniform and carried the obligatory gas mask as she made several trips from the Gare Montparnasse on trains teeming with terrified women, rambunctious children and the sick and elderly. For the first few months after 3 September, Parisians of both sexes barely moved without the compulsory gas mask, so great was the fear of a gas attack. But as several newspapers noted: 'Women in Paris Will Not Forsake Fashion in War'. Some designers seized the opportunity to create ever more ingenious fashion containers for gas masks, and it was not unusual to see the masks in leather or satin-covered boxes or in bags made of various fabrics as women tried matching them to their outfits. Jeanne Lanvin, one of the most popular designers, invented a cylindrical-shaped box with a long strap costing 180 francs, which was much coveted by a few wealthy Parisiennes.

Janet Teissier du Cros, a young Scotswoman married to François, a Frenchman, observed how a handful of fashion-conscious Parisian women managed to remain looking chic in the dark, dirty and chaotic capital. She and her husband had been living in Edinburgh but concluded two days before war was declared that they should return as soon as possible with their small son, André, in order that François could join his regiment to fight. Janet, having chosen to be in France to support her husband, later recalled feeling overwhelmingly that, in spite of the dislocation, uncertainty and upheaval, especially at railway stations, not to fight this time would be deeply shameful. As her sister, married to an American, put it: 'If France and Britain don't fight, however shall I face the Americans?' Janet had studied music before her marriage and, for educated women like her, it was not so much a question now of how to avoid war as of how to win it once it came. Having said goodbye to her husband, she went south as quickly as she could with André to live with her in-laws, optimistic that the war would soon be over. As she boarded one train after another and then had to climb into an open cattle truck, she realized that by that stage 'we were all looking pretty bedraggled. André was so filthy that I doubt whether I would have had the courage to touch him if he had been someone else's child.' But, as she settled on the floor of the cattle truck, she noticed another woman, probably on her way to visit her soldier husband, a true Parisienne dressed in a beautiful black, tailor-made suit with a white lingerie blouse 'that was still really white' and a small black hat which could have come only from Paris. 'She was like a breath from Paris. Though she sat on the floor with us she never lost her air of neat elegance and the sight of her struck guilt into my soul for it reminded me that I had been taking advantage of circumstances to let my standards down, an unpardonable thing in France.'

The couture houses of Paris had shown their fabulous autumn–winter 1939 creations to the world's buyers in April. Now the city's thousands of dressmakers and ancillary workers in their ateliers were busy fulfilling orders. As Lucien Lelong, President of the Chambre Syndicale de la Haute Couture, argued, 'our role is to give France an appearance of serenity; the problems must not hamper the creators. It is their duty to hold aloof from them. The more elegant French women are . . . the more our country will show people abroad that it does not fear the future.'

For those who chose to look, 1939 had proclaimed itself a dangerous year from the start. *Le Jardin des Modes* was not alone among women's magazines in keeping up a pretence of normality by advising its female readers in January 1939 how they too could dress their hair in a little chignon at the nape of their necks 'à la Duchesse de Windsor', or in March giving advice on 'how to embellish, firm up and make younger looking breasts . . . a discovery which French women are passionate about', the magazine insisted. The more upmarket *Vogue* published an advertisement for Helena Rubinstein make-up which proclaimed: 'These days it is the duty of everyone, especially women, to communicate to those one loves, the optimism which results from confidence in oneself.' The interesting logic behind the advertisement was presumably that wearing Helena Rubinstein make-up would help to win the coming war. It was an attitude driven home by editorials in all the magazines that autumn.

Some couture houses had responded to war by introducing military elements into their designs such as frogging, shoulder braid and tassels on the warm coats which were now essential for the long unheated train journeys. A few hats were created to resemble British busbies or French tricornes. But mostly the magazines responded with exhortations to keep up standards for the men's sake. 'For those who are at the front,' declared *Le Jardin des Modes* on its September front page, 'you must stay how they would like to see you. Not ugly.' On its inside pages the magazine explained how all periodicals were required to reduce by 50 per cent the amount of paper they used, but 'we decided in spite of the difficulties that our duty was to show the entire world that French fashion will continue in [these] serious circumstances to guide feminine elegance'.

For as long as they were in print, magazines exhorted Parisiennes to remain 'women who were proud of maintaining a privilege for which all the world envied them, to help fashion overcome the war around them. Fashion will remain Parisienne in its most intimate fibre,' according to an editorial that autumn. 'You will dress yourself simply but elegantly. Those who are at the front want you to be pretty and soignée.' It was a stirring column, telling women they had it in their power to accomplish this essential task: not to allow the luxury industry, one of the vital resources of Paris, to die.

By December the magazines were slightly more sober in tone, attuned to the times, advising women on what to put in the little packages to send their soldiers, how to cook the more economical rillettes, how to knit balaclavas and jumpers or, now that so many budgets were reduced, how to revive an old dress and make it look like this year's. Some asked their readers if they would prefer to have half a magazine appear regularly or have the magazine stay the same size but published half as often. However, by early 1940 the shortages forced most magazines to close down anyway. *Vogue* and *Harper's Bazaar*, despite the difficulties, stayed in production longer but, as Lucien Lelong explained in a November 1939 interview, maintaining the fashion industry was not just about vanity. 'At a time when the country needs foreign currency we must make every effort to increase our export figures. Our overseas clientele has resumed its usual way of life . . . We have another duty. Twenty thousand working women and 500 male employees make their living from Parisian couture. It also has a direct influence on the life of other industries: textiles, silk, furs, lace etc.' Everything must be done to preserve these jobs in Paris, he said. It was an argument he was to make even more stridently and urgently in the months to come. Paris to most people meant fashion, food, cabarets and the Comédie-Française. How these aspects of life were to fare over the next five years was not clear in 1939, but each of them was digging in.

But merely looking elegant and soignée was, of course, never going to be enough. As the American former actress Drue Tartière commented, many of the French soldiers looked pitifully ill equipped for the ordeal ahead, wearing carpet slippers instead of boots. Drue was one of almost 30,000 Americans living in or near Paris before the outbreak of war. She was working at Paris Mondial radio station arranging for Americans to give broadcasts to the United States, intended to convey the difficult atmosphere in Paris. Colette was one of her regular broadcasters, along with the French actresses Mistinguett and Cécile Sorel and the influential American journalist Dorothy Thompson. Although the American Ambassador, William Bullitt, advised all US citizens to leave France, some 5,000 chose to remain in the city either because they had made it their home and loved the country or because they had family ties or both. Since Drue's French husband, Jacques Tartière, to whom she'd been married just a year, was away fighting, Drue hired as her housekeeper a young girl from Alsace called Nadine keen to live in the big city. Just before taking her on, Drue asked her how she felt about the Germans. 'My father,

Madame,' she responded with a straight face, 'always said that there was only one way to cure Germany and that was to kill the women and children.' The response, while comforting, seemed a little extreme to Drue, who took her on all the same. Not many Parisiennes felt quite the way Nadine did towards Germany.

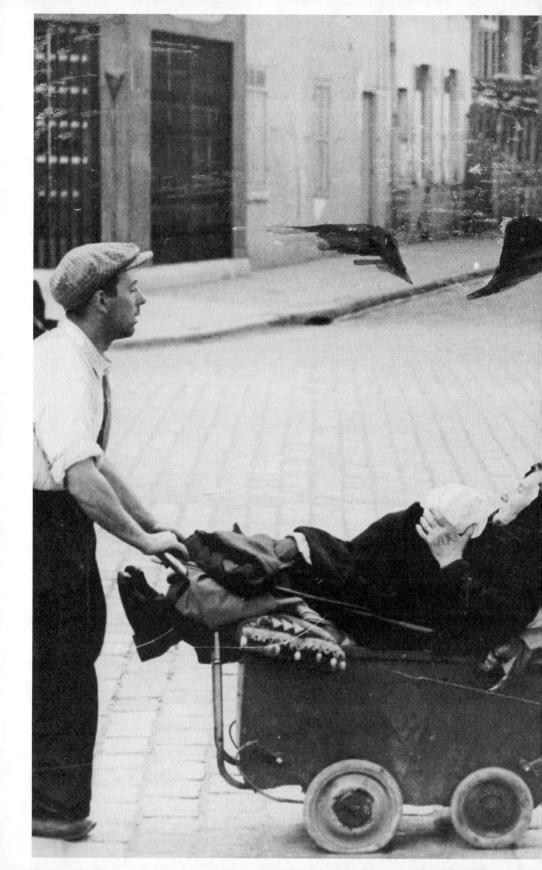

1940

PARIS ABANDONED

France was not alone in suffering an exceptionally severe winter that lasted from mid-December 1939 until March 1940. The cold centre was situated in the Netherlands and northern Germany but the extreme weather conditions were also felt in Finland, Sweden, southern Norway, Denmark, south-western England, northern France, Germany, Hungary, Yugoslavia, Romania, Poland, the Baltic countries and western Russia. Even in northern Spain, temperatures of 0 degrees Fahrenheit (−18 degrees Celsius) were recorded. Some people in France began to wonder if they were living in Siberia, from where the arctic air originated. The ferocious weather encouraged those who believed that the phoney war could not continue and were in any case trying to prepare for catastrophe; ordinary people, many of them housewives, stockpiling essential items such as sugar, flour and tinned food, were shocked to find that water in flower vases turned to ice. But there were also several not so ordinary women who saw the need to offer whatever help they could as quickly as possible.

Early in 1940, Odette Fabius was one of many women from the Parisian haute bourgeoisie who responded to the call for volunteers for a variety of medical and social support services. Odette remembered that during the First World War an entire floor of her family's spacious townhouse had been turned into a temporary hospital while her mother, in starched white nurse's uniform, tended the sick. Four-year-old Odette was encouraged to walk up and down the beds offering cigarettes. Odette Fabius, née Schmoll, was born into one of France's oldest and most illustrious Jewish families, with roots deep in Alsace on one side, in Bordeaux on the other, and was descended from Abraham Furtado, a French politician and one-time adviser to Napoleon Bonaparte. Her father was a high-ranking lawyer who worked in the Palais de Justice, and she and her brother grew up

Odette and Robert Fabius's wedding in 1929

lacking neither parental love and devotion nor material goods. Her golden childhood enabled her to see life as 'a marvellous gift' full of privileges regulated by a British governess called Alice Darling. Darling, who was still with the family in 1940 after thirty-two years' devoted service, ensured that English was Odette's first language. That they were Jewish was simply a fact and did not disturb their daily life.

In 1929 Odette was introduced to Robert Fabius, an attractive man ten years older than her, whose family were antique dealers, or as M. Schmoll disparagingly described them, shopkeepers. It was a profession, however, that was ultimately to save his life. Odette and Robert were married the following year by Paris's Grand Rabbin in a magnificent ceremony at the Grand Synagogue in the Rue de la Victoire, the same synagogue where forty years earlier Captain Alfred

Dreyfus had married Lucie Hadamard. Odette, just twenty, wore a magnificent dress with a thirty-foot lace train made by Lanvin, her favourite designer, and was attended by numerous cousins and friends, including Renée, formerly Van Cleef, daughter of the jeweller. The lavish reception was held at the Hôtel George V.

Within a year a daughter, Marie-Claude, was born and the family moved to an apartment on the fashionable Rue Meyerbeer with enough room for three staff, including an English nanny. But Odette was far from happy with a life that involved nothing more than dinners at the fashionable Boeuf sur le Toit or visits to cabarets, and a husband who, as she soon learned, drank, gambled and kept mistresses. The latter was hardly a surprise to her, since her own father had done likewise. But, in the way of the haute bourgeoisie, he had been discreet. There were few options in the 1930s for a young mother like Odette. Then, in 1937, her beloved mother died and, lacking anyone with whom to discuss how best to live her unhappy life, she visited a well-known psychoanalyst in Paris, Dr Démétrian. She continued the sessions until Dr Démétrian was called up, then suddenly 'for me, life was about to begin'. Odette joined the SSA or Sections Sanitaires Automobiles (mobile health units) as a volunteer ambulance driver. Faced with shortages of both ambulances and drivers, the French Department of War had accepted an offer from the Croix-Rouge Française to help with transportation of wounded soldiers from the battlefield. A brief inaugural ceremony was organized on 24 April 1940 in the Cour des Invalides, following which some units went immediately into action. In fact, the role of these SSA women, many of them countesses and princesses from France's best-known families, went beyond merely picking up wounded British and French soldiers and was also aiding refugees heading south out of Paris and sending much needed supplies to prisoner-of-war camps. It was dangerous and tiring work, allowing almost no sleep for days on end. Those units near the northern France front line, confronted immediately with casualties from fierce fighting in the area, had to undertake day and night driving, as well as the loading and unloading of the wounded, often under sustained German bombing.

The ambulance drivers were subsequently ordered to retreat from village to village in the face of ferocious German attacks. One of Fabius's final assignments was to transport the Red Cross treasury in her ambulance to Bordeaux, an area she knew well and where the government was intending to transfer in the wake of the German invasion. She stopped for a night en route in Orléans, staying in a hotel which was hit by Luftwaffe planes in the early hours; twenty people were killed. Lucky to survive, Odette moved on as soon as she could. 'I did not want to be accused of disappearing with the Red Cross millions.' But although the SSA was formally disbanded in early September 1940, several of the women, having been exposed to fear and danger, subsequently involved themselves in further actions against the Germans by joining some form of inchoate resistance.

The Duchess of Windsor also joined the SSA for a short time and agreed to deliver plasma, bandages and cigarettes to hospitals near the Maginot Line. Wallis admitted: 'I was busier and perhaps more useful than I had ever been in my life.' However, much to the annoyance of the Duke of Windsor, assigned to the British Military mission at Vincennes, just outside Paris, British newspapers were not interested in writing about the activities of his 'courageous' wife, 'billeted within the sound of gunfire', as he proudly tried to tell them. Then, once Germany invaded the Netherlands on 10 May and began to threaten the French defences, the Duke and several of the international set – including the wealthy socialite Daisy Fellowes, Sir Charles and Lady Mendl, the writer and collector Gertrude Stein and her lover Alice B. Toklas – decided it was time to flee Paris. Edward deposited Wallis in Biarritz and returned to Paris briefly to sort out his affairs. By the end of May his need to be with his wife was so overpowering that, leaving their house at 85 Boulevard Suchet in the hands of a German caretaker, he now abandoned his oldest and most loyal friend and ADC, Major 'Fruity' Metcalfe, without a word of warning, forcing him to find his own way back to England without any means of transport. Not surprisingly, Metcalfe saw this as a callous disregard of twenty years of friendship and threatened never to forgive him. 'He deserted his job in 1936, well he's deserted his country now, at a time when every office boy and cripple is trying to do what he can. It is the end,' he told his wife. Some historians have defended the Duke on the grounds that he probably left Paris with the approval – indeed the relieved approval – of the military mission. More significantly perhaps, the Duke understood that, at a time when everyone else seemed to be against the Duchess, he had to be with her to support and defend her. From Biarritz the pair went to La Croë, their home in the Cap d'Antibes, where they heard news of the German advance and the French collapse. It was agreed with the local British Embassy that the Duke and Duchess must get to Spain, without getting caught up with the fleeing French government.

Somehow Edward found time during these last frenetic weeks in 1940 before the invasion to visit Cartier and collect his latest commission, intended as a birthday gift for Wallis on 19 June, and which he had ordered several months previously. On 4 March 1940 he had visited Jeanne Toussaint, Cartier's Design Director, with his pockets full of stones from a necklace and four bracelets, and discussed with her the making of a magnificent brooch in the shape of a flamingo, with startling tail feathers of rubies, sapphires and emeralds and a retractable leg so that Wallis could wear it centrally, without the leg digging into her should she bend down.

Toussaint was one of an unusual group of self-made women responsible for defining good taste and style in late 1930s Paris; women who felt a burgeoning need to break free and express themselves. Before the First World War jewellery had followed certain rigid conventions and traditions but in the 1920s, as women fought for an enhanced role in society, jewellery and clothes reflected this desire for greater freedom. Toussaint was patronized by women who refused to be confined within narrow limits. Her mother was a Belgian lace-maker, but Jeanne – small, slim and dynamic – left her Charleroi home at just sixteen and came to Paris as the young mistress of an aristocrat and one of the first women to be paid for modelling. When her lover abandoned her, she had affairs with several other men, moving in circles of kept women, courtesans and coquettes that flourished in Belle Epoque Paris, circles that included Coco Chanel, who remained a close friend until the end of her life. In 1918, Jeanne met and fell in love with Louis Cartier, one of three brothers who had built up the jewellery firm which was by then flourishing on the

Rue de la Paix. Cartier, with branches in London and New York, famous for its fine platinum settings designed to set off exquisite stones often imported from India or Russia, was at the height of its international success. Louis, forty-three and divorced, wanted to marry Jeanne, but his family was appalled by the idea of him marrying a woman they considered a demi-mondaine, fearing this would impact negatively on the firm. So she remained his mistress and, although she could neither draw nor sketch, he appointed her Design Director, a key position in the company and also in the life of Parisian high society. She could relate to the French custom of indulging *les grandes amoureuses* and to the role played by lavish jewellery in an extramarital relationship, a world from which she and Chanel had so recently emerged. At Cartier (and other Parisian jewellers) it was not unusual for a man to maintain two accounts: one for his wife and one for his mistress. Meticulous records were kept of everything bought and sold, but discretion was paramount. It was imperative that salespeople were trained never to confuse the two, a discipline followed to this day.

Suzanne Belperron, one of the most talented jewellery designers of her generation, was a decade younger than Toussaint, but she too moved to Paris while still in her teens and she too had an instinctive understanding of the women she was decorating. Belperron, born Suzanne Vuillerme in the Jura in 1900 to a family with deep roots in the area, had won prizes at the Institut Supérieur des Beaux Arts in Besançon from the age of eighteen and went immediately to work with Jeanne Boivin, sister of the couturier Paul Poiret and widow of René Boivin, the most famous Parisian jeweller of his day. But at Maison Boivin, Suzanne could never be given credit for her highly individual creations; her work had to remain anonymous, an impossible scenario for a woman of immense talent and a strong personality to match. So in 1932 when Bernard Herz, the well-known Parisian pearl and gemstone dealer, invited her to work for him as Artistic and Technical Director with much greater freedom, she could not refuse. From now on, *Vogue* regularly featured whole pages with 'dresses by Chanel or Mainbocher, jewels by Belperron', thus linking the names of couturier and jeweller in a new way. In the months to follow, the relationship between these two branches of the luxury industry was of key importance. The name

Belperron was suddenly vying for attention with the longer-established Cartier and Van Cleef. Yet little was known about the woman behind the name, a mysteriousness which added to her attraction.

Suzanne had married the engineer Jean Belperron in 1924 and the young couple lived in Montmartre, where they made friends with many avant-garde artists. Her friend, the beautiful Nusch Eluard, actress and occasional jewellery model, wife and muse to the surrealist poet Paul Eluard, was photographed by Man Ray in Belperron creations. However, Suzanne saw clients at her private salon at 59 Rue de Châteaudun in the unfashionable 9th arrondissement. She never had a shop front, but her work – swirls of naturalist leaves and shells, an antidote to the then fashionable Art Deco, and the mixing of precious stones with non-traditional materials such as ebony or chalcedony – was highly sought after by trendsetters such as the Duchess of Windsor, Daisy Fellowes and Schiaparelli. Parisiennes whose trademark was shopping driven by word-of-mouth recommendations knew where to find her and recognized her bold, unsigned pieces. At the same time, Suzanne was becoming famous for her own personal style, her very short hair often covered by a turban, and, although an extremely private person, she was herself photographed by Horst and Man Ray, sometimes wearing magnificent clips, large cuffs or rings on her long fingers. Herz was a handsome man some twenty-three years her senior, with a large country house at Chantilly and an apartment in the Avenue du Président Wilson in the chic 16th arrondissement. As his own children – a married daughter, Mme Aline Solinsky, and a son Jean who was a prisoner of war – were now grown up, he became something of a father figure to Suzanne and quite possibly her lover too. Among her most precious possessions was a white gold and platinum lorgnette from which dangled two heart-shaped charms; inside were two photographs, one of her mother and one of Herz. But Herz, although born in Paris, was Jewish, which meant that from early 1940 Suzanne Belperron was looking into how to transfer the company into her name and run Maison Bernard Herz entirely alone.

Although in 1940 the United States had not yet joined the war effort, the American Hospital in Paris was one of the few organizations that was prepared. Rebuilt after the Great War with 120 beds for medical, surgical and maternity cases and three operating rooms in the wealthy Parisian district of Neuilly-sur-Seine in the west of the city, it had shed its 1920s reputation as an upmarket clinic providing succour for rich or famous Americans such as Ernest Hemingway and the Scott Fitzgeralds to become a first-rate hospital for all Americans in Paris. Now, once again, with the help of Ambassador Bullitt, it had to get ready to become a military facility able to deal with shrapnel wounds, gas attacks or damage from bombs, with a special unit set up for blood donations.

One of the most senior doctors at the hospital was Sumner Waldron Jackson, a genito-urinary specialist from Maine. He and his Swiss-born wife, Toquette, had lived through one war against Germany and, like many in their circle, had been following the news on the radio for the last two years, listening with mounting horror to Hitler's threats. Charlotte Sylvie Barrelet de Ricout, always known as Toquette, came from a well-off family of Swiss Protestants. Her lawyer father had brought his young family to live in France, settling at Enghien-les-Bains just outside Paris, where Toquette grew up with a love of tennis and sailing on the lake at Enghien. She had been working as a nurse since 1914 and met Sumner in Paris when both were at the American Red Cross Hospital Number Two, treating hideously wounded men brought back from the trenches, often barely alive. The romance began, apparently, with a snatched kiss in a linen cupboard at the hospital, and the pair were married in November 1917. He was thirty-two, she twenty-seven. In 1919 they returned to live for a while in Philadelphia. But Toquette was not happy in America, too French to feel at home there, and so after two years persuaded her husband to return to Paris. That he obliged his young wife so willingly is an indication of her forceful personality since the move involved his taking not only French-language but also fresh medical exams. In January 1929 their first and only son Phillip was born, by which time Sumner was working as a surgeon and urologist at the American Hospital and the family were living in an apartment at 11 Avenue Foch in the 16th arrondissement. As the hospital in Paris braced itself for action, its doctors were already working at a makeshift field hospital established in a former casino at Fontainebleau, using it as a dressing station for French soldiers and wounded refugees needing emergency care.

But, however well prepared the hospital might have been, almost everyone was shocked by the speed and efficiency of the German invasion. The Blitzkrieg began on 13 May and swiftly shattered the French faith in their heavily fortified Maginot Line. The Wehrmacht with its superior mechanized Panzer divisions, supported by Luftwaffe dive bombers, bypassed the fortifications and within one month Dutch, Belgian and Norwegian forces had all capitulated, sending refugees streaming over the border into France. British and French forces, similarly overwhelmed, were trapped at Dunkirk. Although in the nine days following 27 May a total of 338,226 soldiers were rescued by a hastily assembled fleet of over 800 boats, the British Expeditionary Force lost 68,000 soldiers during the French campaign and had to abandon nearly all tanks, other vehicles and equipment. Metcalfe always believed that the Duke of Windsor should have remained in Paris until the last minute, overseeing the evacuation on the Dunkirk beaches. 'This would have made him seem a hero not a coward,' Metcalfe's daughter suggested. But the Duke and Duchess had fled Paris on 16 May and made their way to the Hôtel du Palais in fashionable Biarritz, where life was much calmer than in the capital.

On 10 June the government too left Paris for Bordeaux via Tours, the fight not necessarily entirely over, but giving the signal to the population that it was no longer safe to remain in the capital. 'The streets were empty. People were closing their shops. The metallic shudder of falling iron shutters was the only sound to break the silence, a sound familiar to anyone who has woken in a city threatened by riot or war,' was how the novelist Irène Némirovsky described the scene in her realistic account, *Suite Française*. Four days later, on 14 June, the French government declared Paris an Open City, a declaration intended to protect it as long as no resistance was offered by troops or by the population; otherwise the city would be treated as being in the war zone and liable to destruction. Hitler wanted Paris protected, preserved, so that Germany could forge an alliance with it, enjoy its attributes. While never admitting its superiority, and criticizing the depravity and louche habits of French women, he nonetheless wanted every German soldier to experience, once, the pleasures of Paris: 'Jeder Einmal nach Paris' ('Everyone should have his turn in Paris') was the popular phrase used by the Wehrmacht.

On that day, the day the Germans entered the city and hoisted the swastika over the Arc de Triomphe and the Eiffel Tower, there were fourteen recorded suicides in Paris, of which the best-known was that of Dr Thierry Martel, Chief Surgeon at the American Hospital. Martel, aged sixty-five, was a complex man, simultaneously anti-German and anti-Jewish, a decorated veteran of the Great War and a member of Maurras's Action Française. The son of French aristocrats who loudly proclaimed their belief in the guilt of Dreyfus as well as their dislike of the number of nouveau riche Jews, he was also the uncle of Jacques Tartière, the Gaullist *résistant* married to the American actress Drue Leyton. But he had lost a son in the Great War and vowed after that never to speak to a German. Following Martel's suicide, Dr Sumner Jackson took over as Chief Surgeon and directed policy. Already in May the hospital was sheltering downed US and British pilots. No decision was ever taken to become involved in resistance, but Toquette and her sister Tat, while refusing to leave France, agreed that it might be safer for Phillip if they moved south out of Paris and left Sumner alone in their flat.

The response to France's military collapse was chaotic. No official plans had been issued for a mass evacuation, yet almost three million out of Paris's five million inhabitants, including bureaucrats and dip-lomats, clamoured to get out of the city. *Paris-Soir* advised women to wear comfortable flat shoes and robust thick stockings rather than the elegant silk variety. But that did little to dispel the collective panic which was largely based on fear of being taken prisoner. On 9 June, Simone de Beauvoir wrote: 'I took the German advance as a personal threat. I had only one idea which was not to be cut off from [Jean-Paul] Sartre, not to be taken like a rat in occupied Paris.'

Although some of the wealthier Parisians had left as soon as they realized things were going badly, the poorer ones, with no private means of transport, now flooded on to already overcrowded trains, using every inch of space, including the toilets, as additional seating. This use of the toilets caused intolerable problems on long journeys for passengers who needed to relieve themselves. Many women, in the face of dire need, lost their inhibitions and, on at least one occasion when a train stopped, strong men were seen to lift women out through the windows where they then proceeded to raise their skirts and crouch on the ground, embarrassingly close to the train which they feared might move off without them, as they urinated in a row along the railway line. Thousands of other Parisians tried to leave the city using whatever mode of transport they could commandeer. The roads, already congested with Belgian refugees, were now jammed with desperate families, using private cars if they had enough fuel, often with a mattress on the roof in the mistaken belief that this would lessen the impact of a bomb. Others took to bicycles, or walked, pushing prams and occasionally home-made wheelbarrows containing the frail elderly instead of babies. Some historians have estimated that up to ten million French people fled their homes in the wake of the German advance, not always knowing where they were going (south or west was the general direction rather than north, a route that was now impossible). It was a pathetic multitude, those on foot often going as fast as the red-faced, angry drivers uselessly honking horns.

Most of those who left Paris were women, children and the elderly – the men were either working in factories or serving in the army – as schools were closed down early and exams cancelled, family pets destroyed or else left to run wild and be shot by others. What women chose to wear for such a nightmare journey was much commented on. Some, given the extreme heat and believing they would not be on the road for long, wore summer shorts. Others, more cautious, decided that, despite the stifling weather, the only way to avoid carrying luggage was to wear a large proportion of their wardrobe. 'It was quite common to see women wearing lots of layers of clothes, shirt over shirt, skirt over skirt, jackets covered with coats. The whole ensemble would be set off with scarf, gloves and a hat – the dress code for a middle-class woman could not be ignored even if the wearer had become a nomad.'

Although some took advantage of the sunshine to bring out picnics which they ate, once out in the country, by the poplar-lined roadsides, more commonly families ran out of food or were terrifyingly both strafed and bombed by German planes, which flew low over the crowded roads of civilians. Ditches provided little protection.

Such cruelty seemed especially poignant because of the beautiful hot weather and clear blue skies. Yet so dangerous were the air attacks, and so exhausting the task of carrying weary toddlers, that several mothers accepted offers of lifts from strangers for their children and then, unable to track down their children, posted fraught notices seeking information, a clear indication that normal behaviour had been suspended since no one had any idea of the scale or outcome of the unfolding drama. Heart-rending messages begging for news of lost children appeared for weeks afterwards.

Georges Sadoul, a communist journalist, was one of those who mocked the flirtatious behaviour of young women he saw, and their determination, regardless of cost, to maintain their Parisian elegance. He spoke of a certain 'refugee chic' which involved wearing a shirt and narrow trousers with as much make-up as if for an outing on the town. Fellow writer André Fraigneau wrote about one woman he noticed sprinting out of her car to get hold of some precious petrol to use as nail-polish remover; apparently the colour of her hat did not match the colour of her nail polish. But refugee chic did not last long as this vast swathe of humanity could not wash, had little to eat and was barely moving forward. There were elderly women lying sprawled on the roadside, exhausted, unable to go on, and many younger women, promoted to head of the household in the absence of their husbands, simply could not cope. Among the rare accounts of women behaving well at this time came this from the diarist Anne Jacques: 'I can tell you that the women are not destroyed by nerves or by weakness but are sensible and calm. They are helpful to each other and often heroic. School headmistresses have undertaken the evacuation of their schools with perfect calm.'

The desperate and terrifying flight across France, known to history as *l'Exode*, was captured in hundreds of memoirs. Violette Leduc, the novelist befriended and nurtured by de Beauvoir, wrote in her semi-autobiographical novel *La Bâtarde* of how she and her mother had been so terrified of the enemy they were almost paralysed by the idea of moving, so they waited until the very last minute. Rumours were swirling of the enemy's violent behaviour, with stories circulating that the Germans were 'picking up' boys as young as fifteen. So they left Paris at 5.30 one morning when there was only 'silence in the streets, in the buildings a silence as heavy as the grave. Bricks, stones, tar, pavements, churches, benches, squares, bus stops, curtains, shutters all abandoned to their solitude, everything induced such pity. Paris was a human ruin. Where were the dogs, the cats, the flies? Where was everything?'

And then, as Leduc recorded, once families had left Paris behind, the chaos intensified: 'We followed the line of people on each side of the road. Mothers breastfeeding in the ditch, flirty girls in Louis XV heels, chancers in trucks singing and throwing cigarettes at some old guy who ran into the road to pick them up . . . Mountains, complicated constructions on car roofs. A man alone carrying a mattress on his back.' Jacqueline Mesnil-Amar, an assimilated Jewish mother and writer whose husband had been called up, compared the scene as she fled Paris with her baby daughter Sylvie and nanny Marie to 'a burning Pompeii, fleeing the German lava'.

Many contemporary accounts of *l'Exode* poked fun at women, portraying them as weak and vain, thinking only of what they should pack, and there clearly was an element of truth in the accusation. Once the Sandzer family had finally decided they must leave and abandon the lingerie factory, it was too late for Miriam's mother to take any of her jewellery out of the bank as all the banks were closed. Instead, she brought silver cutlery and candlesticks in case it was necessary to trade them for food but decreed no personal luggage at all. The trunk of the car was to be filled with food and drink and several bottles of Napoleon brandy to be used as bribes. But, just as they were about to set off, some elderly family friends, the Samsonowiczes, arrived insisting they must be taken too or they would throw themselves from the Eiffel Tower. Such emotional blackmail was impossible to resist, but then the couple produced a large carton, which they refused to open but said had to come too. After the war, the carton was found to contain a fur coat. While the Sandzers delayed, two other women, former customers of theirs, begged for help as their husbands had been imprisoned in camps. They at least had a car but had not used it for months and neither of them knew how to drive. Then a factory worker with a baby came to plead as well. The Sandzer family group had now grown to ten adults with two unreliable cars, a baby and a large carton between them. In this way they set off to join the long, sad line of people desperate to get out of Paris but clueless as to where their destination should be. The baby did not survive the journey.

Patrick Buisson, author of *1940–1945: Années érotiques*, wrote about *l'Exode*: 'Most of them left in a great hurry and panic, feverishly shutting bags and suitcases. Others prepared methodically as if invited to a weekend house party in the country or an afternoon tea party as depicted by the impressionist painters.' He cites Geneviève de Séréville, fourth wife of the actor Sacha Guitry, who packed dozens of bottles of nail varnish, face cream and perfume because she had at her disposal a Cadillac with a vast boot. Irène Némirovsky likewise writes of Florence, the fictional mistress of a writer struggling over how to pack his manuscripts and her make-up case. If she took both she could not close the suitcase. 'She moved the jewellery box, tried again. No, something definitely had to go. But what? Everything was essential. She pressed her knee against the case, pushed down, tried to lock it and failed. She was getting annoyed . . . For a second Florence hesitated between her make-up case and the manuscripts, chose the make-up and closed the suitcase.'

Sir Edward Spears, Winston Churchill's personal representative to the French government, was also scathing about the behaviour of those he saw fleeing, men and women. 'In most of the convoys I saw there were also cars in which sat ladies whose ample proportions and commanding looks proclaimed them to be wives of senior officers.' Every town and village he passed through appeared to be full of aircrews on the ground with their planes on enormous floats 'or gaping, idle soldiers. They were not in formations, just individuals in uniform, hanging about', wondering what to do or where to go, while the Luftwaffe, swarming overhead, was strafing those on the roads with their pathetic pramloads of possessions. Spears, observing what he called the paralysis of the French people, was deeply critical of Paul Reynaud, Prime Minister following the resignation of Edouard Daladier; concerned only to please his mistress, Reynaud allowed insults from the whole cabinet to pass without reprimand. As everyone was trying to reach Bordeaux, Spears believed that the machinery of the French army had completely broken down – a view shared by many French women who felt increasingly betrayed by the impotence of their men. One young woman* spoke for many when she said: 'The invasion was like rape. To this day when I read about a rape trial I am reminded of the Occupation. This was really violation – violation of my country. It was impossible to remain passive.' Once at Bordeaux, as Spears commented tartly, there were plenty of kept women among the stream of new political arrivals: 'the mistresses of ministers who boasted of such attachments, and most of them apparently did, were here *au grand complet*'. And at the head of the stream was Georges Mandel, the brilliant Interior Minister with whom Churchill had hoped to work should the French government continue the fight from exile, also with a woman not his wife.

But Mandel's 'lady', Béatrice Bretty, was in a different category from those mistresses scorned by Spears. Bretty, approaching forty-seven in 1940,[†] was one of the most senior actresses at the Comédie-Française and extremely popular with audiences. Born Béatrice Anne-Marie Bolchesi into a middle-class family, she decided aged fifteen to become an actress after watching Sarah Bernhardt. She took the name Bretty from *soubrette*, a nickname she was given to describe her type of light soprano voice when she joined the well-known theatrical troupe at around the age of twenty, by then already married to Clément Dangel. It was to be a brief marriage as Dangel was killed at Verdun in 1916, and she never remarried. After almost twenty years of widowhood, in 1935 she met Mandel through his work as head of the French Radio and Television Company and the pair almost immediately became inseparable. Both keen gourmets, they were widely sought after at fashionable dinners in Paris and were often seen together in the finest restaurants. Until Bretty entered his life, Mandel, a widower, had been regarded as a clever loner, dubbed 'the monk of politics'. But, benefiting from Bretty's warmth, he seemed to expand. She became Mandel's regular companion on holidays in Europe as well as at official dinners and public functions.

* This woman began the war as Marie-Antoinette Morat but, when she became a *résistante*, gave her identity to a young Jewish girl on the run and, using false papers, took another name herself, becoming Lucienne Guézennec.

† According to some Comédie-Française documents she was born in October 1893, but there are other dates in the files.

In addition, Bretty took charge of raising his six-year-old motherless daughter, Claude, 'of whose existence almost no one had been aware until that time'.

From the moment of the armistice, Bretty had refused to stay in a theatre whose independence she felt would sooner or later be compromised. She did not hesitate to follow her lover out of Paris, not only putting herself in considerable danger but risking the loss of her valuable pension as a *sociétaire*, or full member of the Comédie-Française. From August 1940 she repeatedly asked for leave of absence rather than retirement, insisting that she was not asking for money because for the moment she did not need it. But at the same time, she believed she had no choice but to leave the state theatre since, once the Nazis were in control, it was impossible for her to live in Paris with a Jewish partner.

Spears, knowing of the couple's deep attachment, assured Mandel that if he flew to England with him the next day, or went in the waiting destroyer, there would be two places. 'There must be an authorised French voice, not pledged to surrender, to guide the French Empire,' he urged. Mandel was torn, fully aware of the consequences for him, a Jew, if he remained in German-occupied France, and yet convinced he must remain precisely because he was Jewish. He believed that if he left France he would be accused of cowardice, of running away, of not being a 'true' Frenchman. But there was little time to debate the issue.

Spears observed a touching domestic vignette at this moment of crisis when he realized that Mme Bretty, 'with her plump pleasant features', was peeping around the door, a calming presence.

> She looked at us both, then I heard her voice for the first and last time, a pleasant, gay, friendly voice which I have not forgotten. Its tone had an inflection of slight urgency and pleading like that of a child asking with arms upheld to be picked up. 'Les malles sont faites, Georges,' it said. The trunks are packed. Whether she had heard an echo of our voices in the great silent chamber and hoped Mandel would accept my offer and was thus hinting she would like him to agree to it, I do not know. The door closed. I never saw him again.

Spears, who believed Mandel to be 'a great man', departed instead with the little-known Under-Secretary for Defence in the French government, a man newly appointed to the cabinet, Brigadier General Charles de Gaulle, who for the moment left his wife, Yvonne, behind in France.

Marshal Philippe Pétain, in a speech to the nation on 17 June, said loftily that he was 'giving to France the gift of my person in order to alleviate her suffering'. The eighty-four-year-old veteran of Verdun was now leader of the new government, the last of the Third Republic, which was to be based in the inland spa town of Vichy. With its myriad hotels and phone links, opera house, bandstand, park and air of unreality, Vichy was the antithesis of smart Paris, which Pétain maintained stood for vice, corruption and debauchery. The following day, broadcasting from the BBC in London, de Gaulle called upon French soldiers, engineers and specialized workers from the weapons industry to join him in London to continue the fight. Not many in France, even including his young niece Geneviève, heard his famous *appel* announcing in dolorous tones that were to become increasingly familiar to those who had access to a radio, 'Whatever happens, the flame of French Resistance must not be extinguished and will not be extinguished.' But for those who did, it was like a magic spell.

'I remember my elder sister, Monique, came running into my room,' recalled Vivou Chevrillon (as she was then), the excitement still in her voice today. '"It's not over," she cried. "There is a way we can resist." She told me all about the *appel* and we told everyone we could. That's how it spread,' explained Vivou, then a seventeen-year-old violin student at the Conservatoire. The girls were both first cousins of Claire Chevrillon – André Chevrillon was their father's brother – and from now on their life of resistance began.

On 21 June, Mandel, Bretty, the now ten-year-old Claude Mandel and their manservant, Baba Diallo, together with twenty-seven other passengers, mostly *députés* who hoped to continue the fight from the French colonies, embarked on the packet boat *Massilia* bound for North Africa. While on board they heard that Pétain had agreed terms for an armistice to be signed on 22 June 1940, at Compiègne, the place chosen deliberately by Hitler because it was the site of the 1918 armistice agreement between a humiliated Germany and a victorious France. There was now a zone of occupation established in most of northern and western France with the bulk of the remainder of the country designated a so-called free zone to be governed by the French. There was also an Italian zone and an Atlantic forbidden zone, as well as a closed zone to the east. An *Ausweis* (travel pass) was required to travel from occupied to non-occupied zone.

When the *Massilia* docked at Casablanca after three days at sea, those on board were treated not as patriots trying to fight on but as deserters. They were trapped. Pétain had Mandel stripped of his parliamentary immunity, and, now his long torment of arrest and imprisonment began, Bretty remained constantly with him as well as caring for Claude. As Spears recognized, she displayed 'the utmost courage and devotion'. They became peripatetic from now on as the Germans seized and looted Mandel's Paris apartment. Yet, in spite of her deep love for the stage, she never once contemplated returning to the theatre during the Occupation.

Meanwhile Prime Minister Reynaud, having refused the opportunity to go to England with Spears, was now, six days after the armistice, desperately trying to reach his holiday home on the Riviera, en route to Washington. The relationship between Reynaud and his mistress, the Comtesse des Portes, with whom he had been living more or less openly for years, was not just a personal scandal but had serious political consequences. According to the US diplomat Robert Murphy: 'When M and Mme Paul Reynaud were invited to dine at the American Embassy, there always was a question which lady would attend? At one dinner both arrived, providing a neat protocol problem. Hélène des Portes was an exceptionally determined Frenchwoman, and her frenzied political activity and doubts about the war were the gossip of Paris. Even after war broke out, she persistently urged Reynaud and his ministers to negotiate peace with Germany.'

Hélène, a fascist sympathizer, 'so violently anti-British that Hitler had once sent an emissary to woo her favours', had long been urging Reynaud to surrender, even going to the lengths of intriguing with a key US diplomat. The disgusted Murphy later recalled: 'I don't think her role in encouraging the defeatist elements during Reynaud's critical last days should be underestimated. She spent an hour weeping in my office to get us to urge Reynaud to ask for an armistice.'

Now that Pétain had taken over, Comtesse des Portes hoped that she and Reynaud could escape to a new life in Washington. But on the way south, with Reynaud at the wheel of a car dangerously overloaded with trunks, suitcases and other pieces of luggage, the car swerved violently when a hatbox was dislodged and fell into the front, obscuring the driver's view. They hit a tree, killing Hélène des Portes instantly. Reynaud, who suffered a minor head injury, apparently told Bullitt: 'I have lost my country, my honour and my love.'[*]

In the subsequent parliamentary debate in the Vichy Opera House on 10 July, Pétain exploited the absence of the opposition *députés* and was granted full powers as head of the new French state. The term *l'État Français* was chosen in deliberate opposition to the French Republic, which it was replacing. Pétain had long insisted that the morals of politicians of the Third Republic were rotten, as the death of Comtesse des Portes surely illustrated. Just a year earlier, when Pétain, then Ambassador to Madrid, was invited to return to Paris and assume political power he remarked, according to Murphy, the American diplomat, 'What would I do in Paris? I have no mistress!' – a somewhat hypocritical remark as he had been a bachelor into his sixties famous for his womanizing. Yet on 12 July he appointed two men to senior positions, neither of whom conformed to the ideal he was promoting of the perfect family. Pierre Laval, the swarthy self-made newspaper-owner who became Vice-President and his designated successor, had but one child, a daughter, Josée, while Fernand de Brinon, the Catholic aristocrat appointed as representative to the German High Command in Paris, had a Jewish wife, born Jeanne Louise Rachel Franck, a Parisienne socialite and divorcee who was to cause her husband some embarrassment in the months to follow.

At the other extreme from women who were preparing to give their lives to the nation were the young female actresses, the mythical and glamorous Parisiennes or 'ambassadors of the new European order',

---

[*] After his discharge from hospital, Reynaud was arrested on Pétain's orders and imprisoned at Fort du Portalet, where the Germans held him until the end of the war. Reynaud was liberated by Allied troops on 7 May 1945.

as the tragic, self-deluding actress Corinne Luchaire described them. In April 1940, two months before Italy declared war against France, the teenage film star was introduced to Count Ciano, Italy's Minister of Foreign Affairs and Mussolini's son-in-law. In her own faux-naïf account she maintained later that, although flattered by his amorous attentions and aware that he was married, she did not realize then that he harboured such dangerous ideas against her own country, merely that, in gallantly paying court to her, he was playing a sort of game. For a while they met daily, but she claimed later that she found herself involved in 'things I did not understand'.

Corinne Luchaire spoke for many when she explained that of course at first she felt uncertain and apprehensive on hearing about the armistice. But within days the German soldiers she met calmed her by their noticeable demonstration of respect as they stood up and saluted. She learned from a hotel chambermaid that 'the Germans in the hotel were not doing any harm, paid for their own drinks and dined at small tables without paying attention to the other clients of the hotel'. Corinne, because of a childhood spent with her mother among Nazis in Germany, was well placed to reassure French women that the Germans were not at all 'the big bad wolves' they had been portrayed as before the war, but were in fact civilized creatures who would bring a sense of order.

Even Youki Desnos, the artist's muse and model at the core of the bohemian artists' circle in Montparnasse, wife of the surrealist poet and journalist Robert Desnos, recorded in her memoirs that at first the sight of Germans and their swastikas made her legs so wobbly she had to sit down on the terrace of Maxim's. Immediately, a German naval officer took a chair next to her, ordered champagne and proposed she should drive off with him to Rouen. According to her explanation, it was all too easy to fall into conversation. 'There I was, having shared champagne with the enemy. Oh *zut alors*! But it was the gospel truth that he had a way with him, that admiral did.' Youki loved Paris so much that she did not want to escape with Robert. 'Having been so afraid, the people of Paris, regaining confidence, began to tease the invaders, harmlessly nicknaming them *Haricots Verts* or *les Frisés*. After the agony of defeat a kind of euphoria reigned.'

Throughout the capital that summer there were similarly easy and relaxed café encounters between well-mannered Germans, not always in uniform, and elegant Parisiennes eager to hear about life elsewhere, angry at being abandoned by their own menfolk and enjoying a mild flirtation. It was just such a chance meeting that led to Johann and Lisette* becoming lovers that summer, though Lisette insisted later that had Johann been in uniform she would not have engaged in conversation. Johann, aged thirty-one, was serving in the Wehrmacht Auxiliary Forces as an interpreter (he had excellent French), and so was often in civilian clothes, which made it easier for them to be seen strolling around the sights of Paris together, walking up the Eiffel Tower (the Resistance had put the lift out of action) and eating in romantic restaurants à deux. Although he was married with two children, something he probably did not immediately reveal to the twenty-seven-year-old Lisette, the couple soon began an affair. By the time Lisette brought Johann home to meet her parents her mother Françoise, a concierge in one of Paris's nineteenth-century apartment blocks near the Hôtel de Ville, was delighted by the man she immediately started to call her son-in-law.

For many of the profoundly demoralized French, the arrival of the German army in June 1940 was almost a relief. What they had feared had now happened and it was not too bad. The German soldiers, well dressed, amiable and often French-speaking, were ordered to behave with restraint and good manners – as many Parisiennes could not fail to notice. 'More than any Frenchman ever did, German soldiers invariably stepped aside politely in the street or in the Métro for us in our nursing uniforms,' recalled the Viennese-born Gitta Sereny, then a teenage nurse without a home and already embarked on the life story in the course of which she would deny her Jewishness. It was a complex part of her survival mechanism which allowed her to comment later that 'the German officers with whom I had to

---

* Names have been changed to protect the families but the original letters between this couple are in the United States Holocaust Memorial Museum, Washington, DC. See Caroline Moorehead, 'Sleeping with the Enemy', *Intelligent Life*, September/October 2013.

negotiate for food, clothes or documents were always courteous and often extremely helpful'.

The most noticeable and most immediate changes for all Parisians were the daily displays of goose-stepping power as the Wehrmacht marched down the Champs-Elysées, the change of time as the clocks were brought forward by one hour so that Paris was on the same time as Germany, the night-time curfew from 10 p.m. until 5 a.m., and the exchange rate, which was fixed at the hugely favourable twenty francs to the Reichsmark, which meant that everything German soldiers could buy in Paris was at a bargain price, especially attractive because much of the produce was unobtainable back home. A few shops took advantage at first by dramatically raising prices. Lancel, for example, upped the price of a suede bag from 950 francs to 1,700 over ten days but were later penalized when the Préfecture de Police, charged with carrying out inspections, discovered the increase. Native Parisiennes were distraught at being priced out of the market by the new German buyers. Helmuth von Moltke, the aristocratic German lawyer drafted into the Abwehr intelligence service (though he was opposed to the Nazis), wrote home to his wife in Berlin telling her how he felt that the influx of Germans, both civilians and army representatives, in Paris made an 'ugly impression . . . One sees high party functionaries with their wives, traversing the town in big cars on shopping expeditions.' He was appalled, he told Freya, by stories of generals travelling to Paris and buying several fur coats. 'The most disgusting are the people from Berlin who come to Paris for a day to stock up on everything imaginable.' On the other hand he described the attitude of the native population as 'reserved . . . but on the whole sickeningly friendly . . . Everybody confirms unanimously that the women . . . were positively queuing up to get a German soldier into bed, evidently from a feeling that he was the stronger and that it was more fun with the stronger man.' Germans played on this attitude, with posters displaying a handsome German soldier gazing at a lost child above the slogan: 'Populations abandonnées – Confiez-vous au soldat allemand!' (You have been abandoned – put your trust in the German soldier).

As the well-brought-up, half-Jewish Simone Kaminker remarked when she first noticed German soldiers: 'They were fantastic – tall, tanned, Wagnerian.' Simone Kaminker, still a teenager in early 1940, not yet the world-famous Simone Signoret she would soon become, was living in Brittany some five hours away from her Paris home when war was first declared. One day four German soldiers from Hanover came to live in the house that she and her mother and younger brothers were renting. Their father, André, had escaped to join de Gaulle in London, but they lied about his whereabouts, insisting that they had no idea where he had gone, he had just disappeared in the upheaval. Her mother assigned the German soldiers tasks such as fetching the water and feeding the rabbits and then, as suddenly as they had arrived, they were gone. In September 1940, Mme Kaminker decided it was time to reclaim the family apartment in Neuilly, just outside the centre of Paris, seven rooms in a splendid, deserted building in a deserted city. Surprisingly, the little Kaminker boys found their toys were still where they had left them. The only other inhabitant of the building was the disagreeable concierge, who complained that the family had not paid their rent for months.

Mme Kaminker now set about organizing Protestant baptisms for the boys while Simone, the eldest child, who had just passed her baccalauréat in Brittany, was sent out to look for work. She felt alone in this smart part of Paris where Pétain was 'a perfect symbol of reassurance for the good French bourgeois' and where so many lives went on as before. 'By which I don't mean to say that they were bad. They were waiting.' The well-to-do Jewish families who might have shared her anguish had left Paris and not returned, whereas the poor Jews of the 3rd and 4th arrondissements had remained. 'But the 4th arrondissement is far from Neuilly-sur-Seine and I knew no one there.' Although Simone harboured dreams of becoming an actress, she needed first to work as the family breadwinner. Remembering a classmate from Neuilly who had become a famous actress while still a schoolgirl, Corinne Luchaire, she went to a premiere to celebrate her success, and Corinne had lightly tossed off a suggestion that she should call her.

Corinne's father was the journalist Jean Luchaire, an old friend of Otto Abetz, the Francophile former teacher who in November 1940, aged thirty-seven, became German Ambassador in Paris. Abetz had married Luchaire's former secretary, Suzanne de Bruyker, so when

Luchaire was asked to edit a new evening paper it was Abetz who ensured that he was paid an enormous salary of 100,000 francs a month, plus expenses, which enabled him to live in great luxury, lunch at La Tour d'Argent and keep expensive mistresses – none of which, according to his loyal daughter Corinne, he had done in the past. Now Luchaire needed an assistant. 'Which is how, without professional qualifications, without knowing how to type and without Jean Luchaire's asking me "where is your father?" . . . I was hired at 1,400 francs a month as the assistant to the personal secretary of the future director of the big collaborationist newspaper, which was to be called *Les Nouveaux Temps*.'

Simone insists she was little more than a glorified office girl who, with her notebook in hand, followed Luchaire around, organized flowers for famous actresses such as Zarah Leander who were passing through Paris, and answered the phone. More than once she took a worrisome call which announced: 'I'm a friend of his sister's.' Simone understood what that meant as Luchaire's sister had a Jewish husband, Théodore Fraenkel. Simone saw many women – 'a whole raft of ladies' – who called in person begging for a personal favour, usually to arrange the release of their prisoner husbands. Simone survived working for this collaborationist paper for eight months, but feared that before long everyone in the office would know about her Jewish father. Her position was therefore dangerous and may also have lost her friends, but crucially it helped her family – so poor that their phone had been cut off after her mother failed to pay the bill – to get through another harsh winter without starving. In September food-ration cards were introduced and everyone had to queue for hours to be given one. But often there was little to queue for other than mangel-wurzels, the dreaded root vegetables. Simone frequently saw her famous friend Corinne breeze into the office on her way to a party, always superbly dressed by Jacques Fath; she 'never failed to remember a kiss for her poor friend relegated to her cubbyhole'.

Slowly, the terms of the armistice began to sink in. The French had to pay for the 300,000-strong German Army of Occupation, amounting to twenty million Reichsmarks per day, paid at the artificial exchange rate. This was fifty times the actual costs of the occupation garrison. The French government was also made responsible for preventing citizens from fleeing into exile. Germany took almost two million French soldiers as prisoners of war – one of whom was Jean Herz, son of Bernard – and sent them to work in Germany. In Paris itself it took little time for new, bold black German signage to appear, with enormous swastikas displayed on the grand boulevards as well as flying from key public buildings such as the Chambre des Députés and the Sénat. On the streets German soldiers patrolling with bulldogs replaced elegant ladies window-shopping with poodles, while the best hotels and houses were swiftly requisitioned and thousands of hotel and restaurant staff were suddenly required to serve Germans.

The Musée du Louvre, which had closed in September 1939 after transporting 3,691 paintings to pre-arranged destinations (mostly chateaux in the Loire), for fear that they might be destroyed by bombs, was now ordered to reopen to give a semblance of normality to the city. But it was only a partial reopening, as few treasures remained and many galleries were entirely empty. Nonetheless the Germans produced itineraries which occasionally led the new visitors to stare at blank walls.

In June 1940, when Hitler made his one and only visit to Paris, flying in suddenly and secretly the day after the armistice agreement had been signed, he briefly visited the mighty art gallery. He is pictured standing among some of the enormous sculptures considered too big or too dangerous to move, all that remained. But the visit was intended to make a statement, because one of Hitler's key war aims was to expropriate French culture, proving the superiority of German culture in every possible way from music to fashion. He wanted to create his own art gallery in Linz, his home town, and this required the expropriation of Jewish-owned art on a massive scale. Later, the Louvre served as a temporary warehouse for artwork stolen from Jewish collectors. A 1943 image shows 170 canvases stacked against a wall, while another shows a hall cluttered with crates containing sculptures and other large pieces. Expropriation, or spoliation, was both an economic necessity – the objects could be sold – but also an essential part of the procedure of dehumanization preceding extermination. It was part of the mechanism of genocide, to disorientate, slowly destroying any sense of belonging by depriving Jews of what they owned. Removing the art was a stage in the process of sucking the lifeblood from Jews, most of whom saw themselves as French first, French above all else, so entrenched in French soil that many of them had fought in the French army or given their sons to the country or even bequeathed their homes to the state.

But nowhere were the effects of the Occupation felt more acutely by Parisians than in their stomachs. After August 1940, when stringent food rationing was introduced, people had to register first with the authorities, then again with an individual baker and butcher, and then had to collect coloured stamps, which the French called tickets, from the local Mairie. During the phoney war several restaurants still seemed to offer, as one American journalist reported, 'a choice between seven kinds of oyster and six or seven kinds of fish, including bouillabaisse followed by rabbit, chicken or curry and fruit salad, pineapple with kirsch or soufflé à la liqueur'. And even in 1940 a select number of Parisian restaurants such as Maxim's, La Tour d'Argent and Le Boeuf sur le Toit seemed able to offer menus that offered similarly fine dining on a grand scale for those in power. But for the bulk of the population, already suffering the effects of a poor harvest made worse by the invasion, once the Germans started to requisition food along with everything else, daily life for those not willing or able to enter the black market involved a painful mixture of hunger and queues. From the outset, the products that were rationed included bread, sugar, milk, butter, cheese, eggs, fats, oil, coffee and fish, and the list lengthened as the war dragged on. And of course the rich, with access to country cousins or the black market, not only did not suffer in the same way but made light of the difficulties. One customer commissioned from Boucheron, the Place Vendôme jewellers, a charm bracelet comprising small cars, each one engraved with the name of a rationed foodstuff. Janet Teissier du Cros, the Scotswoman married to a French soldier, described long queues for food, full of grumbling women often standing unprotected in the rain as they inched forward. 'We all spoke our opinion without restraint,' she wrote, 'and I never even attempted to conceal my origins for it only made them more friendly. When at last my turn came and I was inside the building, going from counter to counter, from queue to queue, for the various cards, I was always in a fever lest some mistake be made and I come away with less than my due.' Those whom Janet resented above all were the women behind the counters, women no doubt as underfed and overworked as the rest. 'They were most of them tasting power for the first time in their lives.'

On 11 October 1940 Pétain made a radio speech in which he alluded to the possibility of France and Germany working together once peace in Europe had been established. In this speech, he used the term 'collaboration', linking the word to the idea of peace with Germany. And that month the Vichy government, on its own initiative, showed what being a collaborationist government meant when it published the first in a series of anti-Semitic measures, the Statut des Juifs, which authorized the exclusion of Jews from the professions, the civil service, the military and the media. It was the beginning of a series of ever harsher exclusions which made living in Paris for Jewish women close to impossible. On 24 October Pétain conducted an historic meeting with Hitler at Montoire, 125 miles south-west of Paris, at which he and Laval discussed with the Führer how Franco-German collaboration would work in practice. For Pétain and Laval, collaboration with Germany, which they believed would soon be the dominant force not just in France but in European affairs, was the means by which France might secure a better place in a post-war Europe. In the short term they also hoped that collaboration would lead to some immediate improvements: the return of most prisoners of war, the continuing safety of the French population, a decrease in the war indemnity France was obliged to pay and, of course, an assurance that Vichy's sovereignty over the occupied and unoccupied zones would be respected.

Thus, as autumn approached, the severity of the new Vichy laws against the Jews forced Suzanne Belperron, like many businesswomen, to understand that if her company was to survive it would now have to be owned by her. Yet such was her determination to remain in Paris that she declined an invitation from Paul Flato, the flamboyant New York jeweller, to move to America. Many others realized that they should now try to escape, although it was fast becoming impossible. Picasso's friend and art-dealer Paul Rosenberg, having already moved out of Paris to the country and having tried to conceal or send abroad as many canvases as possible, left for the

United States via Lisbon on 20 September 1940 with his wife and daughter. Seventy-five years later his granddaughter, Anne Sinclair, once more back in Paris, would tell his story. The family still have not recovered all their pictures.

But some of those who had initially fled Paris now returned to a city which many of them felt had had its soul excised. Rosemary Say, a well-brought-up young English girl who had been working as an au pair in Avignon in 1939, left it too late to escape from the country so that when she finally decided to flee, against the surging crowd and with suitcases and her much treasured hatbox, she could get only as far as Paris. On the train she shared a carriage with a young soldier returning home to his dying mother. After a long and hot journey he suddenly jammed his rucksack against the train door, lifted her, un-protesting, on to the carriage bench 'and without a word being said, we made love. It was brief, perfunctory and almost totally silent. We both felt comforted.' After that, Rosie went on to work at the American Hospital, swabbing down corridors and waiting at table, a post which lasted only three weeks as the Americans decided that employing a British national was a liability. The woman who found Rosemary a new place to stay was Hoytie Wiborg, an American heir-ess and well-known lesbian in pre-war Parisian artistic circles, who proved a good friend.

A silence prevailed in the capital, breached occasionally when a black Citroën Traction Avant – the favourite Nazi car in Paris – screeched terrifyingly out of nowhere. Jean Guéhenno, a writer and teacher who decided he would write, in private, for himself but pub-lish nothing during the Occupation, found the silence of Paris with no birdsong unnerving. All the birds had died when the city's large oil and gas tanks were set on fire as the Germans approached. As the black smoke spread out over the streets and parks, it poisoned everything. 'What is certain is that nothing is moving or singing in the trees behind the house . . . and that adds to our sadness.'

It was the same desperate sadness which young Cécile Rol-Tanguy experienced. In early June, just over a year after her marriage to the Spanish Civil War veteran Henri Rol-Tanguy, their first child, a daughter named Françoise, had suddenly fallen dangerously ill from extreme dehydration. Cécile, twenty-one and alone as Henri was fighting at the front, rushed the baby to the nearest hospital where she died on 12 June, just a few months old. 'I can still remember the terrible pall of burning smoke over Paris and wondering if that was what had made my baby ill. I left her in the hospital overnight and when I went back the next day there was another baby in her bed,' recalled Cécile, closing her eyes as if the shock were yesterday. Still today she cannot talk about the death of her first baby without reliving the agony. To make matters worse, Henri was then arrested as part of a round-up of communists following a French decree, issued by Reynaud's government, imposing the death penalty for those accused of 'demoralizing the army' as the Germans closed in on Paris. Her father, François Le Bihan, an early Communist Party member, had already been arrested. As the country was plunged into chaos, Cécile agreed to resume work typing political pamphlets for the Metal Workers' Union, now forced underground. 'Françoise was buried on 15 June, the day after the Germans entered the city . . . It was only later I realized how work had helped to assuage my terrible grief,' she said.

Towards the end of 1940, following the French surrender, Henri was freed and returned to Paris. But his reunion with Cécile was short-lived. After two comrades had been arrested, he realized he had to go underground, moving around constantly, so the couple spent the rest of the war living apart, meeting whenever they could. Henri, a keen amateur cyclist before the war, mostly stayed with loyal cycling friends who in general were not politically active and therefore not suspect. Cécile from now on was living mostly with her mother.

Although there was not yet any organized Parisian resistance movement, and the most likely resisters, the communists, had been neutered thanks to the Nazi–Soviet Pact, women in Paris nonetheless found they had to adopt an attitude. In little more than a month at least a million and a half French soldiers had been captured and taken as prisoners of war to Germany. Although some would be released over the next four years, often as a result of bribery, favours owed, blackmail or bargaining, others had escaped to England or were in hiding, and those left behind were often the elderly and infirm. Paris became a significantly feminized city, and the women had to negotiate on a daily basis with the male occupier. Many of those whose husbands were prisoners of war had no cash to buy food because in pre-war days it was the husbands who handed them housekeeping money each month from their wages. Stories of women who did not have their own chequebooks and who had to fight with banks and prove their husbands were still alive and held captive were legion. Most decided they would simply try to get along with daily life as best they could and obtain enough food to feed their children, while hoping they would never come into contact with Germans. But if they encountered them there were stark choices to be faced between making friends with the occupiers, especially if they believed Germany was likely to win the war, and indulging in minor acts of resistance such as walking out of a bar if Germans came in, or misdirecting them if they asked the way. Actual sabotage was rare in 1940.

And there were still English women in the city, often governesses or nannies such as Rosemary Say, who after her sacking from the American Hospital was doing the best she could to survive until she could find a way home. She was working a fifteen-hour day, mostly washing up greasy plates, in one of the many police canteens established all over Paris to feed policemen whose families had fled to the countryside to escape the Germans. She received no wages but was fed at the canteen and lived with the concierge. 'The Canteen quickly divided into pro-German and pro-English groups . . . there were fierce arguments and even fights as the pro-German police would curse the English as I served them at table.' Rosemary was desperate to tell her parents she was alive but could not even send them a letter from Paris as these were banned. She begged a favour from a policeman called Laurent who was often in Paris although based in Toulouse. 'The price, of course, was that I was to go to bed with him. We both honoured the arrangement. We walked to a brothel near the canteen and made love in a small room surrounded entirely by mirrors. I still have the letter he wrote . . . from Toulouse.'

The socialist journalist Jean Texcier, shocked by everything he saw in Paris, wrote a list of more than thirty suggestions for women not brave enough to resist actively yet ready to convey to the occupiers that they were not welcome without antagonizing them. For example, a shop with a sign announcing 'Hier Spricht Man Deutsch' was to be avoided even if it was where basic underwear had previously been bought. Go elsewhere, he urged, choose a shop where they did not speak German. Colette, too, advised in her columns that Parisian women should go out only to find food and should stay at home as much as possible. But some, such as waiters, Jews and prostitutes, were denied a real choice. On the day the Germans took control, the best-known brothel in Paris, Le Chabanais, once frequented by royalty, announced with a notice on its door: 'The house will open at three o'clock.' Yet in another part of town a popular brothel for German soldiers behind the Gare Saint-Lazare doubled as a place of safety for downed British airmen on their way to the free zone because 'the Madam and her daughter are ardent supporters of de Gaulle'.

Paris was quickly dubbed the sex capital of the German Reich as more than 200 brothels, famously known as *les maisons closes*, remained open during the Occupation, some offering special effects or catering to unusual requirements, but all of them places of illusion where the social and moral rules of the outside world had been dropped. So deep-rooted were the legalized brothels in France that one Madam was famous for allowing First World War veterans free access on Thursdays. There was an entire specialist lingerie business called Eva Richard built around the brothels as the girls had to buy approved items of alluring underwear from the brothel-owners who made an additional profit. A handful of the most breathtakingly opulent among them – Le Magueryon, Le Sphynx, the One Two Two (at 122 Rue de Provence), as well as Le Chabanais – were reserved exclusively for German officers, although Hermann Göring had his own favourite, Chez Marguerite at 50 Rue Saint-Georges. Luckily, the Jewish Madam at the Chabanais, Marguerite Nathan, swiftly fled to Nice, leaving the house under the control of a deputy, just before the Germans took over the city. There was even a guide specially printed for officers with detailed photographs explaining what they might expect in each and with advice on how to avoid the risk of infection. But at the other end there were some extremely rough, less hygienic houses, and plenty in between, where the girls harboured few romantic illusions. One explained: 'I'd get there at 9 a.m. [and stay] until 2 a.m. After a hundred and seventy tricks your head is spinning around . . . it takes seven minutes a trick – undressing,

dressing and sex included. You give the guy a glass of water, he has an erection, done.'

The brothels, nightclubs and gentlemen's clubs all offered various kinds of entertainment important for the German sense of wellbeing. Some were even called *maisons d'illusions*, an acceptance that they were places where all the social and moral rules were dropped and the girls were trained to make even the guiltiest man feel cleansed. They provided such a thriving mini-economy that one young boy, a Jewish refugee from Vienna, scraped a living, unsuspected for almost two years, with false identity cards stating he was Robert Metzner from Alsace, a not uncommon ruse for those with Germanic accents.* His job was to show German soldiers the sights around the Place Pigalle, Paris's red-light district at the foot of Montmartre.

> As soon as I saw a soldier approach I'd go up to him and say, 'Would you like me to show you a place where you'll be very well entertained?' All the small places wanted more customers. There were two particular cabarets – one called Paradis and the other called Yves – where we got a commission for taking German soldiers depending on whatever they consumed. It saved my life.

The brothel-keepers may have been confident that war would not diminish their clientele, but it was a testing time for Parisian couturiers and jewellers not yet sure who their customers would be in the months ahead, nor where the precious raw materials would come from. Should they close down, or move south to Vichy and protect valuable stock in the face of the German Occupation? Trading in gold was effectively forbidden by the Bank of France after 1940 unless the client supplied the metal themselves; and similarly, if women wanted new fur coats they were required to bring their own furs to be remodelled. But although many ordinary retailers had little stock and empty shelves, haute couture and luxury were far from dead. The designer Nina Ricci, who reopened on 1 July 1940, explained, 'My

---

* Freddie Knoller, at the time of writing aged ninety-three and living in London, was eventually denounced (by a jealous girlfriend) and deported to Auschwitz in October 1943. He survived there until Liberation in 1945.

clients, who had lost everything during the exodus, came to see me to replenish their wardrobes.' At the end of October Lucien Lelong, President of the Chambre Syndicale, presented his new collection, insisting that 'women desired only to dress wisely and with dignity'. This was true for the most part, and from now on clothes for cycling – slacks or divided skirts – were *de rigueur*, as were warm hoods and windbreakers. (By 1943 there were two million bicycles on the streets of Paris, which had a notable effect on fashion.) Lelong won a prize for Parisian elegance by designing a divided skirt ensemble in red, white and blue, the three colours apparently giving a defiant signal to the Germans. However, as the bicycle became the favourite mode of transport for women in the resistance, so their outfits had to attract as little attention as possible.

But from July 1940, when five officers arrived at the Chambre Syndicale headquarters and helped themselves to an archive about the creation and export of Parisian designs, Lelong was constantly fighting. Just as Hitler wanted to steal French art, he also wanted to move Parisian haute couture to Berlin to ensure that Paris was no longer the fashion centre of the world. Lelong, believing that he was defending not only a French workforce but French culture, insisted that Parisian haute couture must be in Paris or nowhere. He went to Berlin in November 1940 to argue his case, claiming that the designers and workers would not be able to produce anything if they were removed from their familiar surroundings, and he won that battle, saving a workforce of roughly 25,000 women, often seamstresses working in specialized fields of embroidery or beading.

By the end of 1940 a round of fancy-dress balls given by the Germans offered an opportunity to sample the best of French couture. One of the most lavish was a New Year's Eve reception at the German Embassy for *le tout Paris*: literature, the arts, politics and the theatre were all represented. Corinne Luchaire, the child turned into a femme fatale by the press, was wearing only white and thought she looked 'very virginal'. Suzanne Abetz, she noted, her father's former secretary now married to one of the highest-ranking Germans in the city, 'was dressed in a rather striking manner, loaded with heavy jewels which had just been bought and to her mind marked her rise in the world'.

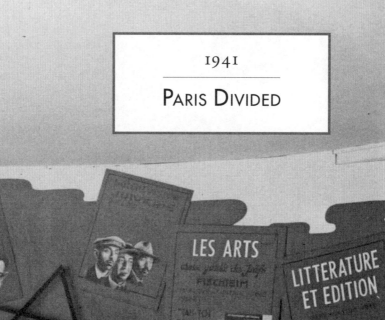

Early in 1941 Léontine Zanta, an influential Catholic intellectual and the first French woman to receive a doctorate in philosophy (in 1914), reminded her female students of their true patriotic duty at this time: to marry, have babies and find fulfilment in the domestic routine.

> Let our young female intellectuals understand this and loyally examine their conscience. I believe that many of them, if they are sincere and loyal . . . will admit that . . . if they didn't marry since they had not found a husband to their taste or because they were horrified by household work, which means that the poor things, in their blindness or their obliviousness, did not see that this was merely selfishness, culpable individualism, and that it was this sickness that was killing France. Today we need to accept the challenge and look life squarely in the face with the pure eyes and direct gaze of our Maid of Lorraine: it is up to you, as it was up to her more than five centuries ago, to save France.

Women, if they wanted once again to become the heroines of national recovery, needed only to make their education bear fruit at home, Zanta urged. 'We are not telling you to give it up, but to give it to your husband for whom you can be the intelligent co-worker, and to your children. Have the courage to endure and be patient. Our leader also advises you to do this and, before criticizing it, act; action will show your true worth more than all your diplomas.'

Zanta's counsel, however extreme it may appear today, was woven into the Vichy fabric of belief that moral collapse was at the heart of the French defeat. The republican slogan *Liberté, égalité, fraternité* was now replaced by *Travail, famille, patrie*. Vichy passed unenforceable laws, clearly flouting the belief in *égalité*, such as that forbidding the employment of married women in the public sector (overturned in 1942 through necessity) and those insisting on a different curriculum for schoolgirls to cover cookery, laundry and domestic hygiene. Vichy's socially conservative policy, reinforced constantly in speeches, placed 'the family' at the heart of policy and elevated the idea of women as mothers and homemakers, making babies and cooking, as the only acceptable version of femininity. For Vichy policy makers, women's primary role was to uphold the family and look pretty to welcome home (an often absent) father. Anything which detracted from that ideal, such as smoking, wearing masculine clothes including trousers or having short hair, was discouraged in both propaganda and laws.*

Corinne Luchaire, no longer able to make films because she was suffering from tuberculosis, now gave similar advice to women from a less academic viewpoint. She now went regularly to a sanatorium in Haute-Savoie where she played bridge and poker, drank champagne, wrote newspaper columns – and still smoked. She was coughing blood, while getting thinner and weaker.

Even in her autobiography she barely spoke of these years in the mountains. She was so truly isolated from the world that it felt like a dream time. For her, the reality was her life back in Paris when she spent her days patronizing couturiers and accompanying her father to official functions. She recalled in her father's weekly journal:

My first reaction was one of revolt against any idea of elegance or novelty. Yet one evening, while I was crossing from one bank to another and observing the Seine, I understood that it was normal to speak once again of elegance. It was impossible that life would not resume, that Paris would not continue with its tradition of elegance, the seduction of the arts and beauty. And for us Parisiennes, after completing our duty, as mothers or in our

---

* The law against women wearing trousers, never enforceable since its introduction in 1800, was finally rescinded only in February 2013, after 213 years. From August 1941 women were not allowed to receive ration tokens for tobacco for reasons of 'moral regeneration' which caused considerable stress for some. See p. 85 for example of Jeanne Bucher.

profession, our role was to put on the costume, the adorable and ridiculous hat covered with flowers, birds, ribbons and feathers whose panache was indispensable to us.

Not surprisingly, the Vichy belief that women were inferior beings who should stay at home made intelligent young women extremely angry, and ripe for recruitment by well-organized communist leaders such as Danielle Casanova, a charismatic dentist who lived on the Left Bank. When the Communist Party was banned, Danielle went into hiding as her husband, Laurent, was a prisoner of war in Germany and they had no children. She spent her spare time campaigning to help orphans from the Spanish Civil War as well as impoverished French workers. She and her friends Maï Politzer and Marie-Claude Vaillant-Couturier were involved in running a pacifist, anti-fascist youth organization called the Union des Jeunes Filles de France (UJFF), which aimed through sporting and cultural activities to help get working-class girls out of their cycle of deprivation. At the outbreak of war they had more than 20,000 members, and many of these volunteered in autumn 1940 to distribute flyers or copies of banned news-sheets such as *L'Humanité*, either by hiding them in prams, giving them to friendly concierges or dropping them into shopping baskets as women queued for dwindling food supplies. By the end of 1940, twenty-five out of thirty women on the National Committee of the UJFF were active members of a fledgling resistance movement. Danielle herself, while still writing for the underground press, helped set up women's committees in the Paris region, and was one of the leaders of the anti-Nazi demonstrations on 8 and 11 November 1940 outside the Collège de France to protest against the arrest of the brilliant physician Professor Paul Langevin. In addition, thousands of college and lycée students defied the ban on public assembly and marched down the Champs-Elysées. As a result, a number of protesters were killed or wounded and more than a hundred were arrested and sent to camps.

Already in February 1941, just six months after the setting-up of the food-rationing system – or *le Systeme D*, as it was known from *se débrouiller* meaning 'to get by or manage', since it largely referred to the way various people got round rationing – women, now responsible as heads of family, became desperate at the hours spent queuing for so little and seeing their families suffering from hunger. Many became ingenious in numerous ways, such as roasting barley and chicory to make ersatz coffee, or keeping guinea-pigs in their apartments to be killed and eaten, or discovering country cousins with vegetables. Making counterfeit food tickets was widespread but illegal, and anyone caught doing so was fined or called in for questioning. Even so, there were occasional food riots, with women turning up at town halls holding their babies high and demanding more milk. On Saturday 22 February there was serious trouble in the central market when the German authorities made a clean sweep of all the potatoes after women had been queuing for them for hours. A riot involving rock-throwing ensued, and as a result all potato distribution was banned for forty days. When potatoes were all there was, losing a ticket which represented a kilo bordered on being a tragedy, as one Parisian mother remembered. Although every patch of public space, including the Tuileries in the very heart of Paris, was turned over to vegetable production, food supply had scarcely improved by the summer. In July a correspondent for *La Gerbe* magazine wrote: 'Eating, and more important, eating well is the theme song of Paris life. In the street, in the Métro, in cafés, all you hear about is food. At the theatre or movies, when there's an old play or movie with a huge banquet scene, the audience breaks into delirious cries of joy.'

But alongside these largely youthful, more or less spontaneous resisters, the first organized resistance movement in France grew up around an unlikely group of middle-class museum curators and librarians. Thirty-eight-year-old Yvonne Oddon, whose father had died when she was a teenager, was head librarian at the Musée de l'Homme, a newly opened museum of anthropology in Paris. She and her Director, Paul Rivet, had decided in June 1940 not to join those fleeing Paris but to remain in the city, keeping the museum open, and in this way demonstrate their refusal to capitulate to the enemy. It may have seemed a small first step, but soon Oddon was sending books and clothing to French prisoners of war, then undertaking to shelter escaping prisoners and helping them cross the demarcation line from the occupied zone into the free zone, putting herself in grave danger. She discovered others who simply wanted 'to do something' – as fellow resister Agnès Humbert said, 'I feel I will go mad, literally, if I don't do something!' – and established contact with the ethnographer Germaine Tillion, with whom she started to discuss possible actions. Working with an escaped prisoner of war, Boris Vildé, and a freed prisoner of war, Anatole Lewitsky, both Russians, the group at the Musée de l'Homme began their resistance activities initially with the sole purpose of defending the anti-racist ideology which was a founding principle of the museum. Mostly, these were not Gaullists, as few of them had been able to hear de Gaulle's *appel* from London. Rather, they were a small group of men and women who met in the museum basement and, by December 1940, were busy distributing leaflets, posters and newsletters, as well as the first issue of their own journal, called straightforwardly *Résistance*.* But even this was hazardous, because it was hard to know who was trustworthy, and it was all too easy for copies of the journal to fall into the wrong hands.

Agnès Humbert, a middle-aged art historian working at the Musée des Arts et Traditions Populaires, who was divorced from the artist Georges Sabbagh with whom she had two sons, acted as secretary and typist for the group. She had heard de Gaulle's *appel* and, as a natural anti-fascist, was determined to heed it when all around her it seemed that men, former soldiers, were behaving as if it was all over. Nonetheless, she was keenly aware of the ramifications of her actions. 'Because of my meddling there will be widows, inconsolable mothers, fatherless children . . . where are all my lofty humanitarian ideals now?' she asks herself. Moments later, when she sees German soldiers removing huge bolts of cloth and many boxes of shoes back to Germany, she knows the answer: 'We simply have to stop them. We can't allow them to colonize us, to carry off all our goods on the backs of our men while they stroll along, arms swinging, faces wreathed in smiles, boots and belts polished and gleaming.'

But, just as swiftly as the resisters had got going, they were denounced to the Gestapo by a priest working as a double agent who

---

* The title was Oddon's suggestion, in homage to the actions of Marie Durand, one of the great icons of the French Protestant world, who resisted religious intolerance in the eighteenth century.

had infiltrated the group. The arrests began in January 1941; Oddon and Lewitsky were captured on 10 February, the others a little later. It was Agnès who in this tense atmosphere nonetheless persuaded Pierre Brossolette, a brilliant teacher who had been sacked from his job by Vichy and was now running a bookstore with his wife as a cover for other activities, to write for *Résistance*. Amazingly, he managed to escape arrest when all the others in the group were picked up, and he took refuge briefly at the Collège Sévigné, where Claire Chevrillon was teaching. This was considered a place of relative safety as most of the pupils, children of academics, were anti-Pétain. But nothing could be taken for granted, even within families, and Claire and Vivou had other cousins on her father's side, the Pelletiers, who were fervent Pétainistes and 'thought it went without saying that all good French citizens were Pétainistes'. These Vichyites had harsh memories of their experiences during the Guerre de Quatorze and so put their confidence in Pétain as one who, they believed, symbolized all the values they had fought for then and 'on which they'd built their lives . . . patriotism, Christian acceptance of suffering, morality tied to work and discipline, dislike of anything revolutionary or disorderly'.

In April Agnès Humbert was arrested while at her sick and elderly mother's hospital bedside and was imprisoned in various Paris jails for the remainder of the year, first in the Cherche-Midi, then in Fresnes and finally in La Santé. After a brief, and somewhat bizarre, military trial, all ten resisters were sentenced to death, but the three women, Yvonne Oddon, Agnès Humbert and Sylvette Leleu, had their sentences commuted to hard labour for life and were deported to Germany. The men were shot on 23 February in a clearing near the fortress of Mont Valérien, overlooking the Bois de Boulogne to the west of Paris, a site now preserved as a monument to the resistance. The German prosecutor remarked to Agnès: 'Madame, if the French army had been composed of women and not men, we Germans would never have gotten to Paris.' The presiding judge, Captain Ernst Roskothen, by all accounts a decent man who hated the job he was forced to do, was profoundly impressed by the courage and demeanour of all the accused. After the Liberation in August 1944, when Roskothen was arrested and briefly imprisoned, Agnès Humbert and Yvonne Oddon petitioned for his release, citing his humanity and respect for those who had appeared before him.

Just before her arrest Agnès had been agonizing over how to earn a living, having been sacked by the Vichy government from her curatorial post as art historian at the Musée des Arts et Traditions. She and a friend came up with the ruse that, before it was too late – given the new aryanization law whereby Jews were prevented from engaging in commercial activities or owning businesses – they should pretend to buy an art gallery belonging to a Jewish dealer while drawing up a private contract with him guaranteeing to return it after the Germans had left. 'The extraordinary upturn in the art market should enable us to earn a very decent living over the months to come,' she wrote. They never got around to it, but others were making fortunes from the frenzied looting of works of art and from the desperation not only of impoverished aristocrats but also of wealthy Frenchmen and women who saw an opportunity to sell heirlooms and raise cash. Paris became an antique-dealer's paradise.

At the very start of the Occupation, a law was passed by the Vichy government declaring that French nationals who had fled the country between 10 May and 30 June 1940 were no longer citizens and their property could be seized and liquidated. The Germans had already passed a similar law for the occupied zone even though theoretically the French were still responsible for law-making. The Vichy administration, believing itself independent and wishing to show it was not merely a Nazi tool, had complained about this on the grounds that, according to the Hague Convention, an occupying power might not interfere with the civil laws of a conquered nation. But even though the German expropriation policy was putting Franco-German relations under increasing strain, Gestapo officers continued removing articles from abandoned Jewish shops and houses, with a list supplied them by Ambassador Abetz of the names and addresses of the fifteen principal Jewish art-dealers in Paris. With French police providing the vans, the Germans now set about removing whatever was still to be found on the premises of the Wildenstein, Seligmann, Paul Rosenberg and Bernheim-Jeune galleries, including books, furniture and even kitchen utensils, as well as the contents of a fine Rothschild residence in the Rue Saint-Honoré. These were taken first to the German Embassy in the Rue de Lille, then to the Louvre to be catalogued and stored. But there were so many thousands of works of art which had been stolen that it was decided instead to use the Jeu de Paume, a smaller museum but deemed by the Nazis to be a more suitable space once the Germany Embassy in Paris could hold no more. By the end of October, more than 400 boxes had been brought in under the overall direction of a taskforce known as the Einsatzstab Reichsleiter Rosenberg (ERR) to undergo a meticulous and systematic classification process in order to decide who was to have what. There were various destinations, but Göring himself, who came to the Jeu de Paume twelve times in 1941 alone, was especially greedy. He was looking for Old Masters, especially those Germanic in origin, both for his own personal collection at Carinhall, his home, and for the planned gallery at Linz, in Austria. Rembrandts, Vermeers and works by Cranach the Elder were favourites, while examples of impressionist and modern art, which the Germans dubbed degenerate, were sold to Swiss dealers in Lucerne and Zurich, who did a brisk trade. The Germans might barter them for Old Masters, while dealers in Paris, in exchange for supplying information, were allowed to choose a selection of paintings. Other works were 'sold' in shady French deals, supposedly to benefit French war orphans. While all the various interest groups were squabbling, the stupefied curator in charge of the Jeu de Paume was the unlikely-looking Rose Valland, a forty-two-year-old spinster who at first, amazingly, was allowed to make an inventory of everything that arrived there and where it went. Her cataloguing skills and attention to detail were to prove invaluable in the post-war search for stolen paintings.

Rose Antonia Valland was born in 1898 in a village near Grenoble, the daughter of a blacksmith. She was a clever scholarship child, winning places at a variety of specialist colleges with the plan of becoming an art teacher. She studied both art and art-teacher training, coming top in one of the competitive exams, and continued studying art history until 1931 when she graduated with a special diploma from the Ecole du Louvre. Finally, aged thirty-four, Valland became a volunteer assistant curator at the Jeu de Paume but, in spite of her myriad qualifications, as a woman she was not eligible for a paid curator's job. By 1941, the ERR was appropriating whatever it could, its job made easier by another law of April that year which gave provisional administrators – officials installed by the Occupation authorities 'to eradicate the Jewish influence on the French economy' – the power to sell Jewish enterprises to Aryans or to liquidate them, with the proceeds going to the state. 'Thus a number of Frenchmen [in the occupied zone only at first] became beneficiaries of an act of spoliation no less direct than the Rosenberg office seizure of Jewish art treasures in Paris at the same time.' Jacques Jaujard, Director of the Musées Nationaux, did what he could to protect Jewish art that had been given to his directorate either as a gift or for safekeeping.

But his protests were largely ignored and, besides the rapacious Germans, French criminal gangs infiltrated as middlemen or informers wherever they saw a possible deal. But once the Nazis had taken over the Jeu de Paume it was Jaujard who ordered Valland to stay on and administer the building. She was there every day for the next four years – other than on four occasions when she was ordered to leave. Each time she managed to return. 'I still don't understand today,' she wrote in her 1961 memoir, 'why I was selected. But once asked, I was determined never to leave. I had no doubt what I had to do.' She was subjected to gruelling questioning from time to time when things went missing, but the most she ever said later about this was that it was 'very disagreeable'.

Effectively, Valland became a spy. Probably the Germans thought the dowdy, bespectacled academic posed no threat, or else they were distracted by other matters and largely ignored her. But although she could no longer openly take note of what came in or out, from March 1941 Valland secretly recorded everything she could, sometimes using shorthand, sometimes 'borrowing' overnight negatives of artwork that had been photographed and surreptitiously returning them, copied, the next morning. She also listened to everything (her ability to understand German helped), in order to send regular reports to Jaujard or his assistants, who had close links with the resistance. Valland noted absolutely everything she observed, not just cataloguing the looted art but recording details every day about who was packing or who was guarding, where the crates were going and when individual Nazis were coming to Paris. She even described the personal intrigues, of which there were many.

As the ERR swelled to a staff of at least sixty, Valland also cast her disapproving eye over all the complicated love affairs developing against a backdrop of increasing madness and secrecy. 'Colonel von Behr had to get rid of his mistress, Mlle Puz, when the Baronne, his real wife, turned up,' she wrote on one occasion. The glass-eyed Baron Kurt von Behr, chief of the ERR, was a notorious womanizer and, since the Baronne was English, matters were even more complicated. When Anne-Marie Tomforde married the ERR business manager, Lieutenant Hermann von Ingram, Valland wrote that 'the young bride did not hesitate to fill her trousseau with objects from various confiscated Jewish collections and to take pieces of furniture from the Rothschild collection or a tea service from the David Weill collection'.

In this sinister atmosphere, in which Jewish dealers were mostly exiled or in hiding, Jewish artists described as degenerate, and the *Pariser Zeitung* – a newspaper conceived, written and handed out by Germans, which made its first appearance in Paris in January 1941 – regularly contained articles glorifying German art and describing all modern art as decadent, it took rare courage for galleries to exhibit works the Nazis decried and openly to support banned artists.

Jeanne Bucher, a divorced grandmother in her mid-sixties, did just that. Several galleries remained open under the Occupation to exploit the flourishing art market, but Bucher was alone in taking the decision that collaboration with the enemy did not have to be a condition of commercial survival. The Jeanne Bucher Gallery was the only gallery during the Occupation to show cubists and surrealists. She dared not advertise her shows so they were never hugely commercial, but she believed it was vital to ensure that cultural and artistic life was not completely controlled by the Germans. 'It is more than my passion – my interest in art is my deepest reason to live,' she wrote to her daughter, Sybille Cournand, then living in America. Jeanne Bucher was born in 1872 into a middle-class Catholic family in Alsace just as the Franco-Prussian War was ending. This informed her understanding of the political situation, as she grew up experiencing the tension of living between France and Germany. Speaking two languages and understanding two cultures enabled her, in the 1920s, to discover German avant-garde artists and promote them. She always tried to help young artists at the beginning of their careers and in this way learned about new movements such as cubism, surrealism, abstraction.

She had married, aged twenty-three, Fritz Blumer, a renowned pianist thirty years older, but the marriage was not happy and in 1901 she fell passionately in love with the poet Charles Guérin. But divorce seemed impossible as Blumer, discovering the liaison, made her choose between her passion and her daughters. She refused to make that choice, deciding instead to wait until her children had grown up and remain on good terms with her husband. But Guérin died tragically young, in 1907, and after that Jeanne continued outwardly to lead an ordinary life, doing the sort of volunteer work at hospitals expected of women of her class during the Great War. But in a letter that she wrote at the end of her life, she explained that the enormous love which Guérin had stirred in her and which she had been forced to suppress had in fact nourished another, more powerful love which she had directed towards art and artists.

After she had at last divorced her husband, Jeanne decided to dedicate her life to modern art and, reverting to her maiden name, moved to Paris. Aged fifty, without significant financial means, she nonetheless embraced a new career and in 1925 opened her first gallery in an annexe of the exhibition shop of Pierre Chareau, the architect and designer. Her first show that year presented works on paper by Jacques Lipchitz, the Lithuanian-born Jewish sculptor, and she soon earned a reputation as one of the key leaders pioneering modern art in Paris. She never had enough money to keep artists under contract but instead used her instinctive ability to spot talent among young artists, and her wisdom to help support them, and to build up as many works as her meagre funds would allow.

In 1936 she moved to a new gallery in the Boulevard du Montparnasse where she displayed works by more established artists in the Montmartre and Montparnasse communities, including Picasso, Joan Miró, Kandinsky, Lipchitz and Max Ernst, as well as the lesser-known. But in 1940, following the invasion, even she was forced to close down and leave Paris for a while. She returned at the end of 1940, reopened her gallery and from then on, defying the Germans in numerous ways, managed during the Occupation to organize at least twenty exhibitions. When the right-wing press attacked the Lipchitz sculpture *Prometheus and the Vulture* (which had been commissioned in 1937 by the French government for the Grand Palais) and demanded its destruction, she responded by organizing an exhibition of his preparatory sketches. Usually, she did not announce her exhibitions in advance so as not to endanger the artists by asking for the required authorizations. But nor could there be any press coverage for her shows while they were running, because many critics were reduced to silence and others dared not express any enthusiasm for modern art.

Bucher's house soon became a centre for intellectual resistance in Paris, visited regularly by Picasso (who was forbidden by the Germans from exhibiting), by members of his circle of painters and by surrealists such as Paul Eluard and Michel Leiris. The gallery took up the first floor of the house, which was set back from the road with a small garden in the front. Georges Hugnet, the multi-talented surrealist poet and graphic artist whom Bucher had met in the course of her first show, took over the ground floor for his printing activities, not least making false papers for other artists in danger, documents which Bucher would hide behind tapestries and under rugs.

In 1940 Bucher published one of the first essays calling for resistance, *Non Vouloir*, written by Hugnet, in a special edition which included four engravings by Picasso. Thanks to her prestige among artists, the house was frequently visited by German officers, usually not in uniform, who poked fun at the modern art on display but often bought it just the same. She wrote to her granddaughter in America about these visits, saying she did not object to the men's nationality as long as they appreciated the art. But on one occasion she lost her temper and asked her visitors, in impeccable German, why they bothered to look at a painting if they thought it was 'bad'. At the same time she took down a photograph of one of Arno Breker's sculptures and stamped on it, shouting, 'That's German art, so look what I do to it.'

People were being arrested for much less. But Bucher was daring in everything she did. She had been exhibiting the paintings and gouaches of the Russian émigré and abstract painter Wassily Kandinsky since 1936 and saw no reason to stop now. But the Germans closed an exhibition of his work at her gallery after just one day.

Sometimes, if the Germans removed from the walls art of which they did not approve, she simply put it away in drawers. Françoise Gilot, the young artist who was to become Picasso's mistress, recalled that she liked Max Ernst's work a lot. 'So I'd go to Jeanne Bucher's gallery before 6 p.m. and then, after it closed, she would show me her Ernst paintings.' In addition, Bucher used the attic rooms of her premises as a safe house in which to hide resisters from time to time. A young medical student, on the run from the Gestapo, was both amused and scared to find he was sleeping in a bed with Braques and Picassos underneath his mattress. But one of her bravest activities was trying to protect the empty properties of those who had been forced to flee, such as Lipchitz and his wife Berthe, who in 1941 thanks to the efforts of the American journalist Varian Fry managed to escape via Marseilles to New York.* The home of the Lisbon-born artist Maria Elena Vieira da Silva, married to the Hungarian Jewish abstract painter Árpád Szenes, who managed to flee in 1940 to Portugal and eventually Rio de Janeiro, was similarly protected by Bucher, who installed friends she trusted to live there as a way of making sure the Nazis did not move in. Henri Goetz, the French-born surrealist, remembered Bucher for the way she disdained the style of fashionable wealthy dealers. 'As for the previews she held,' he recalled, 'nothing could be further removed from the fashionable events of the time: the privileged few were discreetly asked into the kitchen where they were seated on a long bench and served tea and biscuits.'

Bucher found solace in her gallery among the art she loved. She was uncompromising in her determination to continue exhibiting, which she said mattered more to her than food. She refused ever to use the black market. As a long-term smoker she found that not being able to get tobacco – women did not have the right to buy this during the war – was a particular penance. Men could get one packet a week, so her friends, several of whom believed they owed their lives to her, gave her their allowance whenever they could.

*

* Fry volunteered for the Emergency Rescue Committee, which had been set up shortly after the fall of France to rescue intellectuals and others hunted by the Nazis in Vichy, and which saved at least 2,000 people.

'You have to understand that the forms of resistance were innumerable,' explained Jeannie de Clarens (née Rousseau), who had never spoken about her own particular story of resistance until she was ferreted out in 1998 by David Ignatius, a reporter from the *Washington Post*. Jeannie was not at first part of any organized group, but the moment she graduated in 1939 from the Paris Institute of Political Studies, the Sciences Po – top of her class – she had asked the Director to find her some work where she would be 'useful'. But then in 1940 her parents decided it was no longer safe to remain in Paris and her father, a civil servant and former mayor of Paris's 17th arrondissement, took his family to the coastal village of Dinard in Brittany, near Saint-Malo, thinking the Germans would never reach that corner. But soon the enemy arrived in their thousands, preparing for a possible invasion of Britain. So when the local mayor approached M. Rousseau, his trusted neighbour, asking if he knew someone who could speak German to work as a liaison with the army, Jeannie's father volunteered his own daughter, knowing her fluency in German and insisting, 'She wants only to be useful.'

For the next few months Jeannie enjoyed her work. 'The Germans still wanted to be liked then,' she recalled. They were happy to talk to someone whose German was fluent enough to enable them to engage in conversation yet who, they concluded, was surely too young and pretty to understand all that they let spill about names and numbers and plans. Soon the British were receiving so much intelligence about German operations in the Dinard area, partly thanks to Jeannie who had been approached by a local resister, that some Germans believed there must be a well-placed agent there. In January 1941 Jeannie was arrested by the Gestapo and held at Rennes prison for a month. But when a German army tribunal examined her case, the Wehrmacht officers from Dinard defended their charming translator, insisting that she couldn't be a spy. She was released, but clearly there was still some doubt surrounding her and so she was ordered in any case to leave the coastal area.

Now, having acquired the taste for resistance through listening, she went back to Paris where she quickly found a new job acting as an interpreter, this time for a French industrialists' syndicate, a sort of national chamber of commerce for French businesses trying to sell in Germany, with offices on the Rue Saint-Augustin. Jeannie soon became a key member of the organization, a role which involved meeting regularly with the German military commander's staff, whose headquarters were at the Hôtel Majestic. She would visit the Germans almost every day to discuss commercial issues, such as complaints that the Nazis had commandeered inventories and offers from French businessmen to sell strategic goods like steel and rubber to the Germans, and was accumulating a vast amount of basic intelligence. But she felt her information was going to waste.

It was then that she met an old friend, Georges Lamarque, a mathematician several years older than her who remembered her gift for languages and suggested she might like to join him in his work. It was not an entirely chance meeting since Jeannie was travelling on a train to Vichy in a bid to find out what was going on there, instinctively recognizing that there might be an opportunity to use her knowledge but not yet knowing how. So in response to Lamarque's invitation, she unhesitatingly said yes. She told him there were certain offices and departments at the Hôtel Majestic that were out of bounds because the Germans were working in those rooms on special weapons and projects, but she thought that because she was trusted – she was just twenty-one, headstrong and extremely pretty – she could get into those restricted areas. Lamarque made her part of his small *réseau*, or network, known as the Druids, and gave her the codename Amniarix.*

Talking about it later, she said that the information was there for the plucking. 'It was very simple . . . I used my memory. I knew all the details about the plants and commodities in Germany. We were building up knowledge of what they had, what they did; we could keep an eye on what they were doing – "we" being me. And I couldn't be dangerous, could I?'

For the next two years her luck held as she soon met several of the German officers who had been her friends at Dinard and who

---

* The French resistance comprised many different movements and networks, often containing smaller units called *réseaux*, each of which had a specific purpose such as gathering intelligence, sabotage or helping evading airmen find an escape route.

were now working on secret projects. Jeannie was overhearing the most sensitive possible information – tales of special weapons that were being designed in eastern Germany and whose uses she did not entirely comprehend. Both she and Georges Lamarque suspected that she had stumbled upon one of the great military secrets of the war and understood how crucial such information was for the Allies. Lamarque urged her to seek out every morsel she could. But such work came with a high risk factor at a time when most pretty girls her age would be dating, even starting a family. Yet Jeannie felt compelled to do this instead.

Claude du Granrut, now an octogenarian living in the centre of Paris within sight of the Palais-Royal apartment where Colette spent the war years, was a schoolgirl of ten when war broke out. Looking back, trying to understand why some chose the path to resist and others to collaborate, she believes that for her family too it was a straightforward decision. 'My family took another route,' she said. 'I never saw a single German at my home. Pff no! That was very important . . . nor would my parents resort to the black market. But they were desperate for me, the youngest of the family, to grow up healthy so they often sent me away to the country where I could get fresh milk and vegetables.' Mostly life continued as normal for young Claude, who still went with her class to weekly matinées at the Comédie-Française. But she was well aware of the 'complications' many in Paris experienced in making up their minds how to respond. Could one fight the Germans? Or was it best to put up with them in order to continue the cultural life of France with its books, movies, plays and haute couture? Her father, Robert, Comte de Renty, was a veteran of the Great War, a German-speaking businessman involved in agrochemicals, who, she thought in her childhood, went off every day to his office in the Faubourg Saint-Honoré, perhaps lunching at the exclusive Jockey Club, the one place in Paris which German officers did not penetrate. Her immensely elegant mother Germaine, the Comtesse – so chic that all Claude's schoolfriends told her they were jealous of her having such a glamorous mother, 'une vraie Parisienne' – was involved in social work, visiting underprivileged women in the 20th arrondissement in the east of the city, distributing clothes, and sending parcels to prisoners of war. She was not, as Claude wrote of her later in her memoir, *Le Piano et le violoncelle*, someone whose presence could be overlooked. 'She was serene and welcoming to all.' But Claude was only vaguely aware of the welfare visits. 'She was working to maintain France in a certain way and to show solidarity with my father, who was doing much more in the way of resistance. But I did not know that at the time and it was certainly not discussed at home.' In fact, Germaine de Renty and Jeannie Rousseau were friends, but that too Claude did not know until later.

The de Renty family listened to Radio Londres, the BBC broadcasts from London in French, organized by the Free French who had escaped there – 'something we had to be very careful about when other families visited' – and followed carefully what was happening in the rest of the world. What changed for many Parisians in 1941, Claude du Granrut believes, was first the German invasion of Russia in June, followed, at the end of the year, by the American entry into the war as a result of the Japanese attack on Pearl Harbor. 'Little by little, families like ours believed that the war could be won and the Germans defeated.' The Russian invasion not only freed communists to resist but also helped motivate waverers to do something. But there was also a deeper motive for women, she believes. 'For the first time young women decided they had to do something for their country. They couldn't vote or be in the army but they felt the country had been so damaged they wanted to show that as women they could *s'engager*. It was something completely unique.'

Another factor was that by 1941 almost everyone in Paris knew someone who had been arrested. As Germany limbered up in its attempt to eradicate all Jews, Vichy collaboration helped accelerate it. The first wave of arrests took place on 14 May 1941, when 3,710 'foreign' Jews were arrested, followed three months later, after a raid on the 11th arrondissement, by a further 4,230 Jews, both French and foreign; in December 734 prominent French Jews and 250 immigrant Jews were seized. The victims were interned in four camps: at Pithiviers and Beaune-la-Rolande, south of Paris, at Compiègne to the north-east (the only one not run by the French) and at Drancy, an unfinished municipal housing estate on the outskirts of the capital itself. Drancy, lacking basic sanitary facilities and still without windows, was never intended to hold more than 700 but, from the outset, was crammed with thousands of desperate, hungry people held in atrocious conditions.

Anti-Semitism in Vichy may have been different in tone from that in occupied Paris. As Professor Julian Jackson has observed, when Vichy issued its first anti-Jewish statute in October 1940, without any prior request from the Germans, it did so almost apologetically, insisting that the government 'respects Jewish persons and property' and that the statute would be applied in a 'spirit of humanity'. Nonetheless, anti-Semitism for Vichy 'was an autonomous policy with its own indigenous roots'. Pétain's entourage included several fanatical anti-Semites for whom introducing anti-Jewish measures was both a deep-seated belief and a way of winning German favour. In order to coordinate anti-Semitic policy throughout France, the Commissariat Général aux Questions Juives (CGQJ) was set up in March 1941 and run by Xavier Vallat, a zealous anti-Semite and veteran of the Great War in which he had lost his left leg and right eye. One decree followed another in 1941; within twelve months Vichy had issued twenty-six laws and twenty-four decrees* concerning Jews. The second statute against Jews, passed in June 1941, had serious consequences for businesses because it required authorization to sell or take over a company: Jewish businesses had to register, and receivers and administrators were appointed to monitor their conduct. There were criminal penalties for anyone caught engaging in the prohibited activities. Aryanization of businesses in the free zone now matched that in the occupied zone. Decrees imposing quotas on Jewish lawyers, doctors, students, architects and pharmacists were swiftly followed by laws excluding Jews altogether from any profession, commercial or industrial. No payments were ever made for Jewish property as these were regarded as 'ownerless'.

In May 1941 the Germans requisitioned 21 Rue La Boétie, former home of the art-dealer Paul Rosenberg and, with deliberately painful

---

* A statute, or ordonnance, was effectively a law which would normally be ratified by a parliament while a decree was secondary legislation, usually complementary, and gave details of how the law should be interpreted. However, given that Vichy was an authoritarian regime, it did not always follow correct constitutional procedure.

irony, installed there a bizarre organization called the Institut d'Etude des Questions Juives (Institute for the Study of Jewish Questions) – IEQJ – to be run by Captain Paul Sézille, one of Vichy's most uncouth and violent agitators. The IEQJ's main task in 1941 was to arrange an exhibition at the Palais Berlitz entitled *Le Juif et la France* (The Jew and France), which was intended to show the harmful effect Jews had had on France. Sézille explained in the introduction to the catalogue: 'By presenting the Jew in its various manifestations, showing through compelling and carefully selected materials how deep was the Judaic influence on all activities of France, showing the depth of evil that gnawed at us, we want to convince those of our citizens who are still of sound mind and good judgement, how urgent it was to take action.' Ugly posters were displayed at Métro stations and on billboards throughout the city to advertise the exhibition, with further encouragement from loudspeakers strategically placed on boulevards between the Opéra district and the Place de la République.

During the four months when the exhibition remained open, some 200,000 Parisians paid the three-franc entry fee and many others were admitted free. Among those who attended were Marie-Pierre de Cossé-Brissac, born in 1925 to an anti-Semitic French family of noble standing. When she was young, Marie-Pierre's father instructed her: 'Do anything you like, but don't marry a Jew. We're one of the only families of the French nobility not to be Jew-ridden.' During the Occupation, Marie-Pierre's mother hosted high-society parties for Nazi collaborators, gave her child *Mein Kampf* to read and took her to the notorious exhibition with unpredictable results.[*]

Years later, Paul Rosenberg's granddaughter Anne Sinclair examined the few existing pictures of the IEQJ installation and listened to Radio-Paris describing with great pomp the Institute's opening ceremony. 'The wounding words of the speaker are unmistakably

---

[*] In 1945, she fell in love with Simon Nora, a French Jewish resistance fighter. Her furious family managed to have her interned in a Swiss psychiatric clinic, but Nora and some of his resistance comrades freed her and in January 1947 they were married, whereupon Marie-Pierre de Cossé-Brissac's family disowned her (Benjamin Ivry, 'Confronting Father's Mountain of Exaggerations', *Forward*, 13 October 2012).

clear,' Sinclair wrote. '"Today saw the rechristening of the building previously occupied by Rosenberg; the name alone tells you all you need to know."' In the photographs and in the National Sound and Video Archives can be seen the novelist Louis-Ferdinand Céline, 'a star guest with impeccable far-right credentials, parking his bike in front of my grandfather's gallery, on which the name of that formidable new office stands out in capital letters. The porch and the famous exhibition hall are easily recognisable. A huge panel on the wall shows a woman on the ground covered with a French flag, a vulture perched on her belly, with the caption "Frenchmen, help me!"'

In November yet another organization was set up, a Vichy initiative called the Union Générale des Israélites de France (UGIF), arguably the most painful of all as it ultimately forced Jews to administer and take responsibility for their own misery and destruction. The UGIF, to which all Jews living in France had to pay dues, thus not only raised money to help Jews but also, inevitably, was in possession of lists of Jewish names and addresses; it therefore became something of a trap. Those who were saved by being removed from its lists because they 'knew someone' are often ashamed and cannot talk openly of their survival. Historians estimate that the cumulative effect of all these measures meant that already, by the summer of 1941, half the Jews of Paris had been deprived of any means of subsistence.

But Parisian Jews who had fled earlier were now realizing that life in the so-called free zone was little safer. Miriam Sandzer and her parents felt trapped in the south, unable to secure transit and exit visas and all the other necessary paperwork for the family group now swollen to eleven, or to pay for tickets and hotels. As her mother was already ill from the cancer that would soon kill her, it was Miriam who was sent regularly to queue at the Spanish and Portuguese Consulates in Marseilles to seek visas. But progress was agonizingly slow so she decided to visit the Chamber of Shipping, find out what destinations ships were still leaving for and then try to obtain permits for those destinations.

As soon as she learned there were still sailings from Lisbon to Java, she set off for the Consulate of Java where she was granted an interview with the Consul, 'a very handsome man'. He offered to supply her with the necessary paperwork if she could supply him in return with a diamond ring for his mistress; she immediately took off her beautiful platinum and pearl one, but he rejected this as inadequate. Then she managed to secure and pay for eleven visas for Shanghai from the Chinese Consulate, but her plans were stymied because there were no more ships sailing to Shanghai. All the consulates were besieged with desperate people like her, many with forged papers and no money, trying to escape the Nazis. Every opening seemed to finish in a dead end, but only after more of the family group's dwindling resources had been used. Eventually Miriam was persuaded to go alone to Lisbon because she was being watched. Months later most of the group joined her there, and in November 1941, twenty-four hours before they were threatened with expulsion yet again, the British gave them a permit to reside in Jamaica. However, her two brothers had to remain in Lisbon as they were of military age and were required to join the Polish army. The depleted family sat out the rest of the war in the Gibraltar internment camp in Jamaica.*

In Paris itself it was becoming almost impossible for Jews to earn a living in any field, but jewellers especially were in difficulty since they could not acquire the raw materials of their trade. If a client ordered anything in gold they had to supply 100 per cent of the metal themselves and if platinum then 135 per cent. There were ways around this, and much 1940s jewellery was either hollow or lacy openwork or relied on large, semi-precious stones such as amethyst. Cartier turned to making other objects such as clocks, while Boucheron was not the only jeweller to develop a line of mostly silver 'beauty boxes'. Parisian women, determined to flaunt something new and elegant, would take in sufficient quantities of family cutlery to be melted down into a stylish evening clutch bag of silver, possibly with some gold and embellished with a small stone or two on the outside, with special compartments for cigarettes or make-up fitted inside. It was a decidedly outré object, announcing that the user not only was aware of the latest fashions but was demonstrating she was a modern woman, smoking and putting on powder in public, both activities frowned upon in pre-war society.

---

* Miriam finally came to London in 1945 and married her fiancé Ben Stanton.

Bernard Herz, as a wealthy Jew with a large home in Chantilly as well as a Paris apartment and valuable stock, was an early target. It appears that he was harassed and picked up for questioning as early as 1940, but Suzanne Belperron managed to engineer his release through the influence of an actress friend called Rika Radifé, who was married to the actor Harry Baur.* She knew that if the company was to survive it would now have to be owned by her. By 23 January 1941 she had registered a new limited company in her name, Suzanne Belperron SARL, with one associate and with some money lent to her for the transaction by the interior designer Marcel Coard. But the Nazis were ever suspicious of such transactions and Belperron could be under no illusions that the business would from now on be ignored. She too was taken in for questioning and forced to prove through baptismal certificates that the Vuillerme family did not have any Jewish blood.

From 1940, Germans had been making inventories of Rothschild items. According to an 8 December 1941 report by the head of the foreign currency protection command – Devisenschutzkommando – Göring himself wanted to decide on the disposal of the Rothschild family assets when he came to Paris. Among the extensive lists of table silver, knives, forks, spoons and dishes, there were 'pictures and objects of art which were found in a cupboard in the house of the Jewess Alexandrine Rothschild, Paris 2, Rue Leonardo de Vinci. These paintings and objets d'art are to be turned over to the Einsatzstab Rosenberg.' There were a further fifty-two packages of objects of art and jewellery from the property of various members of the Rothschild family, twenty-one of which were to be turned over to the ERR, the other thirty-one to be kept until sent for by Göring 'under lock and key of the foreign currency protection command'.

The Camondo family, known as the Rothschilds of the East as they had come to France from Constantinople in the mid-nineteenth century and were almost as rich, decided in 1941 to complain about the pillaging of their personal art collection and wrote letters to Paul

---

* Baur, thought to be Jewish because of his name, was arrested in 1942. But although he was released when no Jewish origins could be proved, he died shortly afterwards.

Sézille and others. Léon Reinach, husband of Béatrice de Camondo, complained about 'the spirit of hate and jealousy' that was motivating such theft. But to no avail. The family mansion at 63 Rue de Monceau stands today, as then, just the other side of the highly manicured Parc Monceau. The park was developed by a pair of Jewish financiers, Isaac and Emile Péreire, in the 1860s as a suitable area for entrepreneurs and their families to live, and was surrounded by a number of sumptuous mansions owned by Jewish millionaires, including several Rothschilds and Ephrussis; the old-established Paris Jews, who regularly attended the opera, had fine horses and carriages and were determined patrons of the arts. Ironically, the area became something of a ghetto. The Hôtel Camondo is a gem of a house rebuilt by Comte Moïse de Camondo, who at the beginning of the twentieth century demolished the simpler house he had inherited from his parents, intending that the new one should resemble the Petit Trianon of Versailles. Moïse had a keen eye for furniture and objets d'art, especially fine French works of the late eighteenth century. As a young man he was considered something of a bon vivant, but after his wife, the beautiful Irène Cahen d'Anvers, herself the daughter of a wealthy banker, had deserted him in 1897 for the handsome Italian in charge of the stables, Count Sampieri, he became more reclusive. The terms of the divorce – divorce was still considered rather shameful at the time – gave him custody of the couple's two children, Nissim and Béatrice, to whom he was devoted. But in 1917 Nissim, a pilot in the French air force, was killed in a dogfight with a German plane. Moïse, devastated, retreated further into his world of precious objects, often spending days sitting alone in the small room where he displayed his unrivalled collection of Sèvres porcelain.

Béatrice, distressed already by her parents' painful separation, now suffered again with the loss of her beloved brother, and the year after Nissim's death she agreed to an arranged marriage with Léon Reinach, scion of an intellectual and musical family that had been prominent in supporting Captain Alfred Dreyfus throughout his ordeal. They had two children, Fanny and Bertrand, and after her father's death in 1935 they divided their time between an apartment in Neuilly and a luxurious villa on the Riviera, the Villa Kerylos, a magnificent re-creation of a Greek temple. Her father had already in 1924 bequeathed the Parc Monceau house to the state, hoping that such a generous donation would perpetuate the name of the family – motto, 'Faith and Charity' – and link it with the period in French history that he loved. When he died, Béatrice made sure that his wishes were carried out and that the family home, now a museum under the auspices of the Union Central des Arts Décoratifs, was opened on 21 December 1936.*

But Léon and Béatrice soon drifted apart. She was a good-natured woman but had few interests beyond her passion for riding. She became a member of the prestigious Monts et Vallons hunt as soon as women were admitted, and hoped that her life of horses and hunting would continue without interruption irrespective of the political situation. But in July 1941 the Germans had seized several cases of paintings from the Château de Chambord in the Loire Valley, left there for safekeeping by Jewish collectors, including the Reinachs. In one of these crates was the famous Renoir portrait of Béatrice's mother Irène, commissioned by Louise Cahen d'Anvers while she was married to the banker Louis-Raphaël Cahen d'Anvers and at the same time the mistress of Charles Ephrussi.

But as far as the Camondos were concerned the Nazis wanted more than simply objects. When Renoir painted Irène Cahen d'Anvers in 1880 he turned her into a beautiful little French girl with golden curls who had left her Jewishness behind. One critic had written rapturously about the portrait at its first showing: 'One cannot dream of anything prettier than this blonde child, whose hair unfolds like a sheath of silk bathed with shimmering reflections and whose blue eyes are full of naïve surprise.' But the same year Degas, who disapproved of what he saw as Renoir's transformation into a Jewish society portraitist, wrote: 'Monsieur Renoir, you have no integrity. It is unacceptable that you paint to order. I gather you now work for financiers, that you do the rounds with Charles Ephrussi. Next you'll be exhibiting at the Mirliton with Bouguereau!'†

---

* The Cahen d'Anvers family had also donated a villa outside Paris and a great-aunt, Béatrice Ephrussi-Rothschild, had bequeathed the rose-pink villa at Cap Ferrat to the Académie des Beaux Arts.

† A reference Degas intended to be insulting by comparing him with the popular

This tension in French society was never resolved and was now being played out with tragic consequences. Reinach, schooled in the long years of fighting for justice for Dreyfus, believing that rational protests worked and that the Germans would see reason, explained at length to the authorities how both the Reinach and Camondo families had enriched the French artistic patrimony. But when Jacques Jaujard, Director of the Musées Nationaux, doing his best to protect thousands of works of art during the Occupation, forwarded Reinach's letter to Xavier Vallat, the one-eyed head of the CGQJ, the response was that the too-clever-by-half Reinach was arrogant. In any event, the Renoir had already been moved on through dealers, earmarked for Göring's collection in spite of its Jewish subject. Families like the Reinachs now urgently switched from worrying about saving their possessions to saving their lives. Reinach *père* soon moved to Pau with Bertrand while Béatrice, who lived with Fanny, continued for a little longer to ride daily in the Bois de Boulogne and to take part in horse shows and hunts, convinced that she was protected by her equestrian and German officer friends. More than that, the Camondos had given their son as well as one of the most beautiful homes in Paris to the French state, of which they believed they were a part.

It is impossible to quantify how many Parisians were poisoned by the anti-Jewish propaganda and how many were repulsed. But from now on the choice became starker: resist or collaborate. Yet although the majority of the French population entered neither active collaboration nor active resistance – the majority remained 'attentiste' (wait and see) until the end of the war – there is a notable shift at this point. The support for Pétain started to diminish from mid-1941 onwards and the support for de Gaulle and the *résistance* slowly grew from that time.

But whereas in Vichy there was official collaboration, in Paris the ideological collaboration, entertaining the enemy, was becoming

---

painter William-Adolphe Bouguereau and suggesting he might frequent the cabaret-café le Mirliton in Montmartre, owned by Aristide Bruant, friend of Toulouse-Lautrec.

more nuanced and complex. In August *Premier Rendez-Vous* starring Danielle Darrieux became the first successful film of the Occupation produced by Continental Studios, the German-financed film company based in Paris. Continental, set up by Hitler's Minister of Propaganda Joseph Goebbels to give the Germans control over the French film industry, produced thirty full-length films between 1941 and 1944, including some of exceptionally high quality such as *Le Corbeau* and *Au Bonheur des dames*. Almost all were recorded at the Paris Studios Cinema in Billancourt, and several renowned directors worked for the company. The intention was partly to rival Hollywood, as no American films could be shown during the Occupation, and partly, as with fashion and opera, to demonstrate German superiority not only militarily but culturally. Darrieux remarked later that she remembered these years as a time when she was 'totally carefree', when she and her actress friends would have their 'feet done' and 'go to the beauty parlour all the time', a clear indication that Corinne Luchaire was not alone among actresses and performers who had failed, or refused, to realize the gravity of their situation and believed that entertaining was in some ways different.

It was one thing to perform on a French stage but quite another to perform in Germany. From 1941 Goebbels was constantly trying to organize visits by artists to Germany. The first such propaganda trip, a three-week junket touring the country, included Abel Bonnard, Robert Brasillach and Marcel Jouhandeau, the writer admired by Irène Némirovsky (admittedly before he had published in 1938 his notorious pamphlet *Le Péril juif*). Yet even Jouhandeau was not without doubts and wrote about the trip in his diary: 'Why am I here? Because from the time I knew how to read, understand and feel, I have loved Germany, her philosophers, her musicians, and I think that nothing could serve humanity better than our understanding with her.' As Jean Guéhenno commented acidly: 'The species of the man of letters is not one of the greatest of human species. Incapable of surviving for long in hiding, he would sell his soul to see his name in print.'

Yet Jouhandeau was now beyond the reach of Némirovsky, living in Issy-l'Evêque, a village in the Burgundy countryside close to Vichy but in the occupied zone. The days when she had been close to those writers, when she had been part of a literary circle where she was lionized, seemed part of another era; she was now reduced to selling some jewellery and furs – mostly her mother's purloined by Irène when her mother fled the capital* – but was unable to publish any of her writings.

Life in the village appeared on the surface to be calmer for Jews, but through friends and family who were still in Paris and because of her own personal situation Némirovsky would have known of the dramatically deteriorating situation for Jews in the capital. Her publishers, Albin Michel, were sending her monthly payments of 4,000 francs but were nervous of publishing her work. Although her name did not appear on the infamous 'Otto List' (a list of books banned by the Germans which took its name from Otto Abetz), Robert Esménard told Irène that his firm was no longer able to publish her books and ensure their sale. In the circumstances, Irène saw the payments partly as a gesture of compassion and friendship and partly as an advance against sales of her work which they hoped to make after the war. But when Jewish bank accounts were frozen in 1941, Irène and her husband, Michel Epstein, deeply in debt, were worried about how they would continue to live. At this point Irène ingeniously invited Julie Dumot, her father's trusted former companion and an Aryan, to live with them. She told her publishers that this same Mlle Dumot was the author of a novel which in fact she herself had written and therefore it was agreed that payments could be made to Mlle Dumot, who subsequently paid Irène. Némirovsky had now lost her own identity as an author and at times despaired of ever again being published; nonetheless she continued to write every day. Julie Dumot was instructed, in the event that she and Michel were arrested, not only to take care of their two small daughters but also, when the money dried up, to sell the fur coats and silverware.

Later in 1941 other propaganda trips to Germany were arranged. One of the most famous, because the participants were photographed

---

* When Irène's mother, Fanny, learned what had happened to the furs and jewellery she complained, but Irène responded through an intermediary that she had assumed her mother would be thrilled to help her daughter survive.

as they departed from the Gare de l'Est standing alongside uniformed German officers, comprised eleven artists including André Dérain, Maurice de Vlaminck and Paul Belmondo (father of the actor Jean-Paul). They all argued (after the war) that they had agreed to go in exchange for the release of some prisoners of war. However, there is no evidence that any releases followed. One further trip was made in 1941, this time composed largely of musicians, persuaded to go to Vienna in early December as part of a delegation officially intended to celebrate Mozart Week. But the trip ultimately had little to do with Mozart, as even the fascist writer Lucien Rebatet admitted afterwards.

If it was a difficult path for entertainers, the hostesses, especially the three Maries – de Noailles, Bousquet and de Polignac, all pillars of 1930s café society and regulars at Le Boeuf sur le Toit or Maxim's in pre-war years – now found entertaining Germans in their drawing rooms came rather naturally. A number of women made themselves useful to the authorities in this way by introducing Francophile Germans such as Ernst Jünger, Gerhard Heller and Otto Abetz to writers, musicians and artists such as Cocteau, Christian Bérard, Sacha Guitry and others ready to socialize with their new masters. Several regular attendees, having made the connections, then agreed to visit Germany. The outspoken anti-Semites, such as Brasillach, Pierre.Drieu la Rochelle and even Rebatet, mostly did not frequent these fashionable salons.

Few of these hostesses were quite as aristocratic as their names might indicate. As a recent study of café society makes clear, many of the French elite had married American or Jewish money in the previous decades, so there were now few 'pure-bred' aristocrats. Comtesse Marie-Blanche de Polignac was the daughter of the self-made dress designer Jeanne Lanvin and heir to the fashion house her mother had created. Marie-Louise Bousquet, no beauty, was famously derided by Chanel for having the face of a monkey and the mouth of a sewer, but she was the immensely influential editor of the French *Harper's Bazaar*, and a wide variety of cultural and political figures including the cellist Pierre Fournier attended her musical soirées at 3 Place du Palais Bourbon, where her (almost next-door) neighbours were the extremely influential de Chambruns.

Josée de Chambrun, Pierre Laval's adored only child, was stylish and attractive, with olive skin, dark hair and an engaging smile. She had been well educated, spoke excellent English and could play golf and ride, both useful accomplishments. The bond between father and daughter was intense and when she accompanied him, aged twenty, to the United States in 1931 on his triumphant visit as the new French Prime Minister, the American press went wild in their praise for this chic, gay Parisienne. Three years later, at a dinner party, she met an aristocratic lawyer with dual French and American nationality, Count René de Chambrun, known as Bunny, a descendant of the original Marquis de La Fayette, the French aristocrat who fought for America at the time of the Revolutionary War. De Chambrun ran a successful international law practice which boasted Chanel among its clients. His mother was Clara Eleanor Longworth, a relation by marriage of President Roosevelt, who managed to keep the American Library in Paris open during the war. Josée and René were married in 1935, did not have children and were soon indulging in a frenetic social whirl of partying and race-going at the centre of Parisian social life. They knew everyone. As an indication of how useful these evenings were for smoothing Franco-German relations at various levels, the de Chambruns helped provide financial assistance for the Bousquet salon, and Josée introduced the popular film actress and former music-hall singer Arletty to a handsome young Luftwaffe officer, Hans-Jürgen Soehring. Though he was ten years younger than Arletty, she fell passionately and publicly in love and they were seen eating lobsters and oysters together, quaffing champagne and attending the opera, as well as visiting Megève, the ski resort in the Haute-Savoie favoured by Germans and wealthy *collabos*. On one occasion Soehring even introduced Arletty to Göring, on one of the latter's famous shopping trips to Paris. Arletty's collaboration may have been romantic, but that of her friend Josée went deeper than merely accepting and enjoying a way of life in the capital and eating with her father at the best restaurants.

According to the author William Stevenson in his exposé of wartime spying, *A Man Called Intrepid*, Pierre Laval had used his daughter in November 1940 as a courier to take messages to the Vichy Embassy in Washington because she had diplomatic immunity through her husband's work.* He believed she would not attract attention to herself and that her bags, containing documents revealing Vichy post-war aims for France to join a victorious Germany, would not be searched. But when the flying boat was delayed overnight in Bermuda, her possessions were seized.

Stevenson recounts how Josée, 'cold with anger', protested: 'This is an outrage against diplomatic protocol.' But while the arguments proceeded, the papers were photographed for the British before being returned to her, revealing Laval's conviction that Britain was finished. In early 1941 René de Chambrun returned to France, having had little success in his mission to persuade President Roosevelt to send food shipments to alleviate hunger for many thousands of refugees as well as displaced French in Vichy. Disappointed, he returned to Paris with Josée where the couple were swiftly engulfed in a round of lunches and dinners with Otto and Suzanne Abetz, as well as the German consul-general, Rudolph Schleier, and, of course, Arletty. 'For a soldier who resisted the German invasion and a lobbyist who opposed the Germans in the United States, René adapted quickly to the new order that his father-in-law and his wife were introducing him to.'

Marie-Laure de Noailles had the most fascinating, if potentially dangerous, background of all the hostesses who entertained Germans: her father was Maurice Bischoffsheim, the affluent banker of German-Jewish and American Quaker descent. One of her great-great-great-grandfathers was the Marquis de Sade, and her maternal grandmother, Laure de Sade, Comtesse de Chevigné, inspired at least one character in Proust. It was Bischoffsheim money that enabled the Vicomtesse de Noailles to live in such splendour at 11 Place des Etats-Unis in a magnificent *hôtel particulier* built by her grandfather

---

* Count René de Chambrun, godson of Marshall Pétain, son-in-law of Pierre Laval and cousin of Franklin Roosevelt, was impeccably well connected. He served as a captain in the French army until the collapse of France in May 1940 and, from that experience, believed that Britain's Royal Air Force was superior to the Luftwaffe and would ultimately stop Germany from winning the war. He was therefore sent, at the request of U.S. Ambassador William Bullitt, as special emissary to Washington to stiffen his cousin's resolve in providing arms for Britain to resist the Nazis.

Bischoffsheim and which was high on the German list for requisition. Here Marie-Laure danced, placing herself at the centre of
Parisian avant-garde style and acting as the patron and muse of
artists, filmmakers and musicians such as Man Ray, Luis Buñuel,
Alberto Giacometti, Cocteau, Salvador Dalí and Francis Poulenc.
Marie-Laure had remained in this house where she had grown up,
with Serge Lifar as house guest, during the invasion and, thanks to
help from Ambassador Bullitt, who claimed that the property was
American, managed to keep hold of her unrivalled art collection of
Goyas as well as paintings by Watteau, Van Dyck and Mondrian and
several modernist sculptures.

Most notable among the other *salonnières* who contributed to the
illusion that life in Paris was continuing as normal was the glamorous
Florence Gould, born to an American mother and a French father
in San Francisco in 1895. Florence Lacaze had trained as an opera
singer but, after her first marriage ended in divorce, married in 1923
the much older, fabulously wealthy Frank Jay Gould, son of railroad
millionaire Jay Gould, and gave up her operatic studies. The Goulds
lived mostly in the south of France where the couple had built several enormous hotels and casinos, and entertained a wide swathe of
society at their villa in Cannes. When the Occupation began, Frank
bought tickets for them both to go back to America – as Americans
they had ample opportunity to do so. But Florence refused to leave,
and in 1941 she returned to Paris while Frank remained in Juan-
les-Pins. When she discovered that the Germans had requisitioned
both her Parisian homes – a Boulevard Suchet apartment and her
Maisons-Laffitte villa – she brazenly took up residence at the Hôtel
Bristol on the Faubourg Saint-Honoré, a hotel with a reputation for
being able to acquire black-market food.

At forty-six, Florence was still fascinating and beautiful with many
male admirers, and it was now, at the Bristol, that she started her
legendary hostessing career, becoming extremely close to a number
of men, especially Marcel Jouhandeau, whom she first met at Marie-
Louise Bousquet's salon. In order to hide their relationship from his
jealous wife Elise, Jouhandeau invented stories about giving Latin
lessons to a rich American whom he had met at a restaurant called
Chez Florence. History does not relate whether or not she believed

him. Bousquet also introduced Florence to Gerhard Heller, head of the Propagandastaffel, and Heller in turn brought the renowned German writer serving in Paris, Captain Ernst Jünger, whose wife Gretha had remained in Hanover. Jünger had written one of the most powerful memoirs of the First World War, *Storm of Steel*, an account of his time fighting in France and Flanders in 1914–18, a book which Hitler admired. Jünger had been wounded several times, once in the chest by a British bullet, and even though his loyalty was obviously to Germany, he was more philosopher than politician and no mere anti-Semite. Jünger was immediately smitten with Florence and out of delicacy hid her real name in his diaries, referring to her as 'Lady Orpington'.

It was Jouhandeau's suggestion that Florence, who always admitted that she liked authors more than books, established regular Thursday literary salons. These salons, effectively co-hosted by Florence and Jouhandeau in a sumptuous apartment at 129 Avenue de Malakoff, were highly sought after, and sometimes there were as many as fifty guests, ranging from secret resisters such as Jean Paulhan, the artist and designer Christian Bérard and the artist Marie Laurencin* to influential Germans in uniform. Florence herself, rarely seen without several pieces of fabulous jewellery, was a magnetic attraction, almost as much as the free-flowing champagne, cognac and lavish black-market food. Discussion at the salons veered between literature, politics and gossip, the latter often focusing on discussion about Florence's latest affairs. Her behaviour was complicated – behaviour she would have to explain at the Liberation, behaviour for which others were punished when it was described as *collaboration horizontale*. But although Florence was never heard to utter anti-Semitic or even pro-German remarks, it was clear that, thanks to her fortune and her connections with high-ranking Germans, she enjoyed many favours not available to most Parisiennes, including a rare permit to use her car at night during the curfew and a permanent pass allowing her to cross into the unoccupied zone to visit her husband in Juan-les-Pins.

But, despite her cool exterior, Florence Gould was not left entirely

---

* In 1952 she was commissioned by Paul Rosenberg to paint his four-year-old granddaughter, Anne Sinclair.

undisturbed. According to documents unearthed after the war, there was an unsavoury episode when Göring's henchmen inspected the cellars of the Gould villa early in 1941 on the pretext of searching for weapons. None was found, but a valuable triptych and two precious single pieces were discovered, 'everything very old, carved in ivory'. These were taken by the ERR amid protestations from Florence that she had not known of the presence of these objects.

No doubt worried by what else they might seize, 'Mrs Gould declared on the spot that she wanted to contribute the entire stock of wine for soldiers on the eastern front; all the copper and brass, which filled an enormous cellar room, was to go to the German war industry.' But the matter did not end there. A few days later there was a conference with Kurt von Behr of the ERR at which a deal was agreed that, although as an American citizen she was not obliged in any way, she would offer the triptych to Göring, who would in turn present it to the Cluny Museum in Paris, 'to which the Gould family had intended to will it'. In gratitude to Göring for donating the triptych, he was then to have the two single pieces as his private property. But when Göring finally inspected the entire haul he decided that he liked the triptych too 'and ordered that all three were to be brought to Germany'.

Florence and her lawyers had further talks about the collection, but as the author of the report commented, 'they beseeched me to refrain from any further undertaking in order to avoid any difficulties for Mrs Gould . . . such as the possibility of her being sent to a concentration camp'. Florence had been outmanoeuvred. Such threats were especially worrying because in September Vichy's newly established Commissariat Général aux Questions Juives (CGQJ), convinced that Gould was a Jewish name, had been causing difficulties for her husband, who now had to provide baptismal certificates from America proving that he was Christian.

And while Vichy was helping the Nazis with much of the bureaucratic dirty work by forcing registration as a preliminary to rounding up the Jews, suave German officers in Paris could enjoy all that the city had to offer, gastronomically, culturally and erotically. In four years of occupation the Germans spent six and a half million francs on opera tickets alone. They claimed opera as their own, especially Wagner, and there were fifty-four performances of Wagner at the Paris Opéra during the Occupation compared with thirty-five of Mozart. In May, Herbert von Karajan, the young German conductor and Music Director of the Berlin Staatsoper, came to Paris with his Berlin Staatskapelle to perform for the first time at the Paris Opéra. The stars for this gala occasion – two performances of *Tristan und Isolde* celebrating Wagner's birthday on 22 May – were the German tenor Max Lorenz and the French soprano (and Hitler favourite) Germaine Lubin. Staging the opera was an enormous undertaking in wartime as it involved moving scenery, instruments and hundreds of people from Berlin to Paris. Hans Speidel, Chief of Staff of the Military Command in Paris, considered the enterprise a triumph for German logistics as well as culture, always an important goal, and was so enamoured of Lubin that he invited her the following year to perform a concert of Schubert songs, including 'Let Us Make Peace', for his own farewell party when he was posted to the eastern front. 'Now I can go off to war with happiness,' he wrote. Speidel was to remain a friend and supporter of Lubin to the end of his life.

The first performance of *Tristan und Isolde* was reserved entirely for German officers in Paris, and the auditorium became a sea of grey-green uniforms. The second was also quickly sold out, mostly to Parisians with influence who were keen to hear German music. Winifred Wagner, the composer's English-born daughter-in-law and a friend of Hitler as well as of Lubin, attended both and was guest of honour at the glittering after-party. Lubin received rave reviews for her performance of Isolde. Véronique Rebatet, wife of Lucien, a true Wagner connoisseur, was in the audience for the second performance and commented afterwards, 'I never saw a better performance of *Tristan* than the one with Germaine Lubin as Isolde.' Cocteau wrote to Lubin: 'Madame, what you have done for Isolde was such a marvel that I lack the courage to remain silent.'

But not everyone rushed to praise Lubin. The writer of one anonymous letter (the sort that was becoming all too familiar in Paris) accused her of being an 'adored artist who has sold herself'. She always argued that art was not a matter of politics and that she lived only for her art. But there was a fine line between performing and being used by those for whom you were performing. Arguably, Lubin crossed it, but she believed that her friendship with many in the German hierarchy – including a German lover, Hans Joachim Lange, a Wehrmacht officer introduced to her by Winifred Wagner, whom she liked to entertain at her chateau near Tours – gave her useful influence, all the more necessary because everyone now had friends suddenly arrested. Lange was indeed helpful to Lubin personally, securing the release of her son who had been in a German prisoner-of-war camp since 1940. But Lubin's later claims, when facing trial after the Liberation, that she in turn had used her influence to help release her elderly Jewish singing teacher, Marya Freund, from Drancy, were to prove unfounded.

At the end of the year, Corinne Luchaire, having spent the previous six months recovering in a sanatorium, married the French aristocrat Guy de Voisins-Lavernière. He was a shady character who had business relationships with the powerful and dangerous Bonny-Lafont gang, part of the Gestapo Française, the network which supplied the Germans with a wide variety of material objects through black-market contacts and worked with German police to chase Jews and resistance fighters.* There was a ridiculously lavish wedding party but it was the prelude to an extremely brief marriage. Although Mary Pickford had hailed Corinne as 'the new Garbo', she later wrote pathetically: 'No doubt it was my destiny to be involved in major international events without understanding them.'

On Sunday 7 December 1941 the Japanese bombed Pearl Harbor, and within days the United States was at war with Germany. Americans were now enemy aliens in France and subject to arrest. Drue Tartière was allowed to remain in the country since her husband (albeit away fighting) was French and the Germans had not realized that she was in fact the American actress Drue Leyton, for whom they had five times issued a death warrant on air because of the pro-British, anti-German messages she had been broadcasting on Paris

---

* Henri Lafont and Pierre Bonny, part of the corrupt Parisian underworld, took advantage of the Occupation to set up a criminal gang known as the Bonny-Lafont gang headquartered at 93 Rue Lauriston, where they carried out numerous acts of interrogation and torture.

Mondial right up until the fall of France. Drue had decided she would engage in whatever small acts of resistance she could undertake, based in her farmhouse just outside the capital at the edge of the Forest of Fontainebleau, from where she could make regular trips to the centre of Paris to keep in touch with other women who were starting to resist. In September she learned that her husband Jacques had been killed fighting in Syria for de Gaulle's Free French Forces. He had been shot in the back in Damascus by a French Vichyite prisoner-of-war whose surrender he had just accepted. Drue did not know these details immediately but she understood that she had to keep his death a secret from all in her village. If it was known that Jacques had been with the Free French, she would immediately be a suspect herself.

The final months of 1941 saw the resistance, emboldened, now taking to armed action on the streets and organized sabotage. What started in August with a young communist firebrand firing two shots into the back of a German naval cadet, as he stepped into a departing train at Barbès Métro station, continued with further acts of escalating violence in Paris and Lille, as well as strikes at the Renault motor factory in Paris, which meant that Renault were producing a quarter of the vehicles intended for Germany. The repercussions were swift and dramatic. On 20 October, after the Feldkommandant of Nantes had been shot in the back, the Germans put up posters around Paris and elsewhere in France announcing the immediate shooting of fifty hostages, with fifty more hostages to be taken if the guilty persons were not arrested by midnight on 23 October. Almost 150 Frenchmen, mostly communists, were shot in these reprisals and, although both Pétain and de Gaulle urged restraint on both sides, the atmosphere had now changed irreparably. In December the Nazis came up with a further demand, as retaliation for these resistance activities: that French Jews should pay a fine of 1,000 million francs to be collected by the UGIF and that a thousand Jews should be arrested prior to deportation for forced labour in the east. When Otto Abetz, who had a French wife, was informed of the plan he immediately telephoned the German Foreign Office to make sure that the hostages were described not as Frenchmen, but as 'Soviet and Secret Service agents of Judaeo-Communist and de Gaullist origin'.

And so, on 12 December, the Gestapo came for Maurice Goudeket, Colette's Jewish husband, one of 753 picked up that day; he was 'charged with the crime of being a Jew, of having served voluntarily in the last war and of having been decorated', explained a distraught Colette. Writing openly for several occupation and Vichy organs had not been enough to protect her husband. Now, on discovering that Maurice had been taken to the camp at Compiègne, Colette was horrified at the fate that might befall him and used every collaborationist contact she could muster to free him. Her most valuable ally was Suzanne Abetz, who had been introduced by mutual friends and was a keen admirer of her writing. In early February Maurice was released, thanks to the Abetz intervention, and there followed an effusive exchange, with thank-you flowers from Colette and some books from Suzanne Abetz which were delivered by chauffeur and which she wanted signed, along with an invitation to tea for Colette and Maurice. They were well aware this was not the end. For most of the others picked up that day, who finally left Compiègne for Auschwitz on 27 March 1942 with the unhappy distinction of being the first 1,112 deportees from France, it very definitely was.

1942

PARIS RAVAGED

On 20 January 1942 senior Nazi officials gathered at a lakeside villa just outside Berlin. The aim of the meeting, known to history as the Wannsee Conference, was to agree the procedure for the implementation of the 'final solution' to the Jewish question whereby most of the Jews of German-occupied Europe would be murdered. This gave new impetus to the thousands of German officers in France who, in addition to ensuring that everything was being done to ensure military victory, now, at the same time and with the help of Vichy officials, devoted themselves to the relentless task of ridding the country of its Jewish population. Of course not every German in France was aware of the project for mass extermination and some, had they known, would not have supported such a plan. At the top was Carl-Heinrich von Stülpnagel, Commander in Chief in France from February 1942, increasingly an opponent of Hitler who eventually paid for his opposition with his life.[*] But in 1942, fresh from serving successfully on the eastern front where he had ordered many reprisals against partisans and where he was not known for his opposition to mass executions of Jews, he had little room for action. There were other non-Nazis in Paris, but most of them, aware of the risks, toed the line and waited.

In 1933, as soon as Hitler came to power, Ingeborg Helene Abshagen, known as Inga, born into a well-to-do Prussian family, was sent to London to further her education, her parents believing that she should escape the influence of German teachers, who were mostly Nazis. She studied briefly at the London School of Economics under the socialist Jewish professor Harold Laski. When she returned to

[*] A member of the failed July 1944 plot to assassinate Hitler, he was found guilty of treason and hanged in August that year.

Germany, fluent in English, strikingly attractive and with a different worldview from her peers, she easily found a high-powered job working for the Abwehr, German military intelligence, as secretary for its chief, Admiral Wilhelm Canaris. In 1940, immediately after the city fell, she moved with Canaris to Paris, where she lived at the Ritz but worked at the German-requisitioned Hôtel Lutetia during the day.

Inga was emphatic that Canaris was always critical of the Nazi regime from the moment he had witnessed, in Poland in September 1939, what he said were war crimes committed by the SS including the destruction of the synagogue in Będzin and the burning to death of the town's Jewish residents. He warned then that 'Germany will never be forgiven unless some action is taken against these criminals.' Inga thus became close to a group of like-minded Wehrmacht officers in more or less permanent tension with the SS, one of the few German women in Paris working as a double agent supplying false passports to Jews and other persecuted minorities, sometimes delivering these in person. This treacherous work was endorsed by Canaris, who believed that the young and glamorous Inga, looking to all the world like a genuine Parisienne, would evade detection by French police. In 1942 she married a much older senior army officer, Werner Haag, and at the end of the year the pair left Paris for Hungary, no doubt fortunately for her as Paris was by now increasingly dangerous. 'You lived in fear that you were going to be arrested. So I took my father's advice to try to know as little as possible because what you didn't know you couldn't talk about and betray under torture.'

Gisèle Casadesus, then a young mother of two and a hard-working actress at the Comédie-Française, whose audience was always full of non-uniformed Germans, said, 'You never knew who you could trust, so nobody ever spoke about anything that mattered just in case. Food was the constant topic of conversation. What can you eat, how to cook it and where can you get it?'

Although by 1942 Paris was full of German as well as French women, the former never acquired the chic of their local counterparts and in any case most had to wear uniform. Sometimes they were dubbed *Blitzmädchen* or *Blitzweiben* (because they had a stripe, or *Blitz*, on the shoulder), but the favourite French nickname for

them was Grey Mice. These Grey Mice looked with cool dislike on
their local rivals, who, they had been told in advance, were women
of loose morals. The attitude was reciprocated. 'The French were re-
spectful to girls in uniform. We were treated politely by them. Not
with kindness.'

The German women sent to Paris would mostly have been born in
the late 1910s, and food was important for them too. They regarded
the city as a 'Paradise of Plenty'. Although German women had,
unlike French, the right to vote, the Nazi ideology in all other ways
treated them as second-class citizens whose role was to breed; they
faced quotas in universities, and many other aspects of public life
were closed to them. Yet, as they entered their teens in the early 1930s,
having witnessed hyperinflation, mass unemployment and economic
collapse, many of these middle-class girls were loyal supporters of the
Führer. They may have been born malnourished, and they suffered
spells of chronic hunger in 1923–4 and again in 1929–31, so food was
inevitably a concern. But the women were not obsessed in quite the
same way as the German men often were, meticulously documenting in letters home from France what they had had to eat that day
and what they hoped to scrounge the next. Paris was regarded by all
German soldiers as a prized posting, especially compared with the
hardship and privations of being sent to the east. In Paris one could
still get butter, coffee and luxuries such as pâté, confit (of various animals) and salted beef (if you knew where and could pay), as well as
jewellery from Cartier, Boucheron and Van Cleef & Arpels, couture
clothes from Jacques Fath or Maggy Rouff, and even silk stockings,
though they might cost as much as 300 francs on the black market.
But most French women could not afford such luxuries and, once
they had damaged the final pair left in their cupboard, were deeply
concerned about how they were to maintain their propriety since it
was considered distinctly unladylike to be seen without stockings.
The perfumer Elizabeth Arden came up with an answer: a miracle
bottle of iodine dye costing about thirty francs and sold in three
shades: flesh, gilded flesh and tanned flesh. It was advertised as 'the
silk on your legs without silk stockings' and was very popular. Some
women also became adept, in addition, at painting a straight black
line up the calf to imitate the seam of a real stocking.

But you couldn't eat iodine, and food was the overriding preoccupation for everyone. Food was an essential part of French national identity, especially for women responsible for domestic catering. Many Parisians were by now suffering deep hunger, and a generation of babies was in danger of growing up with rickets. Young French girls were sent off on their bicycles to visit distant cousins in the country in the hope that they might at least return with a cauliflower or a few eggs. If they had been sent by train, however, the jostling crowds on the way home frequently meant that an egg or two would be smashed – a disaster. Others, returning with suitcases full of meat, hoped they would not be noticed in the station mêlée. There were soup kitchens where poor people lived on ten francs a day, and special canteens run by the police, or similar bodies, for their own workers, like the one where the British nanny, Rosemary Say, worked until she was taken to the Vittel camp for enemy aliens in May 1941. But those with the money to use restaurants knew how to slip notes surreptitiously under a plate to ensure they would be given food not available to others. Food was an obsession not just because of gnawing hunger nor just because it was the only safe, non-political topic of conversation, but also because of these wild discrepancies. Racketeers were making serious money exploiting whatever they could get their hands on, and small café owners sometimes did a sideline in supplying false identity cards. Those who looked well fed were known as BOFs, *Beurre Oeufs Fromages*, and some of the profits they or their husbands made went back into the city's economy as they were often spent at the couture houses. These 'queens of the black market', as they were known, were laughed at by some of the *vendeuses*, who described them as fat, well-fed women, who 'arrive with pockets full of bundles of banknotes which they do not hesitate to place on the desk of the *vendeuses*. Their manners and language do not exactly match with the tone of couture.'

For ordinary Parisians the black market that was operating in earnest was mostly at Les Halles, although rumours that there was butter at an antiquarian bookseller's, wine at the dentist's or meat at a stationery shop regularly sent women scurrying off in unusual directions. At night women were sometimes seen at Les Halles searching the floor to see if any edible scrap had been dropped. On 31 May

1942 the anger over food supplies burst into the open as a group of largely communist women organized a demonstration to show the Germans 'that we were not afraid', as Lise London later explained. Born Elisabeth Ricol in France in 1916 to illiterate working-class Spanish parents who had been forced to emigrate, Lise had been a communist activist all her life and was now a leader of the Movement of Patriotic Women in Paris. Those who knew her described her as a force of nature, a brave and tireless agitator who put the cause above everything. She had learned her politics as a teenager in Moscow and while there fell in love with Artur London, a tall, handsome nineteen-year-old Czech-Jewish intellectual for whom she immediately left her first husband (the communist Auguste Delaune, who would be executed by the Nazis in 1943). But it was when fighting for the Republican cause in the Spanish Civil War that she learned she could face anything life threw at her. Still only twenty, she survived appalling deprivation and danger in Madrid, but while she was there miscarried a five-month-old baby.

She and Artur moved back to Paris, living under aliases with forged papers, and had another child together, a daughter, Françoise. Then in 1942 Lise helped to instigate a popular uprising against the Nazis in Paris. She had witnessed earlier, small-scale demonstrations in Paris where men had been shot but, as no women had yet been arrested, she was determined to 'give confidence to women so they would want to engage with us . . . and to show that German repression would not end resistance'. Some of the women who joined in were part of organized communist committees but many others did so spontaneously out of desperation. The Rue Daguerre was chosen as it was a busy area with lots of food stores where many people came hoping to buy something to eat, however small; there were several warehouses nearby where products were stored before being sent to the front to feed German soldiers. In the weeks before the riot, Lise worked in secret with her colleagues producing leaflets about the intended action and organizing illegal broadcasts to be heard by other sympathetic groups. She said afterwards that the night before, she and Artur didn't sleep. They made love until dawn. 'We sensed that we weren't going to see each other for a long time, maybe never again,' she told an interviewer in 2011, aged ninety-five.

The disruption when it came involved hundreds of women, and although the Germans up until then had been trying not to shoot women, Lise herself was targeted and would have been hit had a comrade not spotted the danger and shot the German soldier first in the legs. The crowd then dispersed and, in the sniping that ensued, Lise escaped, only to be arrested eleven days later and condemned to death by a Vichy court – the only woman to receive this sentence. However, the fact that she was heavily pregnant with her second child, Michel, saved her from the guillotine. She gave birth in prison, but then had her baby taken away from her, and in April 1943 she was handed over to the Gestapo. Her parents, the elderly and frail Ricols, took care of their grandchildren, Françoise and Michel, throughout the war as Lise was later sent to Ravensbrück concentration camp and Artur to Mauthausen.

Since the German state was determined to ensure that its citizens would be the last in Europe to go hungry, it encouraged them to buy, or often simply take, everything in France that would keep. But when young German girls sent to Paris reported on how exciting it was to be there, the cause of their euphoria was mostly not the food. Ruth A. from Heidelberg wrote, 'Yes, we had it good in Paris – soirées, dances, invitations, wonderful parties. We were simply lucky!' The best part of Parisian life for the Grey Mice was the myriad opportunities for meeting eligible German officers, and Ruth A. met her own husband – a 'charming Viennese' medic – at a special meeting house in Paris run by the Wehrmacht. The couple were married on 10 July 1942, but not in Paris as they had hoped. The city was much too volatile, and in fact on that day a German officer was shot in front of the Madeleine church. But they were able to get travel permits for their families to travel to Lorraine, where her brother was stationed and where the marriage took place. However, Ruth's story illustrates another problem: the auxiliaries quickly acquired a reputation as 'Officers' Mattresses'. In 1942, in order to encourage suitable young single women to sign up to work in Paris, the Germans started to publish propaganda texts which stressed the homely morality of German women compared with the urbane flirtatiousness of the French.

When French women board a train they are 'painted and

powdered. Suddenly we were overcome with such a feeling of un-washed stickiness,' wrote Ina Seidel, a communications worker, adding self-righteously: 'night-time entertainment seems to be the primary industry in the capital of France'. Seidel explained that the Parisian streets were empty at 6 a.m. but 'we are eager to be at our post to relieve our comrades on the night shift and we enter the exchange with a fresh, happy greeting!' What she did not say was that the night-time entertainment was in great demand from her male German colleagues.

Ursula Rüdt von Collenberg spoke without any conscious irony in a post-war interview about life in the French capital for a twenty-one-year-old German girl in 1942 'as the most wonderful and unforgettable time of my youth'. But then she did not have to wear uniform for her job in the French archives, working for the German historian Wolfgang Windelband and living in a huge room, with her own bath and telephone, at the Hôtel d'Orsay. 'I never lived so well anywhere,' she recalled. 'We went to the opera or the theatre, we saw Jean-Louis Barrault and Sacha Guitry and the Grand Guignol; we visited exhibitions in the Orangerie and the Musée de l'Homme.'

Ursula's uncle, Baron Kurt Rüdt von Collenberg, a Luftwaffe general, was living at Neuilly at the time in the requisitioned villa of a Mme Mandel (no relation), where 'he gave fantastic dinner parties . . . with all the right French guests, Marquis so-and-so and Comte tra-la-la. We had good French friends like Daniel-Rops [the Catholic historian who wrote books of religious history] who trans-lated Rilke . . . there was lovely material to be bought for clothes and I found a little White Russian dressmaker. Fantastic deals were being transacted all around on the sly, for wines, food, shoes what have you. We could buy what we wanted, much more than the French.'

As Ursula was well aware, the spring of 1942 offered plenty of opportunity for Germans in Paris to appreciate not just French food and couture but also culture. Jeanne Bucher ignored the prevailing caution and held a show in May for artists including Lurçat, Braque, Léger, Klee and Laurens, even though she could not actively promote the exhibition, which was attended mostly by French. But the major event that month was a massive retrospective show of the work of

Arno Breker at the Orangerie, exhibiting giant figures of supermen representing a Nazi fantasy of Aryan power in Paris. Breker, trained in France but deeply sympathetic to the ideals of the Third Reich, was considered an ideal choice to promote Franco-German loyalty. The young Ambassador Otto Abetz, still only thirty-nine, arranged for Breker to stay in Helena Rubinstein's magnificent and newly expropriated apartment on the Ile Saint-Louis.

Simone de Beauvoir commented in her memoirs that 'almost the entire French intelligentsia' had snubbed the exhibition, but this was far from being the case. The opening events were supported by artists such as Arletty, Sacha Guitry, Serge Lifar and of course Cocteau, who considered himself a personal friend of the great Breker and published a long article detailing why he admired the man so much, a step too far even for many of his artistic circle. As the Vichy Education Minister, Abel Bonnard, delivered some welcoming remarks followed by equally warm words from Pierre Laval, brought back as Prime Minister in April 1942,* no one seemed aware that the bronze for some of the enormous statues on show had been created from the melted-down monuments of Paris itself, or that they had been cast using the forced labour of French prisoners of war. To underline how significant this show was, concerts were arranged beneath the statuary. At the opening celebrations, Germaine Lubin, fresh from performing Schubert lieder as requested at a special farewell concert for her friend and admirer Hans Speidel, was once again the star. In August, the pianists Alfred Cortot and Wilhelm Kempff were chosen to give a magnificent four-handed recital to mark the closing of the exhibition.

Where cultural relations led, personal relationships between German men and French women followed. The actress Gisèle Casadesus was well aware of the Germans in her audience even though most wore civilian clothes and did not frequent the Comédie-Française as much as the opera. 'In the theatre it was normal to be friendly to Germans because they were the audience,' explained

---

* Laval's ill-judged remarks in June that he welcomed a German victory, even though he added the rider which everyone forgot, 'as a means of countering Bolshevism', effectively signed his death-warrant.

Jean-Claude Grumberg, 'but if you wanted to perform you had to swear you were not Jewish.'*

Pretty young actresses were regularly asked out for a drink after a performance even if they were married. Casadesus decided that the best way to avoid having to say no was to make sure she always dashed off with the audience in order to catch the last Métro before the curfew. 'If anyone asked for me, I told my dresser to tell them that I had to hurry home to my children,' she explained; after all, missing the last Métro invariably meant being out after the curfew – a serious crime.

Micheline Bood wrote in 1941, with all the fiery injustice of a teenager, that she had reached the point where she found the French 'no longer men. I am renouncing my country, I no longer want to be French! When you see how one and all have become collaborationist and are licking the boots of the Germans out of fear and cowardice even in my own country.' She described with disgust how one of her friends, fifteen-year-old Monique, 'let herself be kissed by this Boche, who is an enemy in a conquered country'.

But then, in May 1942, she changed her mind and she too started socializing with Germans. She described how on one occasion she and some friends went out with a young officer, not much older than them, who was wearing a white linen jacket 'like Lohengrin' with a shining eagle emblem, and although the other soldiers saluted him, 'the women, the *Blitzweiben* or little Grey Mice, scowled at us'. It was exciting to be taken to smart restaurants and fancy bars and to experience Paris nightlife accompanied by handsome men. She now studied German in order to get a job with the authorities and scrunched up all the letters of denunciation she received before throwing them in the bin. These girls did not see themselves as collaborating any more than Colette did when she recommended turnip juice (which was all one could buy) as a remedy for wrinkles. In different ways, both were ensuring that the population remained quiescent and made the best of the situation.

* Following the law of 2 June 1941 it was necessary to carry a certificate issued by the Commissariat Général aux Questions Juives, proclaiming that the holder did not belong to the Jewish race.

But was sexual collaboration, if genuine attachment was involved, in a different category from that which endangered security by passing on secrets? The question was never adequately addressed in the post-war world and was to cause French women the greatest trouble in the immediate aftermath of the Liberation. By the middle of 1943 almost 80,000 women from the occupied zone were claiming support from the Germans for the children resulting from these liaisons. The French author Patrick Buisson argued that the Occupation encouraged the sexual liberation of women (often lonely wives or abandoned girlfriends) and that the presence of good-looking German soldiers encouraged the development of libido. German military superiority left the French humiliated and in a state of 'erotic shock', he wrote.

Johann and Lisette, the married German Wehrmacht officer and chic French secretary, had continued with their affair for two years in spite of periods when he was sent away on missions and, according to their letters, were more in love with each other than ever. But by 1942 the tense atmosphere of arrests, shootings, deprivation and reprisals had left Lisette full of doubts, which Johann tried to assuage. Her parents may have believed, as she approached thirty still unmarried, that she was bettering herself. But her working-class cousins deeply disapproved of the relationship with *un boche* and wanted nothing to do with her. 'Collaboration?' wrote Johann in one of his letters to her. 'I think it is an illusion. You have to love deeply to understand. Love alone is stronger than patriotism, a love like this one. I love France in you, and you will cherish Germany through me.'

Hélène Berr was also a teenager when war broke out, but with fewer options to make the best of things, as she documented in the elegiac diary which she kept from 1942 onwards. Hélène was dreamy and non-political but the situation was 'obliging' her to take a stance. Her maturity and intelligence are in stark contrast to Micheline Bood's childlike enjoyment of the moment, yet both were young French women from middle-class homes eager to sample life. Berr was born in Paris in March 1921, the fourth child of Raymond and Antoinette Berr, French Jews of enormous culture, sensitivity and intellect who lived in the affluent 7th arrondissement on the Avenue Elisée Reclus.

At the Berrs' country home in Aubergenville on the Seine, summer 1942. From left: Hélène, her mother Antoinette, sister Denise, boyfriend Jean Morawiecki and brother-in-law's sister, Jacqueline Job

The family's Judaism was secular and low key, never denied but not the most central part of their lives. M. Berr was a scientist, a successful industrialist and a decorated soldier of the Guerre de Quatorze, Hélène herself an English student at the Sorbonne and a gifted violinist in love with music, literature and a young Frenchman of Polish Catholic origins, Jean Morawiecki. Brought up like most of the haute bourgeoisie by an English nanny, she was a fierce Anglophile and filled her diary with almost as much about English literature as about the Occupation. It's the juxtaposition of her quartet, playing sublime music, with the horrors she increasingly witnesses around her which gives the diary a particular poignancy. How can a world of Schubert and his 'Trout Quintet' coexist with a world where women have to give birth in the gutter and Jews are forbidden to walk across the Champs-Elysées or to enter theatres and restaurants?

In June 1942 she wrote: 'When I review the week just passed I see a dark sky looming over it, it has been a week of tragedy, a chaotic jumble of a week. At the same time there is something uplifting in thinking of all the wonderful understanding I have encountered . . .

there is beauty in the midst of the tragic. As if beauty were condensing in the heart of ugliness. It's very strange.'

Initially she did not intend her diary to be published, but wrote it rather as a message for Jean, who eventually decided to leave, via the Pyrenees, for England to join the Free French Forces of de Gaulle. Her brother and sister also managed to cross into unoccupied France but she took the firm and conscious decision to stay, initially to support her parents but later as a moral decision on its own, not to abandon the Jewish children she was helping under the auspices of the various Jewish relief agencies. Her choice was to do the right thing, which she did not yet realize would mean certain death because many of the homes were run by the controversial Union Générale des Israélites de France, the organization intended to help Jews but which in the end facilitated their capture and death.

The leaden atmosphere in Paris during the early summer of 1942 provided ample warning of what the full force of the Gestapo could do when it felt threatened. Marie-Elisa Nordmann was a brilliant young chemist who came top of her year when she graduated from the Institut de Chimie de Paris in 1931 and then spent a year in Germany to improve her language skills. She had wanted to be a doctor, a career her protective Jewish mother had not deemed suitable for a young lady, so when fellow chemist Paul Rumpf proposed, she was tempted into marriage at the age of twenty-two, hoping this would give her the independent adult lifestyle she craved but which was hard for a single woman from her milieu to enjoy. But the marriage was unhappy almost from the start and, soon after the birth of their son Francis, the couple divorced. By 1939 Marie-Elisa was living in an apartment with her widowed mother Hélène and her baby, moving in anti-fascist circles, already convinced she had to persuade more of her countrymen about the need to fight the Occupation. She undertook to distribute flyers urging resistance, but she soon realized that something more active was required. So, in spite of the enormous danger and risk to her young son, she agreed to supply mercury from her laboratory for explosives. She was arrested in a round-up of seventy people, many of them women, on 16 May 1942 and taken to a variety of prisons including La Santé, then Romainville and finally, in January 1943, to Auschwitz. She was part of the notorious

'Convoi des 31,000', a series of cattle trucks that took 230 women from a variety of backgrounds and ages whose strength was to be their support for each other. Only forty-nine of them would survive. Insisting that she was a political prisoner, Marie-Elisa managed to hide the fact that she was Jewish, not always possible for men who were caught and it was discovered they had been circumcised. She had learned in August from a secret message hidden inside a packet of cigarettes, just a few weeks after her own arrest, that her mother, devotedly looking after her grandchild Francis, had been taken to Drancy as a civilian hostage and then sent to Auschwitz and gassed, once it was discovered she was Jewish. Francis survived the war, looked after by his uncle and aunt Philippe and Paule Nordmann, as did Marie-Elisa.

In June 1942 all Jews over the age of six in occupied France were ordered to wear a yellow star with the word *Juif* in black inside the star on their outer garments at all times. The procedure for collecting these three cloth badges – which used up one month's worth of textile rations – involved queuing at local police stations and, after signing for receipt of the stars, giving various other pieces of information including an identity card number and home address. Wearing the star enabled all the other punitive laws against Jews to be more stringently enforced, such as not being allowed to go to the theatre, cinema or certain shops until late in the day by which time all the produce had been sold, or to use public phone booths and public parks. In addition, Jews were now restricted to the last carriage of the Métro, but this order was issued by the Préfet of the Paris region with the rider that 'no announcement was to be posted and no information given to the public'. Hélène knew nothing about the rule when she ran for her train on Friday 10 July and was shouted at: 'You there! In the other carriage . . .' By the time she had moved, 'tears were pouring from my eyes, tears of rage and of protest against this brutality'.

A handful of protesters took the decision to wear a yellow star out of sympathy even though they were not Jewish, and called themselves 'Friends of Jews'; some wore a star with the word *Zazou* printed in the middle, the Zazou style being a kind of spontaneous teenage rebellion, more popular with boys than girls, deriving from jazz and anti-fascism. Although the Zazous were spread throughout France, they were concentrated in Paris and met in cafés or basement clubs, mocking the Nazis and their Vichy collaborators. After a government decree that hair should be collected from barber shops to be made into slippers, Zazous grew their hair longer. Cartier even had a customer who commissioned an expensive gold-star brooch to be made as a rather futile grand gesture, but a gesture nonetheless, while one young girl was imprisoned for tying the yellow star to the tail of her dog. Hundreds of Jews, if they thought they could avoid being identified, took the decision not to wear the star at all. Of course they risked being denounced by those who knew they were Jewish, so well-known Jews had little choice other than to write to Vichy, which had not yet imposed the star on its citizens, anxiously requesting that they might be granted special dispensation by Pétain himself.

Claire Chevrillon, hoping that the Parisian authorities had not discovered that her mother was Jewish, advised her to risk not wearing it. But her law-abiding mother decided she should and queued up to buy her three badges. 'First my mother wore the star. Then she took it off. Then she put it on again. She oscillated this way for several months – certainly the worst thing to do – and finally stopped wearing it altogether. Later through the underground I got her a false identity card with the name of Mme Charpentier, which at least allowed her to avoid being caught in a street round-up.'

Some women saw in the regulations an opportunity for revenge or for a meagre payment from the authorities. One anonymous informer wrote about the daughter of M.A., 'a former dancer who was not wearing the star. This person, not satisfied with being Jewish, debauches the husbands of genuine French women . . . Defend women against Jewesses . . . and you would be returning a French husband to his wife.' It was typical of many such letters.

Hélène Berr agonized for herself too but then decided she must obey. 'It is cowardly not to wear the star vis-à-vis people who will,' she wrote. One day a stranger approached her and offered his hand saying loudly, 'A French Catholic shakes your hand . . . and when it's over we'll let them have it.' It was, she felt, the decent thing to do. Similarly she concluded that leaving the country would be an act of cowardice: 'enforced cowardice, it would be cowardly towards the other internees and the wretched poor'.

But on 23 June – 'a radiant morning', as Hélène noted – her father was, without warning, arrested. Hélène was the first in the family to discover that he had been taken from his office for questioning at the Avenue Foch, and she rushed home to tell her mother. The Avenue Foch was a wide boulevard in the heart of fashionable Paris where three magnificent nineteenth-century villas at numbers 82, 84 and 86 had been taken over by the notorious SiPo-SD (Sicherheitsdienst), the counter-intelligence branch of the Nazi SS, as their French headquarters in Paris. Number 84, used for the imprisonment and interrogation of foreign agents captured in France, soon became a byword for cruelty, torture and terror. Later that day the Berr family learned from a surreal conversation with a French police officer, who telephoned to give them further details, that M. Berr had been detained because his yellow star was not correctly stitched on. Mme Berr then explained that she had put it on with hooks and press studs 'so Papa could wear it on different suits. The officer insisted that the press studs were what had prompted Papa's internment. "At the Drancy camp all the stars are stitched on." So that made us realise that he was on his way to Drancy.'

In the boiling heat of the day, so hot that Hélène was 'drenched in sweat', she, her sister Denise and her mother rushed around gathering essentials such as a toothbrush, which they had been told they could deliver to the Préfecture de Police, where he was being held.

> We tramped up endless staircases, along blank-walled corridors with small doors leading off to left and right; I wondered if they were cells and if Papa was in one of them. We were redirected from one floor to another . . . the baggage was heavy. Maman found it hard to get up the top flight of stairs. I told myself: 'Come on now, it'll soon be over.' It was close to excruciating.

After several false starts they found the usually dapper industrialist, without tie, braces or shoelaces, already looking like a man in custody. As the dismal family group sat on a bench Mme Berr started sewing on his star again. 'I was trying to get a solid grip on what was happening,' Hélène wrote. As she took in the scene she reflected: 'You might have wondered what we were all doing there . . . we were among French people.' There was not a German in sight.

And then there was further disorientation, as another three women came in including 'a stout vulgar blonde' with 'a dark-skinned Italian Jew', the foursome probably involved in black-marketeering. 'The four of us were so distant from those poor folk that we could hardly conceive that Papa was a prisoner too.' Raymond Berr was sent to Drancy, although he was eventually released after Établissements Kuhlmann, the giant French chemical company to which he had devoted his entire career since 1919, negotiated his release and paid a substantial ransom. The family knew it was but a reprieve. From now on he was obliged to work from home and could no longer travel, but even that was an extraordinary privilege for a Jew – Berr was the only one in France to whom it was granted.

Less than a month later, on 16 and 17 July, the Vichy government, aiming to satisfy German demands to reduce the Jewish population, arrested some 13,152 Jews, including more than 4,000 children, mostly from Paris, in an operation which they were calling 'Spring Wind'. René Bousquet, Secretary General of the French National Police, knew that using French police in the round-ups would be 'embarrassing' but hoped that this would be mitigated if those arrested were only so-called foreign Jews.* However, as the historian Serge Klarsfeld has revealed (making use of telegrams René Bousquet sent to the prefects of departments in the occupied zone), the police were ordered to deport not only foreign Jewish adults but children, whose deportation had not even been requested, nor planned for, by the Nazis. Pierre Laval maintained that including children in the

---

* Vichy France depended on the loyalty of its police and judiciary, which most of the time was not in question. However, the conundrum for the Vichy regime was that as long as it collaborated with the Germans it could preserve the fig leaf of French sovereignty, but if it resisted it risked provoking German intervention in all areas. For the first two years Vichy nominally administered France while accepting an occupied zone in the north. But it was not that simple as there was a double ruling in the north – one French, one German – but the Germans had the upper hand. Officially the Germans ran only the north, at least until 1942, and France and the occupiers were separate – a fiction which Vichy was determined to uphold.

round-ups was a 'humanitarian' measure to keep families together, a clearly fallacious argument since many of the parents had already been deported. The reality was that this way he not only raised the total numbers but would, he calculated, avoid the awkward situation of leaving Jewish children without parents, who would then be the responsibility of the state. The youngest child sent to Auschwitz under Laval's orders that month was eighteen months old. So terrified were the children that some of them invented the name 'Pitchipoi' for their imagined, unknown destination. The adults accepted it in a feeble attempt to convince them they were going somewhere exciting. Everyone was taken on French buses to the Vélodrome d'Hiver, a bicycle stadium in the shadow of the Eiffel Tower, where most of the victims were temporarily confined for five days in extremely crowded conditions, almost without water as there was only one available tap, with little food and with inadequate sanitary facilities. They were then moved to Drancy, Pithiviers and Beaune-la-Rolande, internment camps managed by Vichy in collaboration with the Germans, before being sent on by train to Auschwitz for extermination. The round-up has been a source of enormous grief in France. It was not until 1995 that French President Jacques Chirac admitted French complicity as French policemen and civil servants had been used for the raid. He urged that 16 July be commemorated annually as a national day of remembrance. It was a ground-breaking moment in French history.

Rachel Erlbaum still lives today in the same apartment in the Marais just across from the Rue des Rosiers where she grew up with her parents and younger brother, a street with many other Jewish families. Her mother took the precaution of hiding during the day, living in the coal cellar, and only going back up to the apartment most nights to see her children. She was there on the day of the round-up. 'At dawn, as soon as they realised something was going on, my parents closed the shutters and told us to keep quiet. By some miracle the police did not enter our building.' Rachel pauses before continuing. 'I can still hear the screams and cries of the babies and other children thrown into the green and yellow buses by French police.'

'La police française,' she repeats, in case there is any doubt about the significance of what she has just said. And then she says it once again with more vigour, so hard is it to comprehend. 'French buses on every street corner. The Germans may have been waiting behind the cordoned-off area but they did not show their faces.' They did not need to. Her schoolfriend Sara Lefkovich was arrested that day. She had been in hiding with her father while her mother was in a different hiding place with her brother. When her father was taken, Sara ran to him and he shouted at her, 'Run away, go, run away, Sara,' but she, wooden, could not move, rooted to the spot in an embrace with her father. She did not want to leave without him. Neither came back. It's a memory Rachel Erlbaum will never forget and which lives afresh whenever she talks about it.

The Reiman family lived not far away in the Rue du Temple when the police came for them – mother Malka, and daughters Madeleine, eleven, and Arlette, nine. Their father had already been arrested and taken to Pithiviers. '"Don't worry," he always told us, "don't be afraid. This is the land of freedom, of Voltaire and Rousseau."' And so it had been until 1940. Abraham Reiman, born in Poland, had built up a successful furrier business and married his childhood sweetheart, Malka, in France in 1929. For ten years the Reimans had enjoyed a bourgeois existence with car, housekeeper and total freedom for the young children to run around in the area meeting friends. When Abraham was arrested in 1941, the enterprising Malka managed to get herself and the girls to Pithiviers and, thanks to the efforts of a kind and sympathetic local French policeman, who arranged for them to stay at his home, they saw Abraham and gave him a parcel of food and clothes. Notwithstanding, in June 1942 he was deported to Auschwitz, where he was killed.

But this time, back in Paris, there was nothing Malka could do. 'I remember my mother shouting and screaming at the police who came to our door and throwing furniture at them. They told us to prepare food and drink for three days. "How ridiculous," my mother replied. "What can we take? As Jews we are barely allowed to buy any food."' Arlette remembers every detail about that hot and humid day, especially how the concierge was watching as the four families in their apartment block left.

Once at the stadium, the situation deteriorated dramatically.

The stench was appalling, unimaginable. You could barely breathe. There was nothing to eat or drink, the few toilets that were in use were quickly blocked, some people were throwing themselves off the top of the wall to commit suicide and women who had their periods were walking around with blood pouring down their legs. I thought these women were dying and had been murdered. I clung to my mother, berating her, 'Where is Zola now and where is Rousseau?' I thought these were real friends of my father's and that they would come and help us. But adults had lied to me. That is what stays in my mind.

There were other heart-wrenching testimonies of children saying a final goodbye to parents they would never see again, some who went mad and behaved violently. When condensation started dripping from the roof one mother was heard to tell her child this was God's tears.

Irène Némirovsky was arrested on 13 July, likewise as part of the Spring Wind operation. French gendarmes came to the house the family had recently rented in the heart of Issy-l'Evêque. Everyone in the village knew that the Epsteins were Jewish long before they had seen them wearing a yellow star (only Elisabeth, the youngest daughter, was exempt), despite the fact that the Epsteins regularly at-tended Sunday mass and that their daughter Denise had had her first communion in the local church. The two gendarmes who came for Irène were polite, gave her enough time to pack a small suitcase with essential toiletries and offered her a chance to say another goodbye to her daughters. She declined, saying 'one adieu is enough', and left behind the manuscript of the great unfinished epic she was working on at the time, written in tiny, spidery handwriting on the paper that was becoming increasingly hard to come by. As she had prophetically told her publisher two days previously, 'I have written a great deal lately. I suppose they will be posthumous works but it still makes the time go by.' They were her last words as a writer.

The book, *Suite Française*, was intended as a symphony with four or five sections. The completed two, 'Storm in June' and 'Dolce', are brilliantly nuanced evocations of how the war was damaging the lives of ordinary people; they show a writer who had developed a deep understanding of humanity, not always visible in her earlier works. Irène by this time seems to have had no illusions about her own fate, the last two years having taken their toll on whatever optimism she may have had in 1940 when she wrote to Marshal Pétain 'with respect and sometimes even with veneration'. She had asked him to grant her special status, having lived in France for more than twenty years, insisting, 'I cannot believe, Sir, that no distinction is made between the undesirable and the honourable foreigners, those who have done everything possible to deserve the royal welcome France has given them.'

Her plea for cultural superiority to save her family strikes an awkward note today, but when she was arrested two years later Michel Epstein clearly thought that, thanks to their influential friends, his wife would be swiftly freed. They managed to exchange a few letters suggesting names of people they hoped would help. But after two days in the local prison Irène was taken to the Pithiviers camp, which by the time she arrived was swollen with arrivals from the Paris round-up. Theodor Dannecker, head of the Jewish section of the SiPo-SD, having promised to deliver a deportation of 40,000 Jews in three weeks, was tightening his grip: no more visits, parcels or releases on health grounds. On Friday 17 July Irène was taken on a dawn convoy to Auschwitz, where, as her biographers put it, 'she was no longer a novelist, mother, wife, Russian or Frenchwoman: she was just a Jewess'. The journey took two days and on arrival she was marked with a tattoo but not gassed immediately because she was young enough to work. She survived until 19 August when an epidemic of deadly typhus swept through the camp and killed her. She was thirty-nine. Her daughters clung on to the manuscript, not realizing the value of what they had in their possession.

The then three-year-old Renée Wartski, by her own admission 'an extremely difficult child', has always known how lucky she was to have survived the round-up. 'I can still remember the look on my mother's face when she heard the Paris policeman knock on the door of the concierge and ask for the Jews on the second floor. Normally I would have screamed.' Renée's father, a naturalized Frenchman who worked in the leather trade, had emigrated from Poland during the First World War when France encouraged such movement, and was now a prisoner of war in Germany. Her mother Fanny was alone with Renée, her nine-year-old brother Louis and her parents, all squashed into a small apartment in a four-storey building down an alleyway off the Rue de Crimée, an old cobblestoned street with cafés on each corner in the 19th arrondissement. 'The quick-thinking concierge told the policeman: "They've left, sorry, gone out of town."

"But why are the shutters open then?"

"Oh," she shrugged convincingly, "you know Jews – strange people – when they leave in a hurry, like that, they don't think." But Renée, aware that she owes her life to the loyal concierge, insists on telling me 'a parallel story, about her mother's sister Sara, a dressmaker who lived in the north of the city and who was denounced by her concierge and deported 'even though she had often made clothes for this concierge's child. Why? I always believed it was just a matter of luck that I was saved and they were not. After my aunt and cousins were taken away the concierge helped herself to all the silver in the flat.'*

In fact, Fanny Wartski had been warned about the upcoming *rafle,* or round-up, as her younger brother, a violinist, had heard rumours thanks to his best friend in the orchestra, a Catholic. But the family had not acted in time. Now she wasted not a moment and the next day courageously paid a *passeur* to whom she had been recommended to take her two young children out of Paris as quickly as possible. They were going to live on a farm in the Alps in the free zone. She would follow when she could. Some weeks later Fanny arranged to hide herself in the back of a goods train transporting coal. She heard dogs sniffing for would-be escapers but she survived and, when the family was finally reunited in Grenoble, her face was covered in so much coal dust that relatives teased her: how could she think to put on mascara at a time like this?

It was brave of my mother to trust the *passeur* as such people sometimes took the money and did not deliver, selling the

---

* Similarly Denise Epstein, daughter of Irène Némirovsky, affirmed in a May 1996 interview that she had seen candlesticks belonging to her mother in the possession of the concierge of their apartment building after the war (Jonathan Weiss, *Irène Némirovsky: Her Life and Works,* p. 196).

children on to the Nazis. We could never discuss this at first. Then, when she did manage to talk about it, she would always laugh when she told the story of how we got out. She tried to make light of it by joking about the coal-dust mascara. It was her way of coping.

After the Vél' d'Hiv round-up, few French people – whether Jews or non-Jews – were left with any illusions about the future. Even Gerhard Heller, after seeing hordes of Jewish children being herded towards cattle trucks at the Gare d'Austerlitz, declared: 'That day my eyes were definitely opened by the horrors.' A handful of young French girls training to be nurses were taken to the stadium and witnessed a corner of the human drama but could not begin to comprehend the epic scale of the tragedy. What could they do beyond ladling out soup? Denise Tavernier, a twenty-three-year-old probationer social worker who had just gained her first degree, was so horrified by what she saw that she protested to the chief of police, telling him he should be ashamed to be French. 'I was threatened with being arrested myself and since no one at the time wanted to hear I kept quiet. But, encouraged by my priest, who told me future generations must know about this, I did write down details of what I saw.' Eventually, when police archives were opened in the 1980s, Serge Klarsfeld read her comments and, in 2013, Denise Tavernier, aged ninety-four and in poor health, was awarded the Légion d'honneur. Another student nurse, present that day, still cannot talk about it.

In the wake of the summer events, arrests were carried out on the flimsiest of pretexts, so that Paris was like a trap which could be sprung at any moment for so many who had something to hide. Train stations were now crammed full of people desperate to get out of the city; men and women were occasionally spotted with baggy overcoats over pyjamas, suggesting that they had had to leave through a back window in a hurry. The Métro and theatre exits were places of infinite danger where the Gestapo, usually in plain clothes, would often be hovering ready to ambush Jews, saboteurs, spies or even random hostages, especially alert for anyone turning round or going backwards at the sight of barriers.

Only very few of those arrested effected extraordinary escapes from the sports stadium; toilets which had windows had been blocked off for use so exits were few. And those who managed to slip out had to find other hiding places swiftly. Cécile Widerman Kaufer was just eleven years old when 'soldiers banged on our door loudly, pointed guns at our heads and forced us to leave our apartment'. She never forgot being driven to the sports stadium, spending several days without food and water and then her father somehow convincing a French guard to let her and her younger sister, Betty, leave the stadium and go with their mother to the nearby Rothschild Hospital. It was the last time they saw their father and elder sister.

> While at the hospital, I convinced a woman to pass a note on to my grandparents letting them know where we were. Next, we persuaded a French guard to let us free from the hospital, while my grandparents arranged for my sister and me to be taken into hiding by a Catholic French woman from Normandy who was already hiding five Jewish children. We called her Mémère, which means grandmother in French . . .
>
> Like the thousands of other hidden children, we went for days without food. I was scared all the time and worried constantly about caring for my little sister. But I promised my mother I'd take care of her. And I still take care of her.

As Cécile told an interviewer in 2012, 'Every July, my stomach churns from the memory.'

Most were taken from the Vélodrome by cattle train to Beaune-la-Rolande. There Malka Reiman, a German-speaker, found a job as a translator in the camp. Working in an office she saw documents which made her realize they would soon be taken from there to somewhere worse, so she came up with a flimsy ruse, telling the authorities that before the round-up she had hidden vital material, furs as well as sewing machines, that would be useful to the Germans. If she was allowed back to Paris with her children she would show them where. Amazingly, they allowed her and the two girls to travel unaccompanied on a military train back to Paris where they were due to be met. Her daughter Arlette recalled:

My mother, realizing that the train was very slow, regularly stop-
ping, saw a chance. She told us, when she gave the nod, we would
have to jump out and lie low between the wooden sleepers and
that we would be fine. We had to trust her. She would come back
to collect us. It was terrifying but we did it. The whole thing
is still today like a dream to me, but she saved our lives. We
then walked into Paris and stayed with a friend until my mother
found a family outside Paris to take us in.

Paris was terrifying for many but, at the same time, social life flourished as usual for the upper crust, *le gratin*, a shrinking number of
privileged individuals.* On the evening of 17 July, the day after the
round-up, Josée de Chambrun was partying with her friend Arletty
and her Luftwaffe officer Soehring, and the next day Bunny, her husband, won at the races at Maisons-Laffitte, while in the evening the
French film actor Raimu was entertained for dinner by the Lavals. It
took more than events at the Vél' d'Hiv to keep Josée away from her
favourite activities for long, whether this was socializing with the stars
or buying hats from Balenciaga or dresses from Schiaparelli. The one
required the other. But she was not alone. Records from Van Cleef &
Arpels show that the Paris showroom continued selling its dazzling
creations in 1942, and not just to Germans. The firm's file cards of
jewellery sales indicate that the purchaser was sometimes a named
German officer, sometimes simply 'Allemand Civil' or 'Officier
Allemand', but there were still many sales to French clients such as the
Faucigny-Lucinge family, whose name appears regularly. Similarly,
when a special couture ration card was negotiated with the Vichy
government, enabling thirty couture houses to continue their creative
work with certain complicated restrictions, it was French women as
well as German who continued to buy. No fashion house was allowed
to produce more than seventy-five outfits and each outfit had controls
on the amount of fabric permitted. Yet Balenciaga saw sales rise by
400 per cent in 1941 and 1942 – although the house was briefly closed

* Janet Flanner estimated that the perfect taste and style of pre-war Paris es-
poused by *le gratin* were maintained by only approximately a hundred people
out of a total population of two million (Flanner, *Paris Journal*, 1944–55, p. 62).

by the Germans in 1944 because it had exceeded its quota. To attend any fashion show during the Occupation one needed a special pass, but – of 20,000 such passes issued – only 200 were given to wives of German officers, many of whom were on the invitation lists of Otto and Suzanne Abetz. The rest went to French women.

But Parisiennes were creative, and many of them had their own dressmaker who would copy high fashion. The twenty-one-year-old Elisabeth Meynard was typical: even though it was summer, she enjoyed wearing a 'smart suit of smooth brown velvet, which my favourite Jewish Polish dressmaker, moonlighting to bring in some extra cash, had made for me with material bought as upholstery fabric'. Jacques Fath, who started trading as a couturier only in 1939, was able to increase the number of his skilled staff from 176 in 1942 (many of them drawn from other houses that had been forced to close) to 193 in 1943 and 244 in 1944. His pretty wife, Geneviève, was a key asset as she was not only photographed in his creations on magazine covers, such as *Pour Elle* in March 1942, but, according to the influential historian of fashion Dominique Veillon, it was she who maintained the crucial business connections with the German purchasing office in Paris's Rue Vernet, ensuring that Fath's creations were reproduced and discussed in the French and German press. There were others in the fashion industry who maintained an equally opportunist, if not actively collaborationist, attitude by joining the Cercle Européen, an ideological centre for those who believed in Nazi ideas, among whom Marcel Rochas is the best-known. Rochas had been suspect ever since he and Maggy Rouff agreed to present a private show to German dignitaries in November 1940. But in 1942, as the elegant Odette Fabius noted, once Jews had been forced to wear the yellow star, 'he no longer greeted even good customers and friends because they were Jewish[,] and crossed the road to avoid catching their eye when he chanced to meet them in the Avenue Montaigne'. Since her own apartment was on the Avenue Montaigne she was especially well placed to observe this.

Other couturiers with a different agenda were equally busy. Comtesse Lily Pastré, two years into the war, was now enjoying her new-found independence. This least political of women, an eccentric who liked to play the saw (much to the consternation of listeners), now relished the opportunity to act as a true and hugely generous patron of the arts. Since 1940 she had poured her money into an organization she had created called Pour Que l'Esprit Vive (May the Spirit Live) to support the artists she had so loved watching and listening to in Paris who were now in difficulty. Among those who benefited from her hospitality were the harpist Lily Laskine, the composers Darius Milhaud and Georges Auric, the pianists Youra Guller and Rudolf Firkušný and the painters André Masson, Victor Brauner and Rudolf Kundera. Pastré went out of her way to seek out Kundera, living in poverty in Cassis, and persuaded him to come to her chateau at Montredon, telling him that where he was living was unworthy of his art. And she agreed to shelter the Jewish lover of Edith Piaf, Norbert Glanzberg. She started arranging nightly concerts at the chateau, which had also become a refuge for fleeing artists, several of whom were waiting for a boat and a visa for America. Most of the latter were being helped by the Emergency Rescue Committee officer Varian Fry, the American journalist who had been sent by this private relief organization specifically to bring artists and intellectu-als out of France. It is estimated that his efforts saved about 2,000 people. Artists looked after by Lily Pastré found not only comfort and stimulation – there was always plenty of food at her table.

One of her most extraordinary actions was in April 1942 when she became aware that the Romanian-born pianist Clara Haskil, often in fragile health, was seriously ill. Clara, approaching fifty, had already survived an emotionally draining escape from Paris, along with other members of the Orchestre National de France. They had taken trains and been forced to walk in the cold and dark until they met a guide, who was paid to lead them through fields and woods to the free zone. But the guide was so frightened him-self that he kept warning his musical charges that the prisons in the neighbourhood were full of people like them who had been caught. Once she had arrived at the Château de Montredon, Clara started suffering from double vision accompanied by severe headaches. Lily realized that this was more than emotional fragility and quickly summoned a talented resistance doctor, Jean Hamburger, who was in hiding in Marseilles. He diagnosed a pituitary tumour pressing on the optic nerve which would soon lead to blindness unless she underwent immediate surgery. Lily therefore organized and paid for a renowned Parisian brain surgeon, Marcel David, who operated on Clara's tumour using only local anaesthesia and cocaine in a room at the old Hôtel-Dieu hospital. During the operation Haskil mentally played Mozart's Piano Concerto in E-flat major as a way of ensuring that the surgery was not damaging her memory or mental abilities. Just three months after that operation, a heavily bandaged woman, looking pale and hunched, emerged in the chateau park and gave a magnificent and emotional rendering of Mozart's Piano Concerto in D minor, thereby earning a reputation as a great Mozart interpreter as well as making medical history by her method of neurological rehabilitation. Everyone who listened that night was moved beyond words by her courage and determination. A few weeks later Lily organized a visa for Haskil to go to Switzerland; there she recuperated with Lily's friend Charlie Chaplin. But on 27 July Lily Pastré set her sights on producing a defiant musical extravaganza that would combine brilliant originality and Parisian elegance – an open-air production of *A Midsummer Night's Dream* for one night only. She saw it as her way of fighting against the current darkness, against 'the constants of grief, failure and the disease of the time', according to her friend Edmonde Charles-Roux.

Christian Bérard and Christian Dior were involved in the set design and costumes for the actors, draping over them whatever was to hand while they were on stage. When stocks of the materials had run out, Lily had the curtains and valuable old wall fabrics taken down inside the chateau. The orchestra comprised twenty exiled Jewish musicians conducted by Manuel Rosenthal, and at the end of the evening all costumes and scenery were burned; this was meant to represent unreality. Only one or two photographs survive to prove it was not just a dream. Lily's son Pierre commented later that his mother, determined to be beholden to no one, derived the greatest sense of freedom imaginable by keeping a flame of Parisian culture alive in Marseilles. A few months later the Germans occupied the city and destroyed much of the old port area where Jews and resisters were hiding in the narrow windy streets.

*

The ramifications of the *rafle* rumbled on throughout the summer. Only a few people made public protests, among them Pastor André Trocmé, the pacifist Protestant minister who often preached against anti-Semitism at Chambon-sur-Lignon, the mountainous village in the Haute-Loire, south-central France, where many risked their lives to save hundreds of Jewish children. Trocmé protested against the Vél' d'Hiv round-up in a public sermon on 16 August, declaring that 'the Christian Church must kneel down and ask God to forgive its present failings and cowardice'.

Hélène Berr wrote that as soon as she had heard the details of the *rafle* she felt guilty 'that there was something I hadn't been seeing and that this was reality'. She noted some facts: 'How some children had to be dragged along the floor, how one whole family (mother, father and five children) gassed themselves to escape the round-up, how one woman threw herself out of a window . . . several policemen have been shot for warning people so they could escape . . . It appears that the SS have taken command in France and that Terror must follow.' But for Berr the real agony was how to respond personally: should she try to leave and abandon struggle and heroism in exchange for dullness and despondency or do something proactive, like many factory girls who lived with Jews? 'They are all coming forward to request permission to marry, to save their men from deportation.' Then, with the painful honesty which makes her diary such a powerful document, she admitted that part of the reason she did not want to leave Paris was her love for Jean.

The round-up was only a partial success for the Germans in terms of numbers of people seized, as only half the Jews intended to be arrested were actually caught. The news had leaked and many Jews went into hiding. But in August 1942 René Bousquet, Vichy police chief, rewarded by the Germans with extra resources, organized several further deportations of Jews from French-administered camps such as Gurs and Rivesaltes in the so-called free zone. These Jews had been turned over to the Nazis by the Vichy authorities in accordance with a deal Bousquet had just struck with SS General Carl Oberg, the man in charge of German police in France. The Bousquet–Oberg accords of 2 July were presented to local officials as giving French police greater autonomy, but this was far from the truth and in reality French police were compelled to comply with German demands. Since the Germans did not have enough manpower in France in 1942 to undertake all these arrests themselves, the question remains: if Vichy had refused to comply at this time would more Jews have been saved? The first of the convoys consisting of Jews from the Free Zone delivered by Vichy to the Nazis according to the Bousquet–Oberg deal, Convoy no. 17, left Drancy for Auschwitz on 10 August 1942 carrying approximately 1,000 Jews, almost all German citizens, over half of whom were women. Three-quarters were gassed as soon as they arrived in Auschwitz. Throughout the month of August, convoy after convoy left the non-occupied zone, heading first to Drancy. New convoys were then formed, not always with the same Jews, which went from Drancy to Auschwitz.

Now it was clear nobody was safe. Those Jews who had convinced themselves that they had lived in France for so long or had contributed so much to the country that they were immune from the threat, that they were somehow protected, were plunged into terror. Many applied for special dispensation to Vichy, making their case for why they should not have to wear the yellow star. On 25 August, Heinz Röthke, the highest-ranking German official in charge of the camp at Drancy, listed twenty-six individuals who had been granted an exemption certificate.

Among those hand-picked to receive protection from Pétain, which meant, among other 'privileges', that they did not have to wear the yellow star, were wives of leading figures such as Lisette de Brinon, née Franck, whose husband, Fernand de Brinon, was the Vichy representative to the German authorities in Paris, and Marie-Louise, Marquise de Chasseloup-Laubat, daughter of the banker Edgar Stern, as well as her sister Lucie, Mme de Langlade. Both had converted to Catholicism years before. But several requests were rejected, including one made by Colette on behalf of her husband, Maurice Goudeket. He escaped on forged papers to the free zone for a while, but then returned and hid in the maid's room above their apartment, believing that Colette could not survive without him. It was a brave gesture.

The request from Béatrice de Camondo Reinach, daughter of the wealthy Jewish banker Moïse de Camondo, was also rejected. That

summer Béatrice had been receiving instruction from a Catholic
priest who, on 1 July, baptized her and four days later confirmed
her into the faith. She continued riding in the Bois de Boulogne
with the German officers from Neuilly she counted as her friends,
and hunting in the forests near Senlis along with her close friends
such as Marie-Louise de Chasseloup-Laubat, a high-profile hunt
member who, unlike poor Béatrice, had been granted a valuable
exemption certificate. Throughout the summer of 1942 Béatrice remained convinced that her brother's death in action, her divorce, her
conversion to Catholicism, her family's gifts to the state and, above
all, her friends in high places would surely protect her. While she
herself was not a collector, she had grown up in an ambience where
collecting French eighteenth-century art, preserving the ancient
French patrimony, was more important than anything else, certainly
religion. She had happily overseen the gift of her family's home and
collections to the state of which she was part and to which she belonged. She continued to feel secure within its boundaries. After all,
her own mother, now Irène Sampieri, permanently immortalized by
Renoir, seemed safe enough, albeit out of Paris. The child with the
shimmering hair was to survive. But the horse-loving daughter was
ultimately abandoned by friends as well as her mother, defined by
her religion.

Béatrice was not alone in discovering that friends were not always
robust. Renée Puissant was born Rachel Van Cleef on 22 October
1896. Her Jewish parents Alfred Van Cleef and Esther Arpels were
double cousins who had married in 1895 in Paris when she was
eighteen, he twenty-two. A generation earlier, Alfred's father Salomon had left Ghent in Belgium after his first wife died and come to
Paris, where he married Melanie Mayer, a linen merchant's daughter.
(Melanie's sister, Theresa, married Salomon Arpels, and Esther was
their daughter.) Salomon Van Cleef joined his father-in-law's linen
business, but when he died in 1883 his son Alfred was only eleven
years old and it was decided that he should be apprenticed to a stone-
cutter. By 1906 Alfred and Esther were ready to open a fine jeweller's
in the Place Vendôme, following the example of Frédéric Boucheron,
who had been the first to establish himself, in 1893, in the area near

the new opera house. From the start they were in competition with Cartier, Chaumet, René Boivin and several others who had shops there. In 1908 they opened a branch in Dinard, followed by branches in other resorts such as Nice, Deauville and, in 1913, the important spa town and centre of much socialite activity, Vichy. There followed a period of rapid social advancement for the family. Esther, who now called herself by the less Jewish and more French name Estelle, served as a nurse during the First World War and was decorated four times for her work, culminating in 1921 when she received the Légion d'honneur.

But Renée, the only child of Alfred and Esther, never enjoyed a good relationship with her mother, who always felt more of an Arpels than a Van Cleef and was possibly jealous that her husband had left Renée rather than herself in control when he died in 1938. Renée was a deeply creative woman with a good business brain and an instinctive understanding of style, but she could not draw, so it was largely thanks to the appointment in 1922 of the designer René Sim Lacaze, who could interpret some of Renée's ideas, that the company had developed its reputation for its innovative designs and daring originality.

At the outbreak of war, when some of the Arpels family were in the United States and others in the south of France, Esther decamped to Cannes. Renée, left in charge of the Paris store, courageously oversaw an aryanization of the business whereby in March 1941 the majority shareholder became Comte Paul de Léséleuc, in a deal which enabled Van Cleef & Arpels to continue trading. Renée, however, had already removed much of the stock in an extremely heavy suitcase to Vichy, where she took an apartment at the Hôtel Parc et Majestic, the principal hotel, which housed Laval on the second floor and Pétain and his entourage on the third. She was alone but felt safe there, convinced she would be protected by her friendship with Josée de Chambrun and with René Bousquet's cousin, Colonel Marty, the trusted administrator of her father, Alfred Van Cleef, who knew both her parents well. So she continued running the shop as a boutique, housed directly below the hotel.*

* When Esther received the Légion d'honneur in 1921 and Alfred the same award in 1922, both certificates were signed by Marty.

Odette Fabius was revolted by what she saw happening in Paris, not just M. Rochas crossing the street to avoid his former Jewish clients but shop windows along the Champs-Elysées displaying grotesque, giant-nosed caricatures of Léon Blum and Georges Mandel. She was torn between looking after her elderly widowed father, who refused to move from his Parisian apartment, and looking after the property in Biarritz which had been in the family for generations. In addition there was her daughter Marie-Claude's schooling and safety to consider. In spite of the movement prohibitions against Jews, Odette repeatedly crossed the country from 1940 until the spring of 1942, buying a fake *Ausweis* whenever she could at a cost of 500 francs each. On one occasion she negotiated an extra four for her Sections Sanitaires Automobiles Féminines (SSA) friends Daisy de Broglie, Marie-Louise de Tocqueville, Claude de Peyerimhoff and Colette Schwob de Lure, a policy which landed her in prison for a week in 1941 when she was denounced. She was released, as she learned later, 'because Sylvia de Talleyrand heard I was arrested and went to the Ritz Hotel to see her friend, the German tennis champion Gottfried von Cramm, who in turn told Otto Abetz . . . and I was freed.' It was only thanks to the intervention of courageous friends with good networks that Fabius was released. But she never knew the name of the person who had denounced her.

Nonetheless, Odette's experiences meant that she discovered an exaggerated form of patriotism which had little to do with the fact that she was Jewish. 'I just felt extremely French with a strong line behind me . . . I had been brought up to be proud of my descent from the Furtado family who came to France in 1680.' She never wore a yellow star because she refused to accept that she was different. She was French and that was her prime motivation in taking on an increasingly dangerous amount of resistance work. After her first spell in prison she went back to the south of France and tried, vainly, to persuade her father to join the family in Cannes. On one of her train journeys she met up with a childhood friend involved in the Alliance resistance network. At first all he asked her to do was deliver a letter. 'I was both seduced by wanting to do it and anxious.' Odette's brother had by now left for London, where he joined de Gaulle's Free French. But that was not an option for her, thanks to her duties as mother and daughter, but she urgently wanted to do something. Although she and Robert were barely living together, he was the father of her child so she had to ask his advice. He was not keen: 'There are fifty million other French people who can do it, why you?'

'Why not me?' she replied.

Robert's view, according to Odette, was that because they were Jewish they had to stay in a corner quietly if they wanted to survive. 'If we didn't have the right to travel then we needed to find another way of surviving.' So she embarked on her resistance career regardless of what Robert thought and soon undertook her first mission in Paris, collecting an urgent letter and delivering it to the south (there was no post between the free and the occupied zones), and combining her visits to Paris with seeing her father. Thus began what she later called the richest period of her life. She worried about her ten-year-old daughter, all too aware that she was not seeing enough of her, so she placed her as a pupil in a Catholic boarding school just outside Vichy, rationalizing that this was the safest place as no one would bomb the provisional capital. Some 60 per cent of the pupils were Jewish, but religion was never mentioned.

Working for Alliance, she was given the codename Biche and reported to Marie-Madeleine Fourcade, known as Hedgehog, a woman no less strong than her and the only woman to head a major network. Odette was engaged in transporting letters, plans and even people across the line. Once she shared a compartment on the train with a German officer who was drinking champagne and toasted the Third Reich. Occasionally Marie-Claude travelled with her, and she risked more than once putting documents and false papers in her daughter's case.

Seventy years later, asked whether she thought it right for a mother to jeopardize her daughter in that way, it seems clear this is a question Marie-Claude has often asked herself. She replied evenly that her mother 'could never have been different. That was who she was.' But she admitted that Odette herself later questioned whether it had been right, as a mother, to undertake resistance work. 'Would it have been better if we'd had a peaceful family life in Le Lavandou, all three of us, or would living in a fixed abode in a group have hastened our departure to Auschwitz? Those were the decisions we faced.'

Odette was not good at taking orders and clashed with the formidable chief, Marie-Madeleine. Odette complained she was being given the boring jobs, however crucial, such as noting the arrival and departures of Lysander aircraft flying from England,* rather than operating from the Grand Hôtel at Marseilles, which was where everything happened, not least foreigners searching for a boat or for a visa from any of the consulates. 'She criticized me and didn't like me,' Odette maintained. So she left Alliance and joined a different resistance network, OCM, the Organisation Civile et Militaire. Almost immediately, she was sent to meet the charismatic leader of the Sailors' Union in Marseilles, Pierre Ferri-Pisani, a forty-one-year-old Corsican well known as the boss of the entire port, to enlist his help in getting regular information about everything going on there. Ferri-Pisani was a self-taught anti-fascist agitator who had fought in Spain for the republican cause and, in 1940, was briefly put under house arrest by Vichy. He knew he was under surveillance and was well protected by his associates. But eventually Fabius was taken to meet him at a rendezvous in the Café des Marins. She had prepared carefully for the meeting, choosing an elegant Lanvin suit but no hat or gloves, contrary to the rules for women of good society. Her one accessory was a copy of *Das Kapital* by Karl Marx, which made Ferri-Pisani laugh. She was immediately struck by the man's imposing presence, charisma and directness. Where was the money to come from to pay for information, he asked? He went away and minutes later returned with a diamond. Odette never knew the provenance but guessed it might have belonged to his wife. He asked, could she sell it anywhere for a good price? So, in early December, Odette made her way to Vichy to visit her friend and former bridesmaid Rachel Van Cleef, now known as Renée Puissant, running the Van Cleef & Arpels boutique. When Odette explained the problem, her friend gave her much more than she had expected or indeed than it was worth. Ferri-Pisani was extremely impressed with his new recruit. Before the year was out, the two had become lovers.

---

* The exceptional ability of Lysanders to land on small, unprepared airstrips behind enemy lines made them invaluable for clandestine missions to place or recover agents in occupied France.

Eight days after this transaction, on 12 December, the body of Renée Puissant was found in the street, officially described as suicide but her death a mystery, probably caused by her increasing realization that no one in Vichy was looking out for her. For more than two years she had managed to maintain a semblance of normality in Vichy, walking along the lakeside and around the park where Pétain went for his daily constitutional with his doctor, Bernard Ménétrel. As the Vichy population swelled to 120,000 (of whom 45,000 were bureaucrats, many of them married), it must have seemed that life was safer than in Paris. Although there were still long queues for food, the prospects for selling jewellery were at least as good as they were in Paris, if not better. In Vichy people took pleasure from playing golf, bicycling and watching horseracing.

But all that changed after 11 November 1942 when German troops occupied the former free zone in response to the successful Allied landings in North Africa. Four days previously US and British forces, commanded by General Dwight D. Eisenhower, began Operation Torch, the amphibious invasion of North Africa. This was intended to ensure Allied control of the Mediterranean, a preliminary to the opening of a second front in Europe which would relieve the pressure on Russia from Axis forces. Although Vichy French forces initially resisted, they were quickly neutralized and had ceased armed resistance by 11 November. Admiral Darlan, formerly Vichy's deputy leader and one of Pétain's closest advisers, defected to the Allies and, as he was in North Africa at the time, ordered French forces there to join the Allies. To prevent the seizure of their Mediterranean fleet by the Germans, the French wrecked their own ships, mostly by capsizing them in the harbours of Toulon, on 27 November.

This only served to emphasize that the armistice agreement of 1940 offered nothing that could justify the Vichy regime. As the Germans could no longer rely on Vichy to remain a neutral state in opposition to the Allies, they promptly occupied the whole of France, north and south. The Vichy administration was not officially disbanded but from now on it was increasingly a tool of German policy, and German repression was more draconian than ever. Any fiction that the unoccupied zone was free was now totally dispelled, and it was hard to see precisely what authority remained with the government in Vichy. In an odd reversal of the regime's moral philosophy, married women, forbidden in 1940 from working in the public sector when husbands were in a position to provide for them, were now allowed to work without the permission of their husbands, so many of whom were either dead or prisoners of war. The country needed the workforce, the wives needed the money, so the laws were repealed.

Quite possibly, when police came to arrest her, Renée panicked, the events of November all too clearly consuming her thoughts, and threw herself out of the window from her third-floor bedroom. According to Arlette Scali, who had grown up with the Arpels family and whose second husband, Elie Scali, had once been one of Renée's lovers, Renée was completely alone in her hotel, depressed and close to a breakdown. 'She could not cope with all the goings-on, all the laws, and had been counting on Colonel Marty – the trusted administrator of her father, Alfred Van Cleef' – to protect her. 'She was not only frightened, she was sick with fright.' She had been humiliatingly forced to move from the Hôtel Parc et Majestic, where all the important Vichy leaders were living, to a third-floor room at the less prestigious Queen's Hôtel, not far away but a move which led her to believe that any protection she might have been entitled to had now evaporated. Unknown to her, however, on 6 November a letter from one Vichy police administrator to another stated in a handwritten postscript with double underlining, '<u>Ne pas inquiéter sur Madame Renée Puissant Van Cleef</u>'. What seems clear is that for her, as for Némirovsky, the final humiliation had been the law which came into force the previous day, requiring all Jews throughout France to wear a yellow star.

It is worth lingering on the connection with Colonel and Mme Marty. In the mid-1930s, when Elie Scali and Renée Puissant were lovers, René Marty had been a good friend of both. He had been *l'homme de confiance* of Renée's father. Now, as a cousin of René Bousquet, the hugely powerful Vichy police chief, he could be extremely useful and indeed was for Elie Scali, providing him with many permits to travel from the free zone to Paris and back to enable him to continue overseeing his apparently aryanized leather business, which was clearly a *vente fictive*, the term used for a false sale.

When the Scalis moved to Graullet, a village in the mid-Pyrenees, after their Paris apartment had been expropriated by the Germans, it was the Martys who ensured that they were protected by introducing them to the police in the Tarn department. In return, Arlette Scali sent to Mme Marty frequent food parcels of eggs, turkeys and whatever else they had access to on their land. They well knew they owed their lives to Colonel Marty and they did not desert him at the Liberation, pleading on his behalf when he was, for a short time only, interned in Drancy.

But it wasn't only Jews who were being picked up in the febrile atmosphere of 1942. One hot morning in September two men came to arrest Drue Tartière while she was gardening. She described them later simply as a huge German soldier and a smaller Frenchman, but Nadine, her housekeeper, told her they were from the local Gestapo. Drue was in dirty overalls, earth between her toes and under her fingernails, but they refused to give her time to wash and change, insisting she had to come immediately. She managed, by offering them a cognac, to delay them just long enough so that Nadine could warn Jean Fraysse, her former boss at Paris Mondial with whom she was by now heavily involved in resistance work. Then, promised that her interrogation would last only an hour, she went off to the local prison. After twenty-four hours without food or drink she burst into the office of the Kommandant and brazenly pulled up her overalls to show him blood trickling down the insides of her legs. Her period had just begun and she made use of it by shouting at him: 'If I am going to spend my life in this filthy hole, at least send to my house and get me some clean clothes and, above all, some sanitary napkins.' The embarrassed Kommandant was shocked into complying with her demands, which gave Drue the chance to contact Nadine and ask her to send urgently not only sanitary napkins and other essentials but a medical certificate which she had cleverly acquired about ten months before stating she had cancer of the womb. From now on she was going to have to fake this condition and starve herself to within an inch of her life.

Drue, together with several other women, had been rounded up because she was American, an enemy alien, and not because, as she had at first feared, they had discovered she was Drue Leyton, the

American actress with a price on her head; or indeed because she and Jean were planning to receive arms, ammunition and other material on her property. She was soon being held at the makeshift camp in the Grand Hôtel at Vittel in north-eastern France, along with other American women she had known in Paris such as Sylvia Beach, whose well-known book shop, Shakespeare and Company, had been forced to close soon after the Occupation with most of the stock hidden upstairs. Drue persuaded the Jewish camp doctor, Dr Jean Lévy, who was also being held hostage, that in order to continue with her resistance work she had to get out. He agreed to play along with her ruse that she had cancer of the womb and, although he had to prescribe medicine to stop her haemorrhaging, told her to throw that down the toilet and instead take the haemorrhage-inducing medicine which she had brought with her as part of a preconceived plan. This made her very weak, and as an experienced actress she had little difficulty in staging fainting fits when the Nazi doctor came by. Dr Lévy quickly became worried that if she went on losing blood at such an alarming rate her health really would be compromised. But in early December the Germans agreed that she could go to a hospital in Paris for the X-ray treatment she kept demanding. Severely anaemic by now, she registered at the Clinique de l'Alma and was told she would require blood transfusions for at least the next year. But, after visiting Dr Lévy's mother to reassure her that her son was alive and well and doing brave things for so many women, she went back to her house outside Paris where she lay low for a while to avoid reinternment.

In September 1942 Béatrice de Camondo wrote a heartfelt letter to a childhood friend she addressed as 'Ma Bonne Moumouche' (Mme de Leusse) in which she gave veiled descriptions of the present fearful situation in Paris and explained that she was preventing her daughter Fanny, who was referred to simply as 'there' (presumably in the unoccupied zone), from coming back to Paris as journeys were too dangerous. Béatrice said that she was still enjoying being able to ride every morning, smelling ferns and leaves, but that she now had to take the train every morning to a new place, closer to Paris, as she had stabled her horse with some new friends. Her divorce was proceeding but she wondered if it was worth the struggle, especially because 'I am <u>certain</u> that I am miraculously protected, that I have been for years but it is only this year that I have understood from where all my blessings come. But will I have enough years to thank God and the Virgin adequately for their protection? I am such a small thing, and such a novice, so unworthy . . .'

Exactly three months later, on 5 December 1942, Béatrice and the twenty-four-year-old Fanny were arrested and taken to Drancy, now overflowing with 2,420 internees. According to some stories the Camondo women were arrested while having tea with a friend, but the official Nazi explanation for their arrest claimed that they had not been wearing their yellow stars, or that they were not in full view. This could be true only if they were outdoors. One week later the two women were joined there by Léon, Béatrice's husband, and Bertrand, her son.

Among the desperate mass of humanity in Drancy was Bernard Herz, the pearl-dealer arrested on 2 November for a second time following a denunciation insisting that he, a Jew, was still running the business. Suzanne Belperron had been arrested the same day, she at her office and private showroom at the Rue de Châteaudun and he at his home at 38 Avenue du Président Wilson. Both were questioned at Gestapo headquarters, and in the car on the way there the policeman showed Belperron the letter of denunciation which alleged that she was running a Jewish business where one could not buy rings for less than 75,000 francs and cited the jewels of Lord Carnarvon. It was the mention of this name that made Belperron realize that she had been set up. A woman had visited her showroom a few weeks earlier asking for a particular type of ring similar to those she had made for Lord Carnarvon, the Egyptologist, before the war but offering to pay no more than 40,000 francs. Belperron told her that such a ring would cost at least 75,000 francs and, according to current regulations, she would need to supply more of her own gold. As the story reveals, Paris had become a city where nobody could be trusted, denunciations were rampant and bellies were filled with foreboding and fear.

1943

PARIS TREMBLES

At dawn on 30 July 1943, Marie-Louise Giraud, aged thirty-nine, was guillotined in the courtyard of Paris's La Roquette prison, having been found guilty of performing twenty-seven abortions in the Cherbourg region. At her trial in a specially convened court, the prosecution stressed her immorality, but to the populace she became a martyr for a cause – people called her a 'maker of angels'. Giraud, who came from a poor family, was married to a sailor with whom she had two children, and had worked as a domestic housekeeper and laundress. Since the beginning of the war she had rented rooms to prostitutes and began to perform abortions, initially on a voluntary basis and without compensation. Vichy, which still had limited civil authority in the occupied capital, had decreed in a special law of 15 February 1942 that abortion was so sinful – it was a crime against state security – that it must be treated as a capital offence. Only a pardon from Marshal Pétain himself could save Giraud's life. But he refused to commute the sentence, and Marie-Louise Giraud thus became the only woman ever to be guillotined in France for the crime of performing an abortion.

Just before the war Dr Jean Dalsace, a friend of the avant-garde gallery-owner Jeanne Bucher, had opened the first birth-control clinic in France, but the war had put a stop to such free thinking and Giraud was victim of a corrupt regime rapidly losing control. Abortions were freely available for the rich who knew where to go and could afford a fee of around 4,000 francs. Arlette Scali, for example, a member of the haute bourgeoisie who had married as a teenager, wrote that her first husband had intended to continue with his lifestyle of mistresses 'but he did not want children . . . when I was pregnant my mother-in-law paid for abortions which were illegal and costly. It was horrible.' At the other end of the social scale the struggling author, later championed by Simone de Beauvoir, Violette Leduc, wrote graphically in her autobiography, *La Bâtarde*, about how difficult it was for a single mother who did not want to keep a child. She made repeated attempts at an abortion, following visits to 'so-called midwives' – back-street abortionists – which left her close to dying and in terrible pain but bolstered by 'my single woman's determination to stand by herself and not to fall'. During a terrible winter without coal and heat, she only narrowly survived after several months in bed at her mother's with ice on her belly, being sick and continually bleeding. Slowly, she learned to walk and live again, though not long enough to see her rackety life, earning money from the black market, and her painful love affair with de Beauvoir translated into a successful film in 2012 called *Violette*.

One of the most controversial films of 1943, produced by the German-owned Continental Studios and directed by Henri-Georges Clouzot, was *Le Corbeau* (The Raven), which tackled the issue of abortion. The film, now a classic, was notable for causing serious trouble to its director after the war and was banned at the Liberation not only because of the Continental connection but because it was perceived by the communist press and by some who had been in the underground as vilifying the French people. *Le Corbeau* is an extremely dark and melodramatic story about the consequences of writing anonymous poison-pen letters. Letters signed by 'Le Corbeau' accuse a doctor of having an affair with the pretty young wife of an elderly psychiatrist and also of practising illegal abortions. The film ends as an ambulance arrives to take away the wife, who has been deemed insane, and the doctor finds the psychiatrist dead at his desk just as he was writing Le Corbeau's final triumphant letter. His throat had been cut by the mother of a cancer patient who had just committed suicide following receipt of one such anonymous letter warning that his cancer was terminal. A powerful illustration of the effect of paranoia on the human psyche.

The film was loosely based on a famous case in 1917, but the relevance in the fevered atmosphere of 1943 to the number of anonymous denunciations being bandied about, revealing that someone was Jewish or in hiding or involved in black-marketeering, added to its heightened air of realism. Denunciations – there had been an estimated three and a half million of them by the end of the war throughout France – acted as a chilling reinforcement of the power of life over death that individual French people could choose to wield during the Occupation. They were made by people from all social milieux, often driven by revenge or by a desire to claim the financial reward, which in some cases was significant. The highest rewards were paid to those denouncing a resister, and could range from 200,000 francs to 15 million. Radio-Paris, the German-controlled radio station, even had a popular programme called *Répétez-le*, which was entirely devoted to letters from listeners denouncing their neighbours, their rivals in business or love, and even members of their own family. The Germans were said to have been amazed by the response to their call for denunciations, even complaining about the workload involved in investigating them all. Many were from women, signing for example as 'a little woman who only seeks to do her duty', pointing out that a particular shop was Jewish-owned and asking if there were any business opportunities available from abandoned businesses.

In 1942 Pétain had weakly denounced the denouncers, but no one took any notice. By July 1943, the execution of the impoverished abortionist Giraud, whose trial had resulted from a denunciation, served to emphasize just how out of touch the Vichy regime had become, regarding abortion as a national plague while legalizing prostitution.

Earlier that year the introduction of the hated Service du Travail Obligatoire (STO) was promoted by Vichy with posters suggesting that Frenchmen who worked in Germany under the scheme were being good fathers by helping to provide for the wives and children they had left behind. But the STO merely added to the general unpopularity of a regime which, it was by now clear, had salvaged nothing from the defeat and was not even a buffer between the French and the Germans. Since November 1942 Vichy had been a mere puppet government clinging to the remnants of power but losing authority. This prompted Vichy in January 1943 to set up its own paramilitary force, the Milice, headed by Joseph Darnand, mandated to fight the resistance and root out Jews and given its own programme for the Nazification of France. Then Drancy, the increasingly overcrowded and unhygienic internment camp in Paris, which had initially been under the control of French police,* loyal to Vichy ideals, was in early July handed over to the Germans. As the Nazis stepped up their Europe-wide mass-extermination policy, the task of running the camp was handed to the loathed and vicious SS Hauptsturmführer Alois Brunner.

The sixty-six-year-old Bernard Herz, from his desperate corner in Drancy, was witness to the increasingly brutal round-ups that were bringing in more and more Jews. All the while he retained the faintest hope that he might any day be summoned to the Rothschild Hospital and from there effect an escape.† Meanwhile Suzanne Belperron, running the jewellery company singlehandedly and at the same time doing her best to get Herz released, was harassed constantly by the Gestapo demanding to see official documents – baptism and burial certificates – proving she was not Jewish. What seems clear today, from a study of the Herz file – innumerable microfilmed pages in the National Archives in Paris showing detailed floor plans made by French officials of Herz's home in Chantilly as well as inventories of his flat and possessions – is that the Germans were determined to seize his assets. On 21 February he wrote to Suzanne, his 'Chère Amie', what appears to be an agonizing final communication from his 'disgusting' prison. In tiny writing on a fragment of brown paper, he thanks her for the little parcels she was sending him, recounts the interminable boredom of Drancy and tells her where to find his will. He ends: 'I do not at all regret staying in Paris, as I thereby

---

* A number of factors had led to mounting discontent among the French police: their workloads had become significantly heavier as they dealt with the growth of resistance, policed the black market and sifted through thousands of denunciation letters, while their numbers had declined partly thanks to the STO. In addition, many had been unhappy about their role in Operation Spring Wind.
† The Rothschild Hospital, often referred to as an annex to Drancy, was situated next to the Picpus cemetery in the 12th arrondissement, the site of a series of mass graves of aristocrats guillotined during the Revolution. In 1797 the land was secretly purchased by Princess Amalie Zephyrine of Salm-Kyrburg, a German aristocrat brought up in Paris who married into the house of Hohenzollern-Sigmaringen, as her brother and lover were both buried there. As a result the cemetery was apparently treated as sacred ground by the Germans, not to be actively policed, and it thus offered a useful escape route.

shortened the time I will spend away from it. If I had my time again, I would do it all again. Forgive me for all the trouble I caused you. It seems I bring you nothing else when what I wanted so much was your happiness. Thank you for everything.' After seven months at Drancy, Bernard Herz was deported to Auschwitz on 2 September 1943, where he was murdered.

But as more ordinary French people now witnessed cruelty and barbarity on a massive scale, and with children often torn screaming from their parents, public opinion slowly turned. Consequently, 1943 saw a steady growth in resistance groups, not only those in the country- side, swollen with fugitives from the forced-labour draft (now known as the Maquis or Maquisards because of the scrubland they often hid in), but also in towns and villages throughout France. Small cells or networks were now growing with various types of subterfuge undertaken. Many individuals simply wanted 'to do something' to thwart the Germans, without necessarily joining a group. Alongside the collaborators, still buying, still eating, many Parisiennes now put their lives on the line.

'We were all amateurs,' recalled Vivou (née Chevrillon), the young music-student cousin of Claire Chevrillon who was desperate to be involved in something more serious than customizing ready-made cork-soled shoes with fabric, important though that was if she was to look chic among her peers in Paris. Vivou had three brothers, one still a schoolboy, but the older two had both left home to join de Gaulle, encouraged by their remarkable mother who, so keen to help them resist, drove her nineteen-year-old son to the Spanish border to help him get out to fight. Like many young women of her circle, Vivou was not a formally registered resister but nonetheless was involved in important and potentially dangerous work creating false identity papers, forging the signature of the Paris Préfet, Amédée Bussière.[*]

Claire was arrested that eventful summer and on her release, after weeks in Fresnes prison, 'it was my buoyant cousin Vivou, twenty, who marched me to a hairdresser on Rue Royale and stayed the whole time laughing and talking nonsense lest I run away'. Another friend

---

[*] In 1946 Bussière was convicted of 'collaboration with the enemy' and sentenced to life imprisonment, but was pardonned after serving five years.

gave a dinner party, which took two days to prepare, to celebrate Claire's freedom. But the constant threat of a knock on the door in the middle of the night meant that for anyone with something to hide it was difficult to sleep. Some remember hearing dogs barking or whining during the night, others the anguished cries of torture victims or of those being arrested. Many people lived with a small bag packed in case they had to make a sudden escape. The uncertainty created by constantly changing hideouts and by often poorly forged identity cards, which would not have withstood close scrutiny, was taking its toll on already frayed nerves. The resistance seemed to be suffering one disaster after another in 1943. The Germans' charm offensive during the first eighteen months of Occupation gave way to repressive control throughout the country, often relying on informers keen to win a promised reward, usually no more than a hundred francs. Many resisters were betrayed and captured in this way, culminating in the arrest in Lyons on 21 June (and subsequent torture and death) of Jean Moulin, the man parachuted back into France and charged by de Gaulle with unifying the various resistance groups under one umbrella. On 27 May the courageous Moulin, known for wearing a scarf wrapped around his neck to hide a previous attempt at suicide, had held the first meeting of the National Council of the Resistance in Paris but was betrayed just a few weeks later. His death along with the arrest of several of his associates was a major blow, leaving the local Gestapo chief Klaus Barbie in total control in Lyons. Paris, larger and with more opportunities for hiding, became a necessary but still intensely dangerous centre for resistance.

Immediately after her release, Claire went back to teaching at the Collège Sévigné, where her pupils treated her as a heroine. But the euphoria was short-lived. On 23 September her flatmate, the beautiful twenty-two-year-old aristocrat Jacqueline d'Alincourt, was arrested at their flat on the Rue de Grenelle after a landlady had denounced one of her contacts. Jacqueline found several Gestapo officers awaiting her when she returned to the flat and she tried to escape towards an inner stairway that led to the roof:

I was overtaken, handcuffed behind my back, and the interrogation began then and there. I tried in vain to overcome the trembling that took hold of me, head to foot, distressed at the idea that the men would notice it. Questions rained down on me thick and fast, and, because I refused to answer, one of them yelled at me, 'We have ways of making you talk!' I answered immediately: 'I am sure you are capable of anything.' I was slapped in the face and the trembling stopped. A feeling of relief came over me. The strength now within me would not abandon me throughout the five long days and nights that awaited me.

Fortunately Claire was out at the time of the arrest but, as the one who had introduced Jacqueline when she first came to Paris from her home in Poitiers two years previously to Jean Ayral, regional head of the Office of Air Operations (BOA) and a close collaborator of Jean Moulin, she was distraught.

Jacqueline was a young widow, her husband having died suddenly in 1941 while he was held prisoner in Germany. Tall and willowy, she had an inner strength partly derived from watching her widowed mother courageously bring up a family of seven. Resentment over her husband's premature death, and anger when she saw a child forced to year a yellow star in Paris, had helped overcome her fear of the enemy. 'Should one resign oneself to bow one's head in submission? I knew that I would rather die. The shock gave me a resolve that nothing would destroy, for the enemy is powerless over him who has no fear of death.' She started work encoding messages to be despatched to London, ensuring that secret agents sent from England had lodgings, some form of professional cover, false papers and ration cards, as well as finding 'mailboxes' where illegal messages from all over France could be transferred. One fellow agent was a friend called Josette, 'a public relations director for a celebrated couturier, highly esteemed by German officers' wives. Thanks to the comings and goings of many women on the fashion house's premises, our couriers passed unnoticed. No one could conceive of resistance activity going on in the heart of this *grande maison* frequented by the upper crust of the army of occupation.'

After her arrest Jacqueline was imprisoned first at 11 Rue des Saussaies, the Gestapo headquarters where prisoners were chained, interrogated and tortured, then at Fresnes and eventually

Ravensbrück. Not surprisingly Claire, who guessed but could not know what torment Jacqueline was suffering, concluded that now she too must commit fully. 'This work had become my chief interest in life.' She resigned her job, moved apartments and went underground, living clandestinely as Christiane Clouet. She could no longer see her parents as to do so would endanger them all.

'For me the strongest memory of that time is not fear, but solidarity, which was stronger than fear,' recalled Vivou.

> When we heard that one of our friends had been arrested we felt we must do something. We didn't feel the drama in the same way that of course our parents did. The most dangerous thing I did was when my friend (and fellow musician) Antoine Geoffroy-Dechaume was arrested and imprisoned at Compiègne camp just outside the city. I wanted him to know we were aware of what had happened and were doing all we could for him. So I went with Antoine's sister, Marie-France, intending to walk around the camp playing a tune on my violin that he would recognize and know it was me. Unfortunately the SS officer outside the camp, a very Aryan type, warned me: 'I do not advise you to do that.' So we went home, but not defeated.

At the same time André Chevrillon, Vivou's uncle and Claire's father, an esteemed member of the French Academy, wrote to René de Chambrun, who he had heard was hoping for a seat in the Academy, and pleaded 'in the name of French music' for Antoine's release – but to no avail. Antoine was deported to Buchenwald on 20 January 1944.

Antoine and Marie-France Geoffroy-Dechaume were part of a family emblematic of the deep-rooted French patriotism that was stirring now, a countervailing force to those dealing on the black market, buying expensive clothes and contributing to the image of normality in Paris. Nominally Catholic, they were both outward leaning, towards England, and fiercely defensive of a certain idea of what France stood for. Their ancestor Adolphe-Victor Geoffroy-Dechaume, born in Paris in 1816, was a sculptor who believed that the Middle Ages were France's golden age, and whose best-known statues adorn the pier of Notre Dame Cathedral. He was buried at Valmondois, an ancient French village just north of Paris on the River Oise, where the family subsequently made their home. Charles, his grandson, a painter, lived in England before the First World War, and became close friends with Winston and Clementine Churchill and their circle. But, having lost a leg in action during that war, Charles decided after his marriage to return to the comfortable old house at Valmondois. Here he could bring up his ten children in an unusual musical, artistic and creative community. The family some-times performed Bach chorales or sang small-scale operas.

Bernard de Gaulle, nephew of the General, who was to marry Sylvie Geoffroy-Dechaume, the youngest in the family, told me about Marie-France, born in 1919 and given the name France to signify her parents' satisfaction with the terms of the Treaty of Versailles. 'Marie-France was an angel,' he says of his sister-in-law. Bernard, a keeper of so many flames, lives today in an apartment in the shadow of the former Cherche-Midi military prison, now a memorial but notorious as the place where Dreyfus was convicted and where, later, several resisters were tortured and shot. It is almost impossible here not to experience a sense of the past enveloping the present. 'There was something heavenly about her which was a mixture of sincer-ity and force,' he adds. Another friend recalled that, after the war, Marie-France could never walk along the Avenue Foch because of her memory of hearing loud cries from torture victims there. Sylvie, born in 1924, was too young at first to take an active role in resisting, and had to live with the torment of knowing that her brother Antoine was a prisoner while another brother, Jean-Pierre, had been captured following Dunkirk but managed to escape and subsequently joined the Maquis in the south. As soon as she was old enough, Sylvie joined him there.

Since 1941 Marie-France had been helping pilots on the run, even taking some of them to hide at Valmondois if they wanted to use Brittany as their escape route. She often worked with a local car mechanic, François Kerambrun, a trusted friend of the family, who would drive the boys in his old truck to a house close to the sea and from there, once they heard the all-clear on the BBC, lead them down a steep cliff (so steep they hoped the Germans would not watch it) to the sea. The whole party then waited in caves for the British to send dinghies which would ferry them out to a ship waiting offshore. On one occasion she bought her charges French newspapers to read on the train from Paris to Brittany but was horrified to see that, as a German inspector arrived, one of them was reading it upside down with trembling hands. Luckily their documents were accepted so they did not have to say anything.

But in mid-1943, on seeing a Gestapo officer leave her Paris building, Marie-France realized that she had to move away immediately. Using a false identity, she was sent with a band of resistance fighters to a small house on the north Brittany coast, in the Saint-Malo region, part of an undercover operation intended, among other things, to sabotage the railways and the roads to prevent the Germans from reaching the coast and transporting arms and ammunition. From then on her work became more dangerous as, in addition to helping evaders, she was involved in preparing to lay explosives on railway lines in readiness for the Allied invasion, a task not initially given to women resisters and which required her to carry weapons.

Although many women were volunteering in 1943, other than communist workers who were used to being organized, most were well educated and well intentioned but with no previous experience of political or military work. In January 1943 Andrée (known as Dédée) de Jongh, founder and a key organizer of the Comet escape line,* and a former commercial artist and nurse who had made thirty-two journeys over the Pyrenees, was betrayed and captured at a farmhouse in the French Basque country. Interrogated and tortured by the Gestapo, Andrée eventually admitted that she was the organizer of the escape network. Chaos ensued in the wake of her arrest, as it was hard to know amid the infiltrations and multiple arrests who could be trusted.

---

* The Brussels-based Comet line was a resistance group intended to help Allied pilots and a few others on the run to escape to Britain by guiding, feeding and clothing them through France, usually down to Bayonne, over the Pyrenees into neutral Spain and then on into British-controlled Gibraltar. The Pat line, named after Pat O'Leary's code name for Albert Guérisse, had a similar function but used different routes, all of which started from Paris, but one went via Brittany, from where men were shipped to Britain.

Elisabeth Barbier, a thirty-one-year-old divorcee living with her mother in the Rue Vaneau in Paris, had been involved in resistance activities since 1940, working with friends in the Mithridate Franco-British network collecting vital information to help plan military operations. But, late in 1942, she and her mother also became involved in sheltering various resisters, downed pilots or evaders – men on the run trying to avoid being drafted into the STO – in their own apartment or in those of friends until they could be moved on. It was enormously risky work, especially if the men were neither French-speakers nor, in the case of North Americans, French-looking. Money was needed to feed and clothe them or to dye their hair. Cigarettes (important to calm nerves) could be bought for them on the black market but they cost between 150 and 250 francs a packet. Drue Tartière, bringing food from the country, went to visit some of these boys, as she described them, often mere teenagers who were bored hanging about, frustrated at not being allowed outside (since they might all too easily give themselves and others away) and who, she believed, did not appreciate what was being done for them.

Occasionally she took them to a barber for a haircut or for walks around Paris, disguising them as best she could in old French clothes and forbidding them to speak. Once she brought her friend Sylvia Beach, the bookshop owner, to amuse them; on another occasion she had to reprimand a young American lieutenant who was behaving badly, reducing his Parisian host to tears. Drue reminded him that these not very well-off Parisians, paid a paltry sum by various resistance groups as it was difficult to get money to them from abroad, were risking their lives every minute of the day and night for him, and she threatened to turn him out into the street to fend for himself if he didn't show more concern and gratitude. Why did the women do it? According to Jeannie Rousseau, those who resisted were 'almost powerless' because they were responding to 'an inner obligation to participate in the struggle'.

Denise Dufournier, a colleague of Elisabeth Barbier and Jeannie Rousseau, had, like them, been involved in resistance activities almost from the outset. 'You either did something or you were a collaborator' is how Denise's daughter explains her mother's viewpoint today. 'She had a very strong moral compass.' Born in 1915 into a family of artists, doctors and intellectuals, Denise was educated at the Lycée Molière, a leading Paris girls' school of the day where many of her friends were Jewish. This made her keenly aware of the increasing injustices, once the German Occupation began. But her parents died when she was just thirteen and her brother sixteen, forcing self-sufficiency on her from an early age. By the time war broke out, she had qualified as a lawyer and, with her brother working in Lisbon as a diplomat, was an unusually independent young woman who was also a published novelist. With few male barristers still working in Paris, she was in great demand. In addition to her day job, she was running enormous personal risks to help Allied airmen forced to bale out over France and keen to get out of the country. But on 18 June 1943 she and Elisabeth Barbier and Elisabeth's mother were all betrayed by their new courier, a man who called himself Jean Masson but was actually a Belgian conman and traitor, Jacques Desoubrie. Denise later recognized him as her betrayer at her first interrogation when he entered the room and sneered at her.

Dufournier, like de Jongh, was questioned first at Fresnes for six months, but she did not break. Fresnes was now a place of terror, where by this time 'the Germans are shooting hostages or people who have been convicted . . . every day'. Jean Guéhenno, citing a source, 'V', wrote in his diary:

the order goes from cell to cell through the gutters, the toilet pipes, the water pipes: 'six o'clock for cell thirty-two' and at the appointed time the whole prison begins to sing the Marseillaise or the song of departure. The prisoners have broken all the windows so the victims can hear their farewell song as they cross the prison yard. The Germans have forbidden all singing. They are going to make examples, torture and execute. Uselessly. The prison continues to sing.

Denise was familiar with Fresnes, as many of the young clients she had been helping to defend had been sent there. She knew she could survive it, and she did. After six months, Denise and Elisabeth Barbier were transported to Ravensbrück, where a new form of torture began.

*

Vera Leigh had by 1943 become a true Parisienne, having lived all her adult life in Paris, working in fashion. But, by virtue of having been born in Leeds in 1903, she was also a British citizen, so she decided she should now get herself back to England where she could be more actively involved in the struggle against the Nazis. Leigh never knew her birth parents because she had been adopted while still an infant by an American businessman and racehorse trainer called Eugene Leigh and his English wife, who took her to live in France. Thanks to the Leighs, Vera grew up around the Maisons-Laffitte stables, where Eugene kept horses. As a child she had wanted to be a jockey, but instead she worked in fashion, first as a *vendeuse* with the milliner Caroline Reboux.

In 1927 Vera went into partnership with a friend, and the pair set up their own hat shop, which they called Rose Valois, in the Place Vendôme. By the time war broke out Vera was a successful businesswoman with a fiancé, Charles Dussaix, a Swiss based in Lyons. It is not clear why they did not marry, but in 1940, when Paris was first occupied, she went to live with him intending to leave immediately for England. But once in Lyons she became involved in helping Allied airmen to escape until that became too dangerous. In 1942, needing to get out herself, she joined one of the underground escape routes across the Pyrenees into Spain. She was briefly interned just outside Bilbao, but eventually arrived in England via Gibraltar and immediately offered her services to the various women's organizations. She was soon picked out by F Section of Special Operations Executive (SOE) because of her perfect French. Her interviewer noted that she was 'a smart businesswoman and commerce was her first allegiance', but thought this would not lessen her suitability for the work they had in mind for her. She was almost forty, and she agreed from now on to drop all contact with her fiancé. According to the official report 'she felt she had jeopardised him enough by letting him hide her while on her way out'.

The SOE had been created by Churchill in 1940 'to set Europe ablaze' by giving support to the local resistance organizations in occupied Europe. Some sixty SOE agents were women, not all of whom were sent into the field. But the forty chosen for F Section were selected partly because it was believed they would blend in better than men in wartime, and could invent a better cover story, especially in Paris where young men were increasingly a rarity.* This was especially important for couriers, carrying messages often for long distances by train or bicycle, and it was thought in London that women who hid messages in their underwear were less likely to be subjected to a body search.

In this tense climate female couriers were a great help to resistance radio operators, as a woman with a transmitter at the bottom of her basket covered with carrots and turnips could pretend she was carrying a heavy shopping bag, whereas a young man carrying a heavy suitcase was immediately suspect and far more likely to be stopped and searched. Nonetheless it was an unprecedented decision for the British to send women into the field, even or especially as volunteers, where they risked capture, brutal interrogation, torture and death. Although Churchill's approval for using women was never official, when Captain Selwyn Jepson, recruiting officer for F Section, told him of the plans, his response – 'Good luck to you' – was always taken as tacit authority. But it could not be revealed to the public at the time that Britain was using women in this way as, under the Geneva Convention, women were not allowed to take on combatant duties so their activities had to be highly secret: one reason why so little was known about many of them until many years later. A team of lawyers was seconded to SOE and it was decided that SOE women should be enrolled into the First Aid Nursing Yeomanry, known as FANYs, partly to give them useful cover to tell family and friends, partly to train them in the use of firearms; and also in the vain hope that if captured they would have some military status to protect them according to the Geneva Convention. The female agents of F Section did not always carry weapons and were expected to exploit their femininity to maximize their usefulness.

* In addition to the nearly two million French soldiers initially kept as hostages to ensure that Vichy would reduce its armed forces and pay a heavy tribute in gold, food and supplies, Germany continually demanded more workers. It has been estimated that by the end of 1943 there were 646,421 French workers in Germany, almost all male as most had been sent to work on railways or on the land or now as part of the STO (see Julian Jackson, *France: The Dark Years*, p. 233 onwards).

Vera underwent immediate training and her commandant reported that she was 'full of guts', had kept up with the men and was 'about the best shot in the party . . . a plumb woman for this work . . . a woman of outstanding ability and courage and determination'. Another report noted that she was very interested in clothes and hated the hideous khaki uniform she had to wear as a FANY. During the night of 13–14 May, Ensign Vera Leigh, codenamed Simone, was flown back to France and dropped east of Tours in one of the small Lysander aircraft, used not only as they could land without runways but because the lone pilot could fly them low, below enemy radar, with only moonlight to guide him along shiny rivers, lakes or railway line before picking up as well as dropping off those who were not parachuting. She was met by Henri Déricourt, F Section's Air Movements officer in northern France, and immediately moved back to Paris where she was to be a milliner's assistant called Suzanne Chavanne working with the Inventor circuit.* With her well-attuned eye for observing fashion, Vera found Paris in many ways unchanged. Women, or at least certain women, were still shopping at the couture houses around the Place Vendôme and the Ritz Hotel, as shown by figures for turnover of couture clothes, as well as surtax paid by customers.† Feeling if not relaxed at least comfortable in her native

---

* SOE operations in France were organized into networks or cells known as Circuits which covered different parts of the country based around three key figures: an organizer, a courier and a wireless operator, almost all of whom were trained in Britain. The circuit organiser then recruited additional local men and women.
† Turnover in 1943 rose to 463 million francs, from 67 million in 1941. The fashion magazines continued to publish photographs of Parisian high society with details of what the women were wearing, at least until February 1943, when the Germans, not wishing to encourage an appetite for clothes its own women could not satisfy, finally banned the distribution of photographs of French fashion. Those regularly buying the latest Parisian couture designs included wives of German officers, wives of Parisian collaborators, journalists, film stars and wives of industrialists with flourishing businesses. Among them were the actress wife of 'Steve Passeur', nom de plume of Etienne Morin, a journalist and dramatist popular at the time who occupied a suite at the Ritz; Françoise Luchaire, wife of Jean; Mme Lisette de Brinon, newly created honorary Aryan; and Josée de Chambrun. They formed a distinct and limited circle of women intent on keeping up their position in society as they attended a plethora of Franco-German receptions.

city, Vera Leigh foolishly even used the same hairdresser she had frequented in pre-war days where they knew exactly who she was, no mere milliner's assistant, and in addition to her SOE work she continued with her former activities, helping Allied airmen hiding out in various Paris flats who needed escorting through France to Spain often via the Comet line.

Like Vera, Noor Inayat Khan, the part-American daughter of an Indian Sufi mystic, who wrote children's stories and had escaped from Paris to England with her family in 1940, was by the end of 1942 eager to get back to England, her adopted country, and be of real use. Against her mother's wishes, she had joined the Women's Auxiliary Air Force (WAAF), having changed her name to Nora and given her religion as Church of England to avoid awkwardness. Influenced by her brother Vilayat, who had joined the RAF, she repeatedly applied for a commission within the WAAF and by October 1942 came to the attention of SOE because of her interesting linguistic qualifications and was called for an interview in November.

Linguistic abilities were key, and Noreen Riols, born in Malta to English parents, was another young woman recruited to F Section in 1943 when she was still a teenager. She believes she was picked simply because she had attended the French Lycée in London. Like many of the women recruited, she was also very pretty. She recounted the story of one courier, Maureen O'Sullivan, always known as Paddy, who was cycling around Paris with a transmitter strapped to the back of her bicycle when she had to stop at a level crossing. To her horror a car full of Gestapo officers drew up alongside. One of them wound down the window and asked her what she had in her suitcase. 'She knew that if she hesitated or appeared flustered she was lost so she gave a big smile . . . and said "I've got a radio transmitter and I'm going to contact London and tell them all about you" . . . the officer smiled back and said "You're far too pretty to risk your neck with such stupidities" and drove off.'

But it wasn't always that easy, nor was the training given to these keen young women always as rigorous as it might have been in view of the need to get agents into Paris as quickly as possible. From the start there were political tensions in London as the other intelligence services, chiefly SIS (the Secret Intelligence Service, also known as MI6), clashed with SOE and its often unorthodox methods; there was also rivalry with the Gaullist organizations in London. Language and appearance were crucial to recruitment, while character and private life were merely taken into consideration. Noor, or Nora as she was now known, was accepted after just one interview, deemed to be 'sure and confident', according to Selwyn Jepson, chief recruitment officer. She joined officially on 8 February 1943 aged twenty-nine, was also enrolled as a FANY and commissioned. Her training, which included fitness instruction and handling explosives, now started in earnest. However, she was not as supple and sporty as Vera and was, it was noted, 'unsuitable for jumping' and 'pretty scared of weapons'. No one doubted her courage, but her examiners stated that she made 'stupid mistakes, always volunteered far more information when questioned' and 'must learn to be more discreet'. There were clearly doubts about Noor's suitability and readiness. Some thought her too emotional, exotic and dreamy and felt that she might therefore be a security risk, but others considered that as she was an excellent radio operator she would be useful. According to her final report: 'she has an unstable and temperamental personality and it is very doubtful whether she is really suited to work in this field'. But Maurice Buckmaster, the Old Etonian F Section head, who was under enormous pressure to provide trained operators, not only believed she could cope but, alongside a comment that she was 'not overburdened with brains,' scribbled: 'we don't want them overburdened with brains.' Whether Noor would have been retained for further assessments, had the shortage of radio operators not been so acute, is impossible to say.

When other women agents training with Noor expressed their doubts, Buckmaster's deputy, the Sorbonne-educated, elegantly mysterious Vera Atkins, stepped in. She took Noor to lunch at a quiet restaurant and told her about the misgivings, insisting that if she stepped back now nobody would know or consider it shameful. But Noor was firm and maintained that nothing worried her other than concern for her mother.

Leo Marks, a brilliant young cryptographer who got to know Noor well during her last weeks in England, was also worried. The system which agents used at that time to receive and transmit messages was code-based around a well-known poem they had memorized which always concerned him as it could be so easily deciphered. Many agents chose well-known poems which the enemy could guess. It was for that reason that in December 1943 he gave a poem called 'The Life that I Have', which he had written himself in memory of his girlfriend Ruth, who had just been killed, to another SOE agent Violette Szabo and which nobody else knew. Nonetheless, if caught and forced to transmit under duress, an agent had, as additional security, both a 'bluff' check to precede the message which was a warning even if it was then followed by a 'true' check, which it was supposed only London could know about. But for Noor, using such a false check would, of course, involve lying to her captors since it was intended to deceive, and when Leo discussed this with Noor she replied, shocked, 'Lie about them. Why should I do that?' Lying went against her religion. Noor insisted that rather than lie she would just refuse to tell them anything no matter how often they asked.

Marks, clearly smitten with the beautiful Noor, was worried that in practice this would mean her enduring unimaginable torture. In an attempt to protect her he gave her a new security check, telling her 'you won't have to lie about it because no one but you and me will know that it exists'. When she went off to practise encoding the messages for him with the new check, 'I prayed . . . that she'd repeat all her old mistakes and that I could write a bad report on her to prevent her from going in.' But she did it perfectly, so Marks wrote Buckmaster the positive report he needed for Noor to be given clearance to fly off at the next full moon. On 16 June, Vera Atkins drove down to Sussex with Noor. At the last minute, just before she flew off, Vera gave her a silver brooch, suddenly removing it from her own suit and pinning it on to her lapel with the words: 'It's a little bird. It will bring you luck.' From now on Noor was Jeanne-Marie Renier, a children's nurse, with a complicated cover story worked out by Atkins herself.

The summer that Noor and Vera Leigh were sent back to Paris, reprisals and arrests were an everyday occurrence as denunciations from collaborators and infiltrators were flooding into Gestapo offices.

One of those suspected by the Allies of being an informant for the SS with a specific brief to foil the activities of SOE was Violette Morris, the bisexual former athlete highly visible thanks to her enormous size, her habit of dressing as a man and the freedom with which she drove her black Citroën car from Paris to Cannes or Nice in the south of France, chauffeuring members of the Gestapo or Vichy officials. She still lived on her houseboat on the Seine, 'where she frequently receives German officers', and although she had handed over the car-parts garage she owned in Paris to the Luftwaffe in 1941 she continued to run it for the Germans, which entitled her to an apparently never ending supply of fuel and other black-market goods. Many of those she drove knew her as 'la fameuse Violette Morris', the former racing driver of the 1920s. She was implicated in a number of arrests in 1943 and prisoners taken to Fresnes shuddered at the mention of her name.

As London knew, the average life expectancy for a wireless operator in this treacherous climate was six weeks. Within ten days of Noor's arrival in Paris the network she was meant to work with had fallen into German hands and was in complete disarray. In early July hundreds of French agents were rounded up and arrested as the Germans infiltrated the circuits. Noor and two others remained at large, one of whom was a former businessman called France Antelme, in his mid-forties, who it seems was captivated by Nora. The pair tried to warn others and hide while the Germans were torturing those agents they had captured in the hope of locating their comrades. One of those captured was Francis Suttill, a half-French lawyer known as Prosper, who was forced to stand for days on end with no food, water or sleep. Infuriated when he would not talk, his captors beat him mercilessly and broke his arm. Although other agents were told by London to escape across the Pyrenees or return by the August moon when a Lysander pick-up could be arranged, Noor was advised to stay in Paris, simply to lie low for a while and not transmit to London even though she desperately wanted to do her duty. Buckmaster saw her as being of key importance if F Section was to have any chance of recovering after this disaster. When Antelme returned home in late July he reported that he had done what he could to orientate Noor and before leaving had placed her in contact with Déricourt, who needed a wireless operator. But Antelme was clearly unsettled and anxious that he had left her in grave danger. When London finally heard from Noor in August and September there was good news and bad. Her morale seemed high, but she was ignoring basic security by sending out messages *en clair* when they should have been encoded. They did not then know that she was contravening another important security regulation by copying into a notebook all the messages she had sent as an SOE operative. She thanked Miss Atkins for the little bird brooch, which she said had brought her luck. F Section concluded that she had settled into the job, and when later they ordered her to return to London she refused to do so until satisfied that Atkins had found a replacement for her, which she never did.

One of the people Noor stayed with that summer while the Germans were on her tail was a friend of the Marié family from Versailles, a woman who was later caught and deported, although Jacqueline Marié, a seventeen-year-old schoolgirl when war broke out, did not realize who Noor was until she heard about her after the war. Jacqueline herself, stirred by an automatic instinct to resist, now began making anti-German drawings, using tracing paper, which she and her elder brother Pierre delivered to what they hoped were reliable houses in the neighbourhood. But she soon started distributing more sophisticated resistance leaflets, including the news-sheets *Le Courrier de l'Air, Témoignage Chrétien* and some issues of *Défense de la France,* the newspaper of one of the most important resistance organizations, which had its own clandestine publishing press. 'It was unacceptable to live in an occupied country,' she says very simply. Her whole family, scarred by memories of her grandfather who had been deported to Germany in the previous war and who never recovered, was involved in some form of resistance.

'One of the most frightening things was emerging from the Métro with a bag full of anti-Nazi leaflets and finding either French or German police waiting at the exit. Sometimes there were alerts at Métro stations as papers were searched lasting for two hours, so then we would walk through tunnels, which had no light in them at all, and leave by a different exit. But often only one station in three was open so you'd keep on walking. That was normal life for a Parisian resister. Everyone was doing it,' she shrugs, making light of the daily terror. Returning home from the centre of Paris to Versailles, where she sometimes distributed leaflets at the nearby Renault factory, she remembers having to take elaborate routes and sneak into buildings or hide in a lobby if the Germans were doing the rounds or if she had missed the curfew. 'At least you heard them approaching as their hobnailed boots made a noise on the cobbled streets of Versailles,' Jacqueline recalled.

Mme Marié, her mother, was involved in one of the most dangerous jobs of all, hiding young people in the family apartment and allowing them to use it for transmitting. 'We never discussed our work even though we knew what the other was doing, nor did my mother ever try to stop me doing this work,' she says. 'I did feel fear.' In addition to distributing leaflets, Jacqueline's job was to find constantly changing places for radio transmissions as the Germans roamed around in lorries with antennae trying to find them.

Geneviève de Gaulle was, like Jacqueline, a young girl with an elder brother when she first joined a resistance group the day they heard Marshal Pétain's 'cowardly surrender' from Bordeaux on 17 June 1940. 'There are moments in life which are completely unacceptable and the invasion of our country by the Nazis was one. My father Xavier [General de Gaulle's elder brother] had made me read *Mein Kampf*, so I knew Hitler's doctrine. I had a great need to do something, so I went to the nearest bridge, over the River Vilaine in Brittany, and pulled down a Nazi flag,' she explained.

It was, like Vivou Chevrillon's attempted violin-playing at Compiègne, or the tearing down of propaganda posters by the newly married Jacqueline D'Alincourt who went out as soon as curfew ended each morning with her three teenage sisters, a small act of resistance on its own but one which soon led to others. In addition, Geneviève was spurred on by the knowledge that her brother Roger, who had crossed the Spanish frontier, had managed to join the Free French Forces of her uncle. She had grown up in a family who identified themselves as strongly Dreyfusard; in addition, having lost her mother when she was four, she had learned to fend for herself from an early age. Wanting to do something as active as her brother, she returned to Paris from Brittany and wrote articles for *La Défense de la France*, usually under the pseudonym Galliard, but she used a variety of false names. She also helped people to escape, mostly would-be fighters who wished to join her uncle in London, through either Spain or Brittany, sometimes travelling to the border with them. She was constantly on the look-out for small pieces of information about German troops or equipment and was also used for delivering packages or false papers.

Jacqueline Marié exaggerated her youth by wearing white ankle socks and carrying her tracts in a school bag. Similarly, Geneviève de Gaulle considered 'it was an advantage that I looked only about sixteen. Once a German official offered to carry a suitcase for me, not knowing that it contained arms. Another time I took hold of the boy I was with and pretended to kiss him, just to look innocent,' she recalled.

But on 20 July 1943 her luck ran out. The then twenty-three-year-old niece of the exiled French leader was picked up by the Gestapo at a bookshop on the Rue Bonaparte where she regularly delivered false identity papers. Like the others, she was transported first to Fresnes, then to Ravensbrück, one of eighty arrested over the next few days, fifty of whom, like her, were young people working for *La Défense de la France*. Jacqueline Marié still remembers the terror she felt that July when scores of members of various resistance groups were arrested, including some she knew. But she continued with her work, trying to be more careful. There was no alternative.

As the Gestapo discovered more names and addresses they tightened their grip everywhere, and fear spread throughout the country. Families who had moved to Marseilles from Paris thinking themselves safe suddenly found themselves endangered but unable to move. Children especially, constantly on the move and changing schools, experienced the fear of their parents without being able to express their emotions, possibly for years. 'It was something so heavy, even if you didn't know what was going on precisely it was so terrible and you had no power over it. It was breaking you,' explained Paris-born Claude Kiejman, whose family moved south in 1940.

Odette Fabius was now involved in a passionate love affair with the Corsican socialist Pierre Ferri-Pisani and, working closely with his resistance network, was inspired to undertake increasingly dangerous activities. Secret action was something of a drug, she confessed, and she delighted in the opportunity to meet people whom she would never have discovered without war if confined to her own society. Writing about Pierre after the war, Odette admitted that the extreme danger and the uncertainty about what would happen the next day heightened their passion. She ran the love affair alongside the resistance work, one feeding off the other, and although she maintained later that it was a 'wartime love affair', she also recognized that at the time 'we took it to the limit, intensely aware that we had to live in the present and were threatened by the future as one or other of us was likely to die before victory. We dreamed and planned our post-war lives . . . we loved each other so deeply . . . we said to each other that at least this absurd war had the merit of helping us find each other.'

Other than their shared patriotism and 'strong souls', they could not have been more different. The war enabled them to put their differences aside. Try as they might to be discreet, all Pierre's associates were aware of the affair. Odette was engaged in various missions in early 1943, but, having just been to Vichy to collect her daughter for the holidays, was hoping that Easter that year would be spent quietly with Marie-Claude at their rented house at Le Lavandou. However, on 23 April she learned that Pierre and some of his team had been picked up. She went immediately to warn the network of eight 'mailboxes' – the courageous people whose houses couriers used for passing on messages collected throughout France to be sent on to London – that they were being watched. Telling twelve-year-old Marie-Claude to wait for her in a cinema while she did this, she set off, promising to return as soon as she could. But at the eighth stop, a coal merchant, the Gestapo were waiting for her. She tried to bluff her way out, saying she could come back another day, the coal was not urgent as it was hardly winter. But it was useless; she was seized and taken to the local prison. Long after the film was over, Marie-Claude eventually gave up waiting for her mother and decided to make her way to family friends where her father, in due course, came to look after her.

Odette spent two months in the local Saint-Pierre prison, insisting she was a political not a Jewish prisoner – a denial which earned her, as an Aryan, the right to a one-hour walk every day. She longed to tell the other Jewish prisoners that, like them, she was Jewish but could not afford to do so 'because I was engaged in an action which went beyond my personality.' While there, by loudly singing 'La Marseillaise' she discovered that Pierre was in the same prison. Then to her great delight they were transferred to Paris together, enduring a three-day train journey in the same compartment. 'In this sad situation here was a moment of unforgettable joy, even happiness, although the word may shock,' wrote Odette.

But at Fresnes she was put into solitary confinement until in October she was deported to Ravensbrück via Compiègne. She did not know that in November her husband Robert was also arrested but he, by insisting that his wife was a Catholic, managed to avoid immediate deportation to Drancy. Instead, because the Germans knew of his expertise as an antique dealer, he was put to work in a camp inside Paris itself, based in the former department store Lévitan, where his job was to sort furniture and works of art stolen by the Nazis. According to his daughter, when he saw his own family's silver pass through he did what he could to bend the cutlery to render it useless for the Germans to whom it was being sent.

Lévitan, at 85–87 Rue du Faubourg Saint-Martin, had been a well-known Jewish-owned furniture store in Paris but was requisitioned by the Germans in July 1943 and used for sorting, repairing and packing stolen items. There was another warehouse at the Austerlitz train station, one at the Hôtel Cahen d'Anvers in the Rue de Bassano, one at the wharf in Bercy and another at the Quai de la Gare. Of these, the Lévitan furniture store in the heart of the city was the best-known, and detainees who worked there were usually those who had (not always permanently) managed to avoid deportation to Drancy and Auschwitz by virtue of insisting on some sort of special privilege, such as being the spouse of an Aryan, wife of a prisoner of war or a 'half-Jew'. Only remarkable objects were sent to Germany. Furniture and small objects were mostly made available for Nazi officials to choose for their homes, while high-quality artworks went, if not to the Jeu de Paume, where more than 20,000 works of art stolen from Jews were recorded and stored, to the Palais de Tokyo and the Louvre.

It is, of course, impossible to estimate how many Parisiennes must have walked past or been aware of what was happening at Lévitan yet continued with their daily life as best they could. However, alongside the terror, so great that some people never dared venture out of their homes, Paris was also, as one German visitor to the city noticed, full of 'elegant ones' who still held sway over the street scene, causing not only men 'but women who want to know what the fashionable ones wear, to glance in their direction . . . Their resourcefulness in remaining fashionable brought colour to an otherwise grey everyday life.'

Bluebell, the Irish dancer Margaret Kelly, now married to the Jewish pianist Marcel Leibovici, was finding life extremely tough. There was never enough food. In 1940 the Germans had taken her, with one child and pregnant with her second, to the internment camp at Besançon. Eventually Count Gerald O'Kelly, the wealthy and influential Special Counsellor at the Irish Legation, extricated her by supplying documents declaring her a Catholic Irish woman, papers that were to prove invaluable in the next few months. Marcel Leibovici, meanwhile, decided to leave Paris for Marseilles, hoping to make life easier for his wife, but she was unwilling to work at the Folies Bergère given the attitude they had taken to her Jewish husband and, in any case, she disliked the way the largely German audience there regarded a visit to the nightclub as the high spot of Paris life. Instead, she put on a small cabaret of her own in the Chantilly, a small theatre in the Rue Fontaine, with just ten dancers on a tiny stage, including two British girls married to French men. But although her clientele here was not German, she attracted black-marketeers who liked to conduct deals over drinks, often hoping to mingle with the girls too. The German authorities clearly had an eye on Bluebell and on one occasion she was invited for an interview with a Colonel Feldman, who wanted her to tour her show in Berlin. She refused, a brave choice, telling him that as she had a British passport and had relatives who were fighting against the Germans, 'I cannot for a moment contemplate entertaining your troops.'

But soon after she heard that Marcel had been arrested, having been denounced as a Jew, and was being held in the Gurs detention camp, by now being used as a transit camp for many Jews before deportation to Germany. She was terrified that the trail would soon lead to her as Marcel's wife, and at six o'clock one morning was woken by two French policemen accompanied by a German in Gestapo uniform who searched her apartment. As they could not find anything incriminating, they did not take her for questioning. Then, news that was both thrilling and worrying; she heard that Marcel had managed to escape and make his way to Paris, thanks to help from a musician friend with resistance contacts who provided clothes and a false identity card for him. For the next two and a half years, Bluebell, effectively a single mother with a demanding job, kept her Jewish husband hidden in various attics and flats, without a piano because of the noise it would make and with only minimal amounts of food because she did not have a separate ration card for him. As he could not go out, he needed reading material and manuscript paper, and his washing had to be done secretly. Hiding a Jew was a crime sometimes punishable by death, and Bluebell daily risked her life on behalf of her husband.

But in the summer of 1943 she was again arrested, this time six months pregnant, and taken to 84 Avenue Foch. Unsurprisingly, the German officer asked where her husband was. In her own account of the interview she said that when she realized she was about to be asked, in English, if her husband would like to see his children again, she responded, via the interpreter, by asking her interrogator if he would like to see his. She was fortunate to get away with such insolent responses and the subject of her pregnancy was avoided. Had she been questioned, she had an answer prepared: that a German should not examine a girl's morals in wartime too closely. Her own explanation for being set free was her ability to tell convincing lies. 'I've never been shifty-eyed. I always looked them full in the face."* On 22 October Bluebell gave birth to her third child, a daughter called Florence, but Marcel was not able to see his new baby.

When Bluebell was desperate for food she would visit Frédéric Apcar in Vaucresson, about an hour south of Paris, who kept her well supplied. Frédéric was now the dancing partner of Sadie Rigal, renamed Florence, the young South African who had met Bluebell when both were interned at Besançon. Sadie had been released from the camp early in 1941 and allowed to return to Paris, but was required to sign in daily at her local police station. A resistance friend had picked her up from the train station, rented her a hotel room and bought her dinner. She was later to hide a revolver for him in return. Sadie began work again at the Bal Tabarin music hall, at first sleeping in the dressing room, since she did not have a pass that allowed her to be out at night. Later, when she had acquired a pass, she used it to assist others. It was at the Tabarin that she met Apcar, with whom she developed first a dance act, 'Florence et Frédéric', and then a relationship. The pair quickly became one of the top dance teams in France, and although the love affair did not last, they became part of an informal resistance network helping Jewish artists and musicians, including Marcel Leibovici. The Hungarian-born Gisy Varga, famous for dancing naked at the Tabarin, sheltered Gilbert Doukan, a Jewish doctor in the resistance with whom she was having a tempestuous love affair. These were passionate times, as one never knew who would be alive tomorrow. Sadie not only hid and transported weapons for the resistance, she also sometimes hid Jews, most of whose names she never knew, in her frequently changing apartments, and sometimes she accompanied nervous, fleeing Jews without papers when they walked from one hiding place to another.

Once back in Paris, Leibovici was occasionally walked by Sadie,

---

* According to this account, as told to her biographer George Perry, she was interviewed by the Gestapo. But 84 Avenue Foch was the headquarters of the SD and the SiPo, the Sicherheitspolizei. As the two were complementary, Bluebell may easily have been mistaken in thinking it was the Gestapo – in fact headquartered at 11 Rue de Saussaies – who interviewed her.

Sadie Rigal, now the French dancer Florence, posing in front of Berlin's Brandenburg Gate while on a controversial performance tour of Germany in 1943. On the far left is her dancing partner and fellow resister Frédèric. Edith Piaf is 3rd from the right

trying to look relaxed, through streets where armed soldiers might suddenly appear – one of the most dangerous but necessary jobs to give air to those in hiding. On one occasion while Sadie was housing two Jewish sisters, escapees from a camp, a policeman followed her from her daily sign-in. As they stood side by side, looking out over the Seine, he warned her that her landlady had informed on her and that the apartment would be searched. Sadie walked the girls to a convent, witnessing on the way there a Nazi raid on an orphanage, in which Jewish children were savagely tossed from upper-storey windows on to the street. The two Jewish sisters eventually reached the south of France, made their way from there to New York and never forgot the woman to whom they owed their lives. The same anonymous policeman warned Sadie a second time, when she was hiding a gun in her apartment.

When 'Florence et Frédéric' were invited along with the singers

Charles Trenet, Edith Piaf and Maurice Chevalier to tour four French prisoner-of-war camps in Germany, Sadie was advised to accept or else she would draw attention to herself by her refusal. She did not believe the German promise that 500 prisoners would be released if they went, but nonetheless managed to use her trip to help in a small way by filling her suitcase on her return with illegal letters from prisoners to their relatives in France. Before they reached Paris, the French artists stopped in Berlin, where they were caught in an Allied bombing raid. In the bomb shelter, the musicians played jazz, causing a debate among the Germans in the shelter. Piaf, Trenet and Chevalier were among many artists who felt compelled to perform to German audiences, trips for which after the war they were viewed as collaborators.

However, as Sadie's decision clearly shows, nothing was straightforward: Trenet, whose song 'Douce France' was performed in front of French prisoners in Berlin in 1943, felt especially vulnerable as a homosexual, while Chevalier, dangerously, was married to a Romanian Jewish actress, Nita Raya, and lived with her in a comfortable villa near Cannes. In 1942 she had brought her parents there to protect them. They survived, but the marriage did not. Nonetheless Chevalier would be forever tarnished by photographs showing him performing in Berlin, though those same photos failed to show that he performed only for French prisoners of war.

Edith Piaf, born Edith Giovanna Gassion, according to legend on the pavement in the Belleville area of Paris, was the child of an impoverished acrobat father and a mother who was a singer. Abandoned by her mother at birth, Edith was for a time looked after by prostitutes in a brothel run by her grandmother. Performing and pleasing men was all she knew. She became a mother herself at seventeen, but when her daughter, Marcelle, died aged two from meningitis, she was apparently so short of money that she had to sleep with a man in order to pay for the funeral. Edith had been 'discovered' in 1935 by nightclub owner Louis Leplée, who dressed her and drilled her, and encouraged her to use the stage name Piaf – the word was Parisian street slang for sparrow – because of her tiny, waif-like appearance which was in stark contrast to the powerful and dramatic projection of her voice.

During the Occupation, Piaf's career in nightclubs and cabarets frequented by Germans flourished. She undertook to register with the German propaganda department, had her lyrics checked (as did all performers) and deliberately maintained good relations with the Nazis, who enjoyed her performances. But she used her popularity to help friends of hers in difficulty and took a number of risks which might have landed her in trouble. One of her most successful hits was a song called 'L'Accordéoniste', originally performed by the Jewish musician Michel Emer, whose escape to unoccupied France she helped pay for, just as she had helped the Jewish pianist Norbert Glanzberg, briefly her lover, who had worked as a jazz musician with Django Reinhardt in 1930s Paris and who was taken in by Lily Pastré to live in her chateau at Montredon for months. Both Glanzberg and Emer survived in hiding until the Liberation. By 1942 Piaf was earning enough to live in a luxurious set of rooms, with heating, in the 16th arrondissement above L'Etoile de Kléber, a well-known nightclub and brothel close to 84 Avenue Foch, the building used by the SiPo-SD to interrogate and torture. The apartment belonged to Madame Billy, also known as Aline Soccodato, a brothel-owner who hid a number of Jews and resistance fighters and whose secretary, a resistance worker called Andrée Bigard, moved in with Piaf under the pretext that she was employed to help the singer.

Piaf sang all over France, with Germans in the audience or not. But it was her performances at prisoner-of-war camps in Germany which were probably her most useful as well as most controversial acts. Of course the tours boosted Piaf's popularity with the German occupiers, allowing them to show the world that French entertainers were happy with the Occupation and life was 'carrying on as normal'. But Andrée Bigard, who went with her on one occasion, maintained that she deliberately had herself photographed with dozens of prisoners during her German trip so that the resistance could use the images to create as many as 120 false identity cards, delivered by Piaf on her next visit, to help those prisoners escape.

And all the while Parisian highbrow cultural life continued alongside the low. In the autumn Vivou Chevrillon was invited to a performance at the Comédie-Française to make up the numbers and, in the foyer, happened to notice an official book lying open with a signature certifying that the work being performed had been passed by the censor. She gave a knowing look to her companion as it was a familiar signature, that of the Paris Préfet Amédée Bussière, one she knew well as she copied it regularly to make false identity cards. The unaccompanied man in the party noticed her surreptitious look of amusement and a few days later contacted her saying he was working for the resistance in Lyons and could she make him a false *carte d'identité*. Shocked, she asked how he knew she was in the business of supplying them. He told her that she had given herself away with that look. A few months later the man, Guy de Boysson, became her husband.

The activities of the Comédie-Française were never far from the mind of Béatrice Bretty, the actress who had gone into 'voluntary exile' with her Jewish lover, the politician Georges Mandel and potential post-war leader of France, deciding that her presence and tasks were more necessary elsewhere. In 1943, when the Schiller Theatre of Berlin was imposed twice on the Comédie-Française stage, she was further disgusted, 'unable to stomach the German accent . . . permeating the prose of Molière'. Invitations had been sent to the *gratin de la collaboration* and other bigwigs in the capital in what the diarist Hervé Le Boterf described as 'a Franco-German festival'.

Bretty had for months been following Mandel as he was sent from one jail to another. While he was in the Pyrenees, held at Fort du Portalet, the nineteenth-century prison built steeply into a cliff face overlooking the Spanish border, she had been able to cook his lunch almost daily and take it to him, as well as caring for his daughter, Claude. She would hide messages from de Gaulle and others in her bouffant coiffure, then use all her acting talent to get past the guards without being searched. The couple were even allowed brief walks together in one of the fortress yards. It was a surreal existence. Mandel had not been given a public trial and neither the resistance nor the Free French attempted to help him escape, partly because the resistance feared vicious reprisals while Bretty believed that de Gaulle was keen to keep him out of London where he would be a rival for Churchill's ear. His followers had discussed some vague plans to help him flee, but it was difficult to arrange anything that involved him descending by rope as he was so unfit. Another plan involved him leaving, disguised in Bretty's cloak, while she waited behind in the cell. But it was not easy to organize an escape for someone so well known and so well guarded. In April 1943 Mandel was taken briefly to a concentration camp in Oranienburg, north of Berlin, where he was kept in solitary confinement but allowed to write letters. From there he wrote a poignant message to Claude, trying to impart to her his philosophy for life. But later that month he was sent to Buchenwald, albeit kept in a small hut set apart from the rest of the camp. His former political opponent, Léon Blum, was already incarcerated there and had been granted permission while in prison to marry Mme Jeanne Reichenbach, who then lived with him. As soon as Bretty heard this she asked, via Fernand de Brinon in Vichy, for similar permission to marry Mandel. But Mandel himself, although her request was forwarded to him, declined. He would not ask for permission to marry on the grounds that he did not want her to share the harsh winter or his fate. He had books and could meet the Blums, with whom he presumably now made friends, and, although he felt very alone and weak, he tried to believe that his torment would end soon with an Allied victory.

In July 1944 he was moved from Buchenwald back to France, to La Santé prison, and his last words to the Blums were: 'Tell Béatrice Bretty and my daughter that I regret nothing of what I have done, that I know I have acted well, and that no matter what happens, they will not have to be ashamed of me.'

In the frenzied summer of 1943, Rose Valland, the courageous would-be curator at the Jeu de Paume, had to watch the burning of some five or six hundred 'degenerate' paintings, many of them stolen, judged by a Nazi-appointed panel of 'experts' to have little artistic or commercial value. There was a huge bonfire in the Tuileries Gardens of works by Picasso, Miró, Léger, Ernst and many others. 'Impossible to save anything,' she wrote to her boss, Jacques Jaujard, on 23 July. But other than keeping him fully informed of what was happening, which she did constantly, there was nothing more she could actually do.

The Germans continued to propagate the illusion that art in Paris was flourishing, and the American heiress Florence Gould was one of those still visiting the various art exhibitions that the Germans allowed, making the most of Paris cultural life and running her salon. But 1943 was a difficult year, even for her. In March she slipped and broke her leg as she was leaving the Montmartre apartment of Louis-Ferdinand Céline, where she often went in the company of the Comédie-Française actress Marie Bell. According to Céline, writing after the war, Gould had wanted to buy his manuscripts but he had refused, 'not wanting to owe anything to the American multi-millionaire'. After the accident, Ernst Jünger continued to visit her, sometimes with Gerhard Heller, and on one occasion, according to Heller, Florence introduced a friend as 'Colonel Patrick', a German from the Lyons branch of the Abwehr. Possibly he was just another admirer, but she may have needed high-level protection as investigations were continuing into whether or not her husband was Jewish, in which case of course he would be arrested and deported and his extensive properties confiscated and aryanized. Frank Jay Gould had sent off for baptism certificates to prove he was Protestant several months before, but it was only in March that the CGQJ, somewhat reluctantly, agreed that as the Goulds were not Jewish their properties could not be aryanized. Nonetheless the Germans seized control of various Gould hotels and casinos on the Riviera, on the grounds that the owner was now an enemy alien, and administered them until the end of the Occupation.

In October, both Noor and Vera Leigh, the SOE women, were arrested. Khan had managed to transmit some twenty messages while on the run but was betrayed to the Germans, either by Henri Déricourt or by Renée Garry. Déricourt was an SOE officer and former French Air Force pilot who had been suspected in London of working as a double agent for the SiPo-SD. Garry was the sister of Emile Garry, Noor's organizer in the Cinema network. Allegedly paid 100,000 francs, Renée may have betrayed Noor out of jealousy because she suspected that Antelme had transferred his affections from her to Noor. At all events, on or around 13 October 1943, Noor was arrested and interrogated at SiPo-SD headquarters, 84 Avenue Foch.

Though SOE trainers had at the outset expressed doubts about her gentle and unworldly character, on her arrest Noor fought so fiercely, even biting the officer trying to arrest her, that the Germans from then on treated her as an extremely dangerous prisoner. Her interrogation lasted over a month, during which time she made two escape attempts. Hans Kieffer, number two in the Paris SiPo-SD, told Vera Atkins in a post-war interview that Noor did not give the Gestapo a single piece of information, but in fact managed after all to lie consistently. Yet although Noor did not give away anything under interrogation and refused to reveal any secret codes, the Germans found her notebooks, from which they gained enough information to continue sending false messages imitating her, a ruse that London failed to spot. As a result, three more agents sent to France were instantly captured by the Germans on landing, among them Madeleine Damerment, a twenty-six-year-old postmaster's daughter from Lille, another SOE agent trained in London.

And on 27 November Josée de Chambrun went with her friend Arletty to watch a gala performance at the Comédie-Française of *Le Soulier de satin*, (*The Satin Shoe*), by Paul Claudel which lasted in its original form for eleven hours but was reduced to a mere four on this occasion. 'Fortunately there is not a pair,' quipped Sacha Guitry. Arletty was equally stirred to wit by the occasion and commented that the audience consisted of 'Les touts: Tout-Paris, Tout-Résistant, Tout-Occupant'. Clearly that was something of an overstatement, since that same day Noor was taken to Germany 'for safe custody' and in complete secrecy imprisoned at Pforzheim in solitary confinement as a *Nacht und Nebel* (literally 'night and fog') prisoner, condemned to disappear without trace. Two days earlier she had tried to make a daring escape with two other prisoners, but although she managed to saw through bars and get out of her cell she was arrested in the neighbourhood. From then on she was kept in chains, not allowed out for the next ten months.

The winter of 1943 was yet again fierce and bitterly cold, worse even, according to some accounts, than the previous icy wartime winters thanks to the lack of coal and the tense atmosphere. By December, the ten-year-old Rosa Liwarrak was totally alone. Her mother had died giving birth to her in 1933. Her elder sisters were in hiding and her father had been arrested in Paris in September. Before his arrest, he had tried to make arrangements with his accountant to look after Rosa and her brother, but the accountant had refused to take the brother as he was circumcised, and the money was now running out for Rosa. So she was put on the last civilian train to leave Paris for Brittany to live with her young stepmother in the country. But the train, which had a swastika on the roof and many German soldiers inside, was bombed by the British just after Rennes, killing hundreds of passengers. Amazingly Rosa (who had now changed her name to the more Breton-sounding Rose Livarec) survived and, as she did not look Jewish, one of the German soldiers on the train agreed to drive her in a jeep to her stepmother's house. Pauline Bohic, who came from a devout Roman Catholic family, immediately fell on her knees when she saw Rosa, declaring it was a miracle: obviously, her prayers to the Virgin Mary had saved her. Within hours Rosa was converted by the local priest and for the next year attended a Catholic school in a local convent. It was, she said years later, such a relief. 'The Catholic Church is very attractive to a child. Jesus is very forgiving and full of compassion. The church is full of lovely songs and pictures and sculptures. It isn't full of rules about things you cannot do.'

Conversion was less help to Béatrice de Camondo Reinach in Drancy, who was constantly writing letters to her mother, Irène Sampieri, who was herself writing to Georges Prade, a fixer, who had close contacts with Jean Luchaire. Contacts were everything in this murky world. Why could he not fix the Camondo situation? Was there nothing left to barter or were they being punished for their earlier sense of security? On 31 March 1943, Georges Duhamel, Permanent Secretary of the French Academy, had asked Fernand de Brinon for clemency for the Reinach family and Brinon had passed on the request to Helmut Knochen, Senior Commander of the SiPo-SD. In response the SiPo-SD concluded that as various German authorities considered Léon Reinach a 'typical and insolent Jew' he should be deported from Drancy forthwith, although Béatrice could be kept longer. She was given a variety of chores, from sweeping and cleaning the floor to peeling vegetables for the soup. Her daughter

Fanny was working in the infirmary acting as a nurse, while Bertrand, although separated in the men's quarters with his father, made himself useful with carpentry.

The musician Marya Freund, who had taught Germaine Lubin, got to know the Camondo family during her own incarceration here at this time and spoke of Béatrice's dignity. Freund, aged sixty-seven, had been arrested on 11 February at her Paris apartment and imprisoned in Drancy for five weeks, until 21 March, when she was transferred to the Rothschild Hospital, thanks to the intervention of the pianist Alfred Cortot. But even Cortot could not arrange Freund's release from the hospital. Freund owed her second escape, and thus her life, to a doctor there who revealed to her a good moment to escape, information she used one day in July by walking out of a door when no one was looking, without coat or gloves (a noticeable deficiency at all times of the year in 1943), to spend the rest of the war in hiding.[*]

By mid-November there were no further negotiations for any of the Reinach family. Léon was one of approximately forty detainees who tried to dig an escape tunnel four feet high and two feet wide out of Drancy. The diggers, split into three teams and using some of the equipment intended for the renovation of the camp, were taking advantage of the temporary absence of Alois Brunner and his commandos, who had gone to arrest Jews in Nice and the surrounding area. On 9 November 1943, before the escape could take place, the tunnel was discovered by the Germans and punishment was severe for those involved. Reinach and both children, Fanny and Bertrand, were taken to the suburban railway station at Bobigny and on 17 November deported in Convoy no. 62 for Auschwitz. It is inconceivable that the local population of Drancy were unaware of the enormous and constant transfers of prisoners and the almost daily arrests and arrivals of thousands of detainees at Bobigny train station, just as it is inconceivable that Béatrice, who remained, 'preparing nourrissons',

---

[*] In one of her hideouts, a cabin in the forest near Montfort-l'Amaury, she finished a diary she had started at Rothschild which was later found by her son, Doda Conrad, while going through papers to write his own autobiography, *Dodascalies: ma chronique du XXe siècle*, Arles, Actes Sud, 1997.

(baby food), according to a 1943 pitiful plan of Drancy,* did not know that this was the final time she would see her children. What is not known is if she was allowed to say goodbye to them, nor how she retained her own will to survive.

Many women that year were seen on trains reading *Gone with the Wind*, which had recently appeared in French as *Autant en emporte le vent* and, as Drue Tartière noted, they often had tears in their eyes as they read of the hardships during another war, the story making their own suffering more poignant to them. 'The people on these trains were now looking very shabby and, since there was a great shortage of soap, the smells in the train were almost overpowering.' It was, in certain circles, now chic to be shabby in France, with some women determined to wear trousers, especially if they were cycling, because they were warm and comfortable and, if left over from a husband who had been killed or taken prisoner, often made sound emotional and economic sense – even though Vichy had declared trousers to be masculine and condemned those who wore them for displaying signs of moral turpitude. 'Only collaborators could afford to dress well,' according to Drue Tartière. Most ordinary Parisiennes became adept at making do, at being 'des virtuoses du secours, du miracle domestique et quotidien'. In other words, they became miracle workers on a daily basis, virtuosos always able to seek and find help when needed, as Colette recognized.

* In this handwritten schedule of 26 July 1943 the Germans have tidily boxed away the Lévys, Kasriels, Dreyfuses, Schwabs, Nathans and others, identifying all their allotted tasks such as bread, vegetables, painting, hygiene and medical. The sense of order, the notion that this was where the Jews belonged, in their boxes, is chilling.

1944 · (January–June)

PARIS AWAITS

On 17 January 1944 at around 8.30 in the evening, an air-raid warning sounded especially loudly in the Marie-Louise clinic at the top of Rue des Martyrs, the street which led to Pigalle with its ever busier nightclubs and brothels. The wailing drowned out the cries of a baby girl, born in the middle of the raid to a young single mother, Madeleine Hardy. Madeleine, twenty-three years old, a poorly paid accounts assistant, had recently had an abortion but badly wanted this child, even though she knew that the father, a married man with whom she was not especially in love, would not leave his wife to become her husband. He, however, a well-to-do and financially secure manager of a calculating-machine business, twenty years older than Madeleine, was madly in love with this statuesque free spirit and so rented a small two-room flat in the Rue d'Aumale, where he continued to visit his mistress and admire his new daughter, Françoise. This arrangement did not displease Madeleine. A few months later she was again pregnant with his child. But this time, with the war still far from over and food in the city as scarce as ever, the father wanted nothing to do with the new baby. Madeleine, being strong-minded, determined to keep the child, another girl (Michèle, born in July 1945), and enlisted the active help of her own mother so that she could return to work. The elder daughter kept her mother's name and, as Françoise Hardy, went on to become one of the country's best-known pop singers in the 1960s. She was scornful of her father and of how little he provided for the family.

Paris was a dangerous place for most of 1944. As long as the Germans stayed, the curfew remained in force and one night, when Françoise's father was caught out too late to get home, Madeleine refused to let him into the flat he paid for, suspecting he had been with another woman. He found shelter, but this was unforgivable behaviour as the Gestapo were ratcheting up the tension in those months, resorting to any excuse or none to arrest people in Paris, aware that the tide of war was turning. Following the German defeat at Stalingrad the previous year, the Russians were now gaining on the eastern front and the Allies, known to be preparing European landings, were also pursuing the Germans from southern Italy after successfully securing North Africa. The resistance in Paris itself was becoming bolder. On one occasion when there was a volley of gunfire in the street, Madeleine threw herself on top of the pram to protect her baby from the bullets.

With arrests accelerating to a frenzy, the Germans needed to move prisoners out of Paris to other camps. Jews, male and female, were mostly transported to Auschwitz via Drancy. But Drancy was overflowing, and tragically, because the Germans had banned Red Cross parcels, the UGIF was forced to take over responsibility for trying to provide better food and welfare and thus was, by its very act of cooperation with the Germans, complicit. The UGIF, although never responsible for preparing deportation lists, did provide a range of services for the Jewish community, knew the whereabouts of many Jews, and housed children in homes known to the Germans which helped facilitate disastrous raids. But its leaders faced an appalling dilemma: if they refused to supply basic provisions such as blankets and shoes as demanded, then Jews doomed to extinction would be sent on journeys to the east under even harsher conditions. The UGIF leaders believed they had no choice and were facing reality.

In March, after she had spent sixteen months in Drancy, the Germans decided it was time to despatch Béatrice Reinach, who was now deported to Auschwitz in Convoy no. 69. She survived there for another ten months until her death on 4 January 1945, two weeks before the camp was liberated. Her mother, Irène Sampieri, who had not been able to save her daughter, inherited what was left of the Camondo fortune but spent it all in the casinos on the French Riviera in the post-war years and died in 1963 aged ninety-one. The beautiful house, proudly donated by her father to the French state, remains as Béatrice's monument, all that is left of the family today.

Hélène Berr, who had initially worked for the UGIF in their offices, was now increasingly concerned to save Jewish children whatever the personal cost to herself. She took on more direct tasks for various illegal and secret networks, which smuggled Jewish children from orphanages and homes to farms, villages and other places of safety outside Paris. These networks included the Oeuvre de Secours aux Enfants (OSE), the organization founded in Russia on the eve of the First World War to help destitute Jews, and the Entr'aide Française Israélite (EFI), some of them operating partially within official UGIF cover, others linked to non-Jewish groups. But the problem for these organizations was that they had still not moved their premises out of legal, easily recognized Jewish institutions. Hélène understood that since the UGIF was German-sanctioned, and had in its possession far too many names, her work risked the taint of collaboration, but her robust sense of morality helped her conclude that working to keep children out of the camps took priority over such personal scruples. This was the most important thing she could do. After the UGIF offices had themselves been raided at the end of July 1943, and all forty-six of the employees found there deported to Auschwitz, Hélène redoubled her own efforts, even going into Drancy itself to help with the feeding and welfare of the internees for two weeks at a time. As the historian David Bellos has concluded: 'About one third of all Jews resident in France were deported and murdered . . . but only one Jewish child in ten perished in the years of German occupation and that was very largely because of the courage and skill of people like Hélène Berr and the kindness and generosity of a vast network of French well-wishers who took Jewish children and hid them.' Notwithstanding, 11,400 French children died.

But on 8 March 1944 Hélène and her parents were arrested at their apartment on the Avenue Elisée Reclus. Most nights they had been sleeping at other addresses, Hélène going to the home of her house-keeper, Andrée Bardiau, to whom she handed her diary, a page or a section at a time, for safekeeping. As Mme Berr had often said to her daughter: 'Things like that must be recorded, to be remembered af-terwards.' Hélène wrote a quick note to her sister before being taken to Drancy and then to Auschwitz, where her parents were murdered within weeks. She survived Auschwitz for eight months but was then shipped to Bergen-Belsen, where she contracted typhus. Too weak to work, she was beaten to death in April 1945, five days before the British liberated the camp.

Women political prisoners, often after several months in Fresnes or the slightly less harsh Romainville, were also now being deported to camps in Germany, a fate they all dreaded. The women rounded up in 1943, including Odette Fabius, Denise Dufournier, Geneviève de Gaulle and Jacqueline d'Alincourt, could only guess what lay ahead when they were transported early in 1944 from Paris to Ravensbrück, the all-women camp some sixty miles beyond Berlin where Jehovah's Witnesses and 'anti-socials' from a variety of countries had been held since the beginning of the war. They knew enough, from rumours that had reached them, of the cruelty they should expect. As to survival, no one could assume that. But as it was theoretically a 'work camp' there was some hope that they might at least be given hard labour in the open air, surely better than being locked into solitary cells in Fresnes? The already weakened women were taken to the Gare de Pantin, a small suburban railway station on the eastern outskirts of Paris, used by the Germans to shift everything they were looting, and were then herded, sixty at a time, prostitutes alongside countesses, lawyers, teachers and cabaret dancers, into desperately overcrowded trucks for the journey north-east to the camp of Ravensbrück. The countesses 'recoiled in horror' from the prostitutes, who had been arrested for allegedly infecting the Gestapo with VD. But the women travelled in their own clothes, and some had been allowed to pack bags which contained luxuries such as powder compacts, eau de Cologne or sausages and cheese, smuggled into the Paris jails by their families. Many tried to scribble notes for loved ones and threw them out of a window in the hope they would be delivered, which, amazingly, they almost always were. But, for most, the journey to Ravensbrück meant enduring at least three days and four nights with neither food nor water and one overflowing latrine can. When they arrived at Fürstenberg, they were greeted by German guards who opened the train doors brandishing truncheons and shouting, 'Quick, quick, five at a time, you filthy pigs.' To reach the actual camp at Ravensbrück, the cold and hungry women had to march through snowy pinewoods, strengthened only by their conviction that the Allied landings were imminent and that the war would soon be over. As Denise Dufournier commented on seeing a German officer with a riding whip who had ordered everyone out during the journey, 'He didn't dare meet our glance for fear of seeing our confidence in our certain victory.'

When they first walked into the camp, before being humiliatingly stripped and often left standing naked for hours, having their heads shaved and all personal possessions seized, the other inmates, the half-starved creatures who seemed like wraiths from another planet, noticed these *Franzöinnen* (French women) – the word, half whispered, raced around the camp – still erect and confident, different from the rest. Some had arrived in ski outfits, smart woollen coats or even furs, and some refused to eat the proffered food, thinking it would poison them, especially after at least one of them suffered severe stomach cramps from eating indigestible raw swede or rutabaga. Others tried to laugh at the mad reality of what they were witnessing. A Polish *blockova*, the block overseer chosen by the SS to police the camp from within (but not always a cruel SS accomplice), remarked how, just before an inspection visit from the Reichsführer of the SS, Heinrich Himmler, 'the whole camp trembles but you French just laugh'. By late 1943 and into 1944, the Polish and Russian women had had years in which to accustom themselves to the barbarity of the regime and so, when French prisoners started arriving in significant numbers at the camp, the older inmates assigned the French some of the worst jobs. The French women thus suffered a double oppression – from the SS and from fellow prisoners. In addition, the French women seemed to lack the physical strength of their Polish and Russian counterparts, who 'kept their flesh and colour and strength far longer as well as their bright, gay and brutal energy'.

Geneviève de Gaulle, on the same convoy as Denise Dufournier and Cecily Lefort, an SOE agent married to a French doctor who had worked alongside Noor, described her feelings on arrival:

When I was in Fresnes there would sometimes be a gleam of light, a response. But as we went into Ravensbrück it was as if God had remained outside. The women already there, some of whom had survived for two years, were living zombies drained of expression. In the glare of the searchlights we could see women carrying heavy containers. I barely noticed their wavering forms, their shaven heads. But I was shocked to the core by the sight of their faces.

She was equally shocked by their bodies, especially those of the seventy-four formerly healthy young Polish women known as *lapins* – one of whom was just fourteen – who had been used for medical experimentation by Nazi doctors, subjected to up to six operations each, including having the bones and muscles in their legs broken, cut out or otherwise damaged. Their wounds were then deliberately infected with bacteria, with the sickening 'justification' that they were experimenting in order to find a cure for battle wounds. The daily sight of these brave, young, suffering women, hobbling around the camp, kept alive for nefarious reasons, was something never forgotten by other prisoners.

Geneviève, prisoner no. 27372, recognized that, as her physical resources were destroyed, her survival would depend on her ability to draw on her inner resources. 'I was obsessed by the certainty that much worse than death was the destruction of our souls, which was the agenda of the concentration camp world.' But she was determined that, if she endured, what she saw would inform the remainder of her life. Nothing in her previous existence could have prepared her for the back-breaking, twelve-hour shifts to which she was now allotted, smashing boulders for road-building wearing only flimsy shifts. Worse was to follow as she was switched to more gruesome tasks, saw friends dying of exhaustion in the night, witnessed beatings and torture and was herself deliberately knocked to the ground and savagely attacked with kicks and blows. As she became progressively weaker, in unbearable pain from untreated pleurisy, scurvy sores and ulcerations to her cornea, she believed her death was imminent. Like everyone in the camp in 1944, she also knew that Germany was going to lose the war, but not when. Support from friends was crucial in remaining alive until that time. On 25 October, her birthday, these friends gathered together all the breadcrumbs they could, mixed them with some sticky mess resembling jam they had been given as part of their rations, and made her a cake decorated with twigs for candles.

By that time, Himmler had realized the significance of this prisoner who was related to the French General. He also erroneously
assumed that Odette Sansom, an SOE agent captured in April 1943,
was a relation of Winston Churchill. To protect herself, as a cover
story when she was arrested, she called herself Mrs Churchill, claiming that her husband, Peter Churchill, the British agent captured
with her, was a nephew of the Prime Minister. But having worked
as Peter Churchill's courier since November 1942, the couple were
by this time indulging in a love affair, a distraction which some in
London believed had resulted in security lapses which led to their
arrests.* For the moment, Himmler wanted both of them to receive
special treatment so that they might recover adequately to be used as
possible bargaining chips.

On 3 October, returning from work exhausted one day, Geneviève
had been summoned to Kommandant Fritz Suhren's office and asked
how she was. 'Very ill, as you can see,' she told him. In response he
told her she was moving to a different block and would in future
work in the relatively comfortable infirmary instead of undertaking the harsh outside labour she had been given. When Geneviève
protested that she did not want to be separated from her friends,
Suhren told her it was an order. So, for a few weeks, she lived in
a privileged block – the 'show block' which could be displayed to
the few visitors – where she had a mattress to herself covered with a
blue and white checked eiderdown, her own towel and a clean camp
dress with a jacket and scarf, and she had her scurvy sores disinfected
in the infirmary. Crucially, she received the surprising bonus of a
few vitamins. At the end of the month she was moved again, to an
isolation cell this time, in the Ravensbrück bunker. But even here she
was, she was told, not being punished, and soon received a package
of medicines including vital calcium tablets. She was hardly well, but
she no longer believed she would die.

Jacqueline d'Alincourt arrived at Ravensbrück a couple of months
after Geneviève, at midnight, and was left to stand upright, frozen
stiff, until morning.

* The pair were married after the war in 1947 and divorced in 1956.

The next day we were ordered by the male and female guards to undress. This was for the first time. We were stripped of everything linked to the human condition: clothing, wedding rings, the few books we had been able to save, the simplest keepsakes, letters, photographs, everything was confiscated. Heads were shaved at random. Naked, penned up, pressed one against the other, all ages thrown together, we went to the showers. We avoided looking at each other before being handed the striped bathrobe, before learning by heart in German the number assigned to each of us, sewed on the sleeve. We no longer had names. I had become number 35243. A red triangle was also sewn above the number: it indicated our category – we were *les politiques*, 'political prisoners'. Now completely stripped, we were cooped up for three weeks in a quarantine block. We got up at three-thirty in the morning and left for roll call, which could last for hours, and stood in the cold of dawn, come rain, snow, or wind. When the siren sounded, marking the end of this torment, we returned to the block, but the space where we were confined was so small that at no time were we able to sit down.

Eventually Jacqueline met up with Geneviève and for the next few weeks – until the latter's removal to the camp's isolation cell for special treatment – these two were to share the same straw mat, buoying each other up as much as possible. 'In this fierce determination to help each other, we found the strength to resist.'

For most camp prisoners, female solidarity was of key importance; a small group of about three to five was the best number for support. But what kept Odette Fabius, designated a 'dangerous terrorist', going was partly worry about her daughter Marie-Claude and partly the memory of her final half-hour at Compiègne with her lover Pierre Ferri-Pisani at the end of January. Pierre had told her he never doubted that after the torment 'we would find each other again and that we would spend the rest of our lives together. "When two people have the privilege to discover each other it is a sacred duty for them to be united whatever damage the union might cause others."' They exchanged trinkets and said goodbye. Had she known that Pierre was being sent to work in the salt mines of Magdeburg, where few survived, her memory of their parting, which she said 'lit up the dark days that were to follow', might not have offered the same solace.

In August 1944, knowing that rumours of the liberation of Paris were true, Odette, 'an irrepressible optimist', decided that she could not stand another day in the camp and would try to escape. She managed to get herself deployed on a work unit clearing rubble following an Allied bombing raid near Fürstenberg. She swapped four bread rations with someone in the camp who had a 'civilian' dress, identified a fellow prisoner who spoke German and, having arranged to go together and in the middle of the day, while the guards were having a siesta in the sunshine, they seized their moment and ran. Knowing there would be an immediate call for two fugitives, they decided to separate for the time being and made their way through the forest in the direction, they hoped, of Berlin. Odette survived for two days and three nights on the run, but then came to a police checkpoint where she had to present her papers. She had none. She tried to bluff but was recognized and taken back to Ravensbrück, where she was now tortured. Stripped naked, she was tied to a table and beaten with fifty lashes on her back before being sent to the bunker for further punishment of six days without bed, clothes or food. Her fellow inmates doubted she would survive. In addition, all French women in the camp were punished. They were ordered to spend twenty-four hours on their knees in the sharp, rough clinker with hands held in the air. Some women thought that the price of resistance in the camp was too high and that therefore compromise, even if it meant working in German factories, was not collaborating.

Geneviève de Gaulle's staunch religious faith offered her a way through this dilemma; it was not unique, but it was unusual enough to be commented on by survivors. Jacqueline Marié, later Fleury, arrested in Paris in February, arrived in Ravensbrück with her mother later in the year and remembers Geneviève's 'extremely profound faith . . . that was the essence of her life. Although she was a militant with a very fiery temper she was not a political animal.' Worrying about her mother gave Jacqueline Marié an additional reason to stay strong, as it did thirty-six-year-old Germaine Tillion. An ethnographer, Germaine was determined to document what she knew the world would find almost impossible to believe after the war, and she was desperately concerned about the survival of her art-historian mother, Emilie Tillion, who arrived early in 1944. Many in Germaine's close group of friends tried constantly to protect Emilie, as survival for older women was naturally much harder. The Germans were eager to gas those with grey hair, swollen limbs or wrinkled bodies deemed too weak to build airport runways in the cold, damp weather, or to march to and from the munitions factory for ten-hour shifts. Whenever there was a selection a younger woman, often Anise Girard, tried to help Emilie Tillion hide, or else there was a deputation to a *blockova* with influence, begging to get names taken off lists. This worked for several months but was becoming harder and harder.

Ravensbrück was a form of hell on earth and not everyone could draw upon religion as a source of strength. Some used whatever means were at their disposal, including the sale of sexual favours, in order to stay alive. One of those who survived by questionable activities was Anne Spoerry, a wealthy young woman of Swiss ancestry, born in France, who at the outbreak of war was training in Paris to become a doctor. Spoerry came from a Protestant family whose wealth derived from textiles in Alsace. She was trilingual, having spent two years at a smart London school, Francis Holland, before embarking on her medical training. Working in Paris, she watched with disgust as the Panzer divisions arrived in the city in 1940 and, soon after, got involved in resistance activities. With a brother, François, working for a resistance cell in the unoccupied south, she decided she could help British operatives in Paris and ran a safe house where they could stay for a short time. But she was betrayed and arrested in March 1943, before taking her final exams and, after months in Fresnes, ended up in Ravensbrück in January 1944.

Spoerry, a small woman with cropped brown hair, was assigned to Block 10, whose *blockova* was the notoriously powerful, cruel and untrustworthy Carmen Mory. It is hard to explain the twisted camp logic that enabled Mory to survive and prosper. She too was part-Swiss, but had lived in Berlin, become a Gestapo agent and been sent to Paris where the French had sentenced her to death in 1940, following a bungled attempt to murder a newspaper editor. However, she was freed after agreeing to spy for the French against the Germans, and in February 1941 was arrested by the Germans as a double agent and sent to Ravensbrück. She was protected in the camp by one of the camp doctors, Percy Treite, who apparently knew Mory's father in Switzerland. By the time Spoerry arrived in the camp she had probably been beaten and raped, which made her additionally vulnerable. Several women testified after the war that Mory quickly became Anne Spoerry's friend, protectress and lesbian lover in Ravensbrück. One of the last survivors of Block 10, the dignified doctor Louise (Loulou) Le Porz, a young tuberculosis specialist from Bordeaux, was disgusted by Mory's behaviour and her total admiration for Treite. She recalled: 'Mory used to receive medicine that she did not distribute . . . food she kept for herself . . . Anne Spoerry was Carmen Mory's slave. She must have been very scared.'

Spoerry soon changed her name to Claude, sometimes Dr Claude. For Loulou Le Porz, the fact that a doctor could behave in the ways Spoerry did made her actions additionally shocking and unforgivable. A young Polish girl with a beautiful voice who was kept in the ward for lunatics 'sang aria after aria, night and day'. This infuriated Mory, said Le Porz. 'I think she must have asked the . . . head nurse [for] the authorisation to make her disappear.' After Le Porz herself had refused to give the fatal injection, 'Claude . . . took the syringe. Yes. She did not hesitate . . . I was dumbfounded. This was a discovery for me. That anyone who is a medical doctor or wants to become one could deliberately execute a patient . . . I can only explain it by her fear of reprisals.'

Violette Lecoq, a talented artist also in Block 10, had worked as a nurse at the front with the French Red Cross at the beginning of the war and joined the resistance soon afterwards. Like many, she had already spent a year in solitary confinement at Fresnes by the time she arrived at Ravensbrück. She, too, was horrified by Mory and Spoerry's behaviour together. 'Carmen Mory was a horrible woman and the little one followed her . . . They were lovers. Lesbians. Dr Claude would do everything she asked her to do.' Once this involved administering a lethal injection to a hunchback. Another time the pair dragged a Polish girl recovering from surgery 'to the toilets where they hit her, splashed her with cold water – all of which advanced her death'. As the Allies progressed towards the end of 1944, Mory was removed to another, less well-known camp. Spoerry never saw her again and was herself transferred to Block 6, where she resumed her real name, Anne, and tried to behave as nobly as she could, aware that the end of the war was approaching or because a woman who started out with noble intentions had finally freed herself from such a powerful and malign influence. She was now responsible for trying to cure typhus and dysentery patients, rather than administering lethal injections, and it was here that she encountered Odette Fabius, who later testified that Spoerry had saved her life by hiding her for three critical months in a sickbed when she emerged from her punishment. According to another account Spoerry opened a rear block window and, by pushing and shoving, helped six sick Hungarian Jews escape the gas chamber. But nobody could guarantee that this change of heart in the last few months would be enough to allow her to complete her medical exams in Paris once the war was over, as she so keenly hoped.

Not surprisingly, at Ravensbrück as in normal life, there were women prepared to steal bread and betray, as well as women determined to support each other; and there were divisions among various groups over who behaved selflessly by sharing food and who did not pull their weight, who could not summon the resources to deal with what faced them, often because their previous lives had comprised nothing but wealth and privilege. Among the new wave of Parisiennes who arrived in August there were some women wearing 'ridiculous dresses they had concocted somehow', including one sporting an Hermès scarf and another a powder compact that she had managed to smuggle through the showers. Yet on the whole these were cheerful women who spread the news that Paris had been liberated, and their compatriots, who had managed to survive the hell of the last few months, marvelled at such gaiety. 'It was as if a little of our former life had slipped illegally into the camp. A breath of France,' wrote Denise Dufournier.

Among the smart summer arrivals from Paris was Elisabeth de Rothschild, born Elisabeth Pelletier de Chambure, the exquisitely chic daughter of wealthy Catholic aristocrats from the Burgundy region whose ancestors included the famous Napoleonic General Laurent Augustin Pelletier de Chambure, and whose father was the local mayor. Elisabeth, known as Lili, was married first to a Belgian aristocrat, Marc Edouard Marie de Becker-Rémy, but she soon embarked on a passionate affair with the handsome, swashbuckling Baron Philippe de Rothschild, owner of one of France's most famous vineyards, Château Mouton Rothschild. Although their daughter, Philippine, was born in 1933 the couple could not marry until 1935, after Elisabeth's divorce had come through. In 1938 Elisabeth and Philippe had a second child, Charles, a severely disabled boy who survived only a few days, and by then the stormy marriage was already foundering. Philippe knew that Lili believed he was to blame for the tragedy. 'She had taken pills to make her sleep all through the pregnancy and she couldn't sleep, she said, because of me.'

Philippe, promiscuous and a womanizer by his own admission, had had numerous affairs before meeting Elisabeth, including one with the Russian-born countess Mara Tchernycheff, who became one of the most notorious Parisian black-marketeers during the Occupation. Mara had been a teenage model for Chanel, then a shop assistant at Schiaparelli before becoming Philippe de Rothschild's mistress in the early 1930s. His connections helped with her brief career in film, but then he married Lili and Mara married a failed actor. Mara survived the war through a highly lucrative alcohol-trafficking partnership with the arch-collaborationist Max Stoecklin, providing Germans with supplies of hard-to-buy champagne, armagnac and cognac. This enabled her to rent a new flat near the Trocadéro, renew her wardrobe and embark on a further affair with an SS officer, Hans Leimer. Later, thanks to her close friendship with another collaborator, the petty criminal Henri Lafont, she had at her disposal a four-storey mansion – 3 bis Place des Etats-Unis – where she ran her own buying office and furnished the floor that became her office with furniture stolen from an abandoned Jewish flat in Rue de Courcelles. German soldiers under Lafont's influence helped her with the removals.* Perhaps it was Countess Mara whom Philippe de Rothschild had in mind when he explained how words like collaboration 'change colour as the years pass'. In his memoirs, *Milady Vine*, he cited a smart Parisienne whom he knew looking

---

* The owners of the flat, a Jewish couple named Panigel, sued the Countess after the war.

back on the war years as a time when 'it was so much more chic to collaborate'.

Rothschild's estranged wife was also consorting with pro-Nazi types who knew where anything could be bought for a price. 'I did not much care for Lili's behaviour during the German Occupation,' he wrote later. His marriage to Elisabeth had initially been one of great mutual passion but soon turned to tempestuousness and mutual recrimination. Early in the war Philippe was imprisoned in Algeria by Vichy forces but the moment he was released, in 1942, he decided he should go to London to join the Free French. Elisabeth, who according to Philippe 'was influenced by some of our former friends who had thrown in their lot with Vichy', did not want to leave France. She reverted to using her maiden name, Pelletier de Chambure, and believed that the Germans would respect her as the daughter of an old French Catholic family. However, the Gestapo – two men in grey suits, according to Rothschild family retainers at 17 Rue Barbet de Jouy who witnessed the arrest – came for her at 8.30 one May morning, three weeks before the Normandy landings. Ten-year-old Philippine had just left for school with her governess. The men charged up the stairs, pushed the butler, Marcel, to one side and shouted outside Elisabeth's bedroom door, 'Open up, Gestapo!'

'"What are you doing here?" we heard her say. They ordered her to get dressed and took her away in a van. Marcel followed on his bicycle.'

Later that day she was brought back and allowed to have some lunch while they searched the house. During this time Elisabeth asked to see Philippine, who was home from school but whom the staff were desperately trying to hide. There was then a discussion among the Gestapo men about whether they should take the child too, but in the end they decided against. Elisabeth, trying to remain calm, said a casual 'goodbye, see you later' to Philippine and then told the Germans imperiously that she had a hairdressing appointment. They disabused her of that notion and drove her away to prison instead. Philippine was swiftly smuggled out of Paris in an ambulance, with her legs in fake bandages, to stay with her grandfather.

Quite why Elisabeth was picked up as the war was ending has never been made clear. She had never become Jewish and was now

separated from her Rothschild connections, or so she thought. It
is possible that the Germans wanted her to reveal the whereabouts
of Philippe, by then back in France fighting with Allied forces and
whose name had been mentioned on the German-controlled Radio-
Paris. According to Odette Fabius, a pre-war acquaintance, the fact
that Elisabeth didn't understand why she was in a camp compounded
her suffering.

Nor did she understand why her erstwhile 'good friend' Fernand
de Brinon, the influential Catholic aristocrat with a Jewish wife who
was Vichy's Ambassador to the occupied zone, did not come to her
rescue. 'She went on her knees at Ravensbrück repeatedly protesting
that she wasn't Jewish even though her former husband was,' Fabius
recalled.

> But that wasn't why she was there; it was for her disagreeable atti-
> tude towards Madame Suzanne Abetz during a fashion parade at
> Schiaparelli. In the company of one of her relations, she took the
> liberty of changing places to take herself further away, knowing
> the Allies were at the doors of Paris and perhaps belatedly trying
> to distance herself from her earlier connections. But she mistimed
> her actions and that evening Otto Abetz had her arrested. I had
> told her to shut up, telling her all the world could hear her and
> judge her, except the Germans, who did not understand and who
> found her exasperating.

The final convoy from Paris which left the city on 15 August, a
swelteringly hot day, brought to the camp another 603 women –
including the British SOE members, Violette Szabo, Lilian Rolfe
and Denise Bloch – packed into wagons for deportation, just ten
days before the city was finally liberated and the same day that the
Allies landed on the Mediterranean coast. Many of these prisoners, women such as thirty-four-year-old Virginia d'Albert-Lake, the
only American-born woman in the camp, Catherine Dior, sister of
Christian; Jacqueline Marié and her mother Maisie Renault, sister of
Colonel Rémy, one of de Gaulle's top secret agents inside France; and
Jeannie Rousseau, who had been arrested some months earlier – but,
as the war dragged on, the Nazi hierarchy concluded that the women

were badly needed to work as slave labour in Ravensbrück's dozens of satellite camps. The Allied invasion, far from convincing Hitler it was all over, stretched weary Axis forces in yet another direction.

Virginia had been picked up on 12 June as she escorted downed airmen to safety as part of her work with the Comet escape line, just days before the liberation of Paris. Everyone involved in this work knew that, as the Allied invasion neared, such work had become ever more critical – and dangerous – not only because a trained airman was a valuable commodity but because his successful return was a huge morale booster for pilots back in England waiting to fly. As Virginia commented later, if she and her friends had known how long they would be held and how brutally they would be treated on arrival, they wouldn't have struggled with all the boxes and luggage they tried to carry with them on the train journey to Ravensbrück but would have ditched them on the journey. By this time the camp was so full – it now held about 40,000 women, rising to 65,000 by the end of 1944, having been designed for approximately 10,000 – that there were no more uniforms for them and they wore whatever was doled out to them, however unsuitable; this rarely included under-wear and never an outer garment of any sort. Jacqueline Marié was issued with a long dress with just one sleeve and a pair of galoshes – size 41 when she was a 36. The clothes had a large X sewn or even painted on, to denote prisoner status. Virginia had her money – sixty francs – confiscated but her jacket, in which she had hidden her engagement ring in a shoulder pad, was, amazingly, kept for her. The flea-infested bunk beds were now occasionally shared by as many as seven women, although some of the new arrivals were not even as-signed a place in one of these but were forced instead to sleep on the floor of a hastily constructed tent, where up to 7,000 malnourished women were crammed together, oozing misery.

Ravensbrück had from the start been used as something of a dump-ing ground – a place to send any women the Germans wanted out of the way. It was from Ravensbrück that the SS 'hired' prostitutes, and forced them to work in brothels in other concentration camps, and those who survived told horrific tales of rape and abuse which sometimes lasted sixteen hours a day. After all, Heinrich Himmler reasoned, the women in those camps were already 'degenerate'. In

1944 he set up three new brothels in Ravensbrück itself but was struggling to find women to work there when his eye fell on the new French arrivals, some of whom had been working as prostitutes.

But the French women prisoners were different. According to one of the Polish women, the influx of young French political prisoners 'coming from a nation that had not known captivity, often, very audaciously, though unwisely, opposed the authorities' orders and with a great deal of bravura'. This opposition took a variety of forms, but by 1944 the intense overcrowding at Ravensbrück meant that rules could sometimes be broken. The Parisian girls learned survival tactics such as lingering in the infirmary queue to avoid work or finding cherished items in the clothing store – which they dubbed 'Galeries Lafayette' – then hiding them under their bunks, now so closely packed together that guards could rarely penetrate to inspect. These treasures included medicines, underwear and – especially valuable – shoes, which were taken from prisoners on arrival. But a potato or a pencil would be preciously guarded too. The French 'organized' themselves and had lectures from Emilie Tillion, for example, on French art and culture. On 11 November about 250 French prisoners at a sub-camp observed one minute of silence as a protest: 'What hope that minute gave us; six machines ceased simultaneously.'

Often it was the countesses who took the lead in mobilizing protests. Jacqueline d'Alincourt was one of those who had arrived with what she believed was an entire brothel from Rouen, uneducated women who suffered especially because they had no idea why they were there. 'They had nothing to hold on to, no religion, no values . . . we in the resistance, we knew why we were there. We had a superiority of spirit, you understand,' she explained. D'Alincourt and her friends helped these women – not always successfully – to resist the brothel work. Yet the bewildered French prostitutes in some ways suffered a double punishment. They never wrote memoirs, were not part of the resistance, and so, in spite of being responsible for several courageous acts during the Occupation, such as sheltering evading airmen in brothels as well as undertaking individual acts of great kindness in the camp, have largely been forgotten by history.

In spite of attempts at solidarity as the biting winds and winter snows hit, several women regularly lost consciousness when forced to stand for hours for roll call, and died on the spot. Others were often too weak by now to be helped to stand. Virginia d'Albert-Lake gradually became seriously ill and emaciated – like almost all the women at Ravensbrück she no longer menstruated, while those who did suffered the humiliation of blood running down their legs as there was no sanitary protection – but said later that she survived the ordeal thanks to an attitude of mind. 'It was a matter of morale. You couldn't let them see you weep. The women who wept at night were usually dead by morning. You couldn't give in.'

Again and again, those who survived cite the importance of female support systems operating within the barbarity. Germaine Tillion, using her training in the systematic study of human beings to try to understand what made the Germans operate in the way they did, was always writing on whatever paper she could find, every day, determined to bear witness. She was also creating a darkly comic operetta, *Le Verfügbar aux enfers*, inventing words and scenes for existing music, but later refused to have it performed lest the world conclude that life in the camp had been soft, with opportunities to make music.* She was a source of great strength to twenty-one-year-old Anise Girard, repeatedly telling her that as she was young she would survive and have many children.† Other women used scraps of paper to write out favourite recipes, even while starving. One of the extraordinary aspects of this barbaric life, when they ate nothing more than watery soup, wild dandelions or stolen bits and pieces, was the need to discuss food – food that they longed for and dreamed of but had not seen for months or even years. In fact, the hungrier and more deprived they became, the more a longing for food appeared to have seized their imagination. Micheline Maurel, a literature teacher, kept a small notebook diary, which she used when she came to write of that first winter: 'Ate nothing . . . first snow. Ate nothing . . . very cold. It is freezing, so sad.' A few weeks later, trembling, dizzy and short of breath, she wrote: 'I wished I could let myself go and dis-

* The operetta received its premiere in Paris in 2007, when Tillion herself at 100 was too frail to attend but had at last agreed to its being staged.
† She did both. In June 1946 she married André Postel-Vinay and the couple had four children.

appear completely. From the depths of this barrack, I prayed God to let me die on the spot. I also called for my mother.' Since soup aggravated her dysentery, it was only tiny morsels of bread from her friend Michelle which sustained her.

Virginia was deeply grateful for the friendship of Toquette Jackson, the French head nurse at the American Hospital picked up in May by the Milice, along with her husband Sumner, Chief Surgeon at the hospital, and their only child, the sixteen-year-old Phillip. The Jacksons had endured numerous French prisons that summer until Toquette was finally deported in the same August convoy as Virginia. By the time she arrived in Ravensbrück she had no idea what had happened to either of her menfolk. 'I have never known a woman with such courage, willpower and vitality,' declared Virginia. Courage helped in facing the daily fear of selection for the gas chamber, but courage alone failed to combat illness, and by the time Virginia was moved to the infirmary she was close to death. Her mother, Eleanor Roush, was writing to the US State Department begging for help, pointing out that 'Virginia is a Gentile, which may be in her favour in view of Nazi standards.' Washington responded that the Swiss-based International Committee of the Red Cross (ICRC) was insisting it had no access to the Gestapo-run camps as its remit was to look after the welfare of military prisoners rather than civilians and, scandalously, therefore could not intervene.

One of the most powerful protests in Ravensbrück involved the spirited Jeannie Rousseau, who (as seen in earlier chapters) had managed to survive a previous spell in prison at the beginning of the war by outwitting the Nazis. For the previous four years Jeannie had been responsible for sending precise reports on the development of Germany's V-1 flying bombs and V-2 rockets, transcribing all she had seen and heard at the house on the Avenue Hoche where she worked with German officers and French industrialists. After work she would go directly to George Lamarque's safe house at 26 Rue Fabert on the Left Bank and write it up. Even if she did not understand the significance of the *Raketten*, Rousseau knew she was party to highly sensitive information and so helped create one of the great intelligence documents of the Second World War.

She admitted later that she felt lonely at times doing this work.

'It's not easy to depict the chilling fear, the unending waiting, the frustration of not knowing whether the dangerously obtained information would be passed on – or passed on in time – recognised as vital in the maze of the couriers.' But her reports helped convince Churchill to bomb the test site at Peenemünde in the Baltic, thereby blunting the impact of a terror weapon the Nazis had hoped would change the course of the war, and were considered so crucial that the author had to be brought to London for questioning. Betrayed by the French guide paid to lead her and other agents through minefields to a waiting boat in a cove, she was arrested and, even though she fabricated a story that she was just there to make money by selling two dozen pairs of French nylon stockings on the black market in Brittany, she was sent to Ravensbrück.

When she arrived at the camp, she knew about the D-Day landings and was determined to give existing prisoners some hope by telling them the war would soon be over and they would all be free. Still only twenty-four, she believed it was her duty to boost morale; with two friends, the older countess Germaine de Renty, who had been working in various resistance activities since 1941, and a communist from Montmartre, Marinette Curateau, they made a pact that they would not carry out work that might support the Nazi war machine. If they were sent to such a factory or work camp, they would organize a protest. Jeannie had been arrested under her false name, Madeleine Chauffeur, which helped her since by now she was insisting that her name was Jeannie Rousseau and that she was not a spy, thereby confusing her captors who did not realize she was the same woman arrested and then released in 1940 in Rennes. 'Fortunately it was a bad interrogation,' she explained coolly.

Soon after her arrival Jeannie and most of the French women who had arrived with her were selected for work at one of the many sub-camps. She was ordered to Torgau, a Heinkel munitions factory 200 miles to the south. Conditions seemed better there but, having made her pact, Jeannie refused on principle to manufacture ammunition which would be used to kill her own people. She went to the camp chief, a fat-faced German, and declaimed in fluent German that, as the women were prisoners of war, the Gestapo had no right under the Geneva Convention to force them to make ammunition. The other women followed her example and said they, too, would refuse. The camp chief responded by threatening to despatch them back to Ravensbrück.

Even when several of the women, Virginia d'Albert-Lake among them, concluded that they were better off staying at Torgau than returning to Ravensbrück, Rousseau urged her fellow prisoners to continue with their gesture of defiance. 'You see I was convinced somebody had to do something. Somebody had to stand up. I decided to do it.' In the intervening decades, Jeannie avoided discussion of her resistance career, including this episode. She knew that some women may have died as a direct consequence of the protest she had fomented, that some of her comrades blamed her, and indeed still do today, for her actions. Yet, as she approached old age, she decided it was time to talk. 'We were so childish, but there you are,' she told one interviewer.

However, she was not alone. Jacqueline Marié was another young *résistante* at Torgau who 'refused to participate in the war effort of a country that we were fighting, working 12 hours a day in a factory to clean shells in bins of acid. It was unhealthy work and exhausting.' But after the protest Jeannie and others were cruelly punished. Jeannie spent three weeks in a punishment cell doused with cold water every morning, then beaten and led back to her cell. Every day the same. Eventually she was returned to Ravensbrück for questioning. If entering Ravensbrück the first time was bad, returning there was unimaginable.

'I would have died that time,' she said, but the Germans could not find the papers for Jeannie Rousseau, because there were none. When they asked her why she had been sent to Ravensbrück, she replied: 'I don't know!' The Gestapo had concluded by now that, whoever she was, she was a troublemaker. So, papers or not, they sent her and her two compatriots as punishment to Königsberg in the east, her third and by far the worst camp. There the women worked outdoors in the freezing snow, hauling rocks and gravel to build an airstrip. They would stumble back to the camp after dark, bitterly cold, for a hot meal of soup. The soup was kept in great vats policed by the head guard – a fat beast of a woman the French called *La Vachère*, or the cowgirl. Being fat was enough of a provocation, but in addition she would taunt the hungry prisoners by kicking the vat of soup until it spilled into the snow and then watch them scavenge in the slush for tiny scraps of food. Jeannie now realized that her own survival depended, bizarrely, on an escape plan which reinstated her and her friends again in Ravensbrück. They hid in a truck taking TB-sufferers back to be gassed and managed to slip away when the truck stopped, and return to the main camp.

Jeannie, convinced that the war would be over by the autumn, did not have any doubts at the time that her protest at Torgau was the morally correct way to behave and would ensure the best outcome. But the cruel winter dragged on. If indeed Paris had been liberated, and the Allies had succeeded in pushing the Germans out of the rest of France while the Soviets were advancing across Poland and Ukraine, why was it taking so long for the women to be rescued? In fact, throughout 1944 even more women were being sent as labour for the hundreds of sub-camps upon which Hitler, ever more crazed in his determination to fight on, had decided his ability to continue the war depended. Even when, in October, French newspapers, no longer under Nazi control, ran interviews with a woman released from Ravensbrück who had directly witnessed fellow prisoners dying from starvation and bodies burned daily in the crematorium, it was proving hard to press for international action. As evidence accumulated in 1944 of gas chambers and other barbarities, the International Committee of the Red Cross continued to insist to those who expressed their horror at what they now knew was happening in Ravensbrück that it had no access to the camp and could do nothing. Its rules governing interference on behalf of civilians forbade it to publicize the women's appeal.*

The Germans had not picked up all the young Parisiennes working for the resistance. Marie-France Geoffroy-Dechaume, now hiding

---

* Ironically, as Caroline Moorehead points out in her history of the Red Cross, although many of the women imprisoned were there largely for their work sheltering and aiding men, it was men on the committee who insisted on doing nothing and the single voice urging action was a woman's (Caroline Moorehead, *Dunant's Dream: War, Switzerland and the History of the Red Cross*, Introduction).

out with her group in her small house on the coast, was actively engaged in planning night-time operations which involved laying mines or planting bombs both on railway lines and by roadsides in response to information they received about German manoeuvres, about what they were transporting and, crucially, about when they would be passing. She learned to make homemade bombs on the kitchen table and sometimes would bicycle around with gelignite strapped to her chest, having secretly fetched the ingredients from elsewhere, then brought them back to the house to assemble into a bomb, all the time looking to any German soldier every inch the innocent country girl. As her daughter recalled, she rarely talked about these activities, but 'I think she relished this role of looking or playing the innocent, knowing all the while that she had the means to blow the *Boches* sky high!'

The group planted their bombs under cover of night and, after months of inaction and waiting, there was a deep sense of satisfaction verging on euphoria when they saw their targets successfully blown up, a feeling that they were finally doing something positive to help their country.

Later, when it was clear that the Germans had been defeated, there were still small groups of German soldiers straggling along the country roads looking weary and defeated. Marie-France and her gang lay in wait and then ambushed some of these; the soldiers all too readily flung their arms in the air, shouting hopefully, 'Camarade!' She had been instructed to disarm rather than kill them and never forgot the look of humiliation on their faces – to be disarmed by a woman!

The Paris all these women had left behind was increasingly a place of terror, consumed by shortages and despair. In the spring and early summer of 1944, even though the Allied invasion was imminent, only a handful of trusted people knew the precise details. But the constant rumours of a coup to remove Hitler fed Nazi paranoia, and in January 1944 Helmuth von Moltke was arrested and sent to a special prison section at the Ravensbrück camp. He was treated reasonably well at first and got to know prisoners such as Carmen Mory, whom he described to his wife Freya as someone who 'told splendid stories' and was 'a magnificent source of information for me'. Geneviève de

Gaulle, during the time she was held in solitary confinement, was also aware of his presence there, but did not know why he was being held.* But the volatility in Paris of random shootings and reprisals intensified into terrifying chaos after 20 July, when the Claus von Stauffenberg plot to kill Hitler failed. As a result hundreds of conspirators and anti-Nazis, who had thrown in their lot with Hitler's opponents, were now rooted out and punished.

And there were summary executions, on all sides, of those thought to have been betraying secrets or people. On 26 April, Violette Morris, the lesbian former athlete and collaborator, was gunned down at the wheel of her Traction Avant on a country road in Normandy with two other collaborators in the car as well as the collaborators' two young children, all killed in a hail of bullets fired by members of the Maquis Surcouf. Violette was fifty-one and was thought to have been responsible for numerous infiltrations of SOE networks and other resistance groups.

Of course the fear and deprivation felt by women in the capital queuing for food were as nothing compared to the suffering experienced by those in Ravensbrück. Nonetheless, alongside the tension there was a genuine sense of hardship in Paris itself because most of the women there had no concept of how much worse it was for the women imprisoned in the camps. Violette Wassem, a young secretary who had worked in Paris throughout the war, said that after four years of Occupation the low point of deprivation came in 1944 when gas and electricity often failed.

> As I was 'Mécanographe' [early electric-typewriter secretary] at that period, I worked during the night. In order to do that, I took the last underground at 9–10pm and returned by the first at 6–7am. We would be given a 'casse-croûte' [snack] at midnight made of a dish of white beans boiled in water (eugh!) and this, for five or six weeks. The newspapers had only a page, perhaps a half.

---

* Helmuth von Moltke was transferred from Ravensbrück to Tegel prison in Berlin on 11 January 1945, tried before the People's Court on 23 January and executed in April. Freya, Caspar and Konrad von Moltke were evacuated to Czechoslovakia, and in the 1960s Freya settled in the United States.

No white machine-paper, but an inferior pink sort . . . Altered or forged coupons were sold for a great price and to increase the value in weight of the bread coupons, for example, one of our employees was scratching out figures and drawing others all day long. I bought some for us, for my family in the countryside and even for a baker friend so as to satisfy his clients and his miller!

Janet Teissier du Cros was, like most other mothers in this period, worried about adequate food and nutrition for her small children, one of whom, lacking adequate vitamins, was now diagnosed with curvature of the spine. By the winter of 1944 life was an hourly struggle to find enough food.

'Our fat allowance, and this covered all fats, was ten ounces a month and dwindled to two ounces that winter of 1944. Adults got no milk – we had a very small allowance of fatless cheese.' Janet kept a note of these figures at the time because it was so little. 'Our bread ration was six ounces a day but often on some pretext or other, reprisals or what not, it was less.' It was impossible to subsist on these rations, eked out only by such carrots, Jerusalem artichokes, swedes (rutabaga) or an occasional cabbage as she could wrest from the market by dint of long queuing as everything involved queuing among grumpy women. What she found as distasteful as the swedes was the lying. 'We were all of us driven to some form of dishonest practice,' she admitted. The elderly living alone suffered most and of course those in hiding. Fake ration cards were rife; once Janet had an altercation at the fishmonger, when she was loudly accused of using a card twice, which she just as loudly denied only to find out that it was her maid who had purloined it the previous day. Such problems were very real to Parisian women, leading to 'a dishonest way of life in full view of the children and in contradiction to all we were striving to teach them'. Those who could not quite bring themselves to use the black market might be tempted by the grey market. 'There were real false cards and false real cards. The first were counterfeits of the real thing, the second and more expensive were genuine bread cards sold in the towns by country people who could obtain wheat illegally and make their own bread.' And it was not only food in demand on the black market. At one fashionable lunch party the guests left their hats and coats on the banquette in the entrance hall and one also deposited two large bars of soap she had managed to buy. But another guest picked them up on her way out, behaviour unthinkable before the war at such a gathering.

In spite of the bitter cold, with no heating and so little gas or electricity that food could rarely be cooked properly, some sophisticated Parisian women, despite the shortages, took pride in being able to produce miracles with their clothes.

> With hardly anything one could still dress well; we turned and remade our dresses and coats; with articulated wooden soles we had magnificent high-heel shoes . . . Hairstyles and hats were fashioned from tulle scaffoldings, veils, flowers, and recycled feathers. With four or five old handbags, one could have one big one made, very chic.

But although there was no silk for stockings, one new source of fabric was now occasionally available: parachute silk. Downed airmen were instructed where possible to bury their chutes but if they could not, women eagerly seized whatever was not torn or damaged, knowing it might provide enough fabric for a blouse as well as several pairs of luxurious camiknickers.

PART TWO

LIBERATION

On 6 June 1944 Allied forces began the long-awaited invasion of northern France. Operation Overlord, codename for the Normandy landings, was the largest seaborne invasion in history, as British, American and Canadian forces landed on a fifty-mile stretch of coast. Fighting was intense, casualties high and progress slower than the Allies had hoped. The town of Caen, a major objective, was not captured until 21 July, and the Allies could not break out beyond Bayeux until 1 August. But, as they advanced towards Paris, many towns saw spontaneous demonstrations of support from the local people, the vast majority of them women, often wearing red, white and blue and kissing every soldier in sight.

The battle for Paris itself began on 15 August. Colonel Henri Rol-Tanguy, commander of the Paris Region FFI (Forces Françaises de l'Intérieur), the umbrella network for the military resistance, led the popular uprising in the city as the police went on strike and the Métro closed. Cécile Rol-Tanguy, the young activist married to Henri, knew in advance that this was the moment and remembers frantically typing out propaganda posters calling for insurrection which needed circulating across the city. The patriotic French – 'all men from 18 to 50 able to carry a weapon' – were urged to join 'the struggle against the invader', promising 'victory was near' and 'chastisement for the traitors', the Vichy loyalists. The Rol-Tanguys, both committed communists, had managed to survive in occupied Paris for four years leading a dangerous and clandestine existence, taking enormous risks while bringing up a young family. They were fortunate not to be arrested, like so many of their fellow fighters. Although Cécile worked as Henri's liaison officer, they could not live together as he was a wanted man, far too well known by the Germans.

In 1942 Cécile's father, François, had been arrested for a second time, this time deported to Auschwitz where he was killed, and the following year Cécile gave birth to a son, Jean. So Cécile and her mother now lived together in a tiny studio with the two children, Hélène, born in May 1941, and baby Jean, struggling to find enough to eat. She remembers being so thin at one point that her culottes fell down. Cécile had to traverse the city for her work, so she sometimes carried Hélène in her arms while hiding weapons in a sack of potatoes which she pushed in the pram. At other times she buried papers underneath the pram bedding, with the baby on top. She had a number of aliases, Jeanne, Yvette and Lucie, and occasionally changed her hairstyle or wore a fashionable turban, but she did little otherwise to disguise herself. Afterwards, she always made light of her activities, claiming she had done nothing special. 'My strength was always in remaining cool. I think that was my character.'

It required all her strength to stay cool during these exceptionally bloody and chaotic eleven days when almost 1,500 Parisians died in the struggle to chase out 20,000 occupying soldiers as well as collaborationist snipers, many of whom were Vichy *miliciens*, firing from rooftops wherever they could. Suddenly rosette merchants appeared on the streets, hoping to make a quick franc or two from women determined to declare their allegiance to the nation by sporting a tricolore rosette in their blouse. At last, on 25 August, Dietrich von Choltitz, the German Military Governor of Paris, emerged from his headquarters in the Hôtel Meurice to sign the surrender documents. Henri Rol-Tanguy and General Philippe Leclerc of the 2nd Armoured Division, de Gaulle's representative, were also signatories. The following day de Gaulle, unmissable thanks to his immense height, made his triumphal walk down the Champs-Elysées with thousands of people shouting 'Vive de Gaulle!' As he walked, he raised his long arms towards the sky, turning first left and then right, as if offering thanks, in a gesture that was to become his hallmark but was completely new to Parisians then. 'For those gathered there,' remarked Elisabeth Meynard, a teacher in charge of a group of schoolchildren that day, 'he was the living symbol of resistance to the enemy invader.' With the odd German or *milicien* sniper taking murderous pot-shots, he then delivered a rousing speech referring, in an immediate attempt to unite the country, to 'Paris liberated by her own people . . . supported by the whole of France'.

But he could not totally deny the contribution made by the brave communist fighters amongst whom Cécile Rol-Tanguy had played an important role, a crucial factor in determining the political future of the country. One of the liveliest post-war arguments, still arousing controversy in the twenty-first century though only a handful of the participants are still alive, has centred on the part played by female resisters – whether women carried weapons or 'merely' acted in support. Clearly, in Paris women under the command of Rol-Tanguy did use weapons, as can be seen in contemporary footage of the Liberation which shows young girls such as the twenty-two-year-old Anne Marie Dalmaso handling a gun as she fights in the action to defend the Hôtel de Ville. Dalmaso had joined the teams of young volunteers especially created to help those affected by the bombing, or evacuated from combat zones.* Madeleine Riffaud, a twenty-year-old communist arrested in July for shooting and killing a German officer in daylight on a bridge overlooking the Seine, was interrogated in Fresnes and even had a date set for her execution but was released in a prisoner exchange and returned to fight in the resistance. On the day after the Liberation Frida Wattenberg, only nineteen, a Paris-born resister working for the OSE and other groups, was immediately sent to the Toulouse office for 'Questions Juives' to retrieve crucial files that would contain details of any Jewish genocide in France. 'When the official asked me what authority I had to claim them I replied: "All I have is my gun," and pointed it at him.' Marie-France Geoffroy-Dechaume, cycling around the Normandy coast with explosives at the ready, handled not only weapons but also bomb-making equipment.

However, in the euphoria of liberation, the abiding image is of women throughout France who now suffered summary justice for what was termed *collaboration horizontale*. Those accused, rightly or wrongly, of having slept with a German, sometimes but not always in exchange for benefits, of having collaborated by providing sensitive information, or merely of having serviced the occupier in the role of

* After the war she volunteered to bring camp survivors suffering from typhus back to France but contracted TB herself and died in 1950 aged twenty-seven.

housekeeper, seamstress or cook, were all seen as women guilty of infidelity to the nation. They were denounced, hectored, brought to their knees, had their heads shaved; some even had swastikas drawn or branded on their bodies and were made to parade half naked through town to display their shame publicly. No one who watched ever forgot the barbarity, as whole villages turned out to cheer young girls being humiliated perhaps for no greater crime than sleeping with a German in return for some silk stockings or a little bit of money. Lee Miller, the US-born photographer and fashion model who had been accredited as a war reporter with British *Vogue*, had flown over to France on 2 August and was making her way up to Paris where 'I won't be the first woman journalist in Paris . . . but I'll be the first dame photographer, I think, unless someone parachutes in.'* Miller was shocked to witness the 'chastisement' of two girls who were shaved, spat on and publicly slapped even though their interrogation had merely confirmed that there was enough evidence for a subsequent trial. 'They were stupid little girls not intelligent enough to feel ashamed,' Lee wrote to her editor, Audrey Withers.

It was a sickeningly misogynistic response. The women – by some estimates as many as 20,000, known to history as *les tondues*, or shaven ones – were punished by the men who had failed to defend them. One of them was Lisette, the French secretary whose long-standing affair with Johann, a married German soldier, was known of by many in her circle. Her pro-German parents, concierges who were helping themselves to clothes in the apartment of a deported Jewish couple, may have supported her, but her own cousins refused to speak to her. She was lucky not to have had further humiliation in the form of branding inflicted on her as payment for the luxuries she had received during the war. But at the same time de Gaulle did not punish the male political or commercial elite who had backed Pétain, seeing them as valuable allies in the fight against communism. The

---

* This was an impressive achievement as British women reporters were not being given official accreditation to report on front-line battles. It was easier for American women, but some, like Martha Gellhorn, still had to resort to ruses to ensure they got to report on front-line action, not just from hospitals, on the post-battle bomb damage.

controversy has gathered momentum in the intervening years as
historians have pointed out how much of the punishment was not
only gender-based, but a question of class and ancient score-settling.
In the terror of the moment there were tragic mistakes. Max and
Madeleine Goa, two young resisters who, having sheltered evading
airmen, were celebrating victory on the balcony of their apartment
in the Avenue d'Italie when shots were fired. The mob below was
convinced they had come from them, so the pair were hauled down
to the street below where Max was lynched, then run over by a tank,
and Madeleine taken away to a prison, locked up until she went mad,
and then murdered.

Of course there were articulate and fierce opponents of the
épuration sauvage – the wave of vicious punishments without trial,
including executions as well as humiliation, that now swept through
France – including men such as Henri Rol-Tanguy and the communist surrealist poet, Paul Eluard, both married to women who had
risked their lives to resist. Eluard, in his 1944 poem 'Comprenne qui
voudra' (Understand if you will), expressed powerfully his disgust at
how, in order not to punish the real culprits, the mob had attacked
defenceless girls who were trembling with fear as they lay with torn
dresses, while the crowd laughed and parents held up children to see
better, many of whom simply did not understand what was happening to the girls nor why. Angered by the sight of a beautiful woman's
hair lying on the pavement in front of a barber's shop in Rue de
Grenelle, Eluard pointed out that they had not, in any case, harmed
anyone else. 'They had not sold France and they often had not sold
anything at all.'

Janet Teissier du Cros, a clear-eyed observer of what defeat meant to
men in France, believed it affected women more tangentially. 'Theirs
was the cumulative humiliation of being little by little degraded to
an exclusive preoccupation with material things, the humiliation
daily renewed of having to beg even for what they bought . . . But
the actual fact of military defeat is, I think, harder for men to bear
than for women and, so long as German troops remained on French
soil, the wound was kept open.'

At the same time, there were also educated people who defended the
head-shaving. Andrée Doucet, a young art student at Les Arts Décos

(sister school to the Beaux-Arts) during the latter part of the Occupation, believed the punishment was 'a shame, yes, but compared with women who had risked everything for France, understandable. They deserved it. And anyway hair grows back. They soon carried on with their lives.' Doucet had been brought up in a suburb of Paris where her father owned the local Citroën garage. She was keenly aware of girls who had been overly friendly to the German occupiers, something her family, fiercely proud of its French identity, had instilled in her to avoid. Once, she had seen a friend of hers walking arm in arm with the local Kommandant and yelled out 'Salle pute!' (Dirty bitch!) – an action which got her arrested. She talked her way out of that situation by saying that what she meant was that the girl had slept with all the French boys in the village. Happily, she was allowed to go free. But the experience terrified her. 'If you didn't live through the Liberation, you can't describe the atmosphere . . . Euphoria in the streets, people screaming with joy and enthusiasm. Head-shaving didn't seem such a huge thing then. It wasn't physical torture.'

The euphoria of Liberation, as other women soon discovered in 1944, could be highly dangerous. Lucienne Guézennec,* the Paris-born *résistante* who had given her real identity to a Jewish girl on the run, was now taking part in the celebrations of Liberation in Lyons. She attempted to intervene when she saw two naked girls trying to protect themselves from a group of loud-mouthed women spitting on them, attempting to hit them and shouting insults at other shaven-headed girls. But Lucienne, although deeply shocked by this mob justice, was herself still weak, suffering from a German bullet that had punctured her lung during a raid on her printing press, as well as once having had her arm mangled in the printing press, and could do little to protect herself when a youth, yelling at her for trying to help the 'sluts', grabbed her and shoved her into an open truck filled with men and women assumed to have collaborated. Luckily 'Lucienne' was soon recognized by people who knew who she really was and she was released. 'Was it for this', she asked herself, 'that so many comrades died? Could this have been the reason for their struggles and sacrifices?'

* See page 51.

Hungry for normality, the native population had quickly accustomed itself to freedom once more. On 17 August Drancy and its sub-camps, including the Lévitan and Bassano sorting centres, were liberated. Those returning from prisons or deportation, still only a trickle in 1944, were soon to recognize that Paris was not prepared to welcome them. It was a situation that was to deteriorate dramatically in 1945 when most of the deportees wearily straggled home.

Irène Delmas, codenamed Maryka, was one of those released in 1944 who started visiting the families of other prisoners, trying to reassure them, and she soon realized the enormous need for a welfare organization to help newly released female prisoners, many with multiple illnesses and physical disabilities compounding the emotional. By September 1944 she had an official organization under way which sent out 700 invitations to former resisters. More than 350 women attended the first general assembly on 14 October 1944, unanimously approving the by-laws and electing an administrative council headed by Delmas. As they came to appreciate the uniqueness of their circumstances and to see that their wartime activism had been little understood or accepted, their conviction grew that no one would speak for them if they did not do so for themselves.

Even as de Gaulle was marching down the Champs-Elysées on 26 August to wild cheers, the artistic *épuration sauvage* was also well under way. That day saw General de Gaulle acclaimed as President of the new provisional government of the French Republic, as agreed by the Allies. De Gaulle would lead a national unity interim government whose most urgent task, until elections could be held, was to continue the war against Germany and deal with the aftermath of four years of Occupation. Almost immediately, in an attempt to halt indiscriminate revenge attacks, it introduced an offence of *indignité nationale*. Those found guilty were reduced to a class of second-rate citizens, deprived of election rights and banned from government service, trade unions, mass media and executive appointments in semi-public companies, as well as, after 30 September 1944, confiscation of property. Such punishment could last for any period from five years to life, to be decided by each court individually. Those who had done more than simply perform and had flaunted their German friends, lovers and contacts were prime targets, and the opera singer Germaine Lubin, who was preparing to sing Gluck's Alceste, was one of the first to be arrested. She had frequently sung Wagner, sometimes at special performances for the Wehrmacht, and had a long-time German admirer, Captain Hans Joachim Lange, whom she had used to arrange the release of her only son, a prisoner of war captured in 1940. Now she was held in prison for most of the next two years without formally being brought to trial. Her treatment reveals the fixation with punishing women who had openly consorted with German men, yet her prison diary, which makes for graphic reading, displays an arrogance and a total failure to understand why she was being detained, an attitude which goes some way to explaining why she was a target.

On 8 September she wrote:

Eight days ago I was arrested for the second time. For ten hours I waited on a leather bench with no back surrounded by dirty men with week-old beards, concierges, laundrywomen, prostitutes. In the corners, garbage was mixed with the hair of women who had had their heads shaved the night before. During the course of the day another four were shaved completely bald except for one on whom, for laughs, they had left a tuft in the middle of her head which hung down like the mandarin's pigtails – so dreadful as to make one shiver. After the fourth woman was shaved I began trembling in uncontrollable fear of being suddenly delivered into the hands of one of these fanatics and ending up bald.

Worse was to follow. Before the year was out she complained of having to share a straw mattress and one blanket with two other women until she was transferred to Drancy, now used for collaborators. Here 'ugliness, dirt, selfishness, cruelty all mingle . . . It is very cold . . . washing with others in freezing water. The indecency of it. Odious people, nauseating smells, coffee tasting like soup from the night before . . . Drancy is an immense material and moral garbage heap. I live in a state of perpetual nausea.'

The film star Arletty, who had seen her popularity soar during the Occupation, when going to the cinema provided not only a form of escapism but one of the few places that was warm and a useful venue for sexual encounters, much cheaper than renting a hotel bedroom, was also now a focus of attack. In 1938 cinema attendances had been gauged at 220 million but rose to over 300 million in 1943. As American and British films had been banned, the French movie industry flourished and 220 or so films were made between September 1939 and the summer of 1945. It was, paradoxically, a golden age for French cinema and a good time for female stars on the screen. Arletty, leading lady of some seven hit films who earned one of the highest salaries in the business, came to symbolize for many what it meant to be a Parisienne who collaborated. She was not just beautiful but funny and sexy in a nonchalant, devil-may-care Parisian way, and believed she had done nothing wrong. She did her job and fell in love. She was proud of her working-class origins, having started life working in a factory before graduating to modelling and music hall, never losing her trademark *parigot*, the working-class Parisian accent.

But she had celebrity status and therefore she could not be allowed to walk free. Even though she had made no films with the German-run Continental Studios, she was now judged as someone who had, quite literally, embraced France's acceptance of the German presence, evidenced by her passionate love affair with Hans-Jürgen Soehring. She had attended events both at the German Embassy and at the German Institute. For much of 1943 and early 1944 she had been making the great Marcel Carné film *Les Enfants du paradis*, in which she starred as the courtesan Garance. When that was finished, Soehring urged her to flee with him, but she refused.

Nonetheless, as the battle for Paris raged, Arletty, now forty-six, was frightened enough to cycle across the city to find refuge with friends in Montmartre. She then moved to a hotel close to the Champs-Elysées where, in October, she was arrested by two policemen. When they asked her how she was feeling that day, she, ever ready with the bon mot, replied: 'Not very *résistante* . . .' She was taken to the dungeon of La Conciergerie, where Marie Antoinette had spent her last weeks before her execution in 1793, and after eleven miserable nights was transferred to Drancy. Arletty had to be seen to have a spectacular trial, but she escaped being shaven or any other serious punishment. She was released a few weeks later, remembered by posterity for her quip that 'Mon coeur est français mais mon cul, lui, est international' (My heart is French but my arse is international). She was later sentenced to eighteen months under house arrest at the Château de la Houssaye in Seine-et-Marne.

Chanel, too, although arrested and questioned by the FFI in August 1944 on account of her well-known love affair with Spatz, Hans Günther von Dincklage, the suspected spy, was quickly released. According to one story, she reported 'with snobbish disdain' afterwards that 'the most ghastly thing about her arrest was hearing her armed captors say "tu" to the doorman.' There has been much speculation about whether or not Churchill himself intervened on her behalf as he felt an attachment to her ever since her affair more than a decade before with his great friend, Bendor, Duke of Westminster. She had written to Churchill in a complicated attempt to arrange the release of her nephew, André, from a prisoner-of-war camp, controversial negotiations which also involved her friend Vera Lombardi in Madrid and another German officer, Captain Theodore Momm, known to Chanel. While there is no proof that her activities were treasonous, they were certainly unsavoury, and it is clear that she was prepared to consort with Germans when it suited her, that she uttered 'long tirade[s] against the Jews' and that she was extremely lucky to escape a more severe prison sentence or worse.

Malcolm Muggeridge, the British journalist turned intelligence officer working for MI6 and sent to Paris after the Liberation, was shocked by the vindictive fury and chaotic conditions he encountered. After a visit to Fresnes, where he was appalled to find five or six women in a cell intended for one, he concluded that the judicial and prison systems were bursting. His main task was to investigate the writer P. G. Wodehouse and his wife Ethel (who became lifelong friends) as well as Chanel, suspected of spying partly because of her association with von Dincklage. The Wodehouses had been living in Le Touquet near Boulogne until the town was captured by the Germans in May 1940, whereupon he was interned in various camps for more than a year. Released in June 1941 on account of his age (he was sixty), he was sent to Berlin where he was joined by Ethel, who had also been detained in France, and agreed to write and record five talks describing his experiences. The talks, entitled

American soldiers queuing in front of 31 Rue Cambon to collect their free bottles of Chanel No. 5.

How to be an Internee without Previous Training, were not political but were intended to be humorous anecdotes about Wodehouse's experiences as a prisoner. They were initially broadcast only to the United States, with which Germany was not, at the time, at war. But they were also later broadcast to England where they caused a storm. The content was not objectionable, but by giving talks on German radio it was felt that he had aided the Nazis. Muggeridge, however, having considered the case, concluded that there was no evidence whatever that he had acted traitorously or had intentionally given any aid to the enemy, and judged that the broadcasts were neither anti- nor pro-German, but just 'Wodehousian'.* Having done that, Muggeridge turned his attention to Chanel and decided that her success in withstanding the first *épuration* assault had been achieved 'by one of those majestically simple strokes which made Napoleon so successful a general; she just put an announcement in the window of her emporium that scent was free for GIs, who thereupon queued up to get their bottles of Chanel No. 5, and would have been outraged if the French police had touched a hair of her head'.

* Wodehouse was never really forgiven in Britain, however, and in 1947 the couple left France for America.

Muggeridge described Chanel at sixty-two as looking 'immensely old and incorporeal; I had the feeling that she might expire that very evening', prematurely aged perhaps as a result of years of taking drugs. In pre-war days she and her confidante Misia Sert had made numerous visits to Switzerland together to various clinics and to stock up on morphine. In January 1942 this became more difficult and her good friend the journalist Boulos Ristelhueber had to make an emergency visit to an all-night pharmacy for opium supplies for Chanel and Misia, both hopelessly addicted. When Muggeridge came to write his report on his evening with her he concluded that 'really there was nothing to say except that I was sure the *épuration* mills, however small they might grind, would never grind her – as indeed proved to be the case'.

Summary justice was occasionally still resorted to on both sides throughout 1944 but punishments were now increasingly organized by courts, however imperfect. Elie Scali, friend and former lover of Renée Van Cleef, who had committed suicide in 1942, now gave evidence in support of René Marty, the Vichy bureaucrat and first cousin of Vichy police chief René Bousquet. Marty had supplied Scali with many official passes enabling him to cross the demarcation line from one zone to another and had turned a blind eye to his business activities. Colonel Marty was subsequently employed by Van Cleef & Arpels after the war where, according to a woman whose mother had worked since 1919 as a polisher at the company, he clearly continued to receive 'de très hautes protections'. Marty was extremely useful whenever there was a problem with various authorities. 'For example, there had been a series of thefts at Van Cleef, of gems and jewellery, and the "Colonel" solved the problem since he deduced that it must be a staff member. All staff were questioned by police and the culprit was discovered.'

At the Comédie-Française, Mary Marquet, one of the company's most revered actresses, was arrested and sent to Fresnes, accused of collaborating. During her trial she admitted contacting Vichy police in 1943 and asking them to prevent her son François from joining the resistance; but, in spite of a severe warning, he did enlist and was arrested and deported to Buchenwald where he died. Marquet was acquitted, perhaps because it was recognized that she had suffered enough, that any mother would try to protect her son, or that she had not passed on secret information to the enemy. Nonetheless she could no longer act with the Comédie-Française and, although she lived until August 1979, her career was destroyed. From then on she was offered roles only in minor films or light comedies and struggled to make a living.

By contrast, Béatrice Bretty had taken the clear decision at the outset that it was not possible to perform in a company which excluded Jewish actors. She had devoted herself to following Georges Mandel where possible and caring for his daughter Claude. Mandel, having declined Bretty's suggestion that they marry in Buchenwald, was subsequently handed over by the Gestapo to the Milice in Paris and, while being transferred from one prison to another by the latter, was taken out of the car and on 7 July 1944 assassinated by them in Fontainebleau forest. A heartfelt letter which he had written to Bretty a few weeks earlier from Buchenwald arrived after his death in which he told her of his anguish at her suffering as much as his own. 'Your affairs touch my heart as strongly as my own . . . Of all the things which I had to suffer before my exile nothing affected me as profoundly as the unprecedented bad behaviour you received at the Comédie-Française . . . so rest assured that as long as I have a breath of life I look forward to the reparations you deserve.' Two months after Mandel's death, Bretty was reinstated at the theatre and on 18 September she was on stage once again playing one of her best-known roles, Toinette in Molière's *Le Malade Imaginaire*. There was rapturous applause at her return.

But as Sadie, or Florence, star of the Bal Tabarin, proved, it was possible to perform without collaborating. Disguised as an attentive, elegant French wife, she had helped escort escapees and Jews past police and soldiers until in the summer of 1944 a German cultural officer warned Frédéric Apcar, her dancing partner and one-time lover, that she was about to be arrested. So she hid in the secluded safe house in the suburbs which Frédéric had used to hide other Jews, such as Dr Gilbert Doukan, a Jewish escapee from Drancy and resistance hero, and Marcel Leibovici, both men Florence had helped. One morning an American tank rolled up, the driver shouting out for directions to Paris. Frédéric and Florence followed the tank to the capital, where they witnessed the final scenes of the Liberation, and with delight saw Doukan now fighting in a French officer's uniform.

Paris that September was a strange combination of rejoicing and retribution. Once the fighting had ceased, the Americans were hand-ing out chocolate, oranges, chewing gum and bananas – luxuries not seen for four years – and for many women in Paris who had endured those grim years of Occupation it felt like the end. But celebrations were premature while the rest of the world was still fighting and the Germans were far from surrendering. Lee Miller, who had been in France less than a month and reported graphically on the battle for Saint-Malo as well as on the 44th Evacuation Hospital – where, she noted, they used both calvados and penicillin – was disappointed to have been refused permission to continue into Germany with the 83rd Division. 'It is very bitter for me to go to Paris now that I have a taste for gun powder,' she told her editor. But she had a scoop because, although she had been allowed only to report on how things were being managed *after* the St Malo battle, in fact the battle was not yet over. 'I sheltered in a Kraut dugout squatting under the ramparts. My heel ground into a dead detached hand and I cursed the Germans for the sordid ugly destruction they had conjured up in the once beautiful town,' she wrote in the unlikely pages of *Vogue*. 'I picked up the hand and threw it back the way I had come and ran back, bruising my feet and crashing into the unsteady piles of stone and slipping in the blood. Christ it was awful.'

Miller's ability to look horror in the face, not to shirk the unmen-tionable, gave her photographs and her writing a raw power shared by few of her colleagues, male or female. It may also have contributed ultimately to her breakdown and her inability to continue with her work once she had had her own child. In the short term it landed her in trouble with the authorities for a couple of days, for going beyond her agreed zone, but then she moved into Paris, the Paris which she knew so well, the Paris of her youthful love affairs. She soon realized that, as well as a comfortable room at the Hôtel Scribe, the international HQ for all journalists, there were endless stories there for her to write.

Also at the Scribe for a short time was Mary Welsh, the journalist from Chicago, accredited to *Time* magazine, who was now in love with Ernest Hemingway. Welsh had been commissioned to write stories of how fashion in Paris was coming back to life and what displays were in the boutique windows already, tame stuff for a war correspondent in Paris that August. But she soon moved into the Ritz with Hemingway, who she found sitting on the bare floor of his bedroom there with some resistance friends, 'intermittently cleaning rifles and sipping champagne'. Hemingway and his small band of irregular fighters which he called the 'Hem Division' – as a war correspondent he knew he was forbidden to command troops – had made their way on the afternoon of 26 August, the day of de Gaulle's triumphal walk, directly to Sylvia Beach's bookshop Shakespeare and Company in the Rue de L'Odéon, which he had known so well from his pre-war days of living in Paris. Sylvia, who had endured six harsh months at the Vittel camp before being released in 1942, dramatically recalled: 'I flew downstairs; we met with a crash; he picked me up and swung me around and kissed me while people on the street and in the windows cheered.' Sylvia and her French librarian lover, Adrienne Monnier, overjoyed after the tense months when their shop had been closed, the precious books hidden from the Nazis upstairs, invited their old friend and liberator up to their apartment to drink with them. Hemingway, however, thought it more important to check for snipers from the roof before moving on with his men to liberate the wine cellars of the Ritz, as he was fond of recalling later.

Lee Miller was more interested in seeing her old friends Paul and Nusch Eluard, as well as Picasso, still in Rue des Grands Augustins. With her sharp eye she noticed bullet holes in buildings, and girls with flowers in their hair, girls offering kisses or riding bicycles or drinking wine – she saw how Parisian girls dazzled. 'Their silhouette was very queer and fascinating to me after utility and austerity England. Full floating skirts, tiny waistlines. They were top heavy with built up, pompadour front hairdos and waving tresses; weighted to the ground with clumsy, fancy thick-soled wedge shoes. The entire gait of the Frenchwoman has changed with her footwear. Instead of the bouncing buttocks and mincing steps of "pre-war" there is a hot-foot long stride, picking up the whole foot at once.' When she asked American soldiers what they thought of Paris they became starry-eyed and told her it was 'the most beautiful place in the world and the people smell so wonderful'. Most were pleased and surprised that Parisiennes 'were so beautifully dressed and amiable instead of lean and hungry and sour'.

Plenty, however, were lean and hungry and sour but, as Miller rightly observed, they were not out on the streets. Those out on the streets celebrating were the dazzling, joyful young girls 'hilarious at their victory in Paris and proud of their battle scars'. These were the Parisians determined to celebrate 'the world's most gigantic party' even if there wasn't any food.

Yet, in the chaos of the Liberation, the Germans were keen to take a final load of looted treasures with them and, as railway workers went on strike, it was not unusual to see German civilians dragging huge bags to train stations only to find no porters. As some dealers tried frantically to escape with one last haul of paintings, it was once more the indefatigable Rose Valland at the Jeu de Paume who rescued five railway wagons of priceless paintings and other works of art. Valland, the woman who had risked her life day after day spying on the Nazi thefts, knew that whatever was left at the Jeu de Paume, some of it even classified as 'degenerate', including much of Paul Rosenberg's collection, had been hastily packed by the ERR into 148 crates, taken on 1 August to the sidings to be loaded on to waiting train number 40044. Five wagons contained some 967 paintings, including works by Picasso, Dufy, Utrillo, Braque, Degas, Modigliani, Renoir, Cézanne, Gauguin, Toulouse-Lautrec; another fifty trucks held miscellaneous belongings confiscated from Jews. She immediately notified Jaujard, her boss, who gave details to the resistance who, through sabotage and various ruses, prevented the fully loaded train waiting in a siding at Aubervilliers to the north of Paris from departing for Germany.

On 27 August a detachment of the French 2nd Armoured Division, which had just been involved in the Liberation of Paris, captured the train led by a young lieutenant, Alexandre Rosenberg, son of the exiled art-dealer Paul. The soldiers banged on the boxcars' doors (holding fire in case there were prisoners inside), and out straggled some old German soldiers who had been assigned to accompany the booty to Germany. Lieutenant Rosenberg found his own family's paintings on the train which he had last seen in their apartment in Paris.

While this was going on, Valland herself was briefly held captive by Free French troops and liberators who suspected her of collaboration. With a machine gun held to her back she was forced to open the storage areas in case she was hiding Germans there. When it was seen that there were none, they released her and she continued with her work. On 24 November the Commission de Récupération Artistique (CRA) was created and Rose Valland named its Secretary, effectively its head. She elected to go to Germany to find the art that had been stolen from France, and for the next five years was a vital liaison officer between the CRA and the French government.

On 20 March 1944 de Gaulle's provisional government had announced that they would, for the first time, allow women to vote once the whole of France was liberated. Before elections could occur, a consultative assembly was created and the General appointed Lucie Aubrac to join as a resistance representative. Aubrac, a daring *résistante* who had organized the escape of her husband, Raymond Samuel, from a Lyons prison by pretending she had to marry him – the man who had made her pregnant – thus became the first woman to sit in a French parliamentary assembly. She too was keenly aware of the gendered response to Liberation as France enjoyed its new-found freedom, and she was determined that the country should resist falling for the simplistic notion that the women had collaborated while the men had fought. She insisted it was women who had given the resistance its breadth and depth – the women who had been the essential mailboxes because they were at home, the women who had become couriers because they looked less suspect carrying suitcases, as well as the women who had daringly used weapons. Not everyone in Paris was ready to hear her voice – most were preoccupied with trying to resume normal life. As the year ended, any rejoicing was muted by the cold, the shortages of food and fuel and the knowledge that at least three million men and women were either dead, missing or still in German prisoner-of-war camps. In the flurry of books, magazines and pamphlets printed as the Liberation was unfolding, one image stands out: a photographic view over the rooftops of Paris, taken on Christmas Day, 1944, during one of the coldest winters of the century, stretches with clarity to the distant horizon. There is no smoke coming from any of the chimneys to mar the view.

1945

PARIS RETURNS

On 1 January 1945 the factory at Torgau fell silent. One day's respite. The women forced to work at Torgau, the munitions factory in eastern Germany used as a sub-camp of Ravensbrück, sometimes believed they could take no more. Jacqueline Marié felt she was immersed in blackness. 'We were so cold: it was minus 20°C outside! Snow covered everything. We were terrified. Fortunately we had no mirror. But I could see my mother and it hurt me to see her legs reduced to bones, sticking out miserably in her ridiculous galoshes that were so heavy. She maintained an incredible serenity, lavishing affection on our young companions. She was also very lucid and, having so many memories of the war of 1914–1918, warned us about the end of the war, and the most dramatic period we might yet have to endure.'

January and February 1945 were among the coldest winter months of the twentieth century in Europe, with blizzards and temperatures occasionally as low as −13 degrees Fahrenheit (−25 degrees Celsius), and the bitter cold remained until the middle of March. Even if the war *was* nearing the end, some of the women in the camps felt they could not continue one more day. They were ill, underfed and suffering a variety of problems from painful sores to blisters, frostbite and gangrene. Sometimes a dead body would be discovered, frozen fast to the ground where it had fallen. One day Virginia found a friend crouching behind rubbish piles, sobbing, 'I want to die. I can't stand it any longer. I want to die.' There was further panic in March for the Parisian workers at Torgau as the Gestapo made an appearance, interrogating them to see why they could not increase productivity. 'While chaos reigned in Germany, the French women felt as if their very low yield was being held responsible for the end of the Great Germany.'

But then without explanation they were locked into cattle wagons and sent to yet another sub-camp. For Jacqueline and her mother, Markkleeberg, near Leipzig, was the fourth and harshest of all camps where, after several days of a cruel journey,

> we were 'greeted' by beatings and the ranting of yet another commander who seemed even crazier than any yet endured . . . We (the 250 French) were parked in a miserable shack . . . The other barracks were occupied by 1,300 Hungarian Jews who had come from Auschwitz or Bergen-Belsen . . . With the French women, SS and kapos [guards chosen by the SS from prisoners] were particularly fierce: at dawn, still exhausted, staggering along, we would work under constant threat of blows as for twelve hours a day we tried to extract stones deeply embedded into a frozen earth. Sometimes we were harnessed to a huge roller that we had to pull on the roads near the camp. At other times, we had to cut down trees in the forest or, more terrible, unload coal trucks all day long. We had no gloves or stockings, no change of clothes, no soap! We were always wet and fed a meagre swede soup with a small, very small, ever smaller piece of bread! The days seemed endless and we often felt like we were about to die on the spot . . . We were no longer even ghosts of women, we were so ugly.

Here, too, they guessed from the bombing of Leipzig which lit up the camp that the end must be near. 'But then the SS, reacting to the bad news, were increasingly fierce. We had little strength left as food hardly contained anything solid any more. How to hold on until our liberators came? Our universe was growing grey, miserable, and I dared not look at my mother and see the degree of physical deterioration.' And yet the desperate desire to survive, in what sometimes felt like a grim race with her captors, persisted.

Geneviève de Gaulle was spared these bitter final months because in late February 1945 she was released from Ravensbrück. Suddenly one morning she was given some odd clothes to cover her emaciated frame: a navy-blue dress with short sleeves, canvas shoes and, extraordinarily, her own coat, handed in when she had arrived. She tied up the few special things she wanted to keep as mementoes in a piece of cloth she had been using as a towel,* and then was sent for an interview with a senior Gestapo officer 'who talks to me about Paris, where he spent a few months and now remembers the time with great pleasure!' The officer's secretary similarly told Geneviève how much she adored Paris and asked her to write a few lines from a popular song in her autograph album – 'for instance, the opening words of a Lucienne Boyer song, I admire her so much'. And then, flanked by two SS guards and a warder, holding hands silently with a fellow prisoner, 'a terribly gaunt woman who seems very old . . . a few stray hairs have grown again on her shaven head', Geneviève went through the camp gateway one final time, trying to ignore the snow and the icy winds. The little group eventually arrived at a Red Cross camp at Liebenau on the Swiss–German border, where she started the long process of recovery in a Swiss sanatorium.

Her companion, a woman who looked 'like Gandhi during the last few moments of his life', was Virginia d'Albert-Lake, released largely thanks to her American mother repeatedly pestering Eisenhower. Geneviève's release had also been requested at the highest levels by her uncle, now head of the French provisional government, who had been informed of the situation by his elder brother, Xavier de Gaulle, the French Consul in Switzerland and Geneviève's father. Geneviève always insisted that her uncle had nothing to do with her release, and indeed she may never have known of his actions. She always maintained he would never have used his influence to favour one member of his own family. But there is now evidence to suggest that he made his concerns known to the ICRC in Geneva in September 1944, who in turn wrote to the German Red Cross, requesting that she be sent to Switzerland to recuperate.

The final months in Ravensbrück were hellish for the Parisian women who remained. Everyone grew weaker, colder, sicker. At the same time, the air raids were more frequent, the guards even edgier, and whispers of the Allied advance grew louder as a smuggled radio had been rigged up in Ravensbrück. By mid-January, as the Russians advanced to within 400 miles of the camp, the killings intensified. And many were killed from sheer exhaustion while working in the

* See p. 369.

polar cold. If the shootings were too slow, the gassings increased. After Auschwitz closed, starting in January 1945 Ravensbrück made use of a small shed as a temporary gas chamber near the crematorium. The women were pushed in, 150 at a time, and then a canister of Zyklon B gas was thrown in from the roof. Witnesses described hearing moaning and crying for two to three minutes and then silence.

This shed was dismantled early in April 1945 and then, according to Countess Karolina Lanckarońska, the Polish resistance fighter and prisoner, 'a machine appeared which resembled a bus and was in the forest near the camp. It was a mobile gas chamber and was painted green.' These mobile gas vans and trucks, painted green so they would be camouflaged in the forest, were a new mechanism in the Nazi machinery of death.

In April, at yet another *Appell* or roll call, both Anise Girard and Emilie Tillion were forced to line up, but this time Emilie was called for selection. Anise ran to tell Emilie's daughter Germaine, successfully hiding under the covers in the infirmary, what had happened. But it was too late. She had been taken, they hoped, to the euphemistically named 'youth camp', merely an annex where prisoners were taken before being killed, but who knew where? In the next few days they heard that she had been gassed. Anise never stopped blaming herself and would weep whenever she spoke about what had happened. Jeannie Rousseau firmly believed that there was nothing anyone could have done. Emilie, she said, had insisted that 'I have always looked my life in the face; I want to look my death in the face.' Releasing her would only have resulted in someone else being substituted. There was much sympathy for all the French prisoners who had done their best to protect this dignified and courageous woman. But in the camp, as in life, there were divisions. Some, like Loulou Le Porz, believed it was for Germaine herself to have shouldered the blame for not staying with her mother until the end.[*]

---

[*] There were other stories of mothers and daughters providing comfort and support for each other. Suzanne Legrand, who had sheltered evading airmen, was most audacious in saving her mother from the gas chamber. When she heard that her mother had been lined up she stole a uniform and, screaming and shouting and slapping her mother, dragged her away from the selection line past the baffled guards. Both survived the war (Caroline McAdam Clark, conversation with the author, 1 October 2014).

By April, a few French women including Odette Fabius and Jacqueline d'Alincourt were released from Ravensbrück thanks to the efforts of Count Folke Bernadotte, a rich and distinguished member of the Swedish royal family and Vice-President of Sweden's Red Cross. In late February 1945, with Hitler determined to exterminate all witnesses to his camps, Bernadotte undertook a risky operation and negotiated with Himmler to release camp victims. He transported them in white buses to recuperate in neutral Malmö in Sweden. Initially, the scheme applied only to Scandinavian citizens, but it was rapidly expanded to save as many victims as possible. Ultimately, more than 15,000 prisoners were released in this way. The last white bus left on 25 April. On that day another 4,000 women were loaded on to a Swedish train, used as a rescue vehicle in addition to the buses and bound for Hamburg, but it broke down outside Lübeck. By the time the freight cars were finally unbolted, four women were found dead inside.

Toquette Jackson, now fifty-six and desperately ill, also owed her rescue to the Swedish Red Cross, eventually sailing to freedom from Lübeck, along with approximately 223 other women from Ravensbrück, aboard the Swedish ship, the *Lillie Matthiessen*, as part of the same rescue operation. Once in Malmö, desperate for news of her husband Sumner and her teenage son Phillip, she trembled as she wrote to her sister that she had 'open wounds on three fingers and no eyeglasses', and could barely hold a pen. 'I also have otitis and my ears run – I can't hear on one side, my feet are swollen and I have terrible dysentery. But after all that my morale is good.' An American Red Cross official reported on 29 April 1945 that, in addition, Mrs Jackson had ulcerated sores on her hands and legs, and required urgent hospitalization to have her ears drained. 'She is little more than a skeleton,' he added. She had been devoured by lice to such an extent that her skin was pockmarked all over from the bites.

Yet her morale was good because she believed her husband and son were still alive. In June, however, she learned the truth. Sumner and Phillip had been taken from Neuengamme concentration camp and, along with 2,000 others, herded below deck on the SS prison ship *Thielbek*, which was strafed by the RAF. Phillip survived by clinging to a piece of wood, searching for his father, who eventually drowned in Lübeck Bay. By July, Toquette was writing to her sister-in-law explaining that as soon as she was able she was going to look for a job, adding: 'Life is very expensive in France and we [she and Phillip] have not the means to live on our income. I want you to know that I never ceased to be in love with Sumner, for whom I had moreover a great admiration and respect. He had such big qualities.'

Toquette was one of the 'lucky' ones. But the outlook was grim for the remainder as the Germans began to force-march as many of their starving captives as could walk, and shot them if they faltered. Jacqueline Marié and her mother were among those, usually in groups of two or three hundred at a time, forced to march westwards as part of the evacuation of the camps undertaken by the Germans, partly in the hope that prisoners would die of exhaustion and partly so that the camps would be deserted when the Allies eventually arrived, leaving no one alive to reveal the barbarity that had taken place within them. The weakened prisoners were hopelessly ill equipped for the evacuation, having suffered months of poor rations, leading to painful hunger and thirst, and having inadequate clothing. The Marié women, feeling like zombies and with bleeding feet, walked from 13 April to 9 May, scavenging herbs where they could. Occasionally, they encountered French prisoners of war, abandoned by their captors and struggling home, who handed them morsels to eat. Or they sucked grass and drank water from puddles, tiny amounts, which ultimately saved them. Too much, and their stomachs could not have coped. But Jacqueline recognized that they would soon collapse and then be beaten to death. They passed Leipzig, followed by Wurzen, Oschatz and Meissen; until they arrived at Dresden, completely flattened by bombs, with escape seemingly impossible. And then in early May they reached the Czech border and saw soldiers of the Red Army. As Jacqueline wrote laconically, they were 'our saviours but also, hélas, violators of our friends'. She was fortunate not to be one of the thousands of cadaverous creatures now brutally raped as the advancing Red Army indulged in an orgy of uncontrolled sexual rampage.

The former teacher and communist Micheline Maurel, who after two years as a prisoner including days when she ate nothing at all, suffered from constant dysentery – and, according to her own description, was little more than stretched skin over painful bones covered with scabies and sores – reported graphically on the Russian soldiers who raped Ravensbrück survivors and who saw even women like her as sexual objects. 'They had no evil intent, no animus whatever against us. Quite the contrary, they were filled with extreme cordiality brimming over with an affection which they had to demonstrate immediately.'

'French? You French, me Russian, it's all the same! You are my sister. Come lie down there!'

Maurel described how they would swiftly have their way with the sick and emaciated women 'with a hearty brotherly laugh' and then be off across the fields. More Russians would find the women and they would have to explain all over again how, in spite of loving the Russians very much, they were ill and exhausted and neither fit nor willing 'to make love'. Only the ulcerated condition of her sores, which she insisted were contagious, saved Maurel herself from being raped. After the war she remarked that the question she was most frequently asked was whether or not she had been raped. 'In the end I regretted having been spared this. Seemingly, by my own fault, I had missed one part of the adventure, to the great disappointment of my audience.' As she astutely explained, the people who posed such questions were little different from those who inflicted the torture. 'Men and women who have forgotten they have a soul.'

Paris itself in 1945 was a very different city without its occupiers. By the time the women who had survived the camps reached the capital, it had been liberated for some nine months and many of its inhabitants were determined to get on with their lives, which meant ignoring these skeletal figures, all too grim reminders of the war they believed was over, suddenly appearing in their midst. Some concentration-camp survivors, returning with heads shaved and camp numbers tattooed on their arms, women so painfully thin and ill that even their families could barely recognize them, found themselves in a city that did not want to acknowledge them.

Simone Rohner, a political deportee freed in April, was deeply traumatized by the hideous symmetry of being shunned anew, mistaken for a *tondue* merely because she had no hair. 'Civilians looked at us with an air of disgust; some insults were flung at us. We looked at each other in surprise. What? France did not know about the deportees? . . . We had to endure scathing words, we cried in rage from it . . . we received a hostile reception . . . [and] we were shocked.'

Almost all the returning women had geared themselves up with joy and exhilaration at the thought of returning to a 'normal life', but were now enraged, disillusioned and distraught to find they were instead greeted with a lack of empathy and understanding. A decision by Henri Frenay, newly appointed head of the Ministry for Prisoners, Deportees and Refugees, implemented by his department to try banning dissemination of information about the deportees, did not help. Frenay, a former resister who well knew the high price women had paid for their actions, was charged with organizing and overseeing the prisoners' return shortly after de Gaulle's provisional government took office in Paris. Yet he claimed that 'inexact information' might result in reprisals for the prisoners and cause unnecessary anxiety for their families. In addition, as part of the 1945 government repatriation programme, Frenay regularly emphasized how essential it was for women to leave their salaried jobs now and allow men to return to their position as *chef de famille* so that former prisoners of war 'could regain their lost self-confidence'.

With few exceptions, the particular experiences of the several thousand French female political prisoners were excluded from the histories of the period. As the French historian Annette Wieviorka has written: 'Reading the wartime memoirs of de Gaulle, one would never know that French women were among those deported and subsequently repatriated. Writing of the prisoners' return, he called it "a grand national event . . . [one] charged with joy . . . when the nation recovered its two and a half million *sons*".'

Superficially de Gaulle's provisional government was overseeing a return to normality. On 29 April French women voted for the first time in municipal elections, following a decree the previous year which declared that 'women are voters and eligible under the same conditions as men'.* Food now appeared in the shops, including bananas, an exotic item for many children who were seeing them for the

---

* This decree did not formally become law until 27 October 1946 when it was definitively adopted into the French Constitution.

first time; however, rationing, queues and squabbles over provisions were still very much in evidence. Occasionally families were reunited and then the fine wine, well hidden in cellars or behind secret walls throughout the Occupation, would be retrieved. But, more often, families learned of loved ones who would never return, and they had little to celebrate.

Almost immediately after the Liberation of Paris, as Allied troops moved into the city, so too did their support teams of diplomats, civil servants, secretaries and journalists, many of whom were astounded by the flamboyance of French fashion. Expecting to see a nation on its knees, they saw instead war-slimmed Parisiennes wearing very short skirts, over-padded shoulders, extravagant turbans (often stuffed with old stockings to make them fuller), loud colours and very high wooden or cork platform shoes. Some Americans were outraged by such showiness while a war was still being fought. But they misunderstood French culture and the belief among some Parisiennes that to look dowdy was a negation of their patriotic duty, when by sporting extravagant costumes they could thumb their noses at the Germans. Some even went as far as to call it 'resisting'. Fashion was, for the French, even after four years of occupation, anything but trivial. For them, remaining stylish provided a beacon of hope for the future. It was a matter of pride to make a dress from old curtains if they could, or to adapt a man's suit if the man wasn't coming home. 'Many French women tried to assert their individuality in defiance of the enemy; they remained as fashion conscious as possible throughout the war in order to retain their pride, boost morale and remain true to themselves, because fashion expressed their identity.'

Lucien Lelong, President of the Chambre Syndicale, who had argued so strongly with the Germans at the beginning of the war to keep French couture Paris-based, now felt the need to write to American *Vogue* defending the extravagance of the first fashion shows after the Liberation: 'For four years we have fought to keep couture alive because it represents a Parisian industry of prime importance and because it was a means of avoiding unemployment for workers and consequent forced labour in Germany and, lastly, to preserve for *la Haute Couture Parisienne* the place it has always had in the eyes of the world.'

It was in this atmosphere that he and colleagues such as Robert Ricci, head of public relations for the Chambre Syndicale and son of the couturier Nina Ricci, dreamed up a brilliantly original scheme to create a Petit Théâtre de la Mode, harking back to an eighteenth-century practice of presenting fashion to the world by means of dressed dolls. The plan was to dress up 170 scaled-down figures, one-third of human size, made of wire with porcelain heads, in clothes fashioned by at least fifty of the great Parisian couture houses, including Cristóbal Balenciaga, Jacques Fath, Jean Patou and Elsa Schiaparelli, all desperate to revive their pre-war fortunes. The dolls, wearing real jewellery designed to scale by Boucheron, Cartier and Van Cleef, and lingerie that could not be seen but which was delicately stitched on, were mounted on sets created by designers such as Jean Cocteau and Christian Bérard. It was an entirely Paris-based initiative, an unashamed attempt to reassert quickly the dominance of French high fashion and to demonstrate the superiority of French creativity. And it was supported by the newly created French Ministry of Reconstruction partly because, while the country's economy was in ruins, it provided employment for the hundreds of ancillary seamstresses and bead-makers, craftsmen and artisans involved in the textile industry, and partly because it was a way of bringing much needed dollars into the country to rebuild its shattered industrial base. For hours, days and weeks everyone worked, often without heat, with little electricity and meagre food supplies, to create the tiny shoes, handbags, belts, gloves and bags, all meticulously crafted – often, given the shortages of fabric, from scraps. Top hairdressers were brought in to create elegant wigs from a mixture of human hair and glass thread.

The show opened at the Louvre in Paris on 28 March 1945, and was enormously popular, attracting more than 100,000 visitors, as well as raising a million francs for French war relief. Plans were put into operation to tour the exhibition, which moved to London in early December, followed by Leeds, New York and San Francisco, as well as Copenhagen, Stockholm and Vienna the following year. For many British women, whose wartime clothes had been guided by comfort, restraint and deliberately sober severity, such a lavish display, often impractical and overtly sexy, was perplexing.

And all the while the trials continued. In the months following the Liberation until 1 July 1949, as part of the *épuration légale* (as opposed to the *épuration sauvage*), the High Court handed down 108 judgements, eighteen of which involved the death sentence. Taking into account other official courts in France, 6,763 people were sentenced to death (3,910 *in absentia*) for treason and other offences. Only 791 executions were actually carried out as, in addition to those who had escaped, several of those sentenced had died in the interim. The majority of defendants were sentenced to *dégradation nationale*, a punishment introduced at the Liberation which involved loss of political, civil and professional rights and that was handed out to those found guilty of *indignité nationale*. The most high-profile of all was the one-day trial at the beginning of the year of Robert Brasillach, novelist, poet, playwright and editor-in-chief of the fascist paper *Je suis partout*. Brasillach, erstwhile admirer of Irène Némirovsky, had launched wounding attacks on republicans, communists, Jews and foreigners. For a time he was France's most envied and reviled writer. But on 19 January 1945, on trial for his life, he was unrepentant, convinced by the scenes of brutality at the Liberation that these 'horrible things show what the Occupation might have been like for four years if there hadn't been calm, collaborationists, a Vichy government'.

Unlike fellow collaborationist journalists and politicians, Brasillach did not make any attempt to flee but decided he would tough it out, insisting that he was a patriot, loyal to the constitutional Vichy government. He was helped by Marguerite Cravoisier, a woman from his home town of Sens in Burgundy, who had been in love – unrequited – with Brasillach for years and, understanding the dangers he faced, had already prepared a hideout for him in the maid's quarters of a building in Paris near the Sénat. Cocooned here for a month, he did not know that an armed-resistance group of the FFI had arrested his mother and thrown her into jail, where she was detained with political prisoners and those accused of *collaboration horizontale*. When he learned this, he immediately handed himself in to the police. His trial, in a special court of justice for treason (for the offence known as 'intelligence with the enemy') revealed something of the hypocrisy raging amid the current vengeful frenzy in Paris. The judge, who had served Vichy, may have thought he could exonerate himself by condemning Brasillach. After twenty-five minutes' deliberation, the jury, all veterans of the resistance Brasillach had so vehemently denounced, called for the death sentence.

One of the new breed of young journalists who wrote about the trial was Arlette Grebel, a twenty-year-old graduate of the Paris journalism college who made her name reporting on the scenes of Liberation for *France Libre*. Grebel was lucky to graduate first in her class at a time of enormous opportunity; the collaborationist press was being closed down and the events on the street were of unrivalled excitement. She was so inexperienced that when she was sent to cover the trial of Charles Maurras, the extreme right-wing philosopher behind Action Française, she did not even know who he was. The Liberation provided a window of opportunity for young women such as Grebel. As Simone de Beauvoir, who was present at the Brasillach trial and who wrote about it in an extended essay the following year, commented: 'to be 20 or 25 in September of '44 seemed the most fantastic piece of luck: all roads lay open. Journalists, writers, budding film makers were all arguing, planning passionately, deciding as if the future depended on no one but themselves.' Grebel, with her little white bobby socks and short skirts, perfectly encapsulated the widespread idea that France had a chance to start afresh with younger people and create a future untainted by wartime rivalries.

De Gaulle, asked to consider a plea for mercy, upheld the sentence, later explaining that 'in literature as in everything, talent confers responsibility'. Brasillach was hanged on 6 February 1945, aged thirty-five. De Beauvoir had refused to sign the petition for clemency, arguing that although she opposed the death penalty in principle, in his case death was justified. But the position of de Beauvoir herself during the Occupation had been far from uncomplicated, and it is tempting to explain her especially intense hatred of intellectual collaborators such as Brasillach in the light of her recognition that he had been active in creating the world in which she too found herself to be complicit. A committed anti-Nazi, she had nonetheless managed to eat well for most of the last four years thanks partly to her relationship with Jean-Paul Sartre, whose mother continued to serve all the best black-market foods while sending her maid to stand in queues. De Beauvoir herself, once she worked for the German-controlled Radio-Paris, also had access to black-market foods which enabled her to entertain guests, including Picasso and Dora Maar, offering them 'bowls of green beans and heaped dishes of beef stew, and I always took care to have plenty of wine'. She and Sartre may have voiced opposition to the occupiers and did not attend the openly German-supported salons of Florence Gould, but de Beauvoir signed the Vichy-inspired oath stating that she was neither a Jew nor a communist so that she could teach, and she continued to publish under conditions of Nazi censorship while other writers refused, thus working within the German system in Paris. Sartre in particular, by stepping into the shoes of Henri Dreyfus-Le Foyer, a Jewish teacher (and a great-nephew of Captain Dreyfus) who had been dismissed from the Lycée Condorcet, arguably profited from the war.

In March came the turn of Florence Gould herself. Recognizing her ambiguous position, she had made a generous donation to the FFI immediately after the Liberation and now invited passing Americans to her Thursday lunches. She still had to face a French investigating magistrate. In the event, she was not interrogated about her friendly relations with Germans, but rather was asked why she had invested in a Nazi-financed bank in Monaco late in 1944. Gould maintained in a sworn statement that she had been blackmailed into becoming a partner in the Banque Charles, claiming that, had she refused, her husband's companies would have had to pay a far larger sum to the Aerobank, a Luftwaffe-controlled bank with links to the Banque Charles. She had acted in the way she had, she claimed, because she believed that 'M. Charles could keep my husband, who was especially threatened, out of danger. He was sixty-seven and in fragile health and I feared he might be forced to leave his home at Juan les Pins and, as an enemy alien, be taken to Germany.' She insisted that her actions had not in any way been 'against the interests of the Allies'. She was not charged, and the salons continued. However, three years later the case was reopened, and a new report gave a more plausible account of the bank's purpose as being not so much to help the German war effort but rather to channel German money abroad either to establish a Fourth Reich or to provide cash in the event of a Nazi defeat. Again Florence was not charged, but this report concluded that she, 'a Franco-American, appears to have enjoyed singular protections during the Occupation and, if it's not certain that she committed the crime of 'intelligence with the enemy', it is certain that we have no reason to congratulate her for her attitude'. Florence was extremely lucky.*

There was, however, a greater sense of urgency in the chase to catch those who had openly fulfilled Nazi policies. In September 1944, immediately after the Liberation of Paris and in some cases before, some Vichy government leaders including Fernand de Brinon (who had managed to shelter his Jewish wife), Pétain, Laval and several senior collaborators such as Céline, Lucien Rebatet, Jean Luchaire and his daughter Corinne had all fled to Sigmaringen, a village in southern Germany where, based in a German castle, they established a government in exile. However, just as American forces were approaching in April 1945 Laval was flown to Barcelona by the Luftwaffe but, under pressure from de Gaulle, the Spanish government delivered him to the American-occupied zone of Austria. There he and his wife were taken into custody, turned over to the French army and flown to Paris, where they were imprisoned at Fresnes. Mme Laval was later released but her husband remained in prison, awaiting trial as a traitor. Pétain handed himself over to French authorities on 26 April.

During his imprisonment Laval wrote his only book, a posthumously published *Diary* (1948), which his daughter Josée, determined to prove his innocence, smuggled out of the prison, page by page. Laval firmly believed that he would be able to convince his fellow countrymen that he had been acting in their best interests all along, a view Josée and her mother held with a passion. 'They lived in a fever, where agony was mixed with hope. They were busy with pleas, interviews, telephone calls, whatever they could do to save Laval from death.' One of those whose help Josée tried to enlist was the

---

* Eugène Charles, the Swiss businessman behind Banque Charles, turned out to have been Count Albrecht von Urach, then working at the German Embassy in Berne, who had been involved in smuggling capital out of Switzerland to the US via the bank in Monaco, where his second cousin Louis II was on the throne. He was interned in May 1945 but escaped further punishment.

celebrated Catholic author François Mauriac, who commented that if ever there was a desperate case this was it. 'I shall never forget,' wrote Mauriac, 'the admirable daughter of Pierre Laval coming to me one evening as if I could save her father ... Pierre Laval had in a way assumed all the hatreds, even those of the partisans of the Marshal. Never was a scapegoat more bitterly condemned – less for what he did than for what he said.'

Josée did her best to assemble the most experienced team of defence lawyers, while her husband, René de Chambrun, having largely spent the war in America, now returned to support his wife and father-in-law. He assured the press that, with enough time to summon documents and witnesses from abroad, Laval could refute all charges. Laval's short trial – one that a number of historians believe today was deeply flawed, reflecting the poisonous political atmosphere in France at the time – began on 5 October 1945 and lasted just over a week. He was found guilty and sentenced to death. Following a failed suicide attempt – Laval swallowed poison so old that it failed to work adequately and he was revived by use of a stomach pump – he was executed by firing squad on 15 October. His was one of just three death penalties imposed on politicians in the following four years.*

The instant the verdict was announced, Josée, apparently, was seized by fright. She was 'stricken like a wounded animal. The brilliant light of those extraordinary eyes was suddenly extinguished as she stared blankly at all those around her and at a fate she could not accept.' But she quickly recovered. Childless, she devoted the rest of her life to the fight to clear her father's name, and to caring for her dogs. In the grounds of the family mansion at Châteldon in central France, she had a well-tended dog cemetery resembling those surrounding ancient village churches. Each pet, having died of natural causes, had its own engraved tombstone. There was Barye (1890), Pompée (1891), Madou (1908), Brutus (1909), all buried before she was born. But then came 'Whisky, 1948–1962, the issue of Soko,

---

* The others were Fernand de Brinon, Vichy's Ambassador in Paris to the German authorities, and Joseph Darnand, head of the Milice. The death penalty for Pétain was not carried out because of his age.

loyal friend of my father'. It was seeing the tombstone for a dog that
had once belonged to Pierre Laval, the man who said in his own
defence that he had encouraged the deportation of children under
the age of sixteen in order that families should not be separated, that
prompted the author Philippe Grimbert, son of Holocaust victims,
to realize that part of his ongoing trauma resulted from the fact that
his dead half-brother and mother had never been remembered properly. The thought that even Pierre Laval's dogs were being honoured
in death so outraged Grimbert that he was inspired to write a bestselling autobiographical novel called *A Secret*.

Josée de Chambrun died in 1992, at which point her husband
handed over her papers to Yves Pourcher, her biographer. According
to Pourcher, her faith in her father was like a religion. 'She never
accepted that he had had a fair trial and battled to the end. She had
a limitless admiration for her father.'

There were not many people, other than daughters and wives, prepared to speak up for those on trial for collaboration. And sometimes
families turned upon one another. Agnès Humbert, a member of the
early Musée de l'Homme resistance group, had survived a sentence
of five years' slave labour at Anrath prison in Germany. Forced to
work in gruesome conditions at a nearby rayon factory where many
workers went blind, she survived against the odds and was freed
by American troops in early 1945. She then worked alongside these
troops for two months, setting up soup kitchens and first-aid posts
for German civilians, returning to Paris eventually in the summer.
There she learned that one of her sons, Jean Sabbagh, a naval lieutenant, had spent two days following the Liberation under arrest in
Bordeaux because of his position there during 1944 in charge of the
Harbour Police. She wrote to Jean: 'Monsieur, I understand that you
[she used the formal 'vous'] were arrested for collaboration with the
enemy. Henceforth you will therefore no longer consider yourself as
my son.' Some months later there was a reconciliation of sorts. But
irreparable damage had been done to the family.

One of those who went out of her way to help a collaborator was
Simone Signoret, schoolfriend of Corinne Luchaire, when she heard
that both father and daughter had been arrested in May and were
awaiting trial in Fresnes. Simone was by 1945 'an actress without a

contract, a future unwed mother'. André Kaminker, Simone's Jewish father, had now returned to France with the Free French to find, as Simone put it, his 'pretty child pregnant thanks to the labours of a director who had never directed anything and, just to round everything off, was the younger brother of Colonel Allégret, who was my father's direct superior in the chain of command that led to General de Gaulle'. Reminding her father how her job at Luchaire's paper *Les Nouveaux Temps* had been so critical for a time in ensuring his family did not starve, she immediately asked him to file a deposition in support of Jean Luchaire, 'the same Luchaire who had provided his family with a livelihood for a little while'.

The Luchaires both spent the rest of that year in various prisons. Corinne, ill from tuberculosis, had tried to commit suicide but remained heedless of the implications of her friendship with Nazis, asking constantly, what did I do wrong, what did my family do wrong? When she complained about how badly she had been treated in French prisons after the Liberation, accusing French officers of speaking to her harshly and not providing enough milk for her baby, she revealed the vacuum in which she had lived during the Occupation, oblivious of how the Germans had treated other detained women. But then, as the deportees now slowly dragging themselves back were soon to find, oblivion was the religion of many others in Paris.

By June 1945 the returnees included both Jews and political prisoners from the camps, as well as prisoners of war. They arrived by the trainload, mostly at the Gare de l'Est, and were greeted by uniformed women recruited to the newly formed Repatriation Service who referred to the prisoners of war as 'the poor boys, the poor boys', while a loudspeaker played 'La Marseillaise'. The writer Marguerite Duras, anxiously awaiting news of her husband Robert Antelme in Dachau, captured a moment when one of these 'ladies', pointing to her stripes, scolded a soldier:

'So my friend – we're not saluting? Can't you see I'm a captain,' she said.
    The soldier looked at her. 'Me, when I see a skirt, I don't salute her, I fuck her.' The lady, in shock, beat a dignified retreat.

Duras conveyed brilliantly in her writings the fevered anguish, 'the throbbing in the temples', of wives waiting for husbands, mothers for sons. Would there be a phone call, a ring on the doorbell, a letter? Would a fellow prisoner bring bad news? Or might he telephone directly, himself, without warning? Was it safe to go out, just in case?

And then she heard from Antelme's friend François Mitterrand (whom she refers to under a pseudonym, Morland):

> I do not know what day it was, it was definitely one day in April, it was not a day in May. At eleven o'clock the telephone rang. It came from Germany, it was François Morland. He did not say 'Hello', it was almost brutal, but clear as ever.
>
> 'Listen to me. Robert is alive. Calm down. Yes. He is at Dachau. Listen again with all your strength. Robert is very feeble to a level that you cannot imagine. I must tell you, it is a matter of hours. He can live perhaps three days, but no longer.'

As it turned out the liberation of Dachau came just in time for the seriously ill Robert Antelme. He survived and returned to France on 13 May 1945. His sister, Marie-Louise Antelme, who had been deported to Ravensbrück, did not return. Duras later recalled the 'smile of embarrassment' of her husband upon their reunion after wartime separation: 'He's apologizing for being here, reduced to such a wreck. And then the smile fades and he becomes a stranger again.' Antelme returned to Paris weighing 86 pounds and for three weeks wavered between life and death. The story 'Did Not Die Deported' plots Duras's agonizing wait for him and the almost more appalling account of tending his damaged and bony body back to health. For months he had eaten nothing but grass and earth. 'Had he eaten solid food on returning from the camp his stomach would have ruptured under its weight.'

Duras deliberately gave graphic details of her husband's bodily functions, and concluded: 'Those who wince at this very moment, reading this, those whom it nauseates – I shit on them. I hope one day they encounter a man whose body will empty out like that through its anus and I hope that man is the most beautiful and beloved and desirable thing they have. Their lover. I wish that kind of devastation on them.'

Many of the women, once released, made their way directly to the Lutetia, the vast, Art Deco hotel on the Left Bank straddling the Boulevard Raspail and the Rue de Sèvres, built in the more confident days of 1910. In September 1939 the hotel housed numerous refugees, including several artists and musicians fleeing to Paris ahead of German forces. But when Paris fell, the Germans requisitioned the hotel, and its fine cellar was enjoyed by German military intelligence, the Abwehr, who used it as a base. At the Liberation it was converted into a chaotic repatriation centre for prisoners of war, displaced persons and returnees from German camps, many of whom had not slept in beds for years and were unable to do so now, some still wearing their striped prison garb. Accounts of relatives coming daily with hopeful eyes to post requests or scan lists are among the most agonizing of all occupation and war stories. They throw long shadows. In many cases the desperation, illness, suicide and death come years later, beyond the timeframe of this book. Few stories in real life had a happy or straightforward ending, as the tale of Marguerite Duras well illustrates. In 1942 she and Antelme had a stillborn child, and soon after this tragedy she began a love affair with a mutual friend, Dionys Mascolo, which continued while Antelme was imprisoned in the camps. In 1945 Mascolo helped nurse Antelme back to health, but Duras and Antelme divorced in 1946 and the following year she and Mascolo had a son, Jean.

As well as losing loved ones, many had to face the further grief on their return arising from the loss of all their possessions, often with no one still alive to help. Looting furniture, not just fine works of art but everyday household objects, predominantly from Jews, had been a major preoccupation of the German occupiers. The confiscation was partly to dehumanize those from whom it had been stolen and partly to provide small luxuries for German citizens at home and soldiers in the colonized east. It was another sphere where the Germans had been assisted by willing collaboration from the Vichy regime and French civilians to create what they considered was a proper process. Although occasionally concierges (and friends, such as Jeanne Bucher in the case of Vieira da Silva) managed to protect empty Jewish homes, when the dwellings were looted it was the concierge, usually female, who was asked to witness the removal of the goods by Parisian removal companies, thus giving authority to the theft; but she might already have helped herself in advance. Between July 1943 and August 1944 nearly 800 prisoners spent anything from a few weeks to a year in one of the storage warehouses, where they were subjected to forced labour, mostly sorting furniture and objects seized by the Germans.[*]

The vast scope of the looting may not have been acknowledged at the time amid the general wartime chaos, but tens of thousands of homes had been completely emptied between 1942 and 1944. A report by Kurt von Behr, dated 31 July 1944, mentions a total of 69,619 dwellings emptied, 38,000 of which were in Paris. As the Germans retreated in the summer of 1944, some goods were simply abandoned in these warehouses, and it was here that the provisional government made a start in the long and painful process of restitution for returnees, almost all of whom were Jewish. Returning small items of furniture was a less traumatic process than giving back disputed homes, as it required no dispossession of current users but, at a time of scarce resources and personnel, reuniting furniture and other objects with their rightful owners was an exceptionally fraught task. Some argued that it might have been easier simply to distribute any abandoned goods to whomever seemed most in need, of whom there were thousands, and, from November 1944, some such warehouses were set up. But it was never enough. When twenty-year-old Frida Wattenberg returned to the family flat in 1944 she found not only the furniture and all personal possessions gone but even the light switches had been dismantled to remove the copper. At the same time as the new government, determined to impose unity on the country, was trying to enforce an *ordonnance* of November 1944 to return expropriated goods, there were also dozens of associations set

---

* Already in 1943 Isaac Schneersohn in Grenoble had begun creating in secret what became the Centre de Documentation Juive Contemporaine (CDJC) with the specific purpose of documenting the seizure of Jewish goods to support restitution claims once the war was over. For a fuller account see Jean-Marc Dreyfus and Sarah Gensberger's *Nazi Labour Camps in Paris: Austerlitz, Lévitan, Bassano, July 1943–August 1944* Oxford, Berghahn Books, 2011.

up that aimed to legitimize certain French wartime acquisitions and make them permanent. The Union Confédérale des Locataires de France petitioned the authorities in August 1945, threatening that if the government attempted to enforce the *ordonnance* it would risk 'strengthening the already existing strains of anti-Semitism in the country'.

However, after many setbacks, including the fact that some 135,000 lots of stolen goods had been sold off before their owners had had a chance to claim them, so that some Jews had to resort to buying their possessions back from the French state as the only way of reclaiming them, legislation was passed and a budget allocated for the newly created Service de Restitution des Biens Spoliés (SRBS).

In addition, two organizations set up to prevent any return of Jewish properties were banned by the government in April 1945. But as Leora Auslander makes clear in her poignant and revelatory article, 'Coming Home? Jews in Postwar Paris', 'These everyday furnishings were only the tip of the iceberg: lying just beneath the surface were the confiscated bank accounts, libraries, art collections, businesses, stocks and bonds and dwellings of Jews resident in France in 1940. Working out restitution or compensation for these goods (and reparations for trauma and loss of life) is still an ongoing enterprise.' Admittedly, France was not the only country facing the post-war problems of homelessness and dispossession, and within France both Jews and non-Jews suffered. 'But the experience of returning Jews was special because, whereas non-Jews were dispossessed by a foreign enemy, Jews were excluded from what they had thought was their home by people they had understood to be their fellow citizens and in some cases, their neighbours . . . Even more painful for returnees was the response of their fellow Parisians to their efforts to come home.'

In the face of strong opposition from those determined to keep hold of their wartime booty – frequently women proud of what they had managed to come by – the system for restoration required returnees seeking to reclaim goods to write explaining their situation, to submit a precise inventory of the contents of their home at the moment of departure and to provide a confirmation from the concierge, owner or manager of the building that the goods had been confiscated. It was made clear to claimants that unless the pillage had occurred in the final phase of the Occupation, that is after spring 1944, it was unlikely that anything would be recovered in Paris because before that most objects had been swiftly shipped out.

As Auslander shows, among the tens of thousands of returnees who filed petitions between the autumn of 1944 and 1947, there was a wide range of claimants, including men and women, French and foreign, rich and poor, very few of whom recovered the objects that had so painstakingly been bought or, freighted with emotion, transported to Paris from other countries or inherited. Historians estimate that only about 20 per cent of the contents of pillaged homes was ever recovered. And yet, this double dispossession struck at the heart of what it meant to be French and what it meant to be surrounded by domestic objects which defined identity, who one was and how one lived. Although men were often the petitioners, the creation of the domestic space was (and remains in many cultures) predominantly a female activity, and the need to recreate, through objects, the life they once had was pressing. As the increasingly hopeless and emotionally fraught petitions continued well into 1947, the sentiment of many changed from hope to anger.

Most returnees, Jews and non-Jews alike, having dreamed of the day they would return to Paris, were filled with deep disappointment when they actually arrived. 'We were, like thousands of deportees, certain that we had been forgotten and above all certain that several people might have wished never to see us again,' Jacqueline Marié recounted. 'There was a general lack of excitement on seeing the deportees return and not knowing who among them had collaborated and who had done nothing. We felt we had returned to a different planet. We had nothing but rags, we weighed 36 kilos and had barely any skin covering our bones.' All the women returnees looked strange – gaunt, wild-eyed and often with shaven heads and a sense of disorientation. Many were also ill and needed months if not years of medical treatment. Jacqueline added, 'We came to the Gare de l'Est where we were given ten francs and taken to the Hôtel Lutetia where we had a room and were given an assortment of ill-fitting clothes and a Métro ticket. But we had to take the mattress off the bed as it was too soft. We were used to a hard floor.' When Jacqueline and her mother returned to the family apartment in Versailles they found it had been looted, but at least it was theirs. M. Marié, Jacqueline's father, was there, still alive, but he had suffered dreadfully and never fully recovered. 'When I recounted what we had been through,' Jacqueline said, 'no one believed us. They thought the camps had a canteen like a "soldiers' mess" to eat in, and we were given beefsteak and chips. It was such a gulf so I stopped talking about what had happened to us.'

Another Ravensbrück returnee, Michèle Agniel, recounted how, since she could barely stand, she was given a permit to jump the queues for rationed food. 'But when I did, a man complained, so I said I had just come back from a concentration camp. He said, "*Mais quand même*, they know how to queue in concentration camps, don't they?" I hit him.' Some tried to explain the gulf of misunderstanding. François Mauriac wrote: 'It is a mistake to think that the public avoids accounts such as this because it has heard them too often. The truth is that it has never listened to a single one to the end, and it makes it clear that it does not want the subject brought up.'

Simone Veil, the Jewish lawyer and politician who had survived Auschwitz but on her return to Paris found her father, her brother and one sister had been killed, spoke of 'being forgotten' as a second death. Marceline Rozenberg (later Loridan-Ivens) felt muted in the same way. 'Don't say anything, they won't understand,' she was told when she arrived back. Just fifteen years old when she was arrested with her Polish-born father, she had witnessed more horror than any child (or adult) could cope with, together with the knowledge that an uncle, who had killed a German in Paris, had subsequently jumped out of a window at the Rue des Saussaies rather than confess under torture. In the next eighteen months she managed to survive three camps: Auschwitz-Birkenau, Bergen-Belsen and finally Theresienstadt.

'When I returned in July 1945 to the Lutetia I had become a savage. I was like a wild child. We were rock hard, like stone – we had to become human again.' Similarly another woman, explaining that the reason she had survived deportation was because she had learned to steal, never forgot how shocked her aunt had been to hear that her well-brought-up niece had become a thief. But in the camps stealing was merely taking whatever you could find in order to survive. It was called 'organizing', and life or death might depend on being able to organize a spoon.

Marceline was able to articulate only much later, aged eighty-six, how after the camps there could be no more humanity inside her: she had killed off the little girl she had been. When she finally wrote her memoir, *Et tu n'es pas revenu* (You Did Not Come Back) – a reference to her adored father – published in 2015, she explained that in order to survive it was necessary to destroy memory. 'If you cried for others, you would drown in tears.' She had, she explained, been forced to do the work of death itself in the camps. She had become death's tool. For years, she was never able to talk of the work she had been forced to do in the camps: dig shallow trenches in which to burn the corpses of women. She would say instead she had dug trenches in which to grow vegetables. Only very recently was she able to admit: 'I didn't have a choice but I did it. And the simple act of doing it has meaning. I participated like the collaborators did.'

Marceline wrote movingly not only of the guilt of survival but of why it was impossible for others, even close family, to understand. 'Very quickly, Mother asked me in a low voice if I had been raped. Was I still a virgin? Good for marriage? That was her question.' She believed that the intense post-war desire to rebuild, to let life continue its course with weddings and babies, even when many of those who should have been there to celebrate were absent, was a Jewish madness. Two years after her release from Theresienstadt, the year her brother married, Marceline threw herself into the Seine. Saved by a stranger, she later suffered from TB and was sent to recover in a sanatorium in Switzerland.

Marceline was one of a convoy of 1,500 sent out to Germany of whom 100 returned, a statistic that illustrates one of the lingering problems in France, arguably never resolved: the disparity among those who came back. Half of those deported for resistance activities returned, but only 3 per cent of the Jews (2,500 out of 76,000 deported), an unwelcome statistic for those in France denying that a genocide had taken place. Yet the attitude which saw resisters as patriots who had been involved in combat entitled to a higher level of compensation than the deported Jews, perceived as victims, persisted at least until the end of the twentieth century in some quarters, and derives from the problem of what the French historian Henry Rousso later identified as *résistancialisme* to describe the myth which exaggerated French involvement in the resistance to the Nazi Occupation and played down the role of collaboration. But it also fed into the notion that to have been deported as a resister was noble, but to have fallen into German hands as a victim was shameful. 'Even the dead, guilty of passivity, were not immune from this shame, for they had allowed themselves to be corralled by the anti-Semitic laws.'[*]

Philippe de Rothschild was another who went to the Lutetia that summer, seeking news of his wife.

> A group of French women had just arrived not long out of Ravensbrück. They looked as if they had risen from the grave. Among them one recognized me. I looked again, it was Tania, Comtesse de Fleurieu, a brave woman in the resistance. She had been very lovely but now all her teeth were smashed. They had beaten her across the mouth. She knew about Lili [Elisabeth], she had been there, in the same hut. Beaten, degraded and too broken to move, Lili had been dragged from her plank bed by the hair of her head and thrown into the oven alive. She died because she had borne my name. There was no doubt about that . . . I did not make any more enquiries and to this day I have never received official notification of her death . . . poor pretty woman, until they came for her that morning her life had been so easy, all silk and roses.

She was the only member of the Rothschild family to be killed in the Holocaust. After the war Odette Fabius had dinner with Elisabeth de Rothschild's sister-in-law, who asked her what had happened in the camp. 'I told her about the work there but she understood nothing. When I said that for two years we had to build roads and clear

---

[*] See also Annette Wieviorka who wrote about the disparity in the way resistance fighters and holocaust victims were commemorated in France in *Déportation et Génocide: Entre la mémoire et l'oubli*.

up dead bodies and shit the sister-in-law said to me: "Hmm . . . she never even carried her own suitcase. How could she carry a spade?" Was she expecting me to smile?'

Many of the prisoners were given ill-fitting clothes for their return, items that had turned up in a hoard confiscated by the camp authorities, but Denise Dufournier, the lawyer, now desperately thin and psychologically damaged like all the others, arrived at the Lutetia via Switzerland in a ballgown. Later, she would enjoy making a joke of this, dark humour being part of her armour in post-war years, as her daughters would come to recognize. Dufournier was both a published novelist and a lawyer used to living independently when she was arrested, which gave her 'a forensic ability to see things clearly and dissect them'. Within months of her return, recognizing immediately the total lack of comprehension on the part of other Parisians, who regularly told her that they had had a 'jolly tough time in the city', she escaped to a cousin's house in Anjou where she had, before the war, written a romantic novel. There she immediately started writing about Ravensbrück.

'She felt she was carrying a burden and had to get it all done before the stories were corrupted. She was determined never to forget.' The book, *La Maison des Mortes*, published in 1945 by Hachette, was one of the first accounts of the camps and therefore bore an extraordinary and horrific freshness as well as being a solemn, factual account thanks to Dufournier's legal training and good memory. She was 'fortunate', as publishers would soon stop accepting such manuscripts from deportees, believing that a largely indifferent public was not yet ready to hear, or would not believe. Dufournier was especially driven by a need to document the atrocious treatment of the so-called *lapins*. These were the young, formerly healthy, Polish girls who had been used for crippling and barbaric pseudo-medical experimentation, such as Hella, who continually suffered in the camp from bits of bone emerging out of her leg. But, having written the book, Denise now wanted to rebuild her life. 'The one thing she longed for was normal family life,' and in 1946 she married James McAdam Clark, a British scientist turned diplomat she had met in London in 1939 and who had served in the Royal Artillery in North Africa and Italy during the war. She even turned down an invitation to attend as a

Denise Dufournier on her honeymoon in Monte Carlo, 1946

witness the Hamburg trials of Ravensbrück guards, which began at the end of 1946. She remained close to Hella for years afterwards; indeed, according to her daughters, all her closest friends after the war dated from that time and were in some way connected to these shared experiences.

Similarly, Germaine de Renty did not at first want to see any of her friends from 'before'. She was one of those only just saved by the efforts of Count Bernadotte and the Swedish Red Cross, who took her, first, to recuperate in Malmö in May 1945, but then she also returned to the Hôtel Lutetia with the standard Métro ticket allowance. Once home, she was unable for months to talk about the horrors she had witnessed.

'She could not speak and I dared not ask,' commented her daughter, Claude. 'I respected her silence. She too slept on the floor at the side of her bed because she was unused to such comforts as a soft mattress and space to turn.' In Ravensbrück she had shared her thirty-inch board with two others, a young student and a communist, and these at first were her post-war friends. 'Slowly she started to recover what initially were automatic responses like getting herself dressed in the morning and making breakfast for her children and then the arrival of her first grandchild. She had to become mother and father as her husband (my father) had perished at Ellrich [concentration camp].'

She said it was painful for all the survivors to 'reconnect with a world which had lived without you, children who didn't know you, families who thought you were dead'. Those who saw her in the camp remembered that what kept her going was a belief that she had to return to bring up her daughter. So Claude understood that their life from then on needed to re-establish the bonds that had been ruptured in the year spent apart, and she recognized too that the most important thing for her mother was the need to listen to those others who had suffered with her the same shame of hunger and dysentery, the fear and ever present despair, in order to try and pick up an ordinary life once again. 'No one who had not witnessed this hell could understand, only those who had, became her new world.' On one never to be forgotten occasion Claude overheard an old friend comment, 'So, life at Ravensbrück wasn't quite so bad as they'd have us believe then?' My mother replied in an icy tone, 'Every morning we had to step across the remains of those who had died in the night as the rats would start with the eyes.'

There was a range of reasons for the women's silence that in some cases lasted their entire lives. Some could not speak of the camps because it was a hell they wanted to expunge from their minds; others because of the shame of surviving, the shame that it might be assumed they had been raped or had collaborated in the camp or the feeling that they were in some way responsible for their fate. They did not want to speak and others did not want to listen. According to the historian Debra Workman: 'Unable or unwilling to believe the accounts, an often indifferent public was not yet ready to hear their testimonies, and by 1947, editors no longer accepted the manuscripts of the deportees.' Fellow historian Annette Wieviorka summarized the nation's difficulty in responding to the deportation in the early post-war years with a statement that the deportees attributed to several editors: 'Enough of cadavers! Enough of torture! Enough of stories of the resistance! We need to laugh now!'

And so, in November 1945, at the first meeting of the survivors' group called ADIR (Association Nationale des Anciennes Déportées et Internées de la Résistance) it was quickly recognized that the organization should be for women only, and only those who had been deported to the camps because of their work in the resistance, and that their first duty should be to testify. They preferred, at a time when the public perception of the resistance was unashamedly masculine, to keep the organization small and focused on allowing members to extend the links established in the camps, to provide moral, medical and social support to all survivors as well as honouring the memory of their dead comrades. They knew that their experience had been peculiar to them and could not be shared with a male group whose suffering might have been equally appalling but was different. This was not about promoting their actions, about which they remained modest, to the world at large. One of their most important activities was always to bear witness on behalf of those who had not survived.*

ADIR grew out of two experiences: on the one hand that of the Amicale des Prisonnières de la Résistance (APR), which united a small group of female resisters who had been imprisoned in Paris during the summer of 1942 and had recruited friends and family members to prepare care packages for women they had befriended in prison, especially for those alone and scheduled for deportation; and on the other hand, the experience of the deportees in Ravensbrück. Having foreseen the difficulties many would face in returning to a normal life, given their grave physical and mental state, they had decided to form an organization as soon as possible to provide aid and support to the survivors.

Geneviève de Gaulle, niece of the new French leader, within weeks of leaving the Swiss sanatorium where she had gone to recuperate, began to hold a series of meetings with prominent Swiss citizens to raise awareness of the deportees' plight and of the need for long-term convalescence that many would require. At the same time fellow deportee Irène Delmas, who had been one of the first to

* This continued into the late twentieth century in the face of neo-Nazis or Holocaust-deniers. Germaine Tillion and Anise Postel-Vinay gave written testimony in 1984, four decades after they had been there, that there had been a gas chamber at Ravensbrück at least from late January or early February 1945 to late April that year, published in *Les Chambres à gaz, secret d'Etat*, Paris, Editions de Minuit, 1984.

be released, was already working to hand out care packages. While in Switzerland, de Gaulle and Delmas met and, realizing that they shared a vision, decided to merge the two groups. The women of the ADIR did not view themselves as agents of change nor as political actors; rather, they identified themselves personally and collectively as 'patriots' – the wives, mothers and daughters of France who had voluntarily taken the same risks as the men in defence of their country; had suffered the same punishments, and now had united to care for one another and obtain the rights and recognition that they had legitimately earned. Their intense wartime experiences transformed these women, and after the war many of them continued to operate outside the traditional roles assumed by French women.

As Debra Workman has explained:

At a time when women in France had only just received the right to vote and still remained legally under the guardianship of their husbands and fathers, the women of ADIR chose to organize themselves on the basis of gender, as formerly imprisoned women resisters, independent of established political parties and direct institutional affiliation. This choice reflected their awareness of their unique circumstances and their belief that their wartime activism had been little understood or accepted. Their conviction that no one would speak for them if they did not do so for themselves determined the 'innovative character' of the ADIR from its inception.

ADIR managed to bridge the huge social chasm among its members, a bridge that had already been built in the camps where countesses and factory workers might share a bed and supported each other in myriad ways, and this remarkable organization became the principal means through which most female political deportees re-established their post-war lives.

It was not just in publishing but in the arts generally that there was a conscious effort to move on, a belief in recovery through renewal. *Les Enfants du paradis* was shot during the German Occupation, mostly in Nice, directed by Marcel Carné, starring Arletty and Jean-Louis

Barrault, and involving the talents of many 'secret' Jews in hiding, including set designer Alexandre Trauner and composer Joseph Kosma, both Hungarian Jews who worked clandestinely under assumed names. Many of the film's approximately 1,800 extras were also Jews for whom the work was valuable daytime cover. Set among the Parisian theatrical world of the 1820s and 1830s, this melodrama took months to make and was constantly running into difficulties – practical, bureaucratic and financial – but was finished at the end of 1944 amid enormous expectations. Given the tempestuous times, the premiere was delayed until 9 March 1945, one of the first after the Liberation when, with the end of the war in sight, it helped to restore national pride in the indomitable spirit of French culture. Hailed as France's own version of *Gone with the Wind*, it sought to demonstrate the supremacy of French cinema over Hollywood. French audiences found the film deeply symbolic, seeing it not just as a homage to love but specifically as a demonstration of the freedom enjoyed by Garance, the main character played by Arletty, a woman loved by four men, to choose whom to love and on her own terms. Ironically, Arletty was by then incarcerated in her chateau as punishment for her relationship with Soehring, and was forced to miss the premiere. Nonetheless, the film was a spectacular box-office hit, shown at the Madeleine Theatre for fifty-four consecutive weeks, and it has since acquired legendary status.

Jeanne Bucher, who had done so much bravely to support modern French art during the Occupation, began the year crippled with sadness by the news that her beloved grandson, Pierre, had been killed in action. Facing the almost insupportable task of continuing to live, she nonetheless immersed herself in work by continuing to organize exhibitions in her Montparnasse Gallery of artists the Nazis had banned. In April she had a show for Nicolas de Staël and another in the spring for Dora Maar, Picasso's spurned and unhappy mistress.

After the Liberation there had been a major Picasso exhibition at the Musée d'Art Moderne which formed part of the Salon d'Automne that year. As Françoise Gilot, the young woman who had recently become Picasso's lover, commented, 'Since Picasso was painter number one on the German index, the first revenge to take on the Germans was to mount a big Picasso retrospective.' Bucher could not afford to compete in this league so she decided to mount a Dora Maar exhibition instead. Primarily this was an artistic decision but it was commercial too as Bucher knew that Picasso would attend. And in the plan there was also an element of sympathy for Maar. Born Henriette Theodora Marković, part Jewish on her father's side, French Catholic on her mother's, Dora Maar was an interesting, talented but troubled woman. Picasso had kept her in a state of constant anticipation – she never knew from one meal to the next if he would want to see her for lunch or dinner. When they first met, Maar was part of the surrealist group of Man Ray, Michel Leiris and Paul Eluard and had been working as a photographer. But gradually, as she grew closer to Picasso, she devoted more and more time to painting, gave up photography and became the subject of many of Picasso's portraits during this period. Some of them were full of torment and anguish but others convey the colourful radiance of her youth and personality and are expressions of optimism, energy and tenderness.

At the time of Maar's exhibition at the Galerie Jeanne Bucher, Gilot was treating Picasso in the same way that he had behaved towards Maar, refusing to show any commitment to him, not seeing him at all for weeks at a time, a policy that had a marked effect as Picasso struggled to insist he would never allow himself to be permanently attached to Gilot. 'I could admire him tremendously as an artist but I did not want to become his victim or a martyr. It seemed to me that some of his other friends had: Dora Maar, for example.' So when Gilot attended the Maar exhibition it was 'because I was interested to see what she was doing and not at all because I thought Pablo might be there. As it happened he arrived only a few minutes after I did.'

The works on display were mostly still lifes, 'very severe most of them, showing just one object. They may have reflected in a measure her community of spirit with Picasso,' wrote Gilot, who was generous in her praise for the work, which she insisted was not derivative. 'She had taken the most ordinary objects – a lamp or an alarm-clock or a piece of bread – and made you feel she wasn't so much interested in them as in their solitude, the terrible solitude and void that surrounded everything in that penumbra.'

Shortly after the exhibition, however, Maar suffered a nervous breakdown. Picasso blamed not his own behaviour for this, but rather Maar's proximity to the surrealists, and she was hospitalized at a Paris clinic where, after lengthy analysis with the psychiatrist Jacques Lacan, she regained some equilibrium.

Aged seventy-three when the war ended, Bucher was rescued in September 1945 by an invitation from the Museum of Modern Art to visit New York, where she spent the next seven months giving occasional lectures about French art during the Occupation and generally promoting some of the modern French artists whose work she loved, such as Vieira da Silva who had had her first show in Paris in 1933 at the Jeanne Bucher Gallery.*

Eight months after the Liberation of the city, what had begun with a vanguard now turned into a battalion of British and American journalists, spies, diplomats, soldiers and support personnel in Paris, who did much to elevate the mood, tantalize with their food parcels and fine stockings, and foster the idea of new beginnings being within reach. Suddenly well-brought-up, middle-class Parisiennes were revelling in dinner and dancing dates with men from a different world. When the Sorbonne-educated Elisabeth Meynard, the newly qualified primary school teacher who had taken her class to cheer de Gaulle, met a tall and handsome British sergeant by the name of Ivan du Maurier, she described it 'as if a strange and mysterious being had just landed on our planet', as in the film *Les Visiteurs du Soir*. Mlle Meynard had been hired by the Paris Welcome Committee, one of several organizations set up, as its name implied, to salute the droves of Allied officers now in the city and introduce them into French homes. While working for them, Elisabeth met Sergeant du Maurier and just six months later on 14 March 1945 the couple were married, with her new husband providing the parachute silk out of which she created a wedding dress. By then Elisabeth, or Betuska, as she had become, had learned that her husband, now restyled Captain Robert Maxwell MC, was in fact a Czech-born Jew who, having lost most of his family in the camps had, he assured her, given up

---

* Shortly after she returned to Paris in the summer of 1946 Bucher was diagnosed with inoperable stomach cancer and died in October that year.

Elisabeth and Robert Maxwell on their wedding day, 14 March 1945

all religious faith. She, coming from a long line of Huguenot Protestants on her father's side as well as having been educated latterly at the free-thinking Collège Sévigné in the Marais, had many Jewish friends which made her open to the idea of marrying someone whose background was so far removed from her own. But above all she fell in love with this charismatic, forceful and unusual man with whom she created a large family and fortune.* By the end of the year they had gone to England.

The need to move on and draw a line under the war was especially strong after the celebrations of VE Day on 8 May when the war in Europe was finally over and General de Gaulle, in sonorous tones, once more reflected on French glory. Buildings may have been heavily pockmarked, wooden barriers still prevented access to some roads and there were even a few plaques with wreaths to mark the spot where partisans had been killed. But an American military policeman now directed traffic around the Place de la Concorde, American bands played in nightclubs, and water flowed once more

---

* Robert Maxwell became one of the world's most successful media moguls. He drowned in 1991, having possibly committed suicide.

from the fountains in the Tuileries Gardens. Americans and British were highly visible since, although the Métro worked, there were still no buses or private cars in the city. While Parisiennes used bicycles, mostly the British and Americans walked everywhere, either from the British army staff HQ in the Faubourg Saint-Honoré, or to one of the hotels requisitioned for the forces such as the Hôtel Bedford in the Rue de l'Arcade (which cost a mere five francs a night), or to the American mess in the Place Saint-Augustin, or to a Red Cross club or restaurant.

And there was, once again, a flurry of activity around the British Embassy itself – a sumptuous and elegant eighteenth-century building, called the Hôtel de Charost and bought by the Duke of Wellington when the Rue du Faubourg Saint-Honoré was a winding road that passed through fields and market gardens. The first post-war British Ambassador was Churchill's friend and supporter, the intensely Francophile politician Duff Cooper, who arrived at the end of 1944 with his beautiful and long-suffering wife Lady Diana. The Coopers, who held numerous dinners, banquets and receptions – as well as occasional ceremonies to decorate (mostly male) members of the resistance – were not enormous fans of de Gaulle, whom they dubbed Charlie Wormwood (as in Gall and Wormwood), nor of his austere Catholic wife Yvonne, who disapproved of ostentation and adultery in equal measure and rarely emerged in public. She made her first official appearance later that year at a wreath-laying ceremony for Armistice Day.

It was at one of the sparkling British Embassy receptions that Duff met Susan Mary Patten, the attractive young wife of a US diplomat, Bill Patten. Susan Mary, not yet thirty, was soon consumed by an intense longing for Duff; he, at fifty-five more than twenty years her senior, was cool. They embarked on an affair which was to last for several years and changed Susan Mary's life dramatically. Cooper was well known for his voracious sexual appetite and juggled a string of mistresses who often became Diana's friends.

In fact it was Diana who had proposed inviting Susan Mary. This intelligent, serious-minded former debutante, born in Rome to a patrician American family, quickly acquired a reputation in Paris as one of the prettiest and most fashionable women of the diplomatic circuit. Carmel Snow, influential editor-in-chief of *Harper's Bazaar*, now returned to Paris, had her regularly photographed for her magazine. Balenciaga was happy to lend her dresses or else let her buy at 'mannequin rates'. She was also a frequent guest of the peripatetic Windsors, still unhappily undecided as to where they would make their post-war home; they were living in hotels and a number of rented houses (where guests remarked the heating was turned up higher than in any other home), as well as having, until 1948, their house in the south of France, La Croë. Through the Coopers, Susan Mary got to know a circle of writers including Evelyn Waugh and Nancy Mitford, rich hostesses like Louise de Vilmorin (another of Duff's lovers) and artists such as Cocteau and Bérard, not to mention politicians and diplomats. Thanks to Duff, she discovered some of the finest Parisian restaurants as well as the most notorious such as Lapérouse, with its small private rooms where French men had been taking courtesans since 1766, or Larue, a favourite of Proust's. Slowly she was learning what you could or could not say at a dinner party, and when once she referred to the need to rebuild Germany, she quickly realized her faux pas as the French and British did not share the American view on this issue. She was also slowly picking up on growing anti-American sentiment in Paris.

Misia Sert, a woman who had known great wealth and been a muse to many men of genius, lamented what she referred to as 'the banality of France becoming Americanised'. She may have outlived her golden years of artistic influence in the city, but she continued to receive guests at tea time in her apartment as she had in the 1930s. Now, since she had friends in both camps, she had to be careful to invite collaborators and resisters on different days, something she resented, as they tried to make adjustments and an uneasy peace with each other. The wounds were every bit as deep and ran along similar lines as they had fifty years previously when she had lived through the violent arguments between Dreyfusards and their opponents.

On 14 December Lucie, the formidable widow of Captain Alfred Dreyfus, died. She was a few months older than Misia Sert. Lucie had spent the Occupation initially in Vichy, but then moved around until she was forced into hiding as 'Madame Duteil' (her sister's married name) in a home run by nuns. In 1944, after the Germans had left, she returned to Paris already in poor health and died, a year later, aged seventy-six. She was buried in Montparnasse cemetery, and on the tomb she shares with her famous husband is also inscribed the name of their much loved granddaughter, Madeleine Dreyfus Lévy. A social worker for the Red Cross, Madeleine had worked for the Combat resistance network helping smuggle other Jews out of France. She was arrested in November 1943, taken to Drancy and then to Auschwitz, where she was killed aged twenty-five. Long shadows indeed.

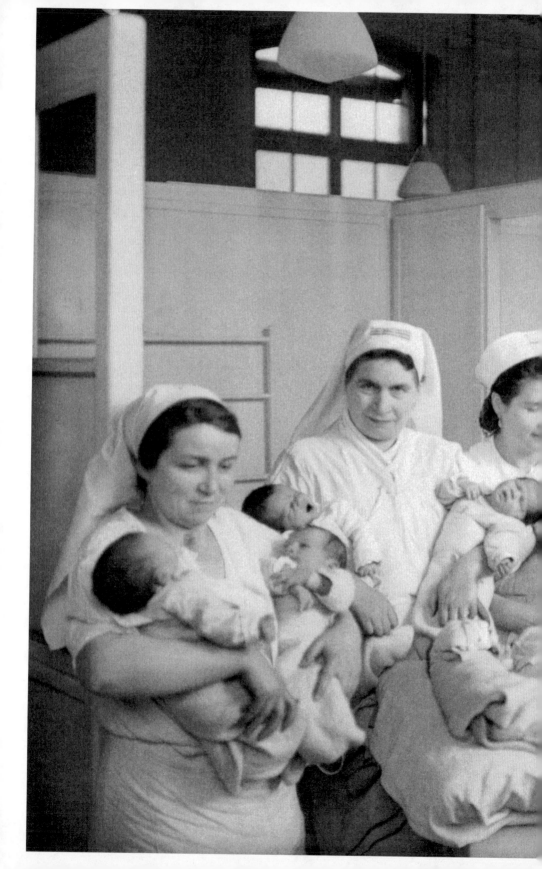

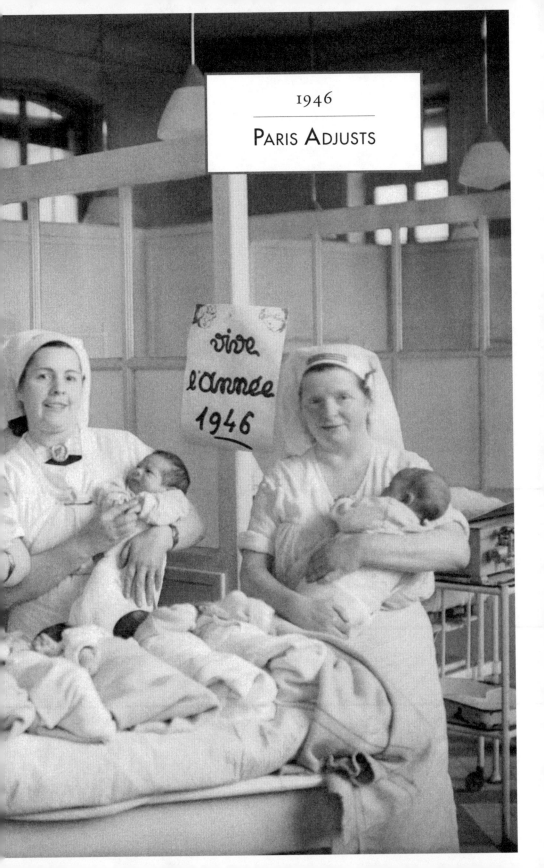

1946

PARIS ADJUSTS

On 9 January 1946, a bitterly cold day, Vera Atkins, an elegant woman with a mysterious past, arrived at Bad Oeynhausen in the British Zone of Allied-occupied Germany. She was determined to secure justice for a small group of women who had given their lives to free France. Atkins, born in Romania in June 1908 as Vera Rosenberg, and briefly educated at the Sorbonne in Paris, was conducting exhaustive investigations into the fate of 'her' women agents, of whom thirteen had been reported missing behind enemy lines, never to return. Thanks to her pre-war contacts with diplomats from many countries, and a talent for languages, Atkins had been taken on in 1941, aged thirty-three, to work as a British intelligence officer with SOE's F Section, successfully concealing both that she had Jewish roots and that she was not a British national. Atkins's job was to recruit and train the agents, assess their suitability and create cover stories for them. She had forged especially close personal relationships with many of the young women agents before they were dropped into France, sometimes giving them intensely personal good-luck tokens, and usually being the last person they saw before boarding the plane for France.

Immediately after the Liberation of Paris, in August 1944, she and Maurice Buckmaster, her boss, had made a brief visit to Paris, staying at the less than impressive Hôtel Cecil in the Rue Saint-Didier, where they were soon apprised that de Gaulle, determined to create the illusion that France alone had organized its own liberation, was ignoring any contribution SOE might have played in the victory. Vera recognized, in the fetid atmosphere of accusation and counterclaim, in which French security police had taken control of the few German records which had been salvaged, that she was unlikely to discover any significant information in Paris itself and returned home to build up files. Among the information she soon received after this trip was news of one of the SOE women, Cecily Lefort, whose poor French accent had always worried Vera, giving an address for her in a camp at Ravensbrück in Mecklenburg, north of Berlin. It was the first time Vera had heard the name Ravensbrück. In fact, Cecily Lefort, who had been ill almost from the time of her arrival in the camp, had been gassed at Ravensbrück in February 1945. Later, Vera learned from witnesses that, just days before her death, Cecily had received a letter from her French husband seeking a divorce. She did not spare Dr Lefort her views of his behaviour.

During the next year Atkins collected and carefully filed details of several arrests and transfers to different prisons, but still lacked confirmation of anyone's fate. Of Noor Inayat Khan, codenamed Madeleine, often referred to as Nora, or Nora Baker, she knew nothing for certain at this point. At the end of 1945, SOE had been wound up but Atkins was only just beginning her own search for the missing agents. 'I went to find them as a private enterprise,' she was to tell her biographer years later. 'I wanted to know. I always thought "missing presumed dead" to be such a terrible verdict.' Atkins, newly promoted to squadron officer in the Women's Auxiliary Air Force and funded by MI6, now began her investigations in earnest, attached to the War Crimes Investigation Unit. In this position she was able to carry out interrogations of Nazis suspected of war crimes and testify as a prosecution witness in subsequent trials. But her priority was always to search for the stories of what had really happened to 'her' missing girls.

Just before leaving for Germany in 1946, Atkins had been in touch with Brian Stonehouse, an SOE agent and artist with a natural aptitude for drawing, a talent which helped him survive four different camps from the time he was first arrested in October 1941.

In June 1944, Stonehouse was a prisoner in Natzweiler-Struthof, a camp in the Vosges which held some 6,000 male prisoners and was the only Nazi concentration camp on French soil. Stonehouse later told Atkins that, although he did not know the precise date, one day around the time of the attempted assassination of Hitler (which had occurred on 20 July 1944) four women, escorted by SS officers, had been marched into the camp, just past where he was working inside the fence on the east side. In fact, several people noticed the girls pass by that afternoon and, while they all remembered something slightly different about them, each of the witnesses commented that they were well dressed, appeared to be in good health and were defiant in their bearing and attitude towards their captors. Stonehouse, eighteen months after the event, dug deep into his memory to supply Vera with drawings and descriptions of the women, one of whom she was easily able to identify as Diana Rowden from the bow she always wore in her hair, and another she thought might have been Noor; 'obviously continental – maybe Jewish', Stonehouse had told her. By the time Vera gave evidence at the specially convened Natzweiler trial, from 9 April to 5 May 1946, she believed that the four victims were Vera Leigh, Diana Rowden, Andrée Borrel and Nora Inayat Khan and that they had all been drugged before being burned alive. But she tried to withhold information to the UK press about their individual identity on the spurious grounds that she wished to spare their families undue grief. More likely, as by now the families were pressing for public recognition of their loved ones' outstanding courage, she hoped to avoid too much press questioning about the recruitment and training of the women.

The one clear fact was that four women were brought to Natzweiler on 6 July 1944 and killed in the camp crematorium the same evening. In a letter to the War Office, Atkins wrote that the four women died by lethal injection, 'probably Evipan, a narcotic, and were immediately cremated. They were unconscious but probably still alive when thrown into the oven.' Various graphic accounts of how the four women had died were heard at the trial. They were all told to undress before being injected and one was heard to ask 'Pourquoi?' and was told 'Pour Typhus.' One asked for a pillow. Several witnesses described hearing groaning as the women were dragged along the floor to their deaths. One of the four clearly woke up from the narcotic and scrabbled and fought to the last to resist being placed, feet first, in the oven. Giving his testimony, camp executioner, Peter Straub, denied everything. But the most shocking

statements came from Walter Schultz, who worked as an in interpreter in the camp's political department. Schultz described how, the
day after the killings, Straub, still drunk from the night before, gave
him a detailed account of what had happened and how the fourth
woman, as she was being put into the oven, regained consciousness.
Straub, pointing to scars on his face, said to Schultz: 'There, you can
see how she scratched me . . . Look how she defended herself.' By the
time Atkins interrogated Straub he still had scars on his face. She
believed they were probably inflicted by Vera Leigh, the oldest of the
four, but there was no proof.

Although Atkins accepted that in the trial her women should
be described as 'spies' – there was no other category for military
persons operating in civilian clothes in enemy-occupied territory
– she had also been concerned that the defence should not therefore be able to claim 'lawful execution'. However, the prosecution
counsel successfully made the case that as the girls were executed
without trial, even if they were spies, this was contrary to the
Geneva Convention and therefore constituted a war crime. Atkins
was reasonably satisfied with the result: the camp doctor and camp
Kommandant were sentenced to death; although Straub was sentenced only to thirteen years in prison at this trial, a few months later
he was found guilty of war crimes in other trials and was hanged
in October.

When the newspapers carried headlines about British women
being burned alive there was a shocked response, especially as the
British public had not previously been aware that any women had
been sent into the field on such dangerous missions. On 18 September 1946 Vera Leigh, the former Parisian milliner, was awarded the
King's Commendation for Brave Conduct. She was, according to the
document proposing her for a posthumous decoration, 'a very gallant
girl. She was secretly terrified by the idea of the mission but still more
terrified by the fear of showing her terror to anyone. She was very
game, very plucky and rather imaginative . . .'

As Vera Atkins remarked later, all the girls in F Section had
different motivations but the one quality they had in common was
bravery. 'You might find it in anyone. You just don't know where to
look.' Bernard de Gaulle, nephew of the General who later married

Sylvie, the youngest Geoffroy-Dechaume daughter, and who knew many *résistantes*, elaborated: 'Those women who gave their lives were not without fear. One of the reasons why the role of women has not been recognized for so long – and it's complicated – is that one lived in permanent fear, one trembled with fear, but nobody wants to talk about fear. People afterwards talk about war in general but it's not "their" war. That is *irracontable* – something they cannot talk about. They are ashamed of having fear.' Odette Churchill was another who admitted later that none of them was without fear in Ravensbrück, but she suggested that it was a question of how they managed it. 'Everybody tried to be a little braver than they felt. All of us had a moment of weakness, we did all cry together at one moment.' Both Odette Churchill and Violette Szabo were awarded the George Cross in 1946 (in Szabo's case posthumously), but Atkins knew that her own work was not over and that in her search to uncover what had happened to all the women she would have to follow up every lead urgently, interviewing prison guards and former prisoners who might help before it was too late and they either died, escaped or were executed. In October she had her honorary commission extended so that she could stay longer in Germany to assist the prosecution in the Ravensbrück trial, which started in December and lasted into early 1947 and beyond.

In mid-January 1946 Charles de Gaulle resigned, to the surprise of many, and retired to the country, ostensibly to write his memoirs. His main task had been to unite the country and to give it back a sense of pride following the humiliating defeat. His determination to create the narrative that France was not one of the defeated countries but a victorious nation gave further strength to his criticism of the Communist Party, which was most in favour of continuing with the *épuration* trials and bringing to justice everyone who could possibly be described as a collaborator. De Gaulle believed that while well-known traitors had to be punished, so-called 'economic collaborators' (occasionally industrialists but more often civil servants and police chiefs) had to be forgiven where possible in order to ensure the continued smooth running of the country. In addition, as Head of State de Gaulle assumed the right to stay executions and, of the 1,554 capital sentences submitted to him, he commuted 998, including all those involving women.

These political machinations go some way to explaining the government's frenzied attempts to stage trials of high-profile collaborators, allowing them to proceed faster than many considered decent, and on 22 February the journalist and editor Jean Luchaire was executed. During his trial the prosecuting counsel began his opening speech by explaining that 'when men committed treason with their pen, their treason was often inspired by fascism. In Luchaire's case, it was inspired by venality and corruption.' He said that the anger that had moved him in other trials was joined by 'disgust'. Luchaire's daughter Corinne, now a divorced single mother with a small child – Brigitte, born in May 1944 after a brief liaison with a Luftwaffe officer, Wolrad Gerlach – wrote pathetically, 'and still it was not all over for me. There was still my trial to come but . . . I remember nothing. I was crying the whole time. I was in mourning for my father.' Corinne, whose golden youth – when she had lived off nothing but champagne and cigarettes – had long since evaporated, had not made a film since 1940, was still battling tuberculosis and was reduced to little more than a character in other people's novels. She had to wait another four long months for her own trial. When it came, a journalist for *Life* reported in an article headed 'The Nazis' Courtesan, French actress-collaborationist, once the toast of Occupied Paris, loses her beauty and citizenship':

> While the court recited a long list of the lovers and parties she had enjoyed, she stood by silently, her pride destroyed, her face aged by dissipation and TB. When the judges sentenced her to ten years of 'National Indignity' without any of the privileges of a French citizen, she could plead only: 'I was young and stupid. I did not realise.'

She had become, according to the *Life* reporter, 'a haggard wreck'. Brigitte, her child, was placed for a time with a family who took in paying guests in Châtel, a village in Haute-Savoie. She went to school in the village and was seen occasionally on the ski slopes in winter.

Those who knew who she was whispered about the mother, the Marilyn Monroe of her day. There were even those who sympathized. According to the French novelist and Nobel Prize winner Patrick Modiano, Corinne, or 'my sister Corinne' as he referred to her, doubtless with his own childhood and dubious father in mind, 'was in a certain sense a victim of her father's adventure . . . an adventure which was nothing in comparison to that of Rebatet or Brasillach'. Modiano, who has created several fictional characters based on Corinne, has pointed out that her father hailed from the political left and was surrounded by Jews in his close family: his brother-in-law Théodore Fraenkel was Jewish, as was his father Julien's third wife, Antonina Silberstein.

> He was led astray into collaboration through a weakness of character and taste for the easy life and a need for money – money which he shared as he was generous in intervening with the Germans to save lives. Fascists like Rebatet and Brasillach hated him and considered him pro-Jewish. Luchaire seemed to me representative of a certain atmosphere and troubled world of Paris in the Occupation, caught up in the black market and which my own father unfortunately was part of in the scheme of things. Luchaire paid for his thoughtlessness with his life.

While the trials attempted to offer justice for those who would never return, the women who had survived often needed more. Early in 1946 the young death-march survivor and *résistante* Jacqueline Marié married Guy Fleury, fellow resister, and her first child was born later that year. 'I saw this not only as a sign of life but as a snub to the Germans. Of all the things that the Germans did, I can never forgive them for what they did to children,' she said.

She and her brother, Pierre Marié, went on to have five children each, and today, as Mme Fleury, she has grandchildren and great-grandchildren, not only a source of enormous pride but a critical part of her recovery. 'When I first returned in 1945 nobody wanted to hear our stories. So after three attempts I stopped. But then I started speaking to my infant son and eventually (in 1961) I started going into schools and since then have never stopped talking about what happened.' Never forget and always bear witness, the twin mantras which motivated many of those who, like her, became involved in the running of ADIR (she is, at time of writing, its President). But as Jacqueline d'Alincourt explained, it was difficult for most of them to talk because it was, quite simply, 'an unspeakable experience. We had no words to express it. Little by little, however, the wall of silence that imprisoned us cracked. Some were bold enough to ask us what happened. The need to speak, to stave off oblivion, became obvious. I still hear the scream of a companion being trucked off to the gas chamber: "Tell it to the world!" Those words will forever echo in my mind.'

Geneviève de Gaulle was also married in 1946 to a man she had met while recuperating in Geneva: Bernard Anthonioz, a publisher from Lyons, a friend of Louis Aragon and André Malraux and a fellow resister. General de Gaulle was a witness at their May wedding and the couple subsequently had four children. One month later in June, ADIR published its first newsletter, *Voix et Visages*, in which Geneviève de Gaulle Anthonioz, as she insisted on being called from then on, wrote to remind fellow *déportées* of the 'virile, effective total' friendship that had sustained them in the camps, 'as it would again as they undertook their new humane tasks'. Initially, the newsletter was devoted to recording fallen comrades but during the following months and years it published a bewildering array of relevant laws and policies concerning the rights and benefits that were due to resisters.

Often more important than the newsletter was human contact, and the organization's Rue Guynemer headquarters provided conversation and companionship for those who called in for the regular Monday afternoon teas. It also helped women to find work or housing, offered advice in dealing with the various government ministries charged with administering benefits, and provided urgent medical care which was often crucial and which the state was not equipped to do. Many of the returning women suffered from a range of illnesses including undiagnosed tuberculosis, typhus, gangrene, dysentery and various infections and digestive ailments. ADIR provided its members with the services of seventeen doctors free of charge, it bought screening equipment for TB, and twice weekly the association's medical personnel offered unlimited consultations and referrals to its members. In addition it subsidized long-term care in convalescent homes, where possible in France and Switzerland. By January 1947 more than 500 women had spent time in one of their homes, sometimes for as long as a year, and by the end of the decade more than a thousand women had benefited from this initiative. Even so, for some this was too late. Among the approximately 40,000 surviving racial and political deportees, nearly 3,000 died within a couple of months of their liberation. And by October 1954, less than ten years after their return, roughly 35 per cent of the deportees had died as a direct consequence of their injuries or maltreatment.

One of those victims was Malka Reiman, the Jewish mother rounded up in the Vél' d'Hiv *rafle* with her two daughters, whose extraordinary courage, resourcefulness and ingenuity had enabled all three of them to escape the camp at Beaune-la-Rolande. Having found a hiding place for her adolescent girls in Vendôme in 1942 with a relatively impoverished Christian family, the Philippeaus, located thanks to her local postman, she then had to find money to pay them, and returned three times to occupied Paris to recover pieces of jewellery and linens that she had hidden. For two years Malka hid in a variety of places, making clothes and food for herself and others to get by. At the Liberation she hoped that her husband Abraham would return, and went endlessly to the Gare de l'Est and the Lutetia, scanning lists, trying throughout 1945 to discover his fate. When she heard that the policeman at Pithiviers, who had shown her family such kindness while her husband was incarcerated there, was now himself facing trial for collaboration, she went to testify in his favour.

But by January 1946, aged thirty-nine, she knew without doubt that Abraham had been murdered at Auschwitz, and from then on she lost the will to live. She stopped speaking, collapsed in the street and suffered ever worsening headaches, unable to contemplate a future without Abraham, her childhood sweetheart. 'She died of a broken heart,' as Arlette Reiman described it. 'I wanted her to live for us, but she was too ill. Her last words were "I need to see Papa. Tomorrow we will be together again."' From now on the two girls were orphans: Madeline, at fifteen, was sent to work, Arlette, thirteen, to boarding school in a village in north-west France near Le Mans where she started her life again as 'la petite orpheline Parisienne'.

The historian Debra Workman believes that ADIR, the association for returnees largely set up by Geneviève de Gaulle, understood the range of diseases resulting from the deportation far earlier than governmental and medical authorities. 'Only in 1953, eight years after their return, did the Ministry for Veterans' Affairs create a special commission to study the pathology of the deportation in order to develop a comprehensive, systematic approach to care for the health needs of those who had been deported.' In addition, the experience of those deported for political reasons and those deported because they were Jews was vastly different. De Gaulle himself never said anything about the Jews nor apologized for their treatment.*

Clearly those deported merely because they were Jews needed their own repatriation organization too. Three weeks after Paris had been liberated, André and Jacqueline Mesnil-Amar helped set up one such information network, the Service Central des Déportés Israélites (SCDI). Jacqueline became editor of its monthly bulletin, using reports from Switzerland, Poland and Belgium in attempts to bring families, sundered by war, together again. For Jacqueline Mesnil-Amar, the hunger and fear of the Occupation while André was in the Jewish Combat organization, a resistance network in the south, as well as the trauma of witnessing the post-war dislocation of survivors, turned her, unusually, from a non-observant Jew into a deeply committed one, 'seized by conscience'. Both she and André – who had so narrowly survived deportation himself by jumping off a train – had grown up in an atmosphere where 'they adored French culture and Latin and Greek took precedence over Hebrew . . .'. Pre-war they had been French citizens first and Jews second. Now they had become just '*Juifs*'. So, deeply concerned also not to

---

* According to one of his biographers, Jonathan Fenby, de Gaulle 'very rarely said the Nazis and I don't know of any reference to the Holocaust' ('Charles de Gaulle and the French Resistance', http://fivebooks.com/interview/jonathan-fenby-on-charles-de-gaulle-and-the-french-resistance/). Others, referencing remarks he made about those who died 'pour La France', point out that such a phrase does not address the suffering of millions of Jews in France.

forget the fate of the foreign Jews, they became ever more immersed in Judaism until, as their daughter Sylvie later wrote, it 'devoured' their thinking. Some of their friends, finding the couple's concerns obsessive, became estranged, and even Sylvie protested that they thought about little else.

But they were not alone. Even in a city where so many of the returning Jews internalized their fate, or else, finding it too painful to speak of, remained silent either to protect their children or, in the inimitable phrase of Romain Gary, chose not to speak 'pour ne pas compliquer les choses'.*

Within a year, her close colleague Andrée Salomon left her work in France for OSE – the Oeuvre de Secours aux Enfants, which had played a critical role in saving Jewish children in France during the Occupation – and emigrated to Israel, where she worked on the OSE archives and tracked the fate of 'her' children, now scattered around the world.

The children who survived now created a special problem. Some 11,600 Jewish children in France had been deported, all of whom perished in the camps, but many had been hidden in France. Vivette Samuel was the daughter of two well-educated Ukrainian Jews who had settled in Paris during the First World War. According to Vivette, who had worked for OSE since 1940 when she was twenty-two, 72,400 under eighteen years old who were not deported survived. About 62,000 of them were able to stay with parents or were directly entrusted by them to institutions or to non-Jewish families, and the issues involved in reintegrating them into a normal life were unprecedented. In addition, the plight of the Jews was, in the post-war context of a continent in ruins, just one problem among many. Thérèse Bonney, the New York-born photojournalist who was the first American to win a scholarship to the Sorbonne, had been documenting for years the appalling conditions in which many children were now living. Already in 1943 her book *Europe's Children* had

* Romain Gary, born in Vilna, educated in Nice, became a pilot with the Free French and coined the phrase in telling the story of his reply when presented to the Queen Mother in England after the war. See http://mayatouviere.com/uploads/3/4/2/3/3423798/la_promesse_de_laube_romain_gary.pdf, p. 23.

been considered shocking. Lee Miller, who moved on from Paris to Germany, witnessed similar horrors and the photographs she took of children in a hospital in Vienna are among the most harrowing and important of her entire wartime oeuvre. She wrote:

> For an hour I watched a baby die. He was dark blue when I first saw him. He was the dark dusty blue of these waltz-filled Vienna nights, the same colour as the striped garb of the Dachau skeletons, the same imaginary blue as Strauss's Danube. I'd thought all babies looked alike, but that was healthy babies; there are many faces for the dying. This wasn't a two months baby, he was a skinny gladiator. He gasped and fought and struggled for life, and a doctor and a nun and I just stood there and watched . . . There was nothing to do but watch him die. Baring his sharp toothless gums he clenched his fists against the attack of death. This tiny baby fought for his only possession, life, as if it might be worth something.

But after the war the problem of abandoned, lost and homeless children became magnified not just in France but throughout Europe. The devastation had left behind it a continent of displaced orphans and homeless children: some 50,000 in Czechoslovakia, 280,000 in Yugoslavia – statistics which cannot easily convey the individual heartache behind them. The UN Relief and Rehabilitation Administration (UNRRA) was by 1947 caring for some 500,000 orphans in Germany alone, many of whom had forgotten who they were or where they came from, or never knew, too young to remember anything about their previous lives and often too emotionally fragile to be told. In the summer of 1945 posters had started appearing on the walls of train stations and post offices across Europe, often put there by the Red Cross, showing pictures of babies and small children with the words: 'Who am I?' Malnourished, wary, sickly, described by one aid worker as 'tired, wan, broken little old men and women', these children became for Jacqueline Mesnil-Amar the symbol of European culture and humanity in disarray. In France, as the war ended, the OSE estimated that there were between five and six thousand Jewish children who were now orphans, whether hidden in non-Jewish homes around the country or over the border in Switzerland or Spain. They needed to be traced, their families and heritage restored.

This was the environment which struck the British novelist Marghanita Laski so profoundly on her frequent post-war trips back to the Paris she loved. She and her husband had not only lived in Paris from 1937 to 1938, they had been married there and knew it well. In addition Laski was well equipped to understand the needs of French orphans at close hand since her own secular, intellectually aware Jewish family had rescued two Jewish refugees from Europe, days before the outbreak of war. *Little Boy Lost*, the bestselling novel that resulted, was not published until 1949 but it describes an all too chillingly familiar France of 1946 'enveloped in a miasma of corruption' where the rules of the black-market economy predominate. Hilary, the anti-hero who has to decide whether or not to take as his own a child from a chilly Catholic orphanage whose identity cannot be proven, asks his resistance friend Pierre how he copes with constantly wondering what everyone did during the Occupation. Pierre tells him that yes, he wonders, 'but automatically now and without caring about the answer. I'm tired with "collaborationist" as a term of abuse; we each did under the Germans what we were capable of doing; what that was, was settled long before they arrived.' Meanwhile, the nuns are weighing up Hilary just as much as he is questioning himself, informing him: 'You will understand that we must be very, very certain that the child is yours before we allow him to pass into a non-Catholic home.'

Some of the wartime schemes to save children had been ingenious and risky, but few had been without consequences, which were now unravelling. María Errázuriz, cousin of Jacques Tartière and now friend of Drue, his widow, had worked closely with Abbé Henri-François Ménardais, the parish priest of Chalmaison just outside Paris, who was deeply involved in the effort to save Jews. He hid whole families in his presbytery, at the orphanage at Chalmaison and at the Château de Tachy there, where nuns from the Fondation Eugène Napoléon resided after their Paris home had been requisitioned by the Germans. Ménardais, a frequent visitor to the Rothschild Hospital, also worked closely with social worker Claire

Heymann. They would meet surreptitiously at the opera, where
Ménardais was, usefully, chaplain to the ballet dancers, known as
les Petits Rats de l'Opéra, and there he would give Heymann dozens
of signed baptism certificates that she could use to reclassify Jewish
children. He even entrusted Jewish children to some Public Aid orphanages, where they would stay until the war's end, as he believed
(correctly) that no one would think of looking for Jewish children
among gentile orphans. In this way Ménardais saved more than 200
Jewish children from the Nazis during the Occupation. But what was
to be done with them all now? Some, like Arlette Reiman, had gone
regularly to church and learned to say mass, but while profoundly
grateful to their Christian saviours they nonetheless still felt Jewish.
Others, mostly younger Jewish orphans who had been baptized for
their safety during the war, now faced complicated futures, as some
Christian institutions argued that, if the mothers had had their children baptized, this was obviously because they wanted them brought
up in the Christian faith.

Baronne Edouard de Rothschild, née Germaine Halphen, not
without experience in dealing with parentless children, took control
of the Rothschild Orphanage immediately after the war when it was
transferred to the Château de la Guette, a Rothschild property in
Villeneuve just outside Paris, where children had been living since
1939. Some children were still being reunited with lost families even
in 1947, a situation charged with trauma given the ordeals that the
survivors had endured. Little professional help was available in this
desperate and unprecedented state of affairs where nobody knew
which was the right or wrong way to behave. Many parents maintained a stubborn silence, thinking that to repress their memories
was best for the child, others made emotional demands on the child
to have their sufferings recognized. Vivette Samuel had found during
the Occupation that one of her most daunting tasks had often been
having to ask for written consent from parents interned at one of the
French camps, such as Gurs, to remove their child, believing this was
the child's only chance of survival. Now one of the most difficult
problems was remembering the promises made to those parents to
have their children raised in a Jewish setting, whether during the
war or, if the parents did not survive, afterwards, when she knew this

might involve a new separation, 'an emotional laceration just as they had found a new serenity. Did we care enough not to traumatize the children again, especially the youngest ones, who had been placed in families that they had emotionally adopted and that hoped to keep them?' Where possible they compromised by keeping the child in the family with the assurance that the child's identity would be preserved. But the problem for children who had been placed in convents was more complex, as some had had themselves baptized and converted. 'Certainly they had been saved and that was the essential thing.' But Samuel recognized that families, however well meaning, were not always the best place for traumatized children in this tragic dilemma:

> Paradoxically, it was possible for children raised in institutions to find differentiated, often beneficial, role models – thanks to their being surrounded by teachers of diverse political or religious allegiance, thanks to the friendship of their peers and also thanks to the efforts made to give them the greatest opportunity possible on the material, educational and moral planes. They shared the same past as the other children of the institution and adapted to that environment better than to families that had sheltered other children.

For some, having remnants of a family survive created its own difficulties. Rosa Liwarrak, aged thirteen in 1946 when she came back to Paris, was now an orphan and still a child in many ways. But she was also a young woman with both a mind of her own and a Catholic stepmother. She had been several times to the Lutetia looking, in vain, for her father. Now she had to continue with her schooling, paid for by OSE. But she was, by her own admission, a disruptive and aggressive child, thrown out of two schools. She recalls being taken by an aunt to a rabbi with the intention of converting her back to Judaism. 'But when he told me all the things I could not do, like switch on a light on the Sabbath because I might offend God, I said to him: "You are telling me I lost all my family in a gas chamber and now mustn't switch on a light in case I offend God?" I pushed my finger into his fat belly button and ran out in disgust.' Today, while acknowledging the role both Catholicism and Judaism have played in her life, she feels ambivalent about all religion.

Rosa, having been born in France just as her parents had arrived in the country from Germany, thought of herself as French. But many of the lost children, the impoverished offspring of east European tailors, knitters, miners and tinkers who had sought sanctuary in France, had never been accepted by that country and had known only fear, exile, hunger, loss and ultimately abandonment or death. How, asked Jacqueline Mesnil-Amar in her painful post-war memoir, can you ever make these children 'normal'? How to give them the childhood they never had? How to stop them regarding adults as enemies, for it was adults who had crushed their parents?

'It's not a gift, but restitution, not charity but justice,' she wrote. It was the duty of adults, she insisted, to care for them in such a way that they would once again belong to the human family. 'We will restore their hope because they are our only hope in a world in which we have failed.'

Odette Fabius, elegantly slim before she was captured, returned skeletally thin. She had been sent from Ravensbrück to Malmö with Toquette Jackson, equally sick and thin, until both were well enough to walk. Odette recovered although needed the help of her sticks for several months. Excited as she was to see Marie-Claude again, she was also shocked to discover that the svelte little girl she had abandoned in 1943, two years later 'had blown up . . . of course still pretty but twice the size since everyone around her had tried to spoil her with food to help her forget the absence of her mother'. Not many women were consulting doctors at this moment, worried about overweight children but, extraordinarily, Odette took her daughter for a consultation with the famous Paris paediatrician Robert Debré, a decision which goes some way towards explaining the iron will of a woman who could survive Ravensbrück. Odette also went to the synagogue in the Rue de la Victoire to attend a memorial service for her murdered aunt and uncle, Raymond and Antoinette Berr, parents of Hélène, the gifted young French woman deported first to Auschwitz then to Bergen-Belsen, where she died in 1945. Odette was appalled to discover there a poisonous atmosphere among those who had survived; some were whispering about who had survived thanks to calling in certain privileges, while others gossiped about who had benefited from the Occupation and how. In this mood, Parisians were not ready to commemorate Hélène Berr's short life, but at least Andrée Bardiau, the family housekeeper who had been with the Berrs for fifty years and had carefully looked after Hélène's diary as it was handed to her page by page for safekeeping, now, on 20 June 1946, passed the manuscript to Hélène's brother, who typed up a copy for the family and gave the original to her fiancé, Jean Morawiecki. Consumed by guilt for abandoning her, he put the diary quietly to one side.

Odette and Robert returned to living together for the sake of their daughter, but now with what she described as an affectionate 'modus vivendi', or total liberty for each of them to pursue their own friendships. As soon as she could, Odette went to Marseilles to visit Pierre Ferri-Pisani. Having thought of him constantly during her time at Ravensbrück, she had tried to prepare herself for their reunion, but even so his dramatic decline and frailty were unimaginable. He had lost forty-four pounds, was partially deaf having stepped on a mine, and was uncertain of himself, having not spoken aloud for a year. At the sight of Odette, he opened his arms for her and then fainted. 'He was emptied of life and energy. He could not understand how I could say that, having lived through an abominable experience, I was trying to find positive aspects of the experience such as the force of friendship.'

The relationship continued for a few more months as Ferri-Pisani travelled to Paris, ostensibly to meet political comrades while he was fighting elections, but also to see Odette and rekindle their wartime romance. He hoped to find a more permanent job that would allow him to come regularly, but then his wife, having only now discovered the relationship, attempted suicide. Odette believed that, without the links that bound them in fighting a common enemy, their relationship was doomed. Ferri-Pisani's post-war style of life was not what she had remembered in 1943. 'Paradoxically our liberation just produced obstacles . . . I realised I was not capable of breaking with all my past life which, now that the war was over, had reawakened in me.' In addition, she had money worries as her husband's business had all but collapsed and family finances were precarious. She decided she had to end the affair with Pierre and in mid-1946, a year after her return from the camps, Odette Fabius accepted a job working for the United Nations in New York. She never saw Pierre again, 'the most brilliant man that I was ever to meet'.

Like Geneviève de Gaulle and Jacqueline Marié, Jacqueline d'Alincourt married in 1946. Her husband was Pierre Péry, a Buchenwald survivor, and the couple decided to live in New York. Several friends had told her she must meet a remarkable American woman called Caroline Ferriday. 'I know you two will understand each other.'

Caroline Woolsey Ferriday was an only child, auspiciously born on 4 July 1902, into a family of wealth and privilege. She was a stunning young woman, a Francophile who spoke fluent French, and was interested in politics from a young age. By the time Hitler came to power she was working as a volunteer in the French Consulate in New York and by 1941 was actively involved in running France Forever, the American support organization to which Micheline Rosenberg, Paul's daughter and the mother of Anne Sinclair, was

Caroline Ferriday, the lifelong Francophile who played a key role
helping the post-war recovery of the Ravensbrück lapins

also committed. Deeply concerned about the suffering of the French people, especially children, she was involved in raising money throughout the war to help orphans and already in 1945 had lists of women and children desperately in need of food, clothing and other support. As she wrote in an emotive appeal on behalf of France Forever shortly after the war: 'Although the Germans suffered a crushing military defeat, Germany will in the long run emerge the victor and it will be Germany who has won the war unless the youth of liberated Europe survive to enjoy the fruits of Victory.' Caroline and Jacqueline became lifelong friends. As Jacqueline recalled, 'Our friendship was sealed after the first meeting when she immediately asked: "What can I do?" She became a sister.' Caroline set up an American friends of ADIR and was constantly looking for ways to help the French victims of the war.

Not surprisingly, those who feared that the justice they faced might not be to their liking also escaped Paris. Chanel, still under a cloud, spent much of 1946 in Switzerland, part of the time with the writer Paul Morand, an active supporter of the Vichy government who knew her well and whom she now commissioned to write her memoirs. She was still indulging, more discreetly these days, her affair with Spatz, described by those who saw him at this time as 'an impoverished, ageing playboy who nevertheless managed to keep up the pretence of wealth'. This charade was largely made possible by Chanel; even after the affair had petered out when Spatz went to live in the Balearics, she continued to remit a monthly allowance. According to Morand's view of Chanel at this time, she was still full of 'brooding fury and barely suppressed energies during her years away from the fashion business that had shaped her life and bore her name'. She was also now fighting in earnest for control of her perfume business, employing the lawyer René de Chambrun, who had been her legal adviser since the early 1930s.

Chanel was neither the first nor the last couturier to realize that extending her brand to perfume could be immensely profitable and did not involve designing new clothes every season. In the summer of 1920 she had met the legendary perfumer Ernest Beaux, who had a laboratory in Grasse in the south of France. According to Bettina

Ballard, the influential editor of *Vogue*, she concocted Chanel N° 5 there in the aftermath of her grief over the death of Captain Arthur Edward 'Boy' Capel, an English polo-player with whom she had had an intense nine-year affair and who had financed her early shops. However, production did not properly begin until 1924 when she was introduced to Pierre Wertheimer, owner, with his brother Paul, of Bourjois, one of the largest cosmetics companies in France. The Wertheimers were a longstanding French Jewish family with some factories, and whose investment in the new company, Les Parfums Chanel, ensured that Chanel perfume and beauty products could be produced in large enough quantities to be sold commercially in Galeries Lafayette and other stores and would make them immensely rich.

But there were arguments from the start. When the company was first established, Chanel herself owned 10 per cent, the Wertheimers 70 per cent with the final 20 per cent going to Théophile Bader, owner of Galeries Lafayette, who had brokered the introduction. But Bader was subsequently bought out by the Wertheimers. Chanel regularly tried to get a greater percentage, which Pierre Wertheimer just as regularly resisted. But even though the perfume was so profitable that Chanel had security and independence for life, the 10 per cent continued to rankle. In 1940 the Wertheimers had to flee Paris and, in order to aryanize the perfume company, handed it to Félix Amiot, a French Christian businessman in whose aviation business they had had a 50 per cent share which they now returned. Chanel was infuriated by the Wertheimers' successful aryanization, since it prevented her from using the opportunity of the Occupation to seize control herself. After the war, Amiot immediately returned the company to the Wertheimers,* which prompted Chanel to initiate legal battles, once again to win a greater share of the company for herself.

---

* But even that did not prevent some believing that, as he had been forced to work for the German aircraft manufacturer, Junkers, to say nothing of selling Chanel perfume to the Germans, he had been a Nazi collaborator. In fact he had set up a resistance network and even tried to build planes for the Free French, but it was his deal with the Wertheimers which may have saved him from prosecution.

So in 1946 she decided to produce samples of her own perfumes with names such as Mademoiselle Chanel No. 1 and No. 2. This obvious challenge to the Wertheimers could not be ignored, and a deal was eventually struck which made her 'unassailably rich'. After May 1947, Chanel received 2 per cent of the gross royalties of perfume sales throughout the world, in the region of $1 million a year. She also received a sum calculated to cover past royalties . . . She was, as one of her biographers put it, now 'wealthy enough to need never work again'.

The return of Jewish companies to their legitimate owners provided plenty of work for lawyers. As part of the long process of regularizing the affairs of Van Cleef & Arpels, on 3 June 1946 the body of Renée Puissant, after four years lying in a Vichy grave, was exhumed by her mother, Estelle Van Cleef, and transported to Nice where it was reburied alongside her father in the Jewish cemetery. The company soon returned to trading from its familiar shop front in the Place Vendôme, but this time it was run by various members of the Arpels family. Although the Van Cleef name was retained, Renée's death, childless as she was, spelled the end of the line for that branch of the family. Some historians of the business have argued that it was the bogus aryanization set in motion by Renée, selling the company to Comte Paul de Léséleuc, which saved it. Without that, the Germans would have confiscated the company for themselves.

While Spatz was being looked after by Chanel, his half-Jewish first wife Catsy, or Maximiliane von Schoenebeck, was faring less well. Having survived various internment camps at the beginning of the war, she was expelled from France and went to Austria to stay with cousins. But at some point towards the end of the war, she returned to her beloved Paris with a new name, only to be arrested once again in 1944 for collaboration. Known to have been involved in the black market, selling lingerie, she spent the following two years in prison, the price for her first marriage to Günther von Dincklage as well as for subsequent relationships with German officers.

'She has had an appalling time,' wrote Allanah Harper, the English-born founder of the French literary review *Echanges* and a close friend of Catsy's half-sister, the writer Sybille Bedford. Harper visited Catsy von Dincklage in September in Paris following the latter's release after almost two years in a French prison. She reported back to Bedford: 'I took her to the Bar in Rue de la Paix, as she said they were the only place that had champagne that was really good. We had three glasses each at 100 francs a glass.' She added that Catsy had been kept in the most filthy conditions, with only bread and water for months.

> She said, typically, that it was amusing in the beginning because the prison was full of Marquises and Countesses who had collaborated, but after a few months they were all let out through influence, but she remained with only 'les femmes de ménage et des grues' [cleaners and hookers]. She thinks she was put in because of her husband, but I think it was for going about with officers. Any rate it could not be for being Jewish as it was after the Liberation she was put in and only came out four months ago . . . I think she feels rather lonely . . . she says she has to work to make money as she has none. She is going to work from next week in a hat shop with a friend.

It was not a story that Sybille, however affectionately she felt towards her sister, and in spite of a fierce belief in justice, was ever comfortable with.

Meanwhile, the British, if they could not ensure justice, were doing their best to promote goodwill between the former allies through the activities of the British Council. Following the success of a big art exhibition featuring John Piper and Graham Sutherland among others, the Council turned their attention to music. Mary Wallington, who had studied French and Italian at Oxford before working in publishing, now aged thirty-two, landed a job in the summer of 1946 as a music assistant with the Council, based at 28 Avenue Champs-Elysées. Other than the constant rain that summer, Mary loved her job, which mostly involved organizing orchestral exchanges and gramophone concerts, or 'séances' as she called them, promoting British music by Purcell, Vaughan Williams and Delius (Delius's *Paris: The Song of a Great City* was a predictably popular choice) and traditional sea shanties, 'which brought a light touch to the end of the proceedings'. Because getting to the office required her to walk down the Rue du Faubourg Saint-Honoré, 'I have done a lot of gloating at the unbelievable shop windows but have been so overpowered that so far have only dared buy 3 pairs of stockings!'

Mary was also well placed to see how ordinary Parisian women, preoccupied as ever with food, were managing the transition to peacetime shopping and cooking. Although she bemoaned the lack of marmalade, soluble sanitary pads and Turkish cigarettes – 'I have plenty of Virginians but Naafi don't rise to Turkish' – she told her 'darling family' that the food was mostly very good with plenty of meat but no salads. She was shocked when invited to dinner one evening to see her profligate hostess throwing a large pat of butter into the frying pan to cook some veal and then mixing even more butter into the noodles. The story well illustrates the terrible disparity between those in Paris who had more than enough to eat (the British, Americans and rich Parisians), while many others in the city were on the verge of starvation. There *was* plenty of meat – but at a price, and butchers were good at exploiting this – while other staples were in short supply. On 1 January 1946 the government had had to introduce bread rationing once more, which led to angry demonstrations as well as violent arguments at bakeries. Women seen to be buying several loaves were sometimes attacked by those still queuing who feared there might not be any left. Once again the black market flourished, and wherever possible, goods – sometimes stolen – and services were bartered. This avoided the cash economy, creating additional difficulties for the government as it tried to collect taxes. One of the most notorious methods of increasing rations was to use the name of a dead relative to acquire an additional ration card. After four years of Occupation, many Parisiennes, cooks and countesses alike, had had time to perfect their forging. Janet Flanner, the US reporter now back in the city sending her 'Letter from Paris' to the *New Yorker*, described the delight of one literary Parisienne 'who, browsing in her attic among pre-war books, found two boxes of pre-war cartridges'. For twenty shells, a neighbourly crackshot brought her back in trade 'two pheasants, a kilo of country butter and a roast of veal'.

However, there was little that anyone could do about the extreme cold weather yet again that winter, especially harsh since there were grave shortages of heating fuel. Public buildings such as theatres were largely unheated. Mary was lucky to attend some of the autumn season's cultural highlights, before the blizzards set in, including what she called 'the great theatrical event of the moment' – Jean-Louis Barrault as Hamlet in a translation by André Gide at the Théâtre Marigny, a production which dismayed Janet Flanner as 'athletic, hearty and hasty', though she realized that no one dared criticize 'the demi-god Gide'.

On 16 October, Mary Wallington was excited to be invited to a gala performance with Marjorie Lawrence, the pre-war Wagnerian rival of Germaine Lubin who had overcome a crippling wartime bout of polio, in aid of establishing penicillin research centres throughout France. Lubin herself was finally brought to trial in 1946, having already served almost three years in prison. In the event, she was acquitted of the most serious accusations after several testimonials were produced from people she had helped during the war. But her career was finished.

'My trial was a complete vindication: I was completely cleared . . . Nobody knows how many prisoners I had released,' she insisted. 'Did anyone bother to ask me why I did not accept Winifred Wagner's invitations to sing in Germany during the Occupation?' Nevertheless she was sentenced to *dégradation nationale* for life (subsequently reduced to five years), confiscation of property, which included a chateau at Tours, and a form of exile which forced her to live with friends in Italy. Lubin did not return to Paris until 1950, by which time she was increasingly bitter about her treatment, claiming that she had been robbed of ten years of her singing career. But she would have derived mild satisfaction had she read Mary Wallington's description of the gala to her parents as 'most elaborately and vulgarly staged with press photographers creeping to the stage to flash cameras in Marjorie Lawrence's face even while she was singing . . . she certainly had the most magnificent voice though unfortunately she had a bad throat and cracked on the high notes at the end of the evening'.

Not everyone was forced to account publicly for how they had lived during the Occupation, but Picasso was one of those frequently questioned. It was known that German soldiers came to visit and even buy from him (or to ensure that he had adequate supplies) as he worked away in his studio in the Rue des Grands-Augustins, a house both shabby and sumptuous that his friends felt suited him so well. André Breton, the surrealist poet who was a friend of Picasso as well as of Eluard, had spent the war years in America. When he arrived back in the summer of 1946 and was reunited with Picasso, he criticized him for his politics *since* the Occupation, in particular for joining the Communist Party. According to Françoise Gilot, who witnessed the unhappy exchange, Picasso told him: 'You didn't choose to stay on in France with us during the Occupation. And you haven't lived through the events we lived through here. My stand is based on those experiences. I don't criticise your position since your understanding of those events was acquired at a different angle from mine . . . I place friendship above any differences of political opinion.'

The breach was never healed, but Gilot was steadfast in her defence of her lover, believing that 'It took a good deal of courage for him to stay there during the war since his paintings had been denounced by Hitler and the Occupation authorities took such a dim view of intellectuals. Many artists . . . had gone off to America before the Germans arrived. It must have seemed wiser to many not to run the risk of staying.' She told how, when she had asked him directly why he had remained in occupied France, he responded, 'Oh I'm not looking for risks to take . . . but in a sort of passive way I don't care to yield to either force or terror. I want to stay here because I'm here. The only kind of force that could make me leave would be the desire to leave. Staying on isn't really a manifestation of courage; it's just a form of inertia. I suppose it's simply that I prefer to be here. So I'll stay, whatever the cost.'

On 27 October 1946 the French constitution was finally changed to include among the basic principles of the Republic the law 'guaranteeing women equal rights to those of men in all spheres', and the national elections a month later in November were the first in which women in France were able to participate. At the same time several magazines were urging women, many of whom had run households as well as holding down jobs during the war, now to return to a time of innocence and femininity, to 'stop making decisions, stop balancing cheque books, stop being aggressively punctual'. But the prevailing feeling was that women could be interested in fashion, beauty, health and décor and still be intelligent enough to have interesting jobs. The new magazine *Elle*, a far cry from the pre-war *Vogue*, catered to this mood and in 1946 hired as its first editor the brilliant thirty-year-old journalist, writer and communicator Françoise Giroud, a liberated woman with a strong social conscience.[*]

And in the spring of 1946, the *loi Marthe Richard* was passed, set to take effect in October, legislation outlawing the legal brothels, which had operated in France since 1804, and pimping, while allowing prostitution itself to remain a lawful activity. Since there were some 7,000 registered prostitutes in France there were justified fears that the law would simply swell the number of those working illegally on the streets and disease would spread. Richard herself, like the new law, was controversial. A former prostitute, she may even have been a double agent, who had spent months profiting in Vichy eventually returning to Paris where it was said that she procured girls for evenings attended by Germans, practised some small-time swindling and eventually joined the resistance, just in time. She became a councillor in 1945 and worked to promote the anti-brothel laws, but her motives seemed dubious to many who saw the new law as an attack on French culture. Among those who lamented the end of the grand Parisian *maisons closes* was the British Ambassador, Duff Cooper – and some commentators believed that, at a time when France was suffering shortages of everything from electricity to potatoes, this should not have been a priority. Was 'Gay Paree', the world's capital of pleasure, succumbing to post-war prudery?

But there were other motives behind the change in the law. One was that the existing system, with its myriad rules and inspections, was open to police abuse and corruption. More significantly, the

---

[*] Giroud went on to become Minister for Women's Affairs under President Jacques Chirac in 1974.

brothels had flourished during the Occupation, as Fabienne Jamet, owner of one of the most notorious, the One Two Two, recalled: 'I'm almost ashamed at having to admit that I'd never had such a good time in my life . . . Those nights of the Occupation were truly fantastic . . . The brothels of France were never as well run and kept as while they [the Germans] were here.' It was not that the girls themselves or even the madams were pro-Nazi or collaborators. A few of the best-known houses had been requisitioned exclusively for officers' use and so the girls who worked there had no choice. But the whole industry was tainted and it was well known that those who wanted the brothels closed down included such bizarre bedfellows as the communists and the de Gaulles. Even though he was no longer in power by the time the law was passed, the General and especially his wife Yvonne loathed the very idea of state-approved brothels in post-war France.

Clearly, closing the brothels was not about supporting women. It had more to do with trying to establish normality in Paris and other cities, and not allowing the Americans to dictate how the city functioned. Just like the Germans before them, American soldiers saw Paris as one 'tremendous brothel', to quote *Life* magazine's reporter Joe Weston. But there was one critical difference: the Germans had regulated the brothels used by their officers, keeping prostitutes under strict medical supervision with weekly doctors' visits to ensure that, in an era when penicillin was not widely available, their men were not infected by syphilis. In the chaotic post-Liberation months the system floundered, as the French could recruit neither adequate medical care nor sufficient police oversight in the face of what came to be known as the 'silver foxhole', a magnet for GIs on leave serviced by women and girls from all over France flocking to the big city hoping to make money. According to Mary Louise Roberts, the author of *What Soldiers Do*, a study of sex and the American GI in France in the Second World War, the French did make an attempt to introduce rudimentary government medical care, which the prostitutes did their best to avoid. 'The treatment awaiting them was at best ineffective, at worst physical torture. Examinations were given under poor lighting and in unsanitary conditions. Often no effort was made to wash the speculum in between examinations, or for that matter to change the linen and the pot of Vaseline. The sickest of the women ended up in locked hospital wards, where nuns did their best to wage a battle against alcohol, bad language, and lesbian sex.'

When American military authorities first took over the Petit Palais, a beautiful 1900 exhibition centre in the centre of Paris, one of the first things they did was put up a large sign announcing distribution of free condoms to US troops. The US military did not really care if a GI had sex with a French woman. What it did care a great deal about was that a soldier did not contract a venereal disease. But the men themselves, who faced violent death every day, were not easily scared by the threat of a curable infection. Since the authorities in 1944 could neither ban brothels nor monitor the hygiene of individual French women, they tried to manage with enormous stocks of condoms. But because supplies could not be well organized behind a rapidly moving army, condoms were often nonexistent and army-issue products generated an endless stream of complaints. Furthermore, some American officers concluded that trying to control the sexual behaviour of a soldier 'operating in a place like France . . . was tantamount to making him eat raw carrots in a steakhouse'.

'In both popular American culture and high diplomatic and military circles, the whore came to represent "Frenchness" itself,' explains Roberts, and selling her body was seen as part of a broader French subservience to American money and power.

Some American soldiers behaved as if, when it came to young French women, anything can be bought. SHAEF's [Supreme Headquarters Allied Expeditionary Force] frustration with French regulation and its inability to see French women as infected as well as infectious had a significant impact on Franco-American relations. Besides reinforcing American prejudices about France as decadent, the 'problem' of VD inspired further condescension, invited American intervention into French affairs, and naturalised the army's 'right' to manage the freedom of the civilian population . . . The supposedly 'infectious' body of the prostitute became the site of a power struggle, but it operated at a more symbolic level as well.

Closing the brothels represented the end of an era, an era when young provincial girls, usually in their early twenties, would be seduced into coming to Paris to seek fame and fortune, often enticed by a man who promised them love and riches, only to find that they had to work to support themselves. A brothel, complete with pimp or madam, was their only option. Some young girls, brought to Paris by a wealthy patron, such as Coco Chanel and Jeanne Toussaint, had made good in the city. But as is shown by the registers from La Petite Roquette (a women's prison used for prostitutes) indicating that fewer than 20 per cent had been born in Paris and its immediate suburbs, most did not fare so well.

With the passing of the new law, furniture from the Belle Epoque bordellos was now auctioned, properties were sold and 'Screw Marthe Richard' was daubed on one famous brothel door as it closed. But the new system, whereby young women in garish clothes were seen plying their trade all too openly on the streets around the Rue Saint-Denis, just as they did in any other city, was not popular either and seemed to threaten Paris with losing its charm – for men at least. As Nancy Mitford wrote (incorrectly of Marthe Richard since she was not a deputy) of the brothels: 'These, having lately been driven underground by the ill-considered action of a woman Deputy, had become rather difficult for a foreigner to find.'

But find them they still did. One of the best-known, which should have closed in 1946 but somehow managed to continue more or less legally as a 'meeting place', was L'Etoile de Kléber, whose upper rooms had housed Edith Piaf and friends for months at a time during the Occupation. Piaf may not have played an active role in any resistance group and she had performed in numerous brothels and nightclubs frequented by Germans or French collaborators or both. Yet, when she was brought before a post-war tribunal, Andrée Bigard had spoken in her favour, and she was forgiven. Her popular song, 'La Vie en Rose', although written in 1945, was not performed in concert for the first time until 1946 and immediately became a huge hit. Similarly, Charles Trenet – allowed to forget his far more questionable behaviour during the Occupation when he had performed at the Folies Bergère and the Gaieté Parisienne, favourite

Wehrmacht haunts – now released 'La Mer', which also became a massive hit. Both songs captured the mood two years after the Liberation: namely that whatever the hardships and pain of war, it was time to move on and forget. Life in Paris was good.

PART THREE

RECONSTRUCTION

1947

PARIS LOOKS NEWISH

By January 1947 Vera Atkins had given evidence at two of the trials organized by the Allies for those high-ranking Nazis held responsible for killing at the various camps that they had managed to capture, hoping both to learn and to see justice done. First was the trial in 1946 of SS officials at Natzweiler-Struthof, where she believed four of her girls had died – Vera Leigh, Diana Rowden, Andrée Borrel and Noor Inayat Khan – and then early in 1947 she assisted the prosecution at the first trial of guards and staff at Ravensbrück, which had claimed the lives of another four – Cecily Lefort, Violette Szabo, Denise Bloch and Lilian Rolfe. But several other agents remained unaccounted for. Just as the Germans had intended for their *Nacht und Nebel* prisoners, they had disappeared without trace. But, two years on from the end of the war, there was now a palpable change of atmosphere as the victorious powers started to turn their energies increasingly towards post-war reconstruction and diplomacy rather than punishing the perpetrators of war crimes.

For Vera it had never been simply a case of retribution. Establishing the truth was a duty she owed her girls. However, some who knew her felt that her grim determination reflected also the guilt she harboured; some agents had been parachuted directly into already compromised circuits, infiltrated by the Germans. Madeleine Damerment, dropped on the night of 29 February 1944, twenty miles east of Chartres, had been seized on landing in an operation arranged by the Germans as part of their *Funkspiel* (radio game), using Noor's captured set. Madeleine was taken to Fresnes, then interrogated at the Avenue Foch SiPo-SD. In May, she was transferred to Karlsruhe civilian jail in Germany with seven other female agents. Quite possibly, Vera's tangled personal circumstances and insecurity – she dreaded her own lack of Britishness being revealed – were part of the reason she had not spoken out earlier and demanded investigations. In addition, she was always deeply loyal to Maurice Buckmaster, head of SOE's F Section, with whom she worked so closely. If she could discover the truth now, she desperately hoped, there was at least a chance of winning posthumous justice for these brave girls.

There is still controversy today about why London continued to send agents as well as money into France when there were concerns that the circuit might have been blown. Some historians believe that Buckmaster was simply careless and overlooked security lapses out of a political need to keep the section's agents in the field. Others conclude that the British were aware of the 'radio games' but played along with the deception so as to distract the Germans in anticipation of D-Day. Yet there is now evidence that Sonia Olschanesky, a Russian-born, locally hired agent working for SOE in France, had warned London on 1 October 1943 of Noor's capture. Buckmaster ignored the warning, worried about the 'reliability' of 'Sonja' (sic). 'Had Sonia's warning been heeded at that time, Dr Goetz's "radio game" would have been exposed and probably halted there and then, saving countless SOE lives,' is the view of one historian. Yet Noreen Riols, who from 1943 onwards worked closely with Buckmaster at F Section HQ in London, is at pains to stress that SOE was constantly making life and death decisions without all the means of instant communication available today. She insists that 'Buck', as she called him, 'was always deeply concerned about his agents and far from careless and uncaring about their fate . . . what critics fail to understand is that SOE was a fledgling organisation; it was unconventional and improvisational since there were no precedents, no previous experience or strategy to help and guide its leaders, no charts, reports or manuals to instruct those in charge. They were obliged to make up the rules as they struggled along.' Either way, the lives of innocent girls were being squandered. The SOE's historian M. R. D. Foot explained later: 'To the question why people with so little training were sent to do such important work, the only reply is: the work had to be done and there was no one else to send.' Leo Marks, having felt such sympathy for Noor during her training, had given her an extra security check to use only if caught, so he was desperately worried when she used it that she must be in enemy hands. 'I said a silent prayer that Noor was having one of her lapses,' Marks wrote later, 'but knew I was having one of my own not to accept the truth.' Buckmaster insisted that London must continue responding to her as if nothing were amiss and that the two-way traffic with her should continue.

But although by early 1947 Vera believed she knew most of what she would ever learn, she was not quite ready to close all her files, especially as she was now starting to receive new evidence about what had really happened to Noor. It was only after the Natzweiler trial that she had seen the name of Sonia Olschanesky for the first time appear in lists of prisoners. But 'Olschanesky', she assumed, while obviously one of the women imprisoned at Karlsruhe, was a name she did not know and quite probably therefore an alias for Noor. Changing names was something they all did and, since Noor had been born in Moscow, she might well have chosen this one, Vera argued.* Some of the most reliable information which helped her finally unravel the last months in Noor's life came from her brother, Vilayat Inayat Khan, who had received eyewitness accounts from two sources – a French girl, Yolande Lagrave, who had met 'Nora' when both were prisoners at Pforzheim secure prison, not at Karlsruhe, in September 1944, and a German woman who had worked at the jail. It was from Yolande that Vera learned that Noor had had her hands and feet constantly manacled, apparently on orders from Berlin as she was considered an especially dangerous prisoner, that she was fed starvation rations, that she was beaten from time to time and that she was rarely allowed to talk to anyone or go outside. Slowly Vera was able to piece together, mostly from interviews with other guards awaiting trial, information about Noor's resilience and dignity in the face of her exceptionally cruel treatment at Pforzheim.

The key breakthrough for Vera came in January 1947 when she was able to interview Hans Kieffer, deputy head of the SiPo-SD in Paris,

---

* Even when she later discovered that Sonia Olschanesky had existed, Vera was never as interested in finding out her story as she was in knowing how Noor had died.

who had finally been run to ground.* Kieffer, she knew, would have interrogated her girls while they were still in Paris, and it was because of him that they were sent to Karlsruhe, his home town. But only Noor, considered a particular risk because she had tried to escape twice, was punished in a solitary cell at Pforzheim and kept permanently in chains. In spite of her barbaric treatment she had refused to give away any information, behaviour which more than anything exasperated her captors. On 11 September 1944 she was driven from Pforzheim to Karlsruhe, where she met up with Eliane Plewman, Madeleine Damerment and Yolande Beekman. They were all then taken to Dachau, where they were kept in separate cells and shot in the early hours of 13 September, but not (as the official version claimed) together, with the four women holding hands as they were shot in the back of the neck. There are different accounts of precisely how Noor was murdered, but – according to information from various sources which Vera appears to have believed, although it was not recorded in the official files – the night before she died Noor was given 'the full treatment'. A German officer, repeating what he had heard from camp officials, told Lieutenant Colonel H. J. Wickey, who worked for Canadian intelligence during the war, that 'Noor was tortured and abused in her cell by the Germans. She was stripped, kicked and finally left lying on the floor battered and bruised. Then in the early hours of the following morning she was shot in her cell.'

However, no one from Dachau stood trial specifically for the executions of Madeleine, Yolande, Noor and Eliane, partly because there was no proof of their demise and no witnesses to describe the killings. Those most likely to have been responsible were either dead themselves or already facing trial for other war crimes. All Vera Atkins could do, once she had discovered what she finally believed to be the truth of Nora's death at Dachau, was to fight tirelessly to have her posthumously awarded a George Cross, the highest civilian award for bravery in Britain. This she did, citing in her recommendation for the award how even Kieffer had wept when he recounted Noor's exceptional courage. The award was granted in 1949.

---

* He was hanged in June 1947, but his trial had nothing to do with the women SOE agents.

Vera herself was demobilized in 1947, and her story continues to fascinate and puzzle. Relatives of those girls unaccounted for found her cold and unemotional, with 'a callous streak' according to her biographer, in stark contrast to her dedication to finding the missing. There is a note in a file now at the National Archives at Kew from the mother of the Paris-born Yolande stating that her daughter was pregnant at the time she was sent into France, while Diana Rowden's mother did not know that her daughter had received the Croix de guerre until the author Elizabeth Nicholas found out while researching her 1958 book, *Death Be Not Proud*. Nicholas also discovered that the fiancé and family of Sonia Olschanesky, who had shown incredible courage by staying on to work as a courier near Paris after the Prosper ring of Francis Suttill had been blown, had never been informed of her fate. Tania Szabo, Violette's young daughter, found Atkins 'cold and distant', and Vilayat Inayat Khan told Vera's biographer that she was 'cold blooded': 'Vera Atkins was the intelligence officer who really wanted to find out what happened, she wanted to sort things out – to be clear about things,' he said. But he believed his sister had been used. Yvonne Baseden, one of those who survived thanks to the Swedish Red Cross, described Vera when she met her on release as 'quite distant – cold almost at first. Suspicious even . . . I think she must have thought – you know – why had I been released? What had I done to be released and not the others? I think that must have been why she was a little wary of me.'

Yet, however keen the French public and government might have been to move on, there were some whose crimes were so heinous they could never be forgiven. Anne Spoerry, or 'Dr Claude', who had been seen on several occasions to execute patients by lethal injection in Ravensbrück, was one such. After the Liberation, Spoerry had returned to Paris hoping to complete her medical exams, but once she was asked to defend the sadistic *blockova* Carmen Mory at the Ravensbrück trials in Hamburg, even though she refused to attend, her anonymity was over. She was swiftly arrested herself on charges of torture and murder, and throughout 1946 and 1947 was summoned to appear in courts in Switzerland as well as before a Free French Forces Court of Honour in Paris, where she was judged by former members of the resistance. Mory, at her trial, accused Spoerry of being the Block 10 murderer, but Spoerry's defence lawyers persuaded the court that this could not be proven, thus absolving her from the most serious charges. Mory was sentenced to death by hanging, but in April 1947 she killed herself by slitting her wrist with a razor blade a week before the sentence was due to be carried out.

Spoerry, at her own trials, tried to deny everything, yet she admitted she had been spellbound by Mory, whom she called a devil. The Court of Honour now found her guilty of different charges: impersonating a doctor, being a traitor to the French and bringing shame on France through her inhumane behaviour. The punishment: exile from France for twenty-five years. Although by now Spoerry had a tropical medicine diploma, she did not yet have her full medical degree because the French Faculty of Medicine blocked it following the Court of Honour verdict. In the wake of this, she decided simply to call herself 'Dr Spoerry,' took a slow boat to Africa and, by 1949, had settled in Kenya where she taught herself to fly and became a much loved flying doctor for the rest of her life. If anyone mentioned the war she flew into a rage. Her good work in Africa no doubt brought her a degree of redemption but, not surprisingly, she never forgot Ravensbrück.

On 12 February 1947, Christian Dior dramatically moved the conversation forward in Paris when he launched his debut haute couture collection. The temperature that day was 21 degrees Fahrenheit (−6 degrees Celsius), but the excited Parisiennes who arrived for his show at 30 Avenue Montaigne were well protected in their mink coats. Marcel Boussac, the cotton magnate who was Dior's backer, was confident that the show would be a success, not simply because of the magnificent floral arrangements organized by his protégé but because of the buzz that had preceded it. The House of Dior had been established only the year before, in October 1946, but it seemed to have captured the widespread political desire to move on and away from the war and to do so in as obviously extravagant a fashion as possible. The eager audience, perched on the edge of their little gilt chairs, watched with delight as the models paraded ninety fabulous outfits of wide skirts, ballerina length, with layers of petticoats accentuated by tiny cinched waists. As the models, full of flounce, flair and feminine drama, twirled and turned on the catwalk, their volu-minous skirts sent cigarette ash flying. To an audience used to tight, short pencil skirts, this opulence was a breathtaking statement. There was an explosion of bravos at the end of the show, so loud that Dior himself was seen putting his hands over his ears. The two doyennes of the fashion press, *Harper's Bazaar* editor-in-chief Carmel Snow and Bettina Ballard of *Vogue*, were both ecstatic in their praise for what was a radical departure in style but nonetheless rooted in Belle Epoque ideas.

It was Snow who exclaimed with delight, 'It's quite a revelation, dear Christian. Your dresses have such a new look,' thereby coining the phrase for what is now seen as the most iconic debut collec-tion of all time. Ballard, not noted for being overly generous in her praise, declared: 'We were witness to a revolution in fashion and to a revolution in showing fashion as well . . . Never has there been a moment more climatically right for a Napoleon, an Alexander the Great, a Caesar of the couture. Paris fashion was waiting to be seized and shaken and given direction. There has never been an easier or more complete conquest than that of Christian Dior in 1947.' Carmel Snow said quite simply: 'Dior saved Paris.'

The American press was united in its view that this was a global fashion revolution, restoring Paris to the pinnacle of haute couture. British journalists who wished to write as rapturously faced a con-flict, because Dior appeared to be signalling an end to austerity and to the wartime fabric restrictions to which British designers were still subject. Alison Settle, then editor of British *Vogue*, was refused permission to mention Dior in her pages at a time when austerity in Britain was biting even harder than it had during the war as a result of the wartime loans the government was now having to pay back. In addition, the New Look's wasp waist and wide hips, even when worn by extremely slim models, depended on firm foundation garments.[*] But most corsetry, regarded as inessential in Britain, was banned under rationing unless required for medical reasons. In short, the

---

[*] Jean Weston, known as Rowlande, who started her modelling career in 1947 Paris for Worth in the wake of the New Look at the age of seventeen, was five foot nine inches tall, weighed a mere 101 pounds and had an eighteen-inch waist.

British feared that the New Look would create impossible demands for additional fabric. When Settle suggested lifting fabric quotas, Sir Stafford Cripps, President of the Board of Trade, roared at her: 'What New Look?'

The situation changed slightly, as the Princesses Elizabeth and Margaret were both captivated by the New Look even though, of course, they were forbidden to flout the regulations. But that autumn, when Dior was in London, the Queen Mother asked for a private show. From then on, British designers found ways of adapting old coats or inserting black velvet bands to give the illusion of extra fabric. The novelist Nancy Mitford, now living on the Left Bank in Paris, wrote to her sister Diana Mosley after seeing the collection, saying that with 'one stroke' Dior's New Look made 'all one's clothes unwearable'. But as Mitford, who had moved to Paris in 1946 in order to be close to her faithless lover, Gaston Palewski, was to discover, wearing such expensive extravagant outfits came with risks, even in Paris. 'People shout *ordures* at you from vans,' she wrote to Eddy Sackville West, 'because for some reason it creates class feeling in a way no sables could.' And when, one month later, Maison Dior decided to hold a photoshoot in the streets of Montmartre, the models found themselves attacked by a group of angry women stallholders who tried to beat one model, pull her hair and tear her clothes off, shouting insults all the while at such conspicuous and excessive profligacy which failed to reflect the hardships they had suffered in recent years or the ongoing shortages of food.

There was another launch at the Avenue Montaigne that momentous day in February. Many of the audience were aware of an exotic perfume, liberally sprayed throughout the premises, to accompany the show. It was called Miss Dior, named after the designer's youngest sister, Catherine Dior. Quite possibly, however, no one at the show was aware of who she was nor of the dangerous resistance work she had been engaged in for three years from 1941 until her capture. Her story has only recently become known, making headline news following the arrest in 2011 of Dior's then creative director, John Galliano, for alleged anti-Semitic remarks recorded in a phone video. At that point the company decided it was time to remind people of 'the values of the House of Dior' by talking of Catherine.

Catherine died in 2008, aged ninety-one, having rarely spoken of her wartime activities. She had been an agent in the Massif Central unit of a resistance network whose main aim was gathering information about German troop and rail movements, production and weaponry, vital knowledge for those involved in active sabotage. According to Gitta Sereny, the Austrian-born writer who worked as a nurse in Paris in 1940 and knew members of 'this elite organisation of more than 2,000 agents – which suffered enormous losses', the group 'was later credited as one of the most dynamic intelligence movements in Europe. By the end of 1942 most of its leaders had been killed by the Gestapo.' Catherine joined the network at the end of 1941, aged twenty-five, persuaded by fellow *résistant* Hervé Papillaut des Charbonneries, whom she met and fell in love with when she went into a shop to buy a radio. A founding member of the network, Hervé was already married with three young children, so the romance was discreet. Another close friend and fellow resister in the same network was Liliane (Lili) Dietlin, 'the epitome of the Parisienne, small, slim, finely boned with that very special elegance of speech, behaviour and, of course, dress that none of us adoptive Parisians could ever emulate'. Lili and Catherine worked as couriers, carrying huge amounts of information, sometimes in their heads if they could memorize it, between sections. When she came to Paris, Catherine would stay at 10 Rue Royale, the apartment used by her brother and his friends. However, in July 1944 she was trapped into a meeting with Gestapo officers, arrested, tortured and deported on the final train from Paris on 15 August to Ravensbrück, where she worked in German munitions factories in notoriously atrocious conditions.

Probably Christian knew of his sister's resistance activities, because immediately after her arrest he used whatever contacts he could to try and get her released. Working at the house of Lelong, he counted among his clients a handful of German officers' wives and he approached them for help. But he was unsuccessful and she was not released until April 1945. When Catherine returned to Paris a month later she was emaciated and ill after eleven months of starvation rations and harsh treatment. But she was one of the lucky ones who recovered relatively swiftly. From now on she lived and worked with Hervé des Charbonneries, building up a business as a *manda-taire en fleurs coupées,* a dealer in the exotic cut flowers of southern France and the French colonies. She and Hervé, who never divorced his wife, would leave at four in the morning to go to Les Halles to buy supplies of fresh flowers to send all over the world. It was a job and a way of life she loved, but perhaps living with a married man was an additional reason for the reticence about her resistance activities.

Two years after her release, her brother named his first scent after her. Catherine was awarded a rare Croix de guerre (normally this was reserved for those in the regular armed forces); she also received the Croix du combattant volontaire de la Résistance, the Croix du combattant and the King's Medal for Courage in the Cause of Freedom (the latter, courtesy of Britain), and she was named a Chevalière of the Légion d'honneur. Not many women were so highly decorated so soon after the end of the war.

But it was not only impoverished Parisiennes who reacted angrily to Dior's New Look. Chanel, who had welcomed the success of the New Look 'with barely suppressed contempt', was motivated not by concern that Dior's lavish designs failed to take account of ordinary women's suffering so much as by jealousy and fury that her own earlier success in sweeping away the corsets women had been forced to wear was now being trumped. 'I make fashions women can live in, breathe in, feel comfortable in, and look young in,' she had declared to Ballard. Now she felt her fashion legacy slipping away. One wealthy Dior client commented that the dress she had just bought was 'the most amazing dress she had ever seen', adding, 'I can't walk, eat or even sit down.'

Chanel, Schiaparelli and Jeanne Lanvin, three enormously influential pre-war female designers, had, it seemed, all had their day. The post-war couture houses were almost exclusively male. During the war, both Dior and Pierre Balmain had learned their trade working for Lucien Lelong. But Balmain now decided to found his own *maison de couture* and in 1947 hired an English woman as his Directrice. Ginette Spanier was married to a French doctor, Paul-Emile Seidmann, and being Jewish had spent most of the war in hiding from the Nazis in occupied France.* They managed to avoid deportation by frequently moving about the country and often went without money or enough food. After the Liberation, Ginette found a job working as a translator for the American army, not least at the Nuremberg trials, while Paul-Emile worked with camp survivors in Paris. Both were decorated for their work. Ginette said later that her character had been forged in the war years. It was the war that had 'confirmed in me all I find most important in life: friends and England and love of warmth and love of life itself. It taught me to fear anything dead and cruel and genteel and therefore lacking in humanity . . . the war taught me to mistrust possessions.' And yet this woman who might have been killed at any instant, who darned threadbare clothes over and over again, never saw fashion as trivial. In Paris it wasn't. As Directrice at Balmain, she was responsible for every human problem throughout the front and back offices, including parts of the company which the public could see and much that they could not, such as feuds between two *vendeuses*, each claiming commission when a dress was sold. This was a significant matter, since Balmain counted among his clients the Duchess of Windsor† and Marlene Dietrich, as well as many other actresses and royalty. Ginette took her job immensely seriously and became something of a legend.

With fashion spearheading the economic revival of France, the twenty-two-year-old Simone Bodin, daughter of a Normandy railway worker, was not unusual in seeking her fortune in Paris. After her father had abandoned the family, Simone and her sister were brought up during the war by their mother, a teacher. As soon as Paris had been liberated, Simone moved to the capital, finding whatever work she could either as a babysitter or as an architect's assistant, but hoping to become a dress designer. A chance introduction to the couturier Jacques Costet led to an offer to model for him, as he

* In one secret location Ginette had come across the British nanny trying to get home, Rosemary Say.
† Wallis shopped at most of the Parisian couture houses and was an early fan of Dior, but she spread her favours widely and also patronized Mainbocher, now back in New York.

admired her fresh-faced, country-girl looks and her slim figure. But when his business floundered, she went to work for Lucien Lelong, having turned down an offer from the less experienced Christian Dior. However, she was soon tempted away from Lelong to work for Jacques Fath, who had flourished during the war and was able to offer her a five-times salary increase.

It was Fath who made her famous, renaming her Bettina because he wanted to convey a modern, American spirit and a brand-new attitude in tune with the post-war ideals. 'He liked that I was different. I was very young, I wore no make-up and I had red hair.' Being a mannequin was still for 'couture only', with no ready-to-wear, but Bettina herself, who had grown up in an impoverished family, was unlike the pre-war, haute-bourgeoise Parisian model, both in looks and in ideals. Bettina's story illustrates one of the greatest changes in the post-war fashion world – the emergence of the professional model, now viewed as a proper career in its own right. The countesses and princesses of high society were being edged out as muses or icons of fashion. Once she had cut her chignon and wore short cropped hair, Bettina became the most photographed face in France, epitomizing the new, chic young Parisienne, or the embodiment of the freedom-loving, modern woman. After a brief marriage in the late 1940s to the photographer Gilbert Graziani, Bettina had numerous relationships with men, including the photographer Robert Capa, but in 1960 was planning to marry Prince Aly Khan. Pregnant with his child, she and Khan were tragically involved in a car crash which killed him and caused the loss of her unborn child.

There was one other voice raised in mild disapproval of Dior's opulence: the designer born Carmen de Tommaso who took the name Marie-Louise Carven. Carven, a petite five foot one, was known for her dislike of old-fashioned Parisian sophistication, or what she saw as the Belle Epoque grandeur of heavy silk and corseted cut, favoured by wealthy older women, that had been revived by Christian Dior. Carven had been designing dresses since she was a teenager in the 1920s and, after studying architecture and interior design at the Ecole des Beaux-Arts in Paris, had courageously opened her own fashion house in the Champs-Elysées in July 1945, immediately the war was over. This was at a time of dramatic fabric shortages throughout

Europe, with almost no raw fibres imported or produced, and mills and factories abandoned or destroyed. Couturiers in Paris could mount a show only if they had small caches of pre-war textiles, or if they had access to supplies, as Dior did through Marcel Boussac with his global empire of cotton textile factories and printing plants.

Marie-Louise Carven, by contrast, was ingenious in her search for every scrap of fabric. For her opening show she was able to make a generous-skirted summer dress, created from a roll of striped mint-green and white cotton found in the attic of a chateau and possibly bought before the First World War, intended for maids' uniforms.* Her dresses were seen as young, fresh and informal in both style and colour, as opposed to the structured gowns of the day which did not flatter small women like her. But more importantly her ideas matched an alternative new mood where fashion became part of everyday living and not just for dressing up to attend a ball. Dior's New Look grabbed the headlines, but arguably it was Carven, one of the first designers to launch a ready-to-wear or *prêt-à-porter* range, whose influence was more far-reaching in changing how women dressed.

Fashion and the film industry had always fed on each other and they continued to do so in post-war Paris. Carven's clothes were in demand from petite stars such as Edith Piaf (who nonetheless insisted on having all the fancy trimmings removed), Leslie Caron, Zizi Jeanmaire and Simone Signoret. Marcel Carné followed his huge success of 1946, the dark thriller *Les Portes de la nuit*, with a project once again starring Arletty, about children who were jailed in pre-war France under horrific conditions. Mysteriously, the film, called *La Fleur de l'âge* and based on the true story of a mass escape that took place on the island of Belle-Ile-en-Mer and of the child hunt that ensued, was never finished. However, it marked the start of a seventy-year career for one of the child actresses who appeared in it, Anouk Aimée. She acquired her first name, Anouk, from a character

* The green and white was so popular that she used it for the packaging of her perfume, Ma Griffe (My Signature), which she launched in 1946 using an aeroplane flying over Paris to release hundreds of tiny parachutes bearing a sample of the scent.

she played in that film; Aimée came later. Still just fourteen, that same year she also had a role in Henri Calef's *La Maison sous la mer*.

Anouk Aimée was born in Paris as Françoise Sorya Dreyfus in April 1932, the daughter of two actors. Her father, Henry Dreyfus, who was Jewish, worked under the stage name Henry Murray, and her mother, Geneviève Sorya, was Catholic. Little is known of the family's Jewish background (they may have been related to Captain Alfred Dreyfus), nor of how they survived during the war, but according to one story Françoise was walking home from school one day in occupied Paris when her classmates shouted out, 'Here's a little Jewish girl for you,' just as German soldiers came by. Fortunately, a 'good' German soldier took pity on her, told her to take off her star and brought her home to her grandmother. She then moved south with her mother, was baptized a Catholic and attended boarding school in Bandol.

No doubt something of the tension of those days always remained with her, and her stunning if disturbing beauty not only made her the ideal actress for Claude Lelouch's *Un Homme et une femme* of 1966 but also equipped her for the central role of a Jewish woman coming to terms later in life with her time at Birkenau as a teenage prisoner in the 2003 film *La Petite prairie aux bouleaux* (The Little Meadow of Birch-Trees). This was based on the real-life experiences of writer-director Marceline Loridan-Ivens, formerly Rozenberg. The film historian Ginette Vincendeau has written that Aimée's films 'established her as an ethereal, sensitive and fragile beauty with a tendency to tragic destinies or restrained suffering'. In recent years, having converted as an adult to Judaism (her mother was not Jewish), Aimée is often referred to as an icon for world peace and reconciliation, but she has not revealed details of her own childhood. At the 2003 screening of the Birkenau film she simply spoke about the importance of documenting this chapter of Jewish history.

Summer 1947 was, according to a young British would-be writer trying to disentangle herself from an unsuitable love affair, 'a summer that will never end, a golden summer of unbroken heat and unclouded blue skies and sunshine: timeless'. Emma Smith had grabbed an opportunity to escape to Paris following a chance encounter in London with one of the five Geoffroy-Dechaume sons. Claude, a jeweller, explained that his family was based in a large, rambling and rather derelict house at Valmondois, north of Paris, and was trying to make ends meet in the difficult post-war climate by taking in English and American students. They needed someone to help with chores such as bedmaking, vegetable-peeling and fetching the early-morning milk and baguettes. Was she interested in such an unpaid post in return for her board and lodging? Emma accepted and moved to Valmondois where she found her new existence basic – her room was illuminated by a single dangling light bulb, had shutters but no curtains, an uncarpeted floor plus bed, chair and table – but more than adequate.

Immersed in this intensely French Resistance family, Emma fell in love not with one son but two: both Denis and Jean-Pierre, the two youngest. After all, both brothers were 'Heroes of the French Resistance', she wrote later of her youthful adoration, 'bravest of the brave, young men who hid up in the hills and fought alongside the gallant Maquis and by their indomitable courage saved the whole world from wicked German fascism. I am bound – am I not? – to adore them both.'

Antoine, the eldest son, the musician friend of Vivou Chevrillon, had, he told her, survived Nazi torture by playing in his head Bach's harpsichord music, while his mother, Mme Geoffroy, had embroidered over the hole in another son's shirt where he had been shot in order to commemorate the wound. Emma was to hear many tales of derring-do that summer, such as how Jean-Pierre had hauled his wounded brother out of hospital minutes before the Germans arrived to take him into captivity. Marie-France, their sister, a heroine decorated by de Gaulle for her work escorting downed airmen to freedom and for cycling with guns concealed beneath onions and gelignite under her coat, passed through Valmondois that summer on her honeymoon with Dermod MacCarthy, a British paediatrician. Sylvie, the youngest of the five daughters, who had also worked in the south with the Maquis (not yet married to the President's nephew, Bernard de Gaulle) was the same age as Emma and became her special friend as they worked together in the kitchen. 'I remember being permanently hungry and thin and feeling there was never quite enough to eat,' said Emma. But the overriding memory of that summer as she immersed herself in French post-war life was the fun she had smoking pungent, wispy Gauloises Bleues cigarettes and drinking '*un petit coup de vin blanc*' at the village bistro, while thinking Jean-Pierre was the handsome prince she had been waiting for. But then, after three months, she was suddenly dismissed. François, the second son who worked in the diplomatic service but was effectively the head of the family, told her she was an extra mouth to feed and the Geoffroy-Dechaumes could no longer afford one of those. Distraught, Emma went home and that autumn, goaded to succeed, wrote her first novel.

Lee Miller, who loved Paris so much, was now back in England, too. She gave birth in September 1947 to her first and only child, Anthony, son of Roland Penrose; she virtually gave up journalism and tried to settle into a new life. To mark the birth, Man Ray, her erstwhile lover when she first came to Paris and responsible for teaching her photography, sent her a signed, original photograph of Nusch Eluard, modelling a Suzanne Belperron bracelet, with a matching ring and brooch. It was a poignant reminder of their pre-war Paris life together when the beautiful Nusch, a muse for and lover of both Eluard and Picasso, had been a jewellery model and one of Lee's closest friends. But Nusch, always physically frail, struggled during the war to find enough to eat and lived with constant anxiety and fear as she and Eluard, both in the communist resistance, were regularly moving homes to avoid the Gestapo. On 28 November 1946, alone in Paris while Paul was away in Switzerland, just after she and Dora Maar had been talking on the phone and making plans to meet for lunch, Nusch suddenly collapsed with a fatal cerebral haemorrhage. It was a terrible loss for many, Paul especially of course, but also for Dora, to whom it seemed that she was losing everyone she loved at the same time. For Lee, it underlined that this was the end of a chapter in her life.

One of the best advertisements for Dior's New Look gowns that year in Paris was Susan Mary Patten, the beautiful and patrician wife of the US diplomat Bill Patten, and Duff Cooper's lover. She had arrived in the city in 1945 and had taken a while to feel at home but was determined to understand it by travelling around, attending some of the collaboration trials and doing her duty as a hostess. Her high-level social connections coupled with her hourglass figure encouraged Christian Dior to lend or even give her dresses on occasion as he knew she made a wonderful model on whom to display his dramatic creations. As they moved from one diplomatic dinner party to another, Susan Mary was intelligent and interested enough to observe the shifting political scene where distrust was growing over increasing Soviet influence and there was controversy over how that was to be countered. In France communists polled five million votes in October 1945, and in the November 1946 national elections they took 29 per cent of the vote. Churchill, although out of power, had made an influential speech the previous year warning of the 'Iron Curtain' that had fallen across Europe, but in general the Americans took the view that German war reparations should not be too heavy and the emphasis should be on rebuilding Germany. But when Susan Mary referred to this one evening at a dinner, Cooper exploded as he, like the French, did not believe that the Germans should be allowed any possibility of rising anew.

In June the US Secretary of State, George C. Marshall, who had been Army Chief of Staff throughout the war, announced a European Recovery Program which would eventually channel $13 billion into Europe to stimulate economic recovery. It was a vital three-year package of aid, if communism was to be countered in Europe. France needed desperately just to improve the daily life of the population, which was suffering serious food shortages once again and an active black market. Nineteen-forty-seven saw yet another severe winter in Paris, this time exacerbated by constant disruption and violence as three million workers went on strike to protest against rising prices and stagnant wages. But there were also communist groups agitating against the Marshall Plan itself. As the disruption spread, telegraph lines were cut and railway lines sabotaged, electricity cut and mail interrupted. One incident involving a train derailment killed sixteen people. However, at the height of the bitter strikes and tension the CGT (Confédération Générale du Travail), one of the country's major unions, called off its strike, enabling dockworkers to return to work just in time to receive the first Marshall Plan shipments from America. *Time* magazine called this scheme of unprecedented beneficence 'the D day of the peace'; others, seeing a weak, vulnerable, insecure continent with little hope of recovery, described it as a lifeline to a drowning man. The veteran journalist Theodore White wrote, 'Like a whale left gasping on the sand, Europe lay rotting in the sun.'

Susan Mary, however fascinated she was by the political environment, had learned that it was beyond her role as the wife of an economic analyst to express opinions, and so it was not on account of her political views that Duff found this twenty-nine-year-old American beguilingly attractive. Yet by May 1947 the pair were indulging – on her part at least – in a passionate affair. Duff, nearing sixty, was flattered and excited but probably not in love; he was still emotionally if not physically involved with Louise de Vilmorin. But Susan Mary had fallen deeply into adulterous love and, as she was to discover, there was no better place than Paris with its upstairs dining rooms and its culture of amorous secrecy to experience such an affair.

However, Duff had known since September that his tour in Paris was ending, and on 10 December the Coopers hosted a magnificent farewell ball at the Embassy. Susan Mary was heartbroken. Duff had once said that when his time was up, 'I shan't mind except for leaving the library' – a magnificent room thanks to Lady Diana enlisting her artistic friends in the decoration, created to house her husband's books. There were several British visitors who attended the ball, including Winston Churchill who could not resist an opportunity to see Odette Pol Roger, of the champagne dynasty, whom he adored, and of course a number of French government ministers. Susan Mary, looking stunning in a Schiaparelli mauve satin and ivory grosgrain gown, stayed until 5 a.m., writing to Cooper later that she would have given anything if 'in return I could have the next five minutes sitting on your lap and be held tight, tight against your heart'. By then, although she did not know it, she was in the early stages of pregnancy. Duff was the never publicly acknowledged father, and he wrote laconically in his diary when told the news that, although Susan Mary had been married for nine years, this was her first child. By the time she saw a gynaecologist she was four months pregnant. There was no question of an abortion; the asthmatic Bill was thrilled and delighted and since Duff would quite clearly never take any particular interest, Susan Mary felt justified in keeping from her son the secret of his parentage. The story of Bill Patten Jr's real father was not revealed until 2006 in a magazine article by the journalist Susan Braudy, more than fifty years after the events in question and two years after Susan Mary's death. Children and the identity of their legitimate parents were a vexing subject for many in 1947 Paris.

1948–1949

Paris Americanized

As the Marshall Plan got under way in Europe, butter, cheese, eggs and other much needed goods at last began reaching ordinary homes, and fresh medical supplies filled hospitals. Every day, 150 or so ships were unloading in port, bringing cargo to Europe. As Paris was the headquarters of the Economic Cooperation Administration (ECA), which was managing the Plan, the liners also shipped in the human cargo, the requisite bureaucracy. Almost 3,000 American men arrived in Paris in the spring of 1948, setting up offices in hotel suites, apartments and *hôtels particuliers*, along with hundreds of women, mostly secretaries but occasionally wives.

After a winter as harsh as any during the war, with coal and gas shortages exacerbated by frequent fog so thick 'it gave you a vague sense of being suffocated', somehow, in the spring of 1948, Paris blossomed again with hope as well as material goods. The cafés were bustling: Sartre, Camus, Picasso or André Breton, regulars at many a Left Bank table, and American jazz players including Charlie Parker and Duke Ellington were performing at other haunts. But it was, in spite of tentative bursts of sunshine, a mixed picture. Paris certainly had not recovered its pre-war status as the foremost centre for art dealers, while a major devaluation of the franc in January 1948 resulted in Americans feeling that Paris shops may have been full of bargains; yet as most, even luxury boutiques around the Place Vendôme, were still resorting to candlelight on alternate days, it was difficult to see.

The British, too, were facing these post-war years of austerity with ration books and stoicism, but a strong domestic Communist Party generating strikes lent an added complication to the French situation. There was a profound fear in 1948 that communism might win the 'Cold War', a new term now being used to describe deteriorating relations between America and the Soviet Union. Nancy Mitford told Evelyn Waugh about her terrors of the Russian invasion: 'I am quite simply frightened. I wake up in the night sometimes in a cold sweat. Thank goodness for having no children, I can take a pill and say goodbye.'

The divisions in French society, even if not discussed, ran deep, not just between Gaullists, who argued that resistance was pure patriotism involving personal sacrifice for the public good, and communists, who believed that resistance embodied an idea of social revolution, but among the many in France who had suffered during the war years, including racial and political *déportés*, Jews who had been in hiding throughout the war, refugees, labour conscripts, foreigners who could not prove French nationality, Gypsies and a miscellaneous population of those whom Vichy had decided were undesirable.

New laws in August 1948 created two different titles for persecution victims: the more prestigious one of *déporté* or *interné de la Résistance* was reserved for resisters and involved higher benefits than the lesser one of *déporté* or *interné politique*, which was for victims without resistance credentials. This distinction meant that Jews, Gypsies and other racial *déportés* were classified as victims, who would not qualify for the higher title; and that women who might, for example, have sheltered evading airmen or others on the run but had not joined one of the officially recognized military formations, also might not qualify. In addition, there was also the question of what constituted a 'combatant' – a word which resonated with military glory from the First World War since resisters who could prove that they were combatants, rather than civilians, were able to claim not only higher financial payments but also certain privileges such as the useful *carte du combatant*. It was for that reason that one woman who had survived Auschwitz described her fellow camp survivors as 'Combatants without Weapons'. She maintained that withstanding Nazi dehumanization was a type of combat. For most women, their activities may have been equally risky and dangerous and in Nazi eyes deserving of punishment, but that did not entitle them to use the word 'combatant'.

The laws, far from resolving issues, merely pushed them aside for a while. Political divisions were also papered over rather than healed. Some believed that the capitalists had profited from the war, as shown by businesses such as Renault, which had collaborated to help the Nazi war machine and so had flourished, while the communists had resisted and suffered. But the communists were able to draw on extra support from, unpredictably, the anti-American right wing, who may not have objected so loudly to the German Occupation but who saw the United States as the new occupying power. Paul Morand wrote to Josée de Chambrun, still belligerently fighting to clear her dead father's name: 'What a tonic to see such magnificent pleasures in the midst of destitute Europe propped up by the Marshall Plan . . . and to enjoy splendid entertainments for which we are indebted neither to a couturier nor to an aunt, pimp, spy or the Coca-Cola Corporation.' Morand's friend, Misia Sert, similarly railed against 'the banality of France becoming Americanized', while the French communist newspaper *L'Humanité* asked: 'will we be coca-colonized?' Even the arch-British diplomat Harold Nicolson joined in, insisting it was not that the Europeans 'were anti-American, just that they were frightened that the destinies of the world should be in the hands of a giant with the limbs of an undergraduate, the emotions of a spinster and the brain of a pea hen'.

But such negative attitudes did little to stem the appeal of Paris for individual American tourists, never sure if they were welcomed, envied or resented or all three, just hungry to enjoy its charms once more aided by the buying power of the strong dollar. The capital was, slowly, becoming a fashionable destination for well-heeled young American girls to visit as part of their education. Norine Murphy, just twenty, and her twenty-two-year-old sister Marilyn were in the vanguard in the summer of 1948 at a time when many American parents felt that the war was insufficiently distant for safety. The Murphy parents were, however, concerned enough that they sewed a supply of dollar bills into the girls' shoulder pads, partly to ensure that they could buy food but also to bribe a border guard should they have to leave suddenly, a real worry at the time. On the *Queen Elizabeth*, the sisters noticed the teenage actress Elizabeth Taylor, almost the only other young woman on board, with her mother, and the three American girls took tea and played cards together most days.

'Paris was a shock,' Norine recalled. 'We arrived in the city in the middle of a coal strike so for several days in the week there was only candlelight. We were issued with bread coupons and told to keep a close watch on our passports because of theft.' Nothing went quite as planned. The sisters were due to continue their travels, by train, to Switzerland, where they were going to study for a year. But after waiting at the railway station for several hours they discovered that their train had already left.

> We tried to call the American Embassy and, not knowing how to use the pay phone, a gentleman stopped to offer his help. We had all kinds of do's and don'ts from our mother and did not know what to do. We noticed he was not French – he told us he was from Russia, but was a White Russian. He kept repeating 'I White Russian!' and we had no idea what that meant but thought it sounded like a good thing. We knew that Russia was a big concern right after the war.

He offered to drive the girls to the American Embassy, and they accepted as he said he wanted to do something 'nice for Americans'. He had a Volkswagen – a car they had never seen before, and it made a big impression on them. When they eventually returned home, Norine and Marilyn never dared tell this story as they knew their parents would be furious.

Then they discovered that the Hôtel George V, where they thought they had rooms, was overbooked due to a UN conference. Arrangements were made instead at the Plaza Athénée but the girls were young, it was after midnight and 'we were very frightened . . . We had no idea that it was such a good hotel and complained. The clerk said if it was good enough for Madame Roosevelt we would be OK.'

Once settled, the girls went shopping, visiting stores whose names resonated from American magazines. They went to Hermès, which that day to their surprise was candlelit, to buy gloves for family and friends, and then on to a delicious lunch of roast duck at Maxim's, 'chosen because that was the only name we knew from catalogues'. Two ladies from the Embassy then took them to a Molyneux show – one of very few fashion houses showing at that time.

At the end of their trip the sisters bumped into a schoolfriend from Illinois, Julie Loeffel, who spoke so little French that she could not even get her sunglasses fixed, so the trio went shopping together at Dior, where Julie was swiftly spotted and hired as a house model. Julie lingered in Paris and was selected to model one of the couturier's most extraordinary ball gowns, the Venus, fashioned from grey silk tulle with a glittering overlay of scallop-shaped petals said to have been inspired by Botticelli's *Venus*, and embellished with small pearl clusters, sequins and crystals. Reluctantly, after a year she returned to live in Glencoe, Illinois.

These young ingénues who knew nothing about life outside the United States may have been cosseted by their parents' deep pockets, but nonetheless were imbued with a spirit of adventure, both excited and repelled by risk-taking. And Julie's story illustrates the powerful, magnetic appeal to Americans of Paris as a thrilling city where dreams could still come true. Barbara Probst Solomon, in early 1948 a young American would-be writer, was obsessed by a certain idea of Paris which she had gleaned from books. She too had an adventurous spirit and was not bothered by strikes or lack of food. Barbara grew up in a privileged, cosmopolitan Jewish family in a magnificent house in Westport, Connecticut, where individualism was encouraged. The family were neighbours of 'Jay' Gatsby, or at least the man she believes was F. Scott Fitzgerald's model for Gatsby. Both parents were highly cultured intellectuals whose lives had been damaged by the First World War, during which her father* had been badly gassed in the trenches near Amiens and so spent three years in an American field hospital recovering, while her older brother had served in the Second. As a sick child, Barbara had spent hours in bed reading illustrated books about Paris, especially *Madeline* by Ludwig Bemelmans, first published in 1939, swiftly graduating to the semi-fictional Proust. From the age of seventeen she had been desperate to go to Paris instead of college in the US; now her parents agreed under one condition: that her artistic mother would accompany her on the transatlantic voyage.

---

* Anthony Probst, a lawyer, had started his career as Woodrow Wilson's campaign manager before serving as a private in the US army.

On board, Barbara and Mrs Probst befriended another mother and daughter, Mrs Mailer and her daughter Barbara, sister of the yet to be famous Norman, who was waiting to greet them as they docked in Cherbourg. Norman and his wife Bea were already settled in Paris, in an apartment near the Luxembourg Gardens, and it was there that the two Barbaras were introduced to a stimulating mixture of artists and intellectuals, including many exiled Spanish dissidents. The exiles were not communists but, according to Barbara Probst, anarchists and socialists, totally at odds with the communists, and therefore vulnerable in France, which could not place them.

Within weeks the teenage girls had been persuaded by Norman to undertake a daring adventure which involved driving across France to Spain in order to rescue two young students held captive in one of the most brutal hard-labour camps run by the Spanish dictator Francisco Franco. Nicolás (son of the historian Claudio Sánchez-Albornoz, President of the Spanish Republic in Exile) and Manuel Lamana were being forced to work as slave labourers in Franco's prison at the Valle de los Caídos (Valley of the Fallen), constructing the vast monument that was to be Franco's tomb. Escapes were extremely rare and firing squads still carried out executions long after the Spanish Civil War was over. Yet, somewhat bizarrely, the girls had agreed to attempt to free the two boys, urged on by Norman, 'who told us he had a car and a plan but it needed Barbara and me to participate. We agreed. He thought two young girls would have a better chance of crossing the border through the mountains because we looked too young, too American to be suspicious. We were just American kids trying to see the world.'

Probst remembers many details of the rescue. Also in the car was a young Spanish student activist, Paco Benet, whose father had been shot dead at the beginning of the Civil War, who knew the country well and spoke French as well as Spanish. 'We had prearranged a meeting place. Nicolás and Manuel had been somehow sent a message telling them to be last in line at the end of the day and that a car would be waiting for them. It helped that, because Spain was too impoverished to provide uniforms for prisoners, they wore regular clothes,' she recalls. While the police searched in the immediate area, the girls drove off to the south with the ex-prisoners and escaped.

By the time the group reached Barcelona, Paco and Barbara Probst had fallen in love, and the pair separated from the others. What's clear from photographs of the time is that Barbara was beautiful as well as clever and well read. She remembers Paco as tall with blond hair, intense dark eyes and 'very brainy'. They returned to Paris, where Barbara enrolled at the Sorbonne and started living with Benet, a relationship which lasted for four years. Like many Americans in Paris at the time, she was shocked by the deprivation she witnessed, never forgetting the disparity between her cushioned life in Paris and that facing most of her fellow students in 1948. She felt guilty about the food parcels which her parents regularly sent, believing it was morally wrong for a foreigner to have access to luxuries denied to the native population, which had suffered so much already.

Alongside her studies at the Sorbonne, she worked hard learning to be a journalist, badgering various editors into taking her stories. 'Nobody wanted to know about the struggle to end Franco's dictatorship after World War Two had ended. It seemed as if everyone had had enough of torture and concentration camps. The Spanish drama was a non-story.' But, as Barbara's life in Paris revolved around groups of dissident Spanish students in exile, she saw her mission as telling the world the story she had learned first hand. One of the motivating factors for her in undertaking the Spanish rescue had been an acute awareness, as soon as she arrived in Paris, that the Jews had had no one looking out for them. 'My mother had several French relatives who had perished in Auschwitz. Only one, Cousin Leah, had survived in hiding. I knew I did not want to look back and think no one had been there for these kids. That was very important for me. That's why I couldn't refuse.'

She felt passionately that the Spanish anti-fascists were now being similarly neglected, a particularly wicked dereliction since the early resistance in France had been fuelled by so many Spanish dissidents, often but not always communists, whose role in the liberation of France was now being downplayed and sometimes totally ignored.

Back in Paris, Benet and Probst started a small underground journal together. Called *Peninsula*, it was smuggled out across the Pyrenees into Spain in an attempt to fight propaganda on both sides. Its motto was 'Neither Franco nor Stalin'. But after four years together, the pair broke up and Probst returned to America, her Paris years remaining a defining fragment of her life from which she dates a lifetime of activism. 'Paris is where I learned to respond to the horror in the world and do something about it. The rest of my working life has been framed by those experiences.'*

While Barbara Probst was feeling guilty about her food parcels, Caroline Ferriday was appealing for all Americans to become a 'package parent' for malnourished French children. 'They are denied milk because there is not enough to go around, rice is an unknown delicacy, butter a luxury for the very rich.' She recounted heartbreaking stories of children whose parents had been killed and who now lacked almost everything. They needed 'kind thoughts as much as food', and she encouraged her fellow citizens to become part of their own 'personal Marshall Plan'.

These stories were in stark contrast to the experience of the thousands of Americans posted to Paris in autumn 1948, who not only had access to Embassy supplies but could afford to eat in decent restaurants. Paul Child, a middle-ranking diplomat married for the last three years to Julia, a native Californian of six foot two who did not speak any French, was expected to promote America to the French, 'to build goodwill between our nations, to reinforce the idea that America was a strong and reliable ally, that the Marshall plan was designed to help France get back on its feet . . . and to insinuate that rapacious Russia was not to be trusted'. Meanwhile Julia, who during the war had worked for the Office of Strategic Services (OSS, forerunner of the CIA), latterly in Sri Lanka and China, was left to explore the Parisian way of life. They experienced

---

* Paco Benet became a distinguished anthropologist, killed in 1966 while on a dig when his jeep crashed in the desert. Probst studied at Columbia, married a law professor, Harold W. Solomon, and wrote a steady stream of novels, essays and memoirs. But she never shed her love of and concern for France and in 1987 reported on the trial of Klaus Barbie, the Butcher of Lyons.

'annoying' shortages – 'coffee rations ran out quickly, cosmetics were expensive and decent olive oil was precious as a gem' – and they had no fridge, so like most Parisians they had to keep milk on a window ledge. The Childs marvelled at being able to eat so well at numerous restaurants for as little as five or six dollars, including a bottle of *vin ordinaire*. Julia was immediately won over by the magnificence of French cuisine, drooling over *sole à la Normande* served with cream, mushrooms, wine, oysters and mussels: 'I had never imagined that fish could be taken so seriously or taste so heavenly.' And she learned how the Parisiennes shopped. 'When you asked at the *crémerie* for a cheese you'd be asked at what time you wanted to serve it to get the ripeness exactly right. The owner would then open box after box, pressing the cheese until she found one that was perfect.' The local *marchand de légumes* taught her not only which vegetables to eat, when and how to prepare them, 'but also about snails and she'd fill me in on so and so's wartime experience and where to get a watch-band fixed'.

By August 1949, recognizing how enraptured she had become by French cuisine, her husband bought for her thirty-seventh birthday the 1,000-page *Larousse Gastronomique*. Two months later she enrolled at the prestigious Ecole le Cordon Bleu in Paris for a year-long course, designed for potential restaurateurs, where most of her fellow trainee chefs were former GIs funded to study cooking by the United States government. Julia Child thrived and, for the remainder of her time in Paris, studied the secrets of good French food until she was ready, with two friends, to set up her own cooking school in France. Later, in 1961, they completed their ground-breaking cookbook *Mastering the Art of French Cooking*, which became a bestseller and even today is often considered a must-have for newly-wed American girls. The book, along with the later hugely popular television show, demystified fancy French cuisine for generations of Americans and probably contributed as much as any diplomat to fostering good relations between France and America and to helping Americans to understand French culture.

But it was not only Americans flocking to Paris. In May 1948 the newly-wed Princess Elizabeth and her husband Prince Philip paid a three-day official visit, which generated enormous crowds cheering them along the Champs-Elysées. Elizabeth was twenty-two and pregnant with the future Prince Charles. It was the first time in her life that she had left British soil. Some Parisiennes, unsure whether to believe rumours that all English women always wore heavy tweeds and carried shooting sticks, wanted to inspect her clothes. They were not disappointed. Her wardrobe had been chosen with enormous care and her jewellery too was admired because the previous year Philip had bought his bride a magnificent diamond bracelet from Boucheron in Paris, which she chose to wear outside her glove on her waving hand. Boucheron had been the favourite of Edward, Prince of Wales, when he was buying for his mistress Freda Dudley Ward in the early 1930s. But Wallis, wanting nothing that was reminiscent of Freda, instructed him to buy her jewellery elsewhere, so Cartier and Van Cleef were patronized. Now Boucheron were back in royal favour once again. Princess Elizabeth laid a wreath at the Tomb of the Unknown Soldier at the Arc de Triomphe and then, opening an exhibition devoted to displaying the cultural links between France and Britain over the centuries, delivered her speech impressively in fluent French. One evening she listened to Edith Piaf performing, another evening the Comédie-Française actress Béatrice Bretty was presented to her at a British Embassy reception. Bretty, now the darling of the company, reminded the Princess of a pre-war meeting in London and the Princess was polite enough to respond that she remembered it well. The only tension during the visit arose from Elizabeth's express wish to attend a performance of Jean-Paul Sartre's current play, *Les Mains sales*, but Embassy officials overrode her wishes, deeming so overtly political a play to be unsuitable.

'Who can resist the legendary lure of Paris – Paris! – with the romantic appeal of its boulevards and buildings, its cafés and squares and bridges over the Seine . . .' exclaimed the writer Emma Smith, who decided to spend the summer of 1948 living on the Left Bank of Paris in a cheap hotel on a corner of the Rue Saint-Sulpice writing her second novel. 'I was totally in love with Paris and France and wanted to go back and impress Jean-Pierre [Geoffroy-Dechaume] with my success,' she explained in 2014, by then in her nineties and very definitely a successful writer. However, Jean-Pierre had fled the city that summer and instead it was Denis who came to take her to the theatre where they listened to a tiny little woman standing in the centre of a bare stage, 'a *chanteuse* who stuns her packed audience with the extraordinary, disproportionately loud harsh volume of her voice . . . singing defiantly, triumphantly'. Denis the resistance hero clearly did not question attending a performance of Edith Piaf even though she had sung to German audiences. Smith would occasionally drink that summer at the Café de Flore and Les Deux Magots, where she remembers glamorous girls with short cropped hair wearing full-length New Look dresses that contrasted with the little shrines appearing in walls with pots of flowers to mark the spot where a brave resister had been shot. 'The flowers were always fresh but nobody would talk about the war. This was a new world and the new world had a great sense of excitement about it, a marvellous feeling of now we are going to do new things.'

By August, the city was in the grip of a heatwave, so Smith took to following 'an undeviatingly simple' daily routine to cope with the temperature. Immediately after a breakfast of croissants and milk at her hotel, she walked with her typewriter to the Ile de la Cité, where she would sit on the flagstones alongside the Seine 'for a whole day of concentrated mental labour'. And there one day a wandering photographer snapped her for the weekly news magazine *Paris Match*. He was Robert Doisneau, and the picture of Smith with her typewriter balanced on her knees appeared on the magazine's centre spread, an illustration of a Parisienne at work. 'I never met him,' Smith says now. 'I would have loved to, because the photograph appears in all his collections.' But the most remarkable thing about the portrait, she insists, is that she appears to have been sitting on stone ground for much of the day. 'I checked the picture recently to see if there was a cushion,' she says triumphantly. 'There wasn't!'

Corinne Luchaire was also writing a book, her self-justificatory memoir published in 1949, which she called *Ma drôle de vie* in obvious homage to her father's newspaper, *Toute la Vie*. The entire book, written with the help of a journalist, was a none too subtle attempt to exculpate her beloved father, revealing how, blinded by the fairytale reflection of her own success, she had totally failed to understand the situation either during the war or five years afterwards. She was caught up in 'a whirlwind of pleasure and easy life', the pinnacle of her success being the opulent wedding, which preceded her ultimately disastrous marriage to Count Guy de Voisins-Lavernière.* Corinne never stopped to question the immense flattery heaped upon her and 'became the agent of a male-dominated political system that knew how to use ingrained attitudes to perpetuate its power'. There was a time when her story, about how an ordinary Parisienne could become a countess, might have been admirable; no longer. She grew sicker and more fragile throughout 1949 and died on 22 January 1950 in a manner both pathetic and dramatic, after a dinner with friends where she could not swallow and was spitting blood. She collapsed in a taxi before she could get to the Parisian clinic which was treating her. She was twenty-eight, uncomprehending to the last, leaving a young child motherless.

There was little that Corinne's remaining family could do to help. Her aunt, her dead father's sister, Ghita Luchaire, married to Théodore Fraenkel, had troubles of her own. She had been in danger during the Occupation because of her Jewish name; now, even though she was Mme Fraenkel, she was scorned because of her despised maiden name. So, as the numbers of young American women visiting Paris grew and grew, in order to make ends meet Ghita Fraenkel, like many, took in American lodgers, one of the few respectable ways to eke out a living.

Reading accounts of the severe culture shock which several of these students experienced in Paris indicates clearly that the city about which Simone de Beauvoir had waxed lyrical when she had lectured in American universities in 1947 did not always measure up, especially so far as public conveniences were concerned. But de Beauvoir had in mind loftier matters, as her groundbreaking feminist work examining the history of female oppression, *The Second*

---

* Patrick Modiano, the French novelist who has long been fascinated by Corinne's life, created in his 1974 screenplay for the film *Lacombe, Lucien* an amoral aristocrat he calls Jean-Bernard de Voisins, who actively worked with collaborators to enjoy the benefits of the black market with his mistress, a failed actress reminiscent of Corinne.

Sex – the standard tome on feminism for several years – was first published in 1949. De Beauvoir was encouraging women to throw themselves into lives that were not defined by gender, to challenge the myth of *l'éternel féminin*, which had predominated before the war, and which so many of them had demonstrably and dramatically destroyed during the war.

It was scarcely oppression, but some of the female students wrote home to express their horror at finding 'squat toilets' in restaurants where you had to carefully place your feet on two pads either side of a porcelain base sunk into the floor, and toilet paper was often nonexistent. Yet even middle-class apartments might have only one shared WC per floor at this time. It was not just that basic foodstuffs were still in short supply, but the city looked shabby and even the grandest buildings were dirty on the outside and dark inside. Almost all the young Americans, while they did not starve, experienced a sense of severe deprivation in Paris alongside the excitement, as well as frequent reminders of the recent war. According to Henriette Nizan, a Jewish writer and teacher who had fled to the US during the war, most American students in Paris tried to be more French than the French. They were the ones who ordered *picon citron* to drink (orange bitters with lemonade) while the natives drank Coca-Cola. 'It was young American girls who influenced young French girls with the fashion for laced sandals and long straight hair, which no one had worn since 1900,' wrote Nizan.

One unknown American who took lodgings with a French family in Paris that year was the twenty-year-old Jacqueline Bouvier, in her junior year at Vassar College and extremely pretty. Finding that Vassar had no study-abroad programme, Jacqueline applied for one run by Smith College, and was accepted.[*] She was in a group of thirty-five students, several of whom lived in dormitories, but Jacqueline's mother, Mrs Auchincloss, 'being a terrible snob', was delighted to discover that, following an introduction from a mutual friend, her daughter could stay in the home of a countess. Germaine de Renty

---

[*] Smith College had been sending women for a year of study in Paris since 1935, but the programme had stopped during the war and did not pick up again until 1947–8.

lived in a large apartment with four bedrooms and one bathroom in the Avenue Mozart in the 16th arrondissement and, although she took two other American students at the same time, Jackie was given the largest bedroom. The de Rentys lived simply and Claude, the youngest daughter, who spoke excellent English as she had just returned from a year in the United States, became a close friend. It was, however, an absolute rule that French must be spoken. Claude was now completing her studies at the Institute of Political Studies and Jackie attended lectures at the Sorbonne. Several of the other Smith girls were staying in homes where strict rules about midnight curfews and no men applied, but in this respect Germaine de Renty was far more relaxed, perhaps because of all she had experienced in Ravensbrück. And she took Jackie everywhere, keen to show her the best of French culture. Jackie remained in Paris until early 1950, perfecting her French and allowing the culture to seep in so deeply that, for the rest of her life, her style in décor and clothes was always considered French.

At the end of the 1940s all branches of the arts were struggling to regain their wartime popularity and funds were scarce. The immediate post-war period was hard for Lily Pastré, the Noilly Prat heiress who had used her chateau to hide Jewish musicians from Paris, and she felt she had lost her sense of purpose. But in 1948, remembering the success of her *Midsummer Night's Dream* extravaganza, she conceived the idea of a music festival near Marseilles, believing that opera lovers should not have to travel to Bayreuth and Salzburg where, in her view, the seats were in any case overpriced.

The first challenge was to find a suitable venue. Working with the impresario and pianist Gabriel Dussurget, she discovered the courtyard of the former Archbishop's Palace in Aix-en-Provence, which they decided would be ideal. Lily funded everything out of her own pocket that first year, spending lavishly and working tirelessly to pull it off. Her inspiration was to engage conductor Hans Rosbaud and his South-West German Radio orchestra, Mozart specialists. 'Three years after the end of the war! The teeth were gritted,' remembered her friend Edmonde Charles-Roux, the journalist and resister descended, like Lily, from a distinguished Marseilles shipping family.

But although this virtuoso idea was a success, one year later Lily Pastré stepped down from the Board of Trustees following disagreements with Dussurget, and from then on she had nothing more to do with the Aix Music Festival.

'It was a great injustice,' commented Charles-Roux. 'Without her, it would have been a different story.' Dussurget now became sole director and ended the sponsorship from the Countess. He disliked her amateurism, the amateurism – or enthusiasm – that had made her chateau at Montredon such an extraordinary artistic haven during the war. He now dismissed her contribution as supplying the 'house party' atmosphere of the festival and was cruel in his criticisms of her, as his memoirs later revealed. Determined to make the post-war festival more professional, Dussurget secured funding from Aix-based institutions and today the event is considered one of the world's top music festivals. His efforts are commemorated with a Dussurget prize, a Dussurget street in Aix and a marble bas-relief of his face. But, however successful, the festival lost some of the quirky charm and spirit of Lily Pastré herself. From then on, although she continued to visit each summer, the Countess appeared either imperious or eccentric to those who did not know her, occasionally even comic. Mostly her name was forgotten and none of her brave wartime deeds publicly recognized, even in her local area, until very recently.* Her last few years were difficult and lonely. She died in August 1974 and, generous to the last, donated a parcel of land next to her chateau to Emmaus, a Catholic organization for the homeless.

But in November 1949 Colette, today a controversial figure who had remained in Paris writing throughout the Occupation, was elected President of the prestigious literary institution, L'Académie Goncourt, the first woman ever to receive this honour. At the opening night of *Chéri*, her own dramatization of her famous novel, she was rewarded with a long and loud round of applause and cheering from the audience. 'Elderly, arthritic, ensconced in a stage box from which only her head was visible – her still mordantly witty face surrounded by its nimbus of radiant hair – she received the acclaim of what is left of the three generations of *Tout Paris*,' wrote Janet Flanner.

* In 2013 there was an exhibition in Aix devoted to her work, *Le Salon de Lily*.

For those who were judged guilty of collaborating, appearing on stage was still considered risky. Mary Marquet, who had not been allowed to return to the Comédie-Française, found it hard to get work. Finally in 1949 she appeared onscreen in a mediocre comedy, but was offered little more than bit parts in second-rate television series. By contrast, her colleague Béatrice Bretty was more popular than ever. One of the longest-serving and best-loved actors in the company, she continued to work there until 1959. But in September 1949, learning that the former French leader Charles de Gaulle was due to speak at the dedication of a monument to her former lover, the assassinated politician Georges Mandel, in Lesparre, north of Bordeaux, she was roused to action. She now released her pent-up feelings of the previous five years and wrote angrily to the *député*, Emile Liquard, who had arranged the ceremony. 'You are disturbing the dead to make of his tomb a political springboard,' she began. Her heartfelt letter was published in full by the local newspaper *Les Nouvelles de Bordeaux et du Sud-Ouest*.

> I am astonished that Gen. de Gaulle is associated with your plans, a man who did not feel obliged to bring from England the necessary aid for Georges Mandel's escape; a man who since his return to France has never under any circumstances spoken the name of this martyr of the Republic; who never on any occasion felt it his duty to pay his respects at his tomb; who never in any fashion has interested himself in his orphan child of fourteen; in short, a man who, by his persistence in this attitude, has clearly shown a total indifference both to the life and to the memory of Georges Mandel. Besides, did he not declare in Algiers that he was not working to whiten sepulchres? Well truly here is one that has no need of it.

Bretty, having fought to support Mandel during the war, was now courageously fighting for his post-war reputation. Yet in his 1994 biography of Mandel, Nicolas Sarkozy criticized Bretty for not doing more, adding that, as she was not Jewish, she had not been in danger. What more could she have done beyond giving up her own career, begging to marry him and share his fate in a concentration camp, looking after his orphan child and writing letters to newspapers pointing out what little effort de Gaulle had made to rescue him? Few women did half as much.

By the end of the 1940s, material conditions in Paris and the rest of France had improved dramatically thanks to the success of the Marshall Plan. According to the renowned Yorkshire-born American journalist Anne O'Hare McCormick, 'anyone who compares the picture today with that of 1947 can hardly believe that such progress could be made . . . a miracle of recovery has been performed'. Her views were echoed by the *New Yorker* journalist Joseph Wechsberg, who wrote in September 1949 that he was pleased to find for the first time since the end of the war that 'my Parisian friends had stopped griping about the black market and rationing and were again discussing passionately and at great length the heady mysteries of *La Grande Cuisine* which, next to women, has always been their favourite topic of conversation'. Not only were Parisians eating well again, but Wallis, Duchess of Windsor, and her friends were buying jewels and couture clothes once more.

In 1948 Wallis bought the star item in Dior's autumn–winter collection, a blue silk velvet gown called Lahore because of its heavy Punjabi-style pearl embroidery. And Cartier's Jeanne Toussaint was busy making jewellery that she knew the Duchess would wear with great panache. In 1948 Wallis bought a panther brooch made of gold and black enamel created around a large emerald. More panthers would follow, including one just a year later; this time the big cat was perched atop an enormous cabochon sapphire. But these were difficult years for Chanel, Toussaint's close friend, who did not show a new collection until 1954, when she staged a comeback of sorts. With her friend Misia Sert, Chanel was by 1949 making regular trips to Switzerland to replenish their drug supplies, journeys they had been undertaking since the 1930s for morphine, relatively easy to obtain in Switzerland.*

---

* For Chanel it may have been little more than a useful sedative, but Sert appeared to need it for oblivion and forgetfulness and had even spent twenty-four hours in prison because of her habit.

But better food and plentiful material conditions failed to hide a sense of foreboding, because much was still not spoken aloud in the continuing battle to decide on the legacy of the war. The overriding establishment view was that in order to preserve unity and keep communism at bay, France had to be seen as a nation of resisters, where resisters were in de Gaulle's phrases 'l'immense majorité' and collaborators a small minority, 'une poignée de misérables et d'indignes'. But the Communist Party was no monolith, as Agnès Humbert, the early resister who had spent the war in German camps, discovered when in 1949 she was awarded the Croix de guerre. Later that year she travelled to Yugoslavia, publishing her impressions and voicing her admiration for its leader, Josip Broz Tito, then estranged from the Soviet Union. As a result she was not only expelled from the women's organization of which she had been President, Les Amies de la Paix (Friends of Peace), but also denounced in the French Communist daily *L'Humanité*.[*]

Lisette and Johann, the forbidden lovers who had both had to face up to punishment, were now trying to rebuild their lives in a postwar world. They were still young, and believed, as they wrote in their passionate love letters, that they were 'entitled' to find happiness after all they had been through.

After her head-shaving, Lisette had been sent briefly to Drancy but was released when she showed the authorities that she had also helped the resistance by providing some useful lists. Johann, having deserted in 1944, had been handed over to the Americans who sent him to Laon, in Picardy, where he was held in a prisoner-of-war camp for German soldiers in France, and then transferred to another camp at Baden-Baden in Germany. Lisette could not bear to remain in Paris alone, 'full of anguish', so she first pursued him to Laon and then, enterprisingly, succeeded in getting herself a secretarial job with the Army of Occupation in Baden-Baden. Finally, in February 1949, Johann won a bitter divorce from his wife and married Lisette, and the couple lived in Germany, trying to earn a living as hoteliers

---

[*] Agnès Humbert died in 1963 and is buried in the cemetery at Valmondois, the village in northern France where the Geoffroy-Dechaume family lived for generations.

for the next thirty or so years. But his children did not want to see him nor meet their new French stepmother and, according to relatives, life was hard, a far cry far from the wartime dream Lisette had nurtured.

The story of Lisette and Johann is in some ways emblematic of the myriad ways French women and German men colluded over the period of occupation merely in order to survive, and the unhappiness that usually followed. That their relatives, even in the twenty-first century, have denied permission for their real names to be used is an indication of the sensitivity still aroused by stories such as theirs. They did not have any children together but, according to some estimates, as many as 200,000 children were born to French mothers fathered by German soldiers during the Second World War. Most never knew their full identity, and, if they did, were ashamed of their German parentage. It was only in the twenty-first century that some started to apply for German citizenship and search for their German fathers before it was too late, which it often was. Fabrice Virgili, author of the most recent study of Franco-German babies, believes there were probably 100,000 of them and that most will have been brought up not only in shame by their mothers alone but never knowing who their father was, 'as in the vast majority of cases these "amours de guerre" ended with the Liberation'.

There were still occasional trials before the decade was out, such as that of Jacques Desoubrie, alias Jean Masson, among others, the traitor and double agent who betrayed Denise Dufournier and was responsible for the capture of as many as 168 Allied airmen. He was arrested in Germany where he had fled soon after the end of the war, swiftly tried and executed in December 1949. And Otto Abetz, Hitler's Ambassador to France, the young man who won his position largely because he was such an admirer of France, was sentenced in 1949 to twenty years' imprisonment for war crimes, in particular for his role in arranging the deportation of French Jews to be gassed. Abetz was released in 1954, but he and his wife Suzanne were killed four years later in a road accident in Germany, which some believe was an assassination organized by former members of the French Resistance.

*

It's not clear what motivated Jacqueline Bouvier to visit Dachau, where she went at Christmas 1949 with one of her friends, not accompanied by her hostess, Comtesse de Renty. Yet perhaps her decision had something to do with the de Renty family conviction of the need for rapprochement between the two age-old enemies. Claude and her mother, unusually for surviving deportees, had already visited Germany in 1946, taking advantage of a cousin working in the army who invited them. Germaine de Renty believed, in spite of everything she had suffered, in the premise of the Marshall Plan that 'we needed to recover alongside Germany with the help of America. My mother always said that's what has to be done. The German people suffered too. Even in Ravensbrück there were German women who suffered.' At all events, Dachau in 1949 was not yet a museum, nor even a memorial, with parts still in use as a camp for Czech refugees and its future a matter of controversy.

How posterity would memorialize the war years was becoming a critical issue. As the 1950s loomed it was clear that the atmosphere was radically shifting. Picasso's Dove, still today the international peace logo, first appeared on posters for the communist-sponsored Peace Congress in Paris in 1949, and remained the iconic symbol of hope and peace in the Cold War years to follow. Yet peace – what so many of those who had engaged in the war now craved above all else as they raised young families – was far from a certainty as the Cold War took hold. Some Americans blamed the French for not repelling the communists in their midst, while many French people criticized Americans as imperialistic.

Even if active fighting was in abeyance, the battle for reputations in 1949 was far from over. As Julia Child and Emma Smith both noticed, there were a few marble plaques now being erected around the city commemorating brave resisters at the spot where they had fallen. But reputations can change over a long period, and in 1857 the publication of Charles Baudelaire's highly erotic poems about decadent women in Paris, *Les Fleurs du mal*, had been greeted with shock and outrage. Baudelaire as well as his publisher were prosecuted under the regime of the Second Empire as an *outrage aux bonnes moeurs* – 'an insult to public decency'. Six poems from the work were suppressed and the pair were fined 300 francs. Now, in 1949, the ban on their publication was lifted and *Les Fleurs du mal* was finally published in France, in full, for the first time.

Epilogue

PEACETIME PARIS

Picasso again. Picasso, the artist of towering genius who produced between three and four hundred paintings plus large numbers of drawings, prints and sculptures during the Occupation years, yet was not allowed to exhibit publicly. Picasso, the artist whose behaviour in Paris during the war is constantly questioned.

Lee Miller believed fiercely that:

> from the point of view of art in Paris, the most valuable contribution has been the fact that Picasso stayed here under the Occupation as an inspiration to others. The fact that he didn't abandon the ship but went on about his business, quietly, unobtrusively, showing himself little in public other than in the immediate vicinity of his studio. He has painted prodigiously during these four years, never accepting anything from the Germans and often pleased to use his ingenuity with new materials as a necessity.

Picasso loved women and needed them to give energy to his life. But he was cruel to individual women, particularly Dora Maar, who died in 1997 aged eighty-nine and whom he never ceased to humiliate. His art always came first. According to Françoise Gilot, this piece of self-knowledge was learned young after he made a crucial promise to God that if his adored little sister, Conchita, recovered from diphtheria he would never paint again. In fact she died but Pablo continued to paint in any case, the promise discarded soon after it was made. Gilot said Picasso only told this story to the women in his life. 'It was a warning that they, like Conchita, would be sacrificed on the altar of art, a fate all of them, except for Gilot, would share.'

This story about the primacy of art above people is in the forefront of my mind as I visit Paris's Picasso museum. The museum, housed in a magnificent seventeenth-century mansion in the Marais district, reopened in October 2014 after five years of delays and infighting following a closure for renovation. I am stunned by the serenity of a 1918 painting of Mme Rosenberg, wife of Picasso's dealer, impresario and friend Paul, and their baby daughter Micheline, who all fled Paris in 1940. This was one of the first pictures the Rosenberg family managed to regain after the war, discovering it in a small museum in Paris after it had been renamed by Göring *Mother and Child*. A gift from Picasso to his dealer, it must have been painted shortly after Rosenberg discovered that his wife had been having an affair with his business partner, Georges Wildenstein, a poignant story recounted in 2012 by Rosenberg's granddaughter, Anne Sinclair, when she too was emerging from a painful personal history. The discovery nearly broke Rosenberg. Sinclair wrote a sensitive account of how her grandparents found a way of living together after that, adding that it helped her understand why her grandfather always appeared burdened. So much turbulence followed that sitting. So much history in one canvas.[*]

The beautiful, talented and sharp-witted Françoise Gilot, Picasso's mistress for ten years from 1943, moved in with him only in 1946. Picasso frequently insisted that one cannot be a real woman without becoming a mother and, in 1947, their son Claude was born; a daughter, Paloma, was born in 1949, the year of the Dove. Yet Gilot's independence was as much irritant as stimulant and when, in 1964, she wrote *Life with Picasso*, an amusing and revelatory book about their life in wartime Paris, an enraged Picasso tried to prevent publication. He failed in his attempt to silence her but, following this debacle, refused to see Claude or Paloma again.

German attempts to impose cultural as well as military supremacy on France, at the same time as drinking from the fountain of French art and literature, is a key theme of this book. The French art scene

---

[*] And that history is still being made as in 2012, following publication of Sinclair's book *21 Rue La Boétie*, the building's current owner organized a marble plaque for the façade bearing Paul Rosenberg's name and that of the artists whose works he exhibited there (Anne Sinclair, conversation with the author 28 October 2013).

flourished during the war as the French, on balance, showed scant inclination to resist the aryanization of the art world. All that was required of artists who wished to exhibit at the Salon d'Automne, for example, was to sign a register stating that they were not Jewish. Although many Jewish dealers had been forced to flee, their collections dispersed, there was no shortage of others ready to step up, notably Martin Fabiani, a Corsican well known as a dealer in Nazi-looted art.

At the end of September 1949 the Commission de Récupération Artistique (CRA), in which Rose Valland had played such a crucial role, was disbanded. It had located some 60,000 artworks, 45,000 of which were returned to their original owners. (At the time of writing there are many thousands of artworks still missing.) After ten years in Berlin, Valland returned to France and became, finally, a curator for the Musées Nationaux. In 1948 the United States had awarded her the Medal of Freedom and the French government awarded her the Médaille de la Résistance and Légion d'honneur, as well as making her a Commandeur of the Ordre des Arts et des Lettres. But this quiet resistance operator, whose actions contributed to saving so much of France's cultural heritage, has not enjoyed the recognition granted to other members of the resistance. Some speculate that the lack of recognition could be because she had no descendants, or, more likely, because she deliberately shunned exposing her private life, one that amid the 1940s glow of praise for resistance heroes was not easy to accept. Her close companion and lover was a British translator and academic, Dr Joyce Helen Heer, born in Liverpool in 1917, who worked at the US Embassy. Or could it be because she was involved in the business of saving not lives but works of art, history valuing the saving of lives over that of worldly goods? Furthermore, because of her professional skills, deep knowledge of art, and refusal to be cowed into submission, Valland was clearly a 'troublesome' presence to certain art dealers and a thorn in the side of some museum professionals. 'Mentioning Valland could have reopened controversies in the art world and called into question the ownership of some valuable pieces kept by the national museums.' Far from being the 'shy, timid curator' depicted by history, Rose Valland was a tireless and vocal advocate for the restitution of artwork. She was able to blend into the background when necessary . . . but she was not afraid to question the methods and actions of anyone at any time.'

In the case of opera, the Germans believed cultural supremacy was already theirs, especially where Wagner was concerned. But Germaine Lubin paid a high price for colluding with this notion, not returning to Paris until 1950 when she sought to resume her career with a recital. Although she met with some sympathy and gave a few further performances, it was a difficult transition, and when in 1953 her son committed suicide, she abandoned public appearances entirely. For the remainder of her life she became a voice teacher, giving lessons at her home on the Quai Voltaire in Paris. Among her notable pupils was the leading soprano Régine Crespin, but by the time she died in Paris in 1979, aged eighty-nine, she cut a sad and lonely figure.

Female performers who had worked in occupied Paris faced the most difficult transition of all, but those whom the public adored and needed were indulged. Although Arletty was forgiven, her wartime liaison was never forgotten and affected her ability to find work. Her first post-war film was not until 1949. When she met Hans-Jürgen Soehring in Paris for the last time that year, she realized that their love affair had ended as he was now married to a German woman with whom he had two sons, and was forging a successful career in the German diplomatic service. In 1960 he was appointed Ambassador of the Federal Republic of Germany to the newly formed Republic of the Congo. Shortly afterwards, during a family outing to the supposedly safe River Congo, he went swimming with his eldest son and disappeared under mysterious circumstances, presumably drowned. His body was never found. Arletty, deeply shocked, went to visit his widow and children in Bad Godesberg. But her own health was not good. Suffering for some time from deteriorating eyesight, by the time she died aged ninety-four in 1992 she was blind. She outlived her lover by thirty-two years.

Although in 1947 Sadie Rigal was declared a 'privileged resident' of France for her resistance activities, she left Paris soon afterwards and started a new life in the United States. She and Frédéric, not merely her dancing partner but the man who had saved her life, toured the United States together in 1948 as 'Florence et Frederic'.

(He dropped the accents from his name here.) This produced an emotional visit from the two sisters whom she had helped escape from Paris to Marseilles and eventually to New York, and who now sought her out to thank her. And while performing her routine at the Copacabana Club in New York, she met and fell in love with a young actor, director and academic, Stanley Waren. She trained a new 'Florence' for the act, remained in New York and married Stanley in 1949. She went on to enjoy a varied career on Broadway and in television, choreographing shows which Stanley directed in Africa, Taiwan and China. For another decade, from approximately 1973 until 1983, Florence Waren was Professor of Theatre and Dance at New York's City College and a dance panellist on the New York State Council on the Arts. It was not until 1996 that, for the first time, she visited her parents' graves in Johannesburg but was nonetheless still reluctant to talk about how she came to be a dancer in Paris and about her daring activities in the 1940s. Eventually in 2003, her son, Mark Waren, directed an award-winning documentary about his mother entitled *Dancing Lessons*. Thus finally did the world learn of her early life in the resistance, when she danced to please German officers quite unaware of her Jewish roots. She was just twenty when war broke out and she chose the path of active resistance. She could have returned home to a peaceful life in South Africa, as her father had urged her to do. Her son said he thought she was often 'very scared. But I don't think it was something she thought much about. It was simply what one did.' She died, aged ninety-five, in 2012.

Edith Piaf became a national treasure; she belonged to Paris, or a certain part of it. In 1961 Janet Flanner described how, at one of Piaf's final Paris performances, the singer shuffled on to the stage, walking with difficulty after a series of accidents and much ill health, dressed in an old black shift looking like a withered tramp, and 'when the thunderous applause strikes her, she mostly acts as if she did not hear it'. Her trademark song, 'Non, Je Ne Regrette Rien', had been released only the previous year, in 1960, but it immediately resonated with many French people who saw it as 'their' song; they had done whatever they had needed to do to survive. Piaf, who was never precise about the number of fake identity papers she had taken with her on tours to Nazi Germany and never spoke about her relationships with the German officers she knew when she lived above L'Etoile de Kléber, died of liver cancer, aged forty-seven, in 1963, predeceasing by one day her friend Jean Cocteau. She was buried in the Père Lachaise cemetery in Paris, next to her two-year-old daughter.

Piaf, like Chanel, has been the subject of numerous films, plays and biographies, and in both cases their tangled lives remain mysterious. Neither was wholly bad nor wholly good, and both made accommodations with the truth. Their lives reflect the duality of Picasso's Minotaur, that mythical half-man, half-beast so important to his art, symbolizing the humanity and bestiality of much human behaviour. Yet there is an unyielding fascination with these two Parisiennes, and there have been regular attempts to uncover the truth about whose side they were really on during the war. (Their own, of course.) Artistic and sexual collusion has always received more attention than economic collaboration; women who performed on stage to a German audience were highly visible and therefore an easy target, while economic collaboration is harder to prove. No post-war government wanted to destroy the seeds of its own recovery with potentially dangerous consequences by punishing those responsible. In the course of researching this book I have interviewed descendants of those whose Jewish or part-Jewish families were probably saved because they owned construction companies or because they manu-factured wire products, including barbed wire – activities critical to the Germans. But why talk about what at the time was necessary to preserve lives, however unsavoury the behaviour may seem today? Better to keep silent.

By contrast, there has been a prolonged and inequitable silence in France about the role of so many ordinary women who in some way resisted the occupiers – like the young woman who, persuaded by her Catholic priest, cycled around Paris distributing anti-German newsletters, or *tractes* as she calls them, an activity for which she could have been imprisoned if caught, yet which was important in persuading others in Paris that they were not alone in opposing the Occupation. Her work was significant enough for her to have pre-served these *tractes* for seventy years and now, in her nineties, she shows me these fragile documents on fading brown paper. They are called *Témoignage Chrétien*.* The ones I see declare that 'France disarmed is momentarily reduced to powerlessness but will not consent to let herself remain like that, to deny her traditions, her hope, her honour and her soul.' They offer a spiritual and patriotic form of resistance against Hitlerism. Yet the woman who risked her life to deliver these asks me not to mention her name.

'Why?' I ask.

'Oh well, what I did was nothing,' she shrugs.

The full names of many other noble French concierges who sent police away knowing there were Jews, resisters or evaders hiding in their buildings will never be known to history. One such was Nana, the brave former concierge who during the Occupation also ran a little shop behind whose displays of soap dozens of wanted men and women hid. Nana tried to do the impossible, and with the help of a chaplain, some nuns and one or other of her 'old aunts' or 'cousins' promised to get parcels to imprisoned resisters like André Amar, husband of Jacqueline Mesnil-Amar. At least posterity knows of her existence.

Only in May 2015, seventy years after the end of the war, were two of the best-known female *résistantes*, Geneviève de Gaulle and Germaine Tillion, friends since Ravensbrück, honoured at a ceremony in France's hallowed Panthéon, a secular mausoleum for the great with its famous inscription to the nation's exemplary men: 'AUX GRANDS HOMMES LA PATRIE RECONNAISSANTE'. In fact the coffins of the two women were buried with only earth taken from their graves but without their remains which, according to family wishes, were to stay undisturbed. In 1964 President de Gaulle, back in office, had arranged for the transfer there of the remains of Jean Moulin, the resistance hero and his own personal emissary who was tortured and murdered by the Nazis in 1943. But until May 2015 the only woman there in her own right was the scientist, Marie Curie.

When President Hollande announced that he was planning a major ceremony to commemorate De Gaulle and Tillion entering

---

* The first number of *Témoignage Chrétien* (in 1941) was the work of Pierre Chaillet, a Jesuit priest trained in Austria and Rome who was shocked by the apathetic response to the Occupation of most French people, including many Catholics.

the Panthéon (two men, Jean Zay and Pierre Brossolette, were also being honoured), the story made headline news because the function of women in the resistance has never been fully acknowledged. It was a far greater role than the one they were allowed in society at the time. After the war, many women were both self-effacing, insisting that they did little more than 'simply' deliver newsletters or act as couriers, and keen to get on with their normal lives – an attitude given official sanction by French authorities – or else concerned to protect children by shielding them from the harsh realities of the Occupation and war. In addition, it was harder for women to prove that they had actually been 'combatants' handling weapons. Only six women (four of them posthumously) were awarded the title Compagnons de la Libération by de Gaulle between 1940 and 1946, out of a total of 1,038,[*] and just 1,090 women received the Médaille de la Résistance (a lesser honour) out of 48,000 awarded in total between 1943 and 1947. But now, with the admission to the august Panthéon of de Gaulle and Tillion, the traditional understanding of how women resisted the German occupiers is being dramatically challenged.

In 1999 I met Mme Geneviève de Gaulle Anthonioz. She had just written her wartime memoirs, having been pressed to do so for years, and was being celebrated as the 'Mother Teresa of France' for her lifetime of work heading a major welfare organization for the homeless which she had helped found, the ATD (All Together in Dignity) Fourth World movement. The organization's aim is to help those who are most marginalized escape the cycle of deprivation by their own efforts, and it therefore focuses on providing street libraries, workshops and training, rather than on handouts.

What was abundantly clear in the time I spent with her, a view reinforced since from meeting many other *résistantes*, is that what they had to endure during the war became the defining experience of the rest of their lives. This is not to say that they could not move on, nor is it simply a matter of who their friends were, but it defined how they lived and what they did. In all her subsequent work, whether for the deportees at ADIR or for the homeless on the streets of Paris,

---

[*] They were Berty Albrecht, Laure Diebold, Marie Hackin, Simone Michel-Lévy, Emilienne Moreau-Evrard and Marcelle Henry.

Geneviève de Gaulle clung to the reality of what had made her life bearable in the camps – several small tokens of friendship which enabled survival and hope.

In the course of our 1999 meeting, a still spritely Geneviève de Gaulle walked over to a chest and took out a large gold box once filled with chocolates. 'Mes petits souvenirs,' she said with a wry smile. 'I do not show these to many people.' Her hands shook slightly – the result of Parkinson's, she told me – as she slowly opened the box and, one by one, pulled out the contents. There were false identity and ration cards, not the ones she was arrested with as she used several; a letter from her father, Xavier de Gaulle, the only one she ever received while incarcerated; and then items of almost unbearable poignancy: a doll with pink dress and beige lace that her friend Jacqueline Péry d'Alincourt somehow smuggled to her, a needle-case made from the stolen leather of a German tank commander's beret, miniature playing-cards she made herself and the small embroidered cloth bag in which she kept her bread ration.

Geneviève suffered forced labour, beatings and semi-starvation during her year in Ravensbrück, as well as witnessing scenes that would haunt her for the rest of her life. She saw a female German guard severing a prisoner's throat with a spade while screaming with hatred. And yet, on her release in 1945, she was determined to do something to improve the post-war world. Despite the obvious advantage of her name, she shunned the prospect of a political career. 'Quite the reverse, I wanted to transcend politics. For me the most important goal in life is to combat misery and exclusion.' In 1957 she was introduced to Père Joseph Wresinski, a Catholic priest working with the homeless and hopeless in Paris's cardboard city. She explained that the expressions in the eyes of those she saw there reminded her so keenly of the haunting eyes of the Ravensbrück inmates that she felt compelled to devote the rest of her life to lobbying on their behalf and building up the ATD.

Jeannie Rousseau – still alive in her elegant nineties at the time of writing – was another whose story has had to wait. She chose to keep silent about her wartime exploits until the *Washington Post* reporter David Ignatius 'discovered' her at a party and persuaded her, in 1998, to give an interview. Realizing how extraordinary her account was, he deposited for posterity a lengthy recorded interview with her at the Washington International Spy Museum. But why wait until almost fifty years after the events? Was it a natural reticence, a question of moving on with life, or the sobering realization which came with age that several women had lost their lives at Torgau as a result of her hot-headed heroism? Jeannie, like many, so young when she first resisted, believes her refusal to accept death or to accept what was happening around her was partly because she was so young. When she finally agreed to talk about her wartime life she simply scoffed at that question. 'I just did it, that's all . . . it wasn't a choice. It was what you did. At the time, we all thought we would die.' As Ignatius put it: 'And that's her answer: Heroism isn't a matter of choice, but of reflex. It's a property of the central nervous system, not the higher brain.'

The notion that resisting was a visceral response was important to many of the *résistantes* who believed fundamentally that resisting the occupier was not for them an act of politics. Their behaviour was above politics, as Geneviève de Gaulle maintained. 'Very few of us were anti-fascist before the war, my mother, Andrée Bès, a Ravensbrück deportee, always insisted,' said Marie-Odile Tuloup, her daughter. 'She could not accept standing by while her country was invaded and while Jews were taken away and murdered.' In other words, it was an automatic response based on her instinctive moral values.

Jeannie Rousseau's behaviour at Ravensbrück offers an insight into the deepest complexities of how good people 'should' react to evil. Not all the other Parisiennes in Ravensbrück felt the same certainty about how to respond to their jailers, and although the camp contained many examples of sisterly support and survival systems, there were, too, compliance with oppression, lying, stealing and cruelty. Faced with depravity, nobility was not always possible. The story of Anne Spoerry, a young woman training as a doctor to save lives, who joined the resistance at the beginning of the war, is particularly fascinating – and horrifying – as it reveals how easily good motives can, under extreme circumstances, all too easily become warped. Spoerry spent the rest of her life in Africa, searching for redemption.

*Odette Fabius and Genevieve de Gaulle, friends since Ravensbrück,
on the occasion of Fabius being awarded the
Officier de la Légion d' honneur in 1971*

The camps provided many Parisiennes with extreme circumstances which tested their moral reflexes. The author of a recent study of Ravensbrück, Sarah Helm, believes the camp has been marginalized for too long in histories of the war, 'and yet it is precisely because this was a camp for women that Ravensbrück should have shaken the conscience of the world . . . Ravensbrück showed what mankind was capable of doing to women.' It also shows what women are capable of doing *for* each other.

War, as always, is a catalyst which gave some Parisiennes, such as Lily Pastré and Odette Fabius, a sense of purpose which they could not always recreate in the post-war years, sometimes with disastrous consequences. It was the war which had brought the very different worlds of Odette Fabius and Pierre Ferri-Pisani to collide, while a sensation of risk fed their passionate relationship. In 1956 Odette and Robert divorced and seven years later, in 1963, Pierre put a revolver into his mouth and committed suicide. Like so many who had managed not to die in the camps, ultimately he was unable to survive in the world – whether from a sense of guilt, humiliation or helplessness. Odette was devastated. She went immediately to Marseilles where she met his son, Charles, a lawyer. He told her that three factors had precipitated his father's decline and death: the first was undoubtedly the rupture with her, the second and third were political disappointments. He tried to regain his position as a powerful union leader, but, facing opposition from a younger generation, lost elections and was caught up in attempts by the CIA – who viewed him as little more than a Corsican gangster – to use him in the battle to control dockworkers in the fight against communism. Odette, removed from that side of his life, wrote after his death: 'Now I realized I had lost not only an old love but the best friend I ever had on this earth.'

The suicide rate of Holocaust survivors is today generally accepted to be almost three times that of the general population.* As the world today is still struggling to try and understand the camps and the mass killings that became the defining events of the twentieth century, it may seem too obvious to state that nobody ever 'got over' the experience of the camps. For many survivors, this meant they had reached a point where they could not continue to live. The Austrian writer Thomas Bernhard explained: 'We're constantly correcting, and correcting ourselves, most rigorously, because we recognize at every moment that we did it all wrong (wrote it, thought it, made it all wrong) . . . that everything to this point in time is a falsification, so we correct this falsification, and then we again correct the correction of this falsification and we correct the result of the correction of a correction and so forth.' Too often suicide became the ultimate correction.

Some survivors managed to continue living, often responding by creating a family, writing books or teaching. Although for decades there seemed to be no appetite for hearing their stories, by the 1980s that had changed markedly. There was a hunger to hear them before the generation that had lived through such evil and terror died out. One of the last films made by the celebrated French film director François Truffaut – and one of his most successful financially and critically – was *Le Dernier Métro* (1980), based on the story of Marcel

---

* And sometimes it is those close to survivors who turn to suicide, such as the younger brother of Marceline Rozenberg who never got over the murder of their father and, at the age of forty-three, killed himself.

Leibovici and Margaret Kelly, whose Bluebell dance troupe had enjoyed great success in post-war Paris. One of the screenwriters was Jean-Claude Grumberg who, as a child, had also known the fear of being hidden because he owed his own survival to his mother's brave decision to hand him and his small brother to a *passeuse* for an unknown destination.

In the attenuated legacy of the Second World War, many reputations were created and destroyed, but occasionally fame came too late for those being celebrated. In 1942, when the novelist Irène Némirovsky was deported, she was a successful and moderately well-known writer in France but little known outside. Two months later, after her husband, Michel Epstein, had also been arrested, the family's two daughters, thirteen-year-old Denise and five-year-old Elisabeth, were briefly picked up but released again, thanks to a German officer who noticed a resemblance to his own daughter. 'He told Julie, our governess: "we're not going to take the children this evening. Go home. We'll come for them tomorrow morning." The governess took the hint. She got in touch with her brother, who was in the resistance, and we were hidden.'

Miraculously, they took with them a small suitcase with clothes and personal mementoes, including some manuscripts filled with minuscule handwriting. 'I did not know what it was, but I knew it was precious to mother,' Denise said later. But the girls put the case away and did not read the contents. They survived the next few years thanks to the courageous actions of a teacher, friends and Julie, who arranged for the girls to be hidden in convents and safe houses until after the war, when they realized that both their parents had been killed. Like many others, they got on with their lives and raised families until, in 1992, the younger daughter, Elisabeth Gille, published an imagined biography of her mother entitled *Le Mirador*, for which she used some of the letters found in the suitcase. There are differing accounts and dates as to precisely when the daughters realized the manuscript existed. But the writer Myriam Anissimov, approached by Denise because she knew Romain Gary who had known Némirovsky, was one of the first in the French literary world who saw the hidden notebooks and, realizing they contained an incomplete novel, suggested publication. The reception was ecstatic.

Némirovsky's harrowing and tragic fate, and the story of how the unfinished work had remained hidden for years in the suitcase, may have contributed to the publicity, but the book, *Suite Française*, was hailed as a masterpiece and has since been translated into dozens of languages. Suddenly, Irène Némirovsky was described as a literary genius and compared to Balzac and Tolstoy, her success crowned by the 2004 award of the prestigious Prix Renaudot, never before awarded posthumously.

In 2014 a film was made of *Suite Française*, bringing her work to a still wider public and helping to show the complex web of what had had to be done to survive. But it also revived arguments about Némirovsky's own blindness to anti-Semitism in France until it was too late; and discussions around whether or not the old-established Jews of Paris had sacrificed the interests and lives of immigrant (or so-called 'foreign') Jews in order to safeguard those of native-born French citizens – a discomfiting argument which risks overlooking who the real enemy was.

Walking around Paris today, one is assailed not only by memorials honouring the role of brave resisters, but also by a number of plaques which finally admit that the French state itself was responsible for taking some Jewish children to their deaths. One of the first in this vein was unveiled on 16 July 1995 at the Gare d'Austerlitz, for the Jews arrested in the Vél' d'Hiv round-up, the same day that President Chirac made his important speech accepting state responsibility for the Vél' d'Hiv tragedy. There are street names that honour those who gave their lives in the fight against the Nazis: Avenue Georges Mandel and Place Hélène Berr are just two among myriad others.

In 2008, more than fifty years after her death, Hélène Berr's diary was finally published. It's an important document not merely because it is all that is left of this talented young woman, so full of musical and literary promise, but also because Berr was so insightful about the nature of the choices facing her and the inevitable catastrophe lurking at the heart of the Union Générale des Israélites de France, the UGIF, itself. This tainted body, neither collaborationist devil nor resistance bastion for Jewish survival it might once have aspired to be, was, as the American historian Richard Cohen subtly argued, an organization with an innate 'precarious duality' at its core. Picasso's

Minotaur again. Eventual publication of *The Journal of Hélène Berr* was largely thanks to the determination of her niece, Mariette Job, who had known of its existence since 1946 when the family housekeeper gave it to Hélène's brother, who passed it on to Jean Morawiecki. In the 1990s Mariette searched in earnest and found an elderly Morawiecki, by then retired as a diplomat and living once more in Paris.

'He gave me the manuscript, which he had been keeping on top of a very high cupboard. It had been a weight almost too heavy for him to bear,' Mariette explained. He agreed to publication which was, after all, what Hélène had wanted, and wrote in the epilogue, 'In that sink of iniquity, Hélène never gave up on the future. She never lost the strength to struggle against the abjection all around her. She preserved her soul and helped her comrades keep theirs . . . May this journal survive down the ages so as to nurture the memory of all those whose words were annihilated.'

One of Hélène's friends, Jacqueline Mesnil-Amar, who also kept a diary, questioned how she herself had been able to continue living when so many of her friends had been killed. 'Is there an element of choice in the ordeal? How is it possible that one is able, in spite of everything, to bear it, even to accept it? Is there a part of ourselves, a point at which we consent to it, as the price we pay to cleanse ourselves of the remorse that lies beneath the web of an almost happy life? A kind of penance . . . is it a betrayal to be alive?' Eventually Jacqueline found a solace in work, helping Jewish *déportées* less fortunate than herself, and in identifying with Jewishness.

Lise London, having survived first the Spanish Civil War, then months in French prisons followed by almost three years in Ravensbrück and the 1945 death march, finally wrote her memoirs in the 1990s, *La Mégère de la Rue Daguerre* or The Shrew of the Rue Daguerre – the name given to her by the Vichy Ambassador to the Nazis in Paris, Fernand de Brinon, when she organized the food riot in that street. She said communism gave her faith and strength to survive prison and torture. 'To be a communist was more than just belonging to a party: it was about faith. There was a religious element to it. We wanted to spread the revolution. When you lost faith, everything collapsed.'

After the war, she went to live in Czechoslovakia, the birthplace of her adored Jewish husband Artur London, with whom she had shared so much over the previous decade. Having survived Mauthausen, he wanted to return to his native land and became a successful communist politician in a Soviet-backed government. However, he fell from grace, was arrested in 1951 and, accused of being a Zionist traitor, had to face a Stalinist show trial. Eventually freed and 'rehabilitated' in 1956, following Stalin's death, he and his family moved back to Paris, where Lise continued to work for left-leaning, progressive causes. In 1970 a play written by him called *The Trial* was made into a film, starring Simone Signoret as Lise and Yves Montand, who had to lose more than thirty pounds in order to resemble the half-starved Artur. The play was based on notes which Lise had managed to smuggle out of his Soviet prison. She was a loyal and brave wife who remained passionate about justice in general and defiant to the end. According to her son, Michel, she rarely mentioned the Nazi camps. But in 2005, after Artur's death, she decided to take her family to Mauthausen. 'It was very emotional for her but she didn't lose her composure. She showed the grandchildren the barracks, the ovens and the striped pyjamas as if it were the most natural thing in the world.' In her final interview she said she was still a communist, 'but not in a political sense any more: I tore up my membership card. I remain a communist out of loyalty to all those comrades who shared our dreams, and who died for freedom.'

But among the plethora of volumes published in recent years, not all enhanced reputations. Bernard Ullmann, the journalist son of Lisette de Brinon by her first husband, waited until 2004 when he was eighty-two to publish a disturbing book about how his Jewish mother had survived the war married to a leading anti-Semite such as Fernand de Brinon. Lisette, born into an assimilated family of bankers, became a hostess of enormous sparkle and superficiality in pre-war Paris, and converted to Catholicism shortly after divorcing her first husband, Claude Ullmann. She always believed that, although anti-Semitism existed in France, 'it couldn't reach people like us'. Ullmann vividly describes how, the day before he was smuggled out of France in 1942 in the trunk of his mother's car so that he could fight in North Africa – a ploy part-organized by his stepfather

– he watched the deeply anti-Semitic film *Jew Süss* and was then taken for dinner at La Tour d'Argent by de Brinon. When de Brinon rose to prominence under Pétain, he protected Lisette and her two sons as long as they remained out of sight, but it was protection of which Ullmann grew deeply ashamed: ashamed of himself and his good manners in never facing up to the man who was his mother's husband; ashamed that this was the man to whom he owed his life. In 1947, Ullmann had the good grace to visit de Brinon in prison as he prepared for his trial for treason, days before he was executed by firing squad. Lisette, who had herself been briefly held in Fresnes, always remained loyal to her husband's memory, continuing to call herself the Marquise de Brinon as she socialized in Paris with friends from Vichy until she died, broke, in a Paris nursing home in 1982.

In 1992 a new edition of Denise Dufournier's book *La Maison des mortes* was published with a 'reflection' by the author, prompted partly by the number of letters she had received from mothers of the pilots whom she had helped to escape, young men who were often killed on their next sortie. The women wanted to thank her for looking after their sons when they needed help. But she was also motivated by what she perceived as a lack of comprehension, especially in England, about how much women like her had done. 'It would be so nice if the English could understand that we did run massive risks.' Like many women who resisted the Occupation, Denise Dufournier went for many years without official recognition of those risks. In her own case, marriage to a British diplomat precluded her from receiving a foreign award until he retired, whereupon she was, finally, made an Officier of the Légion d'honneur. But others did not receive official recognition until the closing years of the last century or even into the twenty-first. Pearl Witherington, one of the most famous of the SOE women, who actually commanded her own *réseau*, the Wrestler network amounting to almost 3,000 men at one point, rejected the offer of a civil MBE with an icy note pointing out that 'there was nothing remotely "civil" about what I did. I didn't sit behind a desk all day.' She later accepted a military MBE and in 2004 was presented with a CBE by the Queen, who told her at the ceremony: 'We should have done this a long time ago.' Finally in 2006, more than sixty years after she parachuted back into France,

Witherington was awarded her parachute wings, an award which she considered a greater honour than either the MBE or the CBE.

One of the most painful controversies I encountered throughout the research for this book is the distinction between Parisiennes deported because they chose to resist, who were therefore decorated by the state on their return, and Parisiennes deported because they were Jewish, and were therefore victims. Vivette Samuel volunteered for the children's organization OSE during the war and subsequently for the deported women's organization ADIR. She wrote sensitively of the great love and admiration she had for the women she met at ADIR, but also of the misunderstandings she encountered. 'Because they had fought in the resistance network I heard them express only contempt for the racial deportees. I had nightmares about it but . . . at the end of my three-month probationary period [at ADIR], I decided to stay.' But, as my interviewees constantly reminded me, 'C'est très compliqué,' and sometimes the divide even fell within families, as it did in the Jacob family. Denise, later Vernay, although Jewish, worked as a *résistante* and was deported to Ravensbrück; but Simone, later Simone Veil, along with her mother and her other sister Madeleine, were all taken to Auschwitz-Birkenau as Jews. Mme Jacob, the girls' mother, died of typhoid in March 1945 after surviving the death march, while Madeleine survived the camps but was killed in a car crash in the 1950s. Vernay, on returning from Ravensbrück, was made Commandeur of the Légion d'honneur and awarded numerous other medals including the Grand-Croix of the Ordre national du Mérite, the Croix de guerre 1939–1945 avec palmes and the Médaille de la Résistance avec rosette. Veil, however, although she had a glittering political career, best known for her determination to legalize abortion in France – the law was finally passed in 1975 after bitter debate – was awarded the Légion d'honneur only in 2012, albeit the Grand-Croix, the highest level. 'We were only victims and not heroes,' she complained in 1993. 'What we experienced mattered little, something people did not fail to tell us in a brutal way, even those belonging to the associations of former resisters.' Veil also faced virulent personal attacks comparing the legalization of abortion to the Holocaust; one parliamentary *député* asked if she would agree to the idea of throwing embryos into crematorium ovens.

And, as historians weigh up the tally of what exactly France is responsible for, it needs pointing out that while the Vichy government deported a shocking number of Jews living in France – 76,000 out of a population of 330,000* – to their deaths between 1940 and 1944, on the other hand the proportion of Jews – approximately 25 per cent – deported from France was much lower than that deported from Belgium, Norway or the Netherlands, where it was as high as 73 per cent. This disparity, often described as the French paradox, is often used to defend the Vichy State as well as the French population, which undoubtedly worked hard to rescue many thousands of Jews. But in a sense that misses the point, which is that had Vichy and its accomplices in the French population not collaborated so actively, thousands of Jews would not have been sent to their deaths, especially in 1942, when the Germans alone did not have the resources to do this effectively.

But war, of course, is neither about merely statistics nor about playing with reputations. War destroys lives. Toquette Jackson never fully recovered her health after Ravensbrück and lived quietly at the family home at Enghien-les-Bains, outside Paris, until she died in 1968 at the American Hospital, where her husband Sumner had worked so tirelessly. She had been continually ill, too sick to return to nursing or even to work at all, although she had talked about having a small business in Paris as a way of affording life in the city. She struggled, but retained both her dignity and her courage and was decorated with many awards, including the Croix de guerre, the Croix du combattant volontaire and, in 1946, Chevalière of the Légion d'honneur, promoted to Officier in 1964. No amount of medals could, however, compensate for loneliness. Some days she wrote in her diary simply: 'Nobody came . . .' In the event Phillip, her son, looked after his mother. He too was highly decorated, testified at the War Crimes Tribunal at Hamburg in May 1946, studied to be an engineer, married and brought up a family. At the time of writing he is a resident of Les Invalides, the distinguished home

---

* According to the Mémorial de la Shoah the figures are a synthesis of the latest estimates by historians at the Yad Vashem memorial in Jerusalem and the United States Holocaust Memorial Museum in Washington.

for war veterans in the centre of Paris, where we met to discuss his mother.

Wallis and Edward, the Duke and Duchess of Windsor, no matter how hard they tried, failed to shift perceptions of themselves in the post-war world as defeatists or, worse, as Nazi sympathizers, and were from then on purposeless exiles, part of European café society moving from one reception to another. From time to time Wallis complained to the British Ambassador that her husband was not being informed of current events or invited to official receptions, or both. Hoping in vain that the British royal family would see fit finally to give Wallis her royal initials – HRH – thus ensuring that she was curtseyed to and therefore enabling the couple to return to England unashamed, they declined to find a permanent home anywhere else. New York, Canada (Edward had a ranch in Alberta) and the south of France, where they continued to rent their heavily staffed, pre-war villa La Croë, were all considered. They became an isolated element of post-war Paris life, or of a certain part of it, *le gratin*, invited to fashion shows, to jewellers and in Wallis's case to the Elizabeth Arden beauty salon, which she especially liked as she rarely paid and was always given her own robe with the initials SAR (*Son Altesse Royale*) – the French version of royal initials – on the pocket. But waiting to see what would happen in Britain was an unsettling existence, so in 1948 they rented 85 Rue de la Faisanderie, a palatial building where some of the decoration had been created by Wallis's pre-war friend Elsie de Wolfe, but for which neither of them felt any particular affection. And then, after the coronation of Queen Elizabeth II in 1953, when it became clear that the royal family's attitude towards Wallis had not softened, they decided to settle in Paris.

They accepted an offer from the French government to live at 4 Champ d'Entraînement, a fine three-storey, turn-of-the-century mansion in the Bois de Boulogne, a house which came with four acres as well as its own history, having been expropriated from Renault after the war on the grounds that the motor manufacturer had collaborated. Louis Renault had initially refused to produce tanks for the Germans but ended up making trucks. In the poisonous atmosphere of the Liberation, he was arrested on 23 September 1944 and taken to Fresnes, where he died in 'mysterious circumstances' a

month later, awaiting trial. The company was then nationalized by
General de Gaulle, who briefly lived in the Bois de Boulogne house
himself – his wife, the ever modest Yvonne, described it as 'a degree
above what I would have liked'. It was offered to the Windsors on
a fifty-year lease for a peppercorn rent and it was here that Wallis
undertook some grand entertaining (the Duke died in 1972). It was
not until the 1980s that the formidable lawyer known as Maître Suzanne Blum came to dominate the Duchess's life. During the Second
World War, Suzanne Weill (as she then was) and her lawyer husband
managed to escape to New York, returning to Paris in 1945. From the
moment she established her law practice in Paris, Maître Blum began
acquiring a remarkable list of clients, mostly prominent figures in
the film industry, but she also defended Bernard Faÿ, the prominent
collaborator, protector and friend of the American writer, Gertrude
Stein. In her spare time, under a pseudonym, Maître Blum wrote
detective stories. Her own complicated life would have provided a
good plot.

But while the Windsor reputation was suffering, Florence Gould
managed to keep hers intact and, in spite of her success as a hostess
entertaining well-known anti-Semites, to overcome taints of collaboration. She died in 1993 and left the bulk of her fortune to establish
the Florence Gould Foundation, an American charity devoted to
supporting the arts, especially Franco-American cultural exchanges.
New York boasts a Florence Gould Hall and San Francisco a Florence Gould Theatre.

Many buildings in Paris, as much as people, were swiftly busy
reinventing themselves. Just as the prison at Fresnes was used in
1945 to house collaborators awaiting trial, often holding prisoners
in the same cells where resisters had been locked up before them, so
Drancy too continued to function in the immediate post-war period
but with different inmates. Then slowly, as 1940s France found itself
confronted with an accommodation crisis, the buildings there, the
La Muette complex, were returned to their original purpose: housing. Since 1976 there has been a large and powerful monument at
the entrance to the buildings dedicated to Drancy prisoners and created by Shelomo Selinger, a former Jewish deportee of Polish origin.
Just beyond is a symbolic freight car of the same type as those used

to transport the deportees to their deaths. But visiting Drancy, so recognizable from photographs of the days when it was an overflowing sink of inhumanity, is a deeply disconcerting experience. When I asked a resident of the flats how he could live in a place of such sorrow and pain he looked at me strangely before replying, 'But everywhere in Paris has a history. Mostly there are places where Germans lived. Surely this is better than that?'

Some battles, far from ending, were just beginning in the 1940s and dragged on for decades. The passionate Francophile Caroline Ferriday, who never married and devoted her life to helping those who had suffered in France, took on the fight for compensation for the young Polish *lapins*, the girls, now often deformed women, who had been the subjects of hideous experimentation by the Nazis in Ravensbrück. Informed of their plight by Jacqueline Péry d'Alincourt, who had befriended a number of *lapins* in the camps, Ferriday was horrified to discover that as the women now lived in communist Poland, with whom the West Germans did not currently have diplomatic relations, they were not eligible to be included in the compensation agreements for Nazi victims, which started to pay out reparations from 1952 onwards. They were abandoned and ignored in the post-war world, many of them requiring constant medical treatment for a range of chronic conditions including cardiac illness, hepatitis and cystitis, not to mention financial assistance. Yet, despite her forceful arguments, Ferriday could not bring about a change in the German position. For nearly twenty years she fought and wrote articles about them and invited them to stay with her at her beautiful family home in Bethlehem, Connecticut. In 1959, nearly fifteen years after the end of the war, thirty-five of the women came to the United States for medical treatment, Ferriday having played a crucial role in convincing them to travel as well as helping to raise the funds. In the early 1960s, following a series of articles in US newspapers which Ferriday helped orchestrate, the West German government bowed to international pressure and full indemnities were finally granted to 136 of the most severely handicapped survivors, while the rest received partial compensation.

Life under oppression, whether at Ravensbrück, in Vichy or in Paris, revealed what women were capable of *in extremis*. 'Indignation can move mountains,' declared Germaine Tillion. 'France in 1940 was unbelievable. There were no men left. It was women who started the Resistance. Women didn't have the vote, they didn't have bank accounts, they didn't have jobs. Yet we women were capable of resisting.' Jeannie Rousseau took the path of resistance, Elisabeth de Rothschild took another, Renée Puissant a third. Yet few people at the time saw themselves as having choices or making decisions, neither *résistantes* nor vegetable-sellers who needed to be paid in order to live; nor black-marketeers who saw opportunities waiting to be seized; nor Jewish mothers who gave their children away; nor women of *le tout Paris* who had lunches and bought fine clothes; nor singers, dancers and prostitutes who continued with the work they were trained or accustomed to do. Many of the latter maintained that even had the French denied social contacts to the Germans during the Occupation, nothing would have been different, and arguably daily life would have been more painful for the French. Life had to go on. Indeed, to deaden Paris in that way risked punishing Parisians more than Germans, they believed. Most just tried to get by however they could.

But what seems so clear today is that there *were* choices. Writers, artists and performers had to submit their work to German officials for permission to show it. Inevitably this meant submitting to compromise and collaboration in varying degrees. Silence or leaving the country was, for some, an option; performing but not socializing after the performance was another; turning a blind eye to behaviour of which they disapproved was the easiest. For some women the choice involved little more than a decision to wear an outrageous hat or to walk out of a restaurant. For others it involved making a deal or a sexual exchange. But surviving in occupied Paris for many women demanded some sort of choice, some sort of decision, about how they would accommodate living with the Germans. It is not for the rest of us to judge but, with imagination, we can to try to understand.

Notes

Prologue: Les Parisiennes

xvii   up to the age of eighteen: La Loi du 18 Mars 1942, on 'l'enseignement ménager familial'.

xix   'no escape line could keep going at all': Edward Stourton, *Cruel Crossing: Escaping Hitler across the Pyrenees*, Doubleday, 2013, p. 78.

xix   'me about choice?': Jean-Claude Grumberg, conversation with author, 9 November 2013.

xx   'one of them': Gabriel Josipovici, *A Life*, London Magazine Editions, 2001, p. 93.

xx   'How could you not do it?': Jeannie, Vicomtesse de Clarens (née Rousseau), video interview with David Ignatius, courtesy of the International Spy Museum Archive, Washington, DC.

xx   'our weapons were born of love': Dédée de Jongh, quoted in Stourton, *Cruel Crossing*, p. 192.

1939: Paris on the Edge

6   'the result is sheer genius': quoted in Ruth Franklin, 'A Life in Good Taste: The Fashions and Follies of Elsie de Wolfe', *New Yorker*, 27 September 2004 (http://www.newyorker.com/magazine/2004/09/27/a-life-in-good-taste).

6   'to defy the fates': Elsa Schiaparelli, *Shocking Life: The Autobiography of Elsa Schiaparelli*, Dent, 1954, p. 110.

7   'a little sad': http://vb.com/dior/aimeedeheeren/ August 2012.

9   'all the cheering was for her': Marjorie Lawrence, *Interrupted Melody: An Autobiography*, Sydney, Invincible Press, 1949, p. 123.

10   'not considered an additional crime': Janet Flanner, *Paris Was Yesterday, 1925–1939*, New York, Viking, 1972, p. 216.

11   'were particularly chic': Schiaparelli, *Shocking Life*, p. 109.

11   'civilised good time,' she wrote: Flanner, *Paris Was Yesterday*, p. 220.

12   'the nineteenth century': Richard Kreitner, 'Bastille Day and the Concept of Progress in 1939', 14 July 2014, *The Nation*

13   'everybody collects at Maxim's': Noël Coward to Gladys Calthrop, *The Letters of Noël Coward*, ed. Barry Day, Methuen, 2007, p. 378.

13 'time for fashion': Adelia Sabatini, 'The House that Dreams Built', *Glass Magazine*, pp. 66–71.

13 'pour espionnage': Archives Départementales du Var, 158 W 848.

14 'practically anything, which is very important': Noël Coward to Gladys Calthrop, Day, *Letters of Noël Coward*, p. 379.

15 'it's not in my temperament': Robert Lavigue, 'Panthéonisations résistantes . . . On l'a échappé belle!', 20 February 2014, http://lavigue. blogspot.gr/2014/02/pantheonisations-resistantes-on-la.html.

17 'to an overseas destination': Miriam Mania Stanton, 'Escape from the Inferno of Europe', ed. Ben Stanton, unpublished ms, courtesy Professor Lawrence Goldman, p. 8. See also http://www.amazon.co.uk/ Escape-inferno-Europe-Miriam-Stanton/dp/09530007707.

17 'How could I just go?' she later wrote: ibid.

18 'Joseph left immediately': Jacqueline Péry d'Alincourt, 'Surviving Ravensbrück: "Forgive, Don't Forget"', https://www.utexas.edu/cola/ insts/france-ut/_files/pdf/resources/Pery.pdf.

20 'the most imposing of obstacles': Jonathan Weiss, *Irène Némirovsky: Her Life and Works*, Palo Alto, Calif., Stanford University Press, 2006, p. 73.

20 'The climate is quite changed!': 'Les Nouvelles Littéraires', 4 June 1939.

22 'the end of happy life': Claire Chevrillon, *Code Name Christiane Clouet: A Woman in the French Resistance*, trans. Jane Kielty Stott, College Station, Tex., Texas A & M University Press, 1995, p. 3.

23 'only as an exceptional measure': quoted in Hanna Diamond, *Women and the Second World War in France, 1939–48: Choices and Constraints*, Routledge, 1999, p. 19.

29 'Will Not Forsake Fashion in War': *Melbourne Argus*, 6 December 1939.

30 'someone else's child': Janet Teissier du Cros, *Divided Loyalties: A Scotswoman in Occupied France*, Hamish Hamilton, 1962, p. 24.

30 'an unpardonable thing in France': ibid.

30 'does not fear the future': Dominique Veillon, *Fashion under the Occupation*, Oxford/New York, Berg, 2002, p. 6.

31 an editorial that autumn: *Le Jardin des Modes*, September 1939.

32 carpet slippers instead of boots: Drue Tartière, *The House near Paris: An American Woman's Story of Traffic in Patriots*, New York, Simon & Schuster, 1946, p. 13.

1940: Paris Abandoned

39 'about to begin': Odette Fabius, *Un Lever de soleil sur le Mecklembourg*, Albin Michel, 1986, p. 47.

40 'Red Cross millions': Fabius, p. 55.

40 'in my life': Wallis Windsor, *The Heart has its Reasons*, Michael Joseph, 1956, p. 228.

40 'sound of gunfire': Duke of Windsor to Bernard Rickatson-Hatt, Thomson Reuter archives, n.d.

40 'is the end': Philip Ziegler, *King Edward VIII* Collins, 1990, p. 417.

45 'not a coward': Davina Eastwood in conversation with the author, 2 October 2014.

46 'like a rat in occupied Paris': quoted in Hanna Diamond, *Fleeing Hitler: France 1940*, Oxford, Oxford University Press, 2007, p. 6.

47 'the wearer had become a nomad': Patrick Buisson, *Années érotiques*, p.51.

48 'of their schools with perfect calm': quoted in ibid. p. 54.

49 'fleeing the German lava': Jacqueline Mesnil-Amar, *Maman, What Are We Called Now?*, trans. Francine Yorke, Persephone Books, 2015, p. 28.

50 'and closed the suitcase': Irène Némirovsky, *Suite Française*, trans. Sandra Smith, Chatto & Windus, 2006, p. 19.

50 'wives of senior officers': Edward Spears, *Assignment to Catastrophe*, vol. 2, p. 237.

50 'in uniform, hanging about': ibid.

51 'impossible to remain passive': Margaret Collins Weitz, *Sisters in the Resistance: How Women Fought to Free France, 1940–45*, New York, John Wiley, 1995, p. 2.

51 'were here *au grand complet*': Edward Spears, *Assignment to Catastrophe*, vol. 2, p. 243.

52 'had been aware until that time': John Sherwood, *Georges Mandel and the Third Republic*, Palo Alto, Calif., Stanford University Press, 1970, p. 186.

52 'guide the French Empire,' he urged: Spears, *Assignment to Catastrophe*, vol. 2, p. 316.

53 'how it spread': Vivou de Boysson: conversation with the author, 23 January 2015.

54 'an emissary to woo her favours': Noel Barber, *The Week France Fell: June 10–June 16 1940*, Stein & Day, 1976, p. 29.

54 'to ask for an armistice': William L. Shirer, *The Collapse of the Third Republic: An Inquiry into the Fall of France in 1940*, New York, Simon & Schuster, 1969, p. 813; and Barber, *The Week France Fell*, p. 223.

55 'I have no mistress!': quoted in Hal Vaughan, *Doctor to the Resistance: The Heroic True Story of an American Surgeon and his Family in Occupied Paris*, Washington, DC, Brassey's, 2004, p. 177.

56 'the other clients of the hotel': Corinne Luchaire, *Ma drôle de vie*, repr. Paris, Dualpha Editions, 2003, p. 127.

56 'a kind of euphoria reigned': David Pryce-Jones, *Paris in the Third Reich*, New York, Holt, Rinehart & Winston, 1981, p. 19.

58 'and often extremely helpful': personal information from Tom Bower, whose mother was a child in Vienna with Sereny and witnessed her removal from school on account of her being Jewish.

58 'on everything imaginable': Helmuth James von Moltke, *Letters to Freya, 1939–1945*, New York, Alfred A. Knopf, 1990, p. 97.

59 'I knew no one there': Simone Signoret, *Nostalgia Isn't What It Used to Be*, Weidenfeld & Nicolson, 1978, p. 41.

60   'relegated to her cubbyhole': ibid.

62   for those in power: Ian Ousby, *Occupation: The Ordeal of France,
      1940–1944*, John Murray, 1997, p. 116.

63   'first time in their lives': Teissier du Cros, *Divided Loyalties*, p. 253.

64   'We both felt comforted': Rosemary Say and Noel Holland, *Rosie's War:
      An Englishwoman's Escape from Occupied France*, Michael O'Mara Books,
      2011, p. 53.

64   'that adds to our sadness': Jean Guéhenno, *Diary of the Dark Years,
      1940–1944: Collaboration, Resistance and Daily Life in Occupied Paris*,
      trans. David Ball, Oxford, Oxford University Press, 2014, p. 20.

66   held captive were legion: Nicole Alby, conversation with the author, 17
      July 2015.

66   'I served them at table': Say and Holland, *Rosie's War*, p. 70.

66   'he wrote . . . from Toulouse': ibid., p. 83.

67   'ardent supporters of de Gaulle': Agnès Humbert, *Résistance: Memoirs of
      Occupied France*, Bloomsbury, 2008, p. 35.

68   'he has an erection, done': *Paris Brothel* BBC Storyville film by Mark
      Kidel, 2008.

68   'It saved my life': Freddie Knoller, conversation with the author, 18 March
      2015.

69   'to replenish their wardrobes': Veillon, *Fashion under the Occupation*,
      p. 23.

69   'wisely and with dignity': ibid. p. 23.

69   'her rise in the world': Luchaire, *Ma drôle de vie*, p. 139–40.

1941: Paris Divided

73   'more than all your diplomas': Francine Muel-Dreyfus, *Vichy and the
      Eternal Feminine: A Contribution to a Political Sociology of Gender*, trans.
      Kathleen A. Johnson, Durham, NC, Duke University Press, 2001, p. 231.

75   'panache was indispensable to us': quoted in Melanie Hawthorne and
      Richard J. Golsan, *Gender and Fascism in Modern France*, p. 78.

76   'delirious cries of joy': *La Gerbe*, July 1941, quoted in Alexandra
      Taylor, 'Part IV: France <3 Food – Adapting to the Ration
      System', https://tayloralexandra.wordpress.com/2012/02/18/
      part-iv-france-3-food-adapting-to-the-ration-system/.

77   'don't do something!': Agnès Humbert: *Resistance, Memoirs of Occupied
      France*, Bloomsbury, 2008, p. 11.

77   'belts polished and gleaming': ibid., p. 28.

78   'anything revolutionary or disorderly': Chevrillon, *Code Name Christiane
      Clouet*, p. 123. Even at the height of the Second World War brother and
      sister André Chevrillon and Adeline Pelletier were still arguing about the
      Dreyfus affair and whether or not there should be a retrial (ibid., p. 124).

78   'have gotten to Paris': Collins Weitz, *Sisters in the Resistance*, p. vi.

79   'months to come,' she wrote: Humbert, *Résistance*, p. 32.

81   'the French economy': Gerald Feldman and Wolfgang Seibel (eds),
        *Networks of Nazi Persecution: Bureaucracy, Business and the Organization
        of the Holocaust*, Oxford, Berghahn Books, 2004, p. 70.

81   'in Paris at the same time': Robert Paxton, *Vichy France: Old Guard and
        New Order, 1940–1944*, New York, Alfred A. Knopf, 1972, p. 76.

81   it was 'very disagreeable': Lynn H. Nicholas, *The Rape of Europa: The Fate
        of Europe's Treasures in the Third Reich and the Second World War*, New
        York, Alfred A. Knopf, 1994, p. 136.

82   'from the David Weill collection': Archives Nationales, Carnets RV folio
        115 18/10/43.

82   then living in America: Jeanne Bucher to Sybille Cournand, 7 December
        1934, Family Archives, courtesy Galerie Jeanne Bucher Jaeger, Paris.

83   directed towards art and artists: ibid., p. 66.

84   'look what I do to it': ibid., p. 62.

85   'show me her Ernst paintings': Alan Riding, *And the Show Went On:
        Cultural Life in Nazi-Occupied Paris,* Duckworth Overlook, 2012,
        p. 171.

85   'served tea and biscuits': Henri Goetz, 'My Life, my Friends', http://
        henrigoetz.com/index.php?/tests-goetz/my-life/.

86   'resistance were innumerable': David Ignatius, 'After Five Decades a Spy
        Tells her Tale', *Washington Post*, 28 December 1998.

87   'I couldn't be dangerous, could I?': Jeanne, Vicomtesse de Clarens, video
        interview with David Ignatius, International Spy Museum Archive,
        Washington, DC.

88   'fresh milk and vegetables': Claude du Granrut, conversation with the
        author, 8 September 2014.

89   'welcoming to all': Claude du Granrut, *Le Piano et le violoncelle*, Paris,
        Editions du Rocher, 2013, p. 65.

89   'discussed at home': Claude du Granrut, conversation with the author, 8
        September 2014.

90   'spirit of humanity': Julian Jackson, *France: The Dark Years 1940–1945*,
        Oxford University Press 2001, p. 354.

92   '"Frenchmen, help me!"': Anne Sinclair, *My Grandfather's Gallery: A
        Legendary Art Dealer's Escape from Vichy France*, trans. Shaun Whiteside,
        Profile Books, 2014 (first published in France as *21 Rue La Boétie*, Grasset,
        2012), pp. 33–4.

92   'a very handsome man': ibid, p. 355.

94   Miriam Mania Stanton, 'Escape from the Inferno of Europe', ed. Ben
        Stanton, p. 59.

94   foreign currency protection command – Devisenschutzkommando:
        http://www.nizkor.org/ftp.cgi/imt/nca/ftp.cgi?imt/nca/nca-06/
        nca-06-3766-ps.

96   mistress of Charles Ephrussi: *Irène Cahen d'Anvers*, oil on canvas, now in
        Zurich's Bührle Collection.

96   'exhibiting at the Mirlitons with Bouguereau!': Elizabeth Melanson, 'The
       Influence of Jewish Society Patrons on Renoir's Stylistic Transformation
       in the Mid-1880s', *Nineteenth-Century Art Worldwide*, vol. 12, issue
       2, Autumn 2013 (http://www.19thc-artworldwide.org/autumn13/
       melanson-on-renoir-and-the-influence-of-jewish-patrons).

98   'our understanding with her': Frederic Spotts, *The Shameful Peace: How
       French Artists and Intellectuals Survived the Nazi Occupation*, New Haven/
       London, Yale University Press, 2010, p. 46.

98   'his name in print': Guéhenno, *Diary of the Dark Years*, p. 38.

100   'café society makes clear': Thierry Coudert: *Café Society, Socialites,
       Patrons, Artists,* Flammarion, 2010.

102   'against diplomatic protocol': William Stevenson: *A Man Called Intrepid*,
       Lyons Press, 2009, pp. 323–6.

102   'introducing him to': Charles Glass: *Americans in Paris: Life and Death
       under Nazi Occupation*, HarperCollins, 2009, p. 173.

105   documents unearthed after the war: my thanks to Alan Riding for
       showing me these.

105   'a concentration camp': Report prepared by the German army in France,
       1942, concerning removal of French art objects through the German
       Embassy and the Einsatzstab Rosenberg in France. http://www.nizkor.
       org/ftp.cgi/imt/nca/ftp.cgi?imt/nca/nca-06/nca-06-3766-ps.

106   'with Germaine Lubin as Isolde': Pryce-Jones, *Paris in the Third Reich*, p.
       262.

106   'the courage to remain silent': Alan Riding, *And the Show Went On:
       Cultural Life in Nazi-Occupied Paris*, Duckworth Overlook, 2012,
       p. 156.

106   'who has sold herself': Patrick Bade, *Music Wars 1937–45*, East and West
       Publishing, 2012, p. 72.

107   'without understanding them': Luchaire, *Ma drôle de vie*.

109   explained a distraught Colette: Judith Thurman, *Secrets of the Flesh: A
       Life of Colette*, Bloomsbury, 1999, p. 454.

1942: Paris Ravaged

114   'against these criminals': Inga Haag quoted in Martin Childs, 'Co-
       conspirator in the plot to assassinate Hitler', *Independent*, 11 January
       2010.

114   'betray under torture': ibid.

114   'where can you get it?': Gisèle Casadesus, conversation with the author, 22
       January 2015.

116   'the tone of couture': Veillon, *Fashion under the Occupation*, p. 121.

117   'repression would not end resistance': Lise London, interview with José
       Fort, *L'Humanité*, 2 August 2014.

117   she told an interviewer in 2011, aged ninety-five: Jesús Rodríguez, 'The
       Last Female Veteran', *El País*, 20 December 2011.

118 where the marriage took place: Rosemarie Killius, *Frauen für die Front: Gespräche mit Wehrmachtshelferinnen*, Leipzig, Militzke Verlag, 2003, pp. 118–22.

118 flirtatiousness of the French: Ina Seidel and Hanns Grosser, *Dienende Herzen: Kriegsbriefe von Nachrichtenhelferinnen des Heeres*, Berlin, Wilhelm Limpert-Verlag, 1942.

119 'a fresh, happy greeting!': ibid.

119 'the Musée de l'Homme': Ursula Rüdt von Collenberg, interview with Pryce-Jones, *Paris in the Third Reich*, p. 244.

119 'much more than the French': ibid.

120 had snubbed the exhibition: quoted in Laurence Bertrand Dorléac, *Art of the Defeat: France, 1940–1944*, trans. Jane Marie Todd, Los Angeles, Getty Publications, 2008, p. 91.

120 the forced labour of French prisoners of war: Nicholas, *The Rape of Europa*, p. 182.

121 'swear you were not Jewish': Jean-Claude Grumberg, conversation with the author, 9 November 2013.

121 'home to my children,' she explained: Gisèle Casadesus, conversation with the author, 22 January 2015.

122 'Germany through me': Caroline Moorehead, 'Sleeping with the Enemy', *Intelligent Life*, September/October 2013 (http://www.intelligentlifemagazine.com/content/features/anonymous/sleeping-enemy).

125 'protest against this brutality': Hélène Berr, *Journal*, trans. David Bellos, MacLehose Press, 2008, p. 92.

126 'caught in a street round-up': Chevrillon, *Code Name Christiane Clouet*, p. 59.

126 'a French husband to his wife': David Rousset, *Le Pitre ne rit pas*, Paris, Christian Bourgeois Editeur, 1979, p. 39.

126 'and the wretched poor': Berr, *Journal*, pp. 77, 83.

127 'It was close to excruciating': ibid., p. 69.

128 'Papa was a prisoner too': ibid., p. 72.

130 'they did not show their faces': Rachel Erlbaum, conversation with the author, 16 July 2015.

131 'That is what stays in my mind': Arlette Reiman, conversation with the author, 18 July 2015.

131 'one adieu is enough': Weiss, *Irène Némirovsky*, p. 155.

131 'time go by': Olivier Philipponnat and Patrick Lienhardt, *The Life of Irène Némirovsky, 1903–1942*, trans. Euan Cameron, Chatto & Windus, 2010, p. 375.

132 'welcome France has given them': ibid., p. 115.

132 'she was just a Jewess': Philipponnat and Lienhardt, *The Life of Irène Némirovsky*, p. 377.

134 'It was her way of coping': Renée Fenby, conversation with the author, 2 October 2013.

134 'definitely opened by the horrors': quoted in John Rogister, review of Yves Pourcher, *Pierre Laval vu par sa fille, d'après ses carnets intimes* (Paris, Cherche Midi, 2002), *Parliaments, Estates and Representations*, vol. 25, issue 1, 2005, p. 251.

134 'talk about it': anonymous, converation with the author, 9 September 2014.

135 'my stomach churns from the memory': Cécile Widerman Kaufer, interview with *Huffington Post*, 17 July 2012.

136 'a family outside Paris to take us in': Arlette Reiman in conversation with the author, 18 July 2015.

137 'material bought as upholstery fabric': Betty Maxwell, *A Mind of my Own: My Life with Robert Maxwell*, Sidgwick & Jackson, 1994, p. 169.

137 'meet them in the Avenue Montaigne': Veillon, *Fashion under the Occupation*, p. 101.

139 her friend Edmonde Charles-Roux: Michel Enrici, 'Edmonde Charles-Roux parle de la Comtesse Lily Pastré', *Culture 13*, http://www.culture-13.fr/agenda/edmonde-charles-roux-parle-de-la-comtesse-lily-pastre.html.

140 'save their men from deportation': Berr, *Journal*, p. 95.

141 as soon as they arrived in Auschwitz: Thomas Fontaine, 'Chronology of Repression and Persecution in Occupied France, 1940–44', *Online Encyclopedia of Mass Violence*, 2007, http://www.massviolence.org/chronology-of-repression-and-persecution-in-occupied-france, citing Serge Klarsfeld, *Le Mémorial de la déportation des Juifs de France* (Paris, Beate and Serge Klarsfeld, 1978; re-edited in the 'La Shoah en France' collection, Paris, Fayard, 2001, 4 vols), p. 699.

144 'I was freed': Odette Fabius, *Un Lever de Soleil sur le Mecklembourg*, Paris, Albin Michel 1986 p. 76.

145 false papers in her daughter's case: Marie-Claude Hayman, conversation with the author, 17 November 2014.

145 'Those were the decisions we faced': Fabius, *Un Lever de soleil*, p. 89.

148 'she was sick with fright': Arlette Scali, *Une Vie pas comme une autre*, Neuilly-sur-Seine, Michel Lafon, 2003, p. 146.

148 'sur Madame Renée Puissant Van Cleef': 1684 WM, Commissariat de Police de Vichy.

151 'such a novice, so unworthy . . .': cat. Mahj no. 243, *La Splendeur des Camondos de Constantinople à Paris 1806–1945*, Musée d'art et d'histoire du Judaïsme, 2009, p. 150.

151 they were not in full view: Centre de Documentation Juive Contemporaine (CDJC), XLVI-485, rapport du 24 Mars 1943. Paris, Mémorial de la Shoah.

151 supply more of her own gold: Sylvie Raulet and Olivier Baroin, *Suzanne Belperron*, Antique Collectors Club, 2011, p. 48, citing a letter which Suzanne wrote after the Liberation.

1943: Paris Trembles

155   'It was horrible': Scali, *Une Vie pas comme une autre*, p. 74.

156   film in 2012 called *Violette*: Peter Bradshaw, '*Violette* Review – Fine Biopic of Simone de Beauvoir's Protégée', *Guardian*, 2 October 2014 (http://www.theguardian.com/film/2014/oct/02/ violette-review-biopic-simone-de-beauvoir).

157   from 200,000 francs to 15 million: André Halimi, *La Délation sous l'Occupation*, Paris, Editions 1, 1998, p. 20.

157   available from abandoned businesses: Mémorial de la Shoah, September 2013, *La Spoliation des Juifs: une politique d'état 1940–1944*.

159   'Thank you for everything': facsimile, 21 February 1943, reproduced in Sylvie Raulet and Olivier Baroin, *Suzanne Belperron*, Woodbridge, Suffolk, Antique Collectors Club, 2011.

159   'talking nonsense lest I run away': Chevrillon, *Code Name Christiane Clouet*, p. 104.

161   'days and nights that awaited me': Jacqueline Péry d'Alincourt testimony. 'Surviving Ravensbrück: "Forgive, Don't Forget"'.

161   'the upper crust of the army of occupation': Péry d'Alincourt, 'Surviving Ravensbrück: "Forgive, Don't Forget"'.

162   'my chief interest in life': Chevrillon, *Code Name Christiane Clouet*, p. 115.

162   'but not defeated': Vivou Chevrillon, conversation with the author, 23 January 2015.

163   'sincerity and force,' he insists: Bernard de Gaulle, conversation with the author, 28 March 2014.

164   did not have to say anything: Colonel Rémy, *La Maison d'Alphonse*, Paris, Librairie Académique Perrin, 1968, pp. 305–11, for an account of these activities. Claire Chevrillon, in her account of her friend's activities (Claire Chevrillon, *Code Name Christiane Clouet*) p. 209, refers to an 'okay on the BBC', indicating there might have been a coded message sent, but most likely she means they were using a wireless.

165   'to participate in the struggle': introduction to R. V. Jones, *The Wizard War: British Scientific Intelligence, 1939–1945*, Coronet Books, 1990, cited in David Ignatius: 'After Five Decades a Spy Tells her Tale', *Washington Post* interview, 28 December 1998.

165   'strong moral compass': Caroline McAdam Clark, conversation with the author, 1 October 2014.

166   'The prison continues to sing': ibid.

167   'while on her way out': The National Archives, Kew, HS 9/9/10/3.

168   a body search: Sarah Helm, *A Life in Secrets, The Story of Vera Atkins and the Lost Agents of SOE*, Abacus, 2005, p. 10.

168   as tacit authority: Roderick Bailey, *Forgotten Voices of the Secret War, An Inside History of Special Operations During the Second World War*, Ebury Press, 2008, p. 39.

169   'outstanding ability and courage and determination': ibid.

170   '"such stupidities" and drove off': Noreen Riols, *The Secret Ministry of Ag. & Fish: My Life in Churchill's School for Spies*, Macmillan, 2013, p. 39.

171   'pretty scared of weapons': Basu, *Spy Princess*, p. 95; see also Noor's personal file, The National Archives, Kew, HS 9/836/5.

171   'suited to work in this field': Basu, *Spy Princess*, p. 117.

171   'overburdened with brains': ibid.

172   'to prevent her from going in': Leo Marks, *Between Silk and Cyanide: A Code Maker's War, 1941–45*, Stroud, The History Press, 2008, p. 329.

172   'It will bring you luck': Jean Overton Fuller, Madeleine: the Story of *Noor-un-nisa Inayat Khan*, Gollancz, 1952, p. 139.

173   'she frequently receives German officers': archives BCRA (Bureau Central de Renseignements et d'Action), Vincennes, Côte PO86618.

175   'streets of Versailles': Jacqueline Fleury, née Marié, conversation with the author, 28 March 2014.

175   'I did feel fear': Jacqueline Fleury, née Marié, conversation with the author, 28 March 2014.

175   'pulled down a Nazi flag,' she explained: Geneviève de Gaulle Anthonioz, interview with the author, 19 December 1999.

176   'just to look innocent,' she recalled: ibid.

176   'It was breaking you,' Claude-Catherine Kiejman, conversation with the author, 18 February 2014.

177   'helping us find each other': Fabius, *Un Lever de soleil*, p. 117.

178   'beyond my personality': Fabius, *Un Lever de soleil*, p. 128.

178   'the word may shock': Fabius, *Un Lever de soleil*, p. 137.

178   to whom it was being sent: Marie Claude Hayman, conversation with the author, 17 November 2014.

179   'an otherwise grey everyday life': Franz Roden, 'Paris 1943: Eindrücke dieses Sommers', *Das Reich*, no. 31, 1 August 1943.

180   'contemplate entertaining your troops': George Perry, *Bluebell: The Authorized Biography of Margaret Kelly, Founder of the Legendary Bluebell Girls*, Pavilion Books, 1986, p. 116.

185   'permeating the prose of Molière': Bretty, *La Comédie-Française à l'envers*, p. 91.

185   'a Franco-German festival': Hervé Le Boterf, *La Vie parisienne sous l'occupation, 1940–1944*, Paris, Editions France-Empire, 1974, pp. 126–7.

186   'ashamed of me': John Sherwood, *Georges Mandel and the Third Republic*, Stanford University Press, 1970, p. 288.

186   nothing she could actually do: Riding, *And the Show Went On*, p. 166; http://www.diplomatie.gouv.fr/fr/sites/archives_diplo/schloss/sommaire_ang.html.

187   the Lyons branch of the Abwehr: Riding, *And the Show Went On*, p. 266.

187   their properties could not be aryanized: Préfecture de Calvados to CGQJ, 22 March 1943.

188 'Tout-Paris, Tout-Résistant, Tout-Occupant': Rogister, review of Yves Pourcher, *Pierre Laval vu par sa fille*, p. 251.

189 'rules about things you cannot do': Rose Livarec (Lady Rosa Lipworth, CBE), conversation with the author, 29 May 2015.

191 'Only collaborators could afford to dress well': Tartière, *The House near Paris*, p. 224.

191 'du miracle domestique et quotidien': Colette, *L'Etoile Vesper*, Geneva, Editions du Milieu, 1946, p. 23.

1944: Paris Awaits

197 'took Jewish children and hid them': Berr, *Journal*, p. 285.

198 'recoiled in horror': Sarah Helm, *If This Is a Woman: Inside Ravensbrück: Hitler's Concentration Camp for Women*, Little, Brown, 2014, p. 348.

199 'confidence in our certain victory': Denise Dufournier, *La Maison des mortes: Ravensbrück*, Paris, Julliard, 1992, p. 349.

199 'but you French just laugh': Helm, *If This Is a Woman*, p. 351.

199 'their bright, gay and brutal energy': Virginia d'Albert-Lake, 'My Story', *An American in the French Resistance*, pp. 142–6 and xxv.

200 'by the sight of their faces': Geneviève de Gaulle Anthonioz, *God Remained Outside: An Echo of Ravensbrück*, Souvenir Press, 1999, p. 8.

201 'as you can see,' she told him: ibid., p. 24.

202 'we found the strength to resist': Péry d'Alincourt, 'Surviving Ravensbrück: "Forgive, Don't Forget"'.

202 '"the union might cause others"': Fabius, *Un Lever de soleil*, p. 149.

203 doubted she would survive: email to the author from Georgina Hayman, Odette Fabius's granddaughter, 19 November 2014.

203 'she was not a political animal': Jacqueline Fleury (née Marié), conversation with the author, 28 March 2014.

205 'She must have been very scared': John Heminway, 'A Legendary Flying Doctor's Dark Secret', *Financial Times*, 21 May 2010.

205 'her fear of reprisals': ibid.

205 'all of which advanced her death': ibid.

206 'ridiculous dresses they had concocted somehow': Dufournier, *La Maison des mortes*, p. 86.

206 'A breath of France,' wrote Denise Dufournier: ibid., p. 86.

207 'she couldn't sleep, she said, because of me': Philippe de Rothschild, *Milady Vine: The Autobiography of Philippe de Rothschild*, ed. Joan Littlewood, Century Hutchinson, 1985, p. 119.

208 'so much more chic to collaborate': ibid., p. 18.

208 'Marcel followed on his bicycle': ibid., p. 182.

209 'the Germans, who did not understand': Fabius, *Un Lever de soleil*, p. 73.

211 'a great deal of bravura': Helm, *If This Is a Woman*, p. 377.

211 'six machines ceased simultaneously': excerpt from testimony of Maguy Saunier, Geneva, July 1945, ADIR Archives, Bibliothèque de

Documentation Internationale Contemporaine (BDIC), Paris. http://www.histoire-politique.fr/index.php?numero=05&rub=sources&item=7.

211 'a superiority of spirit, you understand,' she explained: Helm, *If This Is a Woman*, p. 378.

212 'You couldn't give in': Jim Calio, 'Afterword', *An American Heroine in the French Resistance: The Diary and Memoir of Virginia D'Albert-Lake*. ed. Judy Barrett Litoff, Fordham University, 2006, 242–246.

213 'I also called for my mother': Micheline Maurel, *Ravensbrück*, Anthony Blond, 1958, p. 102.

213 'courage, willpower and vitality,' commented Virginia: *An American Heroine in the French Resistance*, ed. Litoff, p. 170.

213 'in her favour in view of Nazi standards': d'Albert-Lake family papers cited in ibid., Appendix 2, p. 252.

213 one of the great intelligence documents of the Second World War: her report appears in *The Wizard War* by Reginald Jones, head of Britain's scientific intelligence efforts during the war.

214 'in the maze of the couriers': ibid.

215 'I decided to do it': Helm, *If This Is a Woman*, pp. 425–6.

215 'but there you are,' she told one interviewer: Jeannie, Vicomtesse de Clarens (née Rousseau), video interview with David Ignatius, International Spy Museum Archive, Washington, DC.

215 'It was unhealthy work and exhausting': Jacqueline Fleury, History Policy no. 05, ADIR Archives.

215 Every day the same: Helm, *If This Is a Woman*, p. 426.

217 'to blow the *Boches* sky high!': Sophie MacCarthy, conversation with the author, 14 October 2015.

217 'information for me': Helmuth von Moltke, *Letters to Freya, 1939–1945* p. 88.

219 'to satisfy his clients and his miller!': Violette Wassem, 'Violette's Story: Paris – Life during the Occupation', July 1997, http://timewitnesses.org/english/~viol2.html.

219 'and make their own bread': Teissier du Cros, *Divided Loyalties*, pp. 241–253, for a discussion of clothes and food shortages.

220 'one could have one big one made, very chic': ibid.

1944: Paris Shorn

226 'that was my character': Cécile Rol-Tanguy, conversation with the author, 20 January 2014.

226 'resistance to the enemy invader': Maxwell, *A Mind of my Own*, p. 201.

227 '"pointed it at him"': Filmed interview with Frida Wittenberg, *Après la Shoah, Rescapés, Réfugiés, Survivants 1944–1947*, Exposition Mémorial de la Shoah, January – October 2016.

228 Lee wrote to her editor, Audrey Withers: Lee Miller to Audrey Withers, 26–27 August 1944, Field Press Censor, *Lee Miller's War, Beyond D-Day*, Thames & Hudson, 2005, ed. Antony Penrose, p. 65.

229   'and then murdered': Matthew Cobb, *Eleven Days in August*, Simon & Schuster, 2013, p. 352.

229   'Comprenne qui voudra': The full text can be found in Paul Eluard, *Au Rendez-vous allemand*, Paris, Editions de Minuit, December 1944 with a frontispiece portrait of the author by Picasso. Later editions, such as that held by the Chadwyck-Healey Liberation Collection 1944–1946, Cambridge University Library, published in 1945, added more poems, including some that had previously been published clandestinely.

229   'sold anything at all': Eluard's poem appeared initially in *Les Lettres Françaises*, 2 December 1944, with this commentary:

229   'the wound was kept open': Teissier du Cros, *Divided Loyalties*, p. 236.

230   'It wasn't physical torture': Andrée Doucet, conversation with the author, 30 January 2014.

230   'for their struggles and sacrifices?': Collins Weitz, *Sisters in the Resistance*, p. 298.

232   'and ending up bald': Spotts, *The Shameful Peace*, p. 201.

232   'a state of perpetual nausea': ibid., p. 202.

234   'her armed captors say "tu" to the doorman': Arthur Gold and Robert Fizdale, *Misia: The Life of Misia Sert*, Vintage Books, 2002, p. 296.

234   'long tirade[s] against the Jews': ibid., p. 288.

234   a more severe prison sentence or worse: Justine Picardie, *Coco Chanel: The Legend and the Life*, HarperCollins, 2010, p. 262.

235   'a hair of her head': Malcolm Muggeridge, *Chronicles of Wasted Time*, vol. 2: *The Infernal Grove*, Fontana, 1975, p. 267.

236   'as indeed proved to be the case': ibid., p. 269.

236   'the culprit was discovered': Jean-Jacques Richard, correspondence with the author, 22 August 2015.

237   a company which excluded Jewish actors: Jean-Pierre Thibaudat, 'Le Jour où Copeau a exclu les acteurs juifs du Français', *Libération*, 2 january 1995 (http://www.liberation.fr/culture/1995/01/02/le-jour-ou-copeau-a-exclu-les-acteurs-juifs-du-francais_117860).

237   'the reparations you deserve': Bretty, *La Comédie-Française à l'envers*, p. 98.

238   'a taste for gun powder,' she told her editor: Lee Miller to Audrey Withers, August 26–7 1944, quoted in *Lee Miller's War*, ed. Antony Penrose, p. 65.

238   'Christ it was awful': Quoted in *Lee Miller's War*, ed. Antony Penrose, p. 50.

239   'and sipping champagne': Mary Welsh Hemingway, *How it Was*, p. 110.

239   'the windows cheered': Quoted in Charles Glass, *Americans in Paris*, p. 408.

239   'lean and hungry and sour': *Lee Miller's War*, pp. 69- 71.

239   'most gigantic party': *Lee Miller's War*, p. 67.

241   from any of the chimneys: Charles Chadwyck-Healey, 'The Literature
       of the Liberation 1944–1946', *The Book Collector*, March 2015, referring
       to a photograph by Roger Schall in The Chadwyck-Healey Collection of
       Liberation Literature, Cambridge University Library.

1945: Paris Returns

245   'we might yet have to endure': Jacqueline Fleury, 'Témoignage de
       Jacqueline Fleury (née Marié)', http://lesamitiesdelaresistance.fr/lien17-
       fleury.pdf.
245   'I want to die': Helm, *If This Is a Woman*, p. 525.
245   'for the end of the Great Germany': Fleury, 'Témoignage'.
246   'we were so ugly': ibid.
246   'the degree of physical deterioration': ibid.
246   released from Ravensbrück: Debra Workman, 'Engendering the
       Repatriation: The Return of Female Political Deportees to France
       Following the Second World War', http://quod.lib.umich.edu/w/
       wsfh/0642292.0035.017/--engendering-the-repatriation-the-return-of-
       female-political?rgn=main;view=fulltext, note 13.
247   'on her shaven head': de Gaulle Anthonioz, *God Remained Outside*, pp.
       37–8.
247   'the last few moments of his life': ibid., p. 39.
247   sent to Switzerland to recuperate: Helm, *If This Is a Woman*, p. 535.
248   'was painted green': quoted in Helm, *If This is a Woman*, p. 575.
248   'look my death in the face': ibid., p. 511.
248   'with her mother until the end': ibid., p. 551.
249   'my morale is good': Vaughan, *Doctor to the Resistance*, p. 143.
249   'more than a skeleton': Vaughan, *Doctor to the Resistance*, citing Jackson
       Family Archives, p. 195.
250   'He had such big qualities': ibid., p. 160.
251   'who have forgotten they have a soul': Maurel, *Ravensbrück*, pp. 138–9.
252   'we were shocked': quoted in Workman, 'Engendering the Repatriation'.
252   'could regain their lost self-confidence': quoted in Regula Ludi,
       Reparations for Nazi Victims in Postwar Europe, Cambridge, Cambridge
       University Press, 2012, p. 62.
252   'two and a half million *sons*'': quoted in Workman, 'Engendering the
       Repatriation'.
253   'fashion expressed their identity': Katell Le Bourhis, 'Vive la Différence',
       Connoisseur, January 1991, pp. 76–9; and interview with the author, 16
       January, 2014.
253   'in the eyes of the world': quoted in Le Bourhis, 'Vive la Différence'.
255   'calm, collaborationists, a Vichy government': Alice Kaplan, *The
       Collaborator: The Trial and Execution of Robert Brasillach*, London,
       University of Chicago Press, 2000, p. 73.
256   'no one but themselves': ibid., p. 74.

256   to be complicit: Sonia Kruks, *Simone de Beauvoir and the Politics of Ambiguity*, Oxford, Oxford University Press, 2012, p. 158.

257   'to have plenty of wine': Carole Seymour-Jones, *A Dangerous Liaison*, Century, 2008, p. 280.

257   'be taken to Germany': Riding, *And the Show Went On*, p. 268.

258   'congratulate her for her attitude': Archives Nationales, Paris, 20 September 1948, Parquet de la cour de justice du département de la Seine information suivie contre Banque Charles, 511 409.

258   'to save Laval from death': J. Kenneth Brody, *The Trial of Pierre Laval: Defining Treason, Collaboration and Patriotism in World War II France*, Piscataway, NJ, Transaction, 2010, p. 237.

259   'than for what he said': ibid.

259   'at a fate she could not accept': ibid., p. 243.

260   'a limitless admiration for her father': interview with Yves Pourcher, 9 January 2009, on French website http://bibliobs.nouvelobs.com/essais/20090109.BIB2772/josee-la-fille-unique-de-laval-avait-une-admiration-sans-limites-pour-son-pere.html.

260   'consider yourself as my son': Antoine Sabbagh, 'Sir, you will no longer consider yourself my son', *Guardian*, 11 July 2009 (http://www.theguardian.com/lifeandstyle/2009/jul/11/antoine-sabbagh-family-nazis-resistance).

261   'with a livelihood for a little while': Signoret, *Nostalgia Isn't What It Used to Be*, p. 96.

261   'beat a dignified retreat': Marguerite Duras, 'The War (Rough Draft)', *Wartime Notebooks and Other Texts*, trans. Linda Coverdale, MacLehose Press, 2011, p. 127.

262   'the throbbing in the temples': ibid., p. 120.

262   'three days, but no longer': ibid.

262   'he becomes a stranger again': Ian Buruma, *Year Zero: A History of 1945*, Atlantic Books, 2013, p. 139.

263   'that kind of devastation on them': Marguerite Duras, 'Did Not Die Deported', *Wartime Notebooks and Other Texts*, trans. Linda Coverdale, MacLehose Press, 2011, p. 213.

264   38,000 of which were in Paris: *A qui appartenaient ces tableaux?* exhibition catalogue published jointly by the Israel Museum, Jerusalem, and Musée d'art et d'histoire du Judaïsme, Paris, 2008.

264   remove the copper: *Après La Shoah, Rescapés, Réfugiés, Survivants 1944–1947*, Exposition Mémorial de la Shoah, January – October 2016.

265   'existing strains of anti-Semitism in the country': Renée Poznanski, *Etre juif en France pendant la Seconde Guerre Mondiale*, Paris, Hachette, 1994, p. 675.

265   'still an ongoing enterprise': Leora Auslander, 'Coming Home? Jews in Postwar Paris', *Journal of Contemporary History*, vol. 40, 2005, pp. 237–59.

265   'their efforts to come home': ibid., p. 240.

266   of pillaged homes was ever recovered: ibid., p. 248.

267   'We were used to a hard floor': Jacqueline Fleury, all the above from conversation with the author, 28 March 2014.

267   'I hit him': Helm, *If This Is a Woman*, p. 642.

267   'does not want the subject brought up': François Mauriac, Introduction to Maurel, *Ravensbrück*, pp. 5–7.

267   'we had to become human again': *Being Jewish in France, Comme un Juif en France*, two-part TV documentary written and directed by Yves Jeuland, 2007, jewishfilm.org/Catalogue/films/beingjewishinfrance.htm.

268   'you would drown in tears': Marceline Loridan-Ivens (née Rozenberg), *Et tu n'es pas revenu*, p. 35.

268   'I participated like the collaborators did': Marceline Loridan-Ivens, interview, *Sunday Times*, 17 January 2016.

268   'That was her question': Marceline Loridan-Ivens, *Et tu n'es pas revenu*, p. 45.

269   'corralled by the anti-Semitic laws': Caroline Moorehead, Preface to Jacqueline Mesnil-Amar, *Maman, What Are We Called Now?*, p. xiv.

269   'so easy, all silk and roses': Rothschild, *Milady Vine*, p. 189.

270   'Was she expecting me to smile?': Fabius, *Un Lever de soleil*, p. 73.

270   'determined never to forget': Caroline McAdam Clark, conversation with the author, 1 October 2014.

270   'was normal family life': ibid.

271   of her friends from 'before': Granrut, *Le Piano et le Violoncelle*, p. 19.

272   'the rats would start with the eyes': ibid.

272   'We need to laugh now!': Workman, 'Engendering the Repatriation'.

274   'of the ADIR from its inception': ibid.

276   'Dora Maar, for example': Françoise Gilot, *Life with Picasso*, Virago Press, 1990, p. 77.

276   'only a few minutes after I did': Gilot, *Life with Picasso*, p. 79.

276   'everything in that penumbra': ibid., p. 79.

280   'the banality of France becoming Americanised': Gold and Fizdale, *Misia*, p. 296.

1946: Paris Adjusts

286   her views of his behaviour: Sarah Helm, *A Life in Secrets: The Story of Vera Atkins and the Lost Agents of SOE*, Little, Brown, 2005, p. 271.

286   'to be such a terrible verdict': ibid., Prologue p. xxii.

287   'maybe Jewish', Stonehouse had told her: ibid., p. 205.

287   'when thrown into the oven': Squadron Officer Vera Atkins to War Office from HQ British Army of the Rhine, 15 April 1946, The National Archives, Kew, HS 9/910/3.

288   'Look how she defended herself': Rita Kramer, *Flames in the Field*, p. 119. Straub, the camp executioner, is sometimes referred to as Strauss, presumably because the German double SS resembles a B. See also The National Archives, Kew, WO 235/336.

288   able to claim 'lawful execution': Helm, *A Life in Secrets*, p. 241.

288   'very plucky and rather imaginative . . .': The National Archives, Kew, HS9/910/3.

288   'You just don't know where to look': Helm, *A Life in Secrets*, Prologue, p. xxi.

289   'They are ashamed of having fear': Bernard de Gaulle, conversation with the author, 28 March 2014.

289   'cry together at one moment': Rita Kramer, *Flames in the Field: The Story of Four SOE Agents in Occupied France*, Michael Joseph, 1995, p. 106.

290   'inspired by venality and corruption': Gisèle Sapiro, 'Portrait of the Writer as a Traitor: The French Purge Trials (1944–1953)', trans. Jennifer Birkett, 2006, https://erea.revues.org/257.

290   'I was in mourning for my father': Luchaire, *Drôle de vie*, p. 242.

290   'I did not realise': 'The Nazi's Courtesan', *Life*, 24 June 1946.

290   on the ski slopes in winter: private information, 20 April 2015.

291   'Luchaire paid for his thoughtlessness with his life': Patrick Modiano, 'Lettre à Thierry Laurent', http://lereseaumodiano.blogspot.co.uk/2011/11/lettre-thierry-laurent.html.

291   'what they did to children,' she said: Jacqueline Fleury, conversation with the author, 28 March 2014.

292   'never stopped talking about what happened': ibid.

292   'echo in my mind': Jacqueline Péry d'Alincourt, *Surviving Ravensbrück* http://www.utexas.edu/cola/history/_files/downloads/features/pery-jacqueline-memoir.pdf.

292   'new humane tasks': June 1946, *Voix et Visages*, (1) ADIR archives held at BDIC.

293   '"Tomorrow we will be together again"': Arlette Testyler (née Reiman), conversation with the author, 18 July 2015.

294   'of those who had been deported': Workman, 'Engendering the Repatriation'.

294   become just *Juifs*: Sylvie Jessua-Amar, 11 February 2016. Panel discussion at Mémorial de la Shoah.

296   culture and humanity in disarray: Caroline Moorehead, Preface to Jacqueline Mesnil-Amar, *Maman, What Are We Called Now?*, p. xvii.

297   'enveloped in a miasma of corruption': Marghanita Laski, *Little Boy Lost*, Persephone Classics, 2008, p. 225.

297   'pass into a non-Catholic home': ibid., p. 89.

299   'the essential thing': Vivette Samuel, *Rescuing the Children: A Holocaust Memoir*, Madison, University of Wisconsin Press, 2002, pp. 132–3.

299   'families that had sheltered other children': ibid., p. 133.

300   she feels ambivalent about all religion: Lady Rosa Lipworth, CBE, conversation with the author, 29 May 2015.

300   'in a world in which we have failed': Mesnil-Amar, *Maman, What Are We Called Now?*, p. 190.

300   'forget the absence of her mother': Fabius, *Un Lever de soleil*, p. 220.

301   'such as the force of friendship': ibid., p. 227.

302   'the most brilliant man that I was ever to meet': ibid., p. 231.

302   'I know you two will understand each other': Jacqueline Péry-
       d'Alincourt's memorial address, 24 April 1990, on the death of Caroline
       Woolsey Ferriday.

303   'to enjoy the fruits of Victory': SOS from Caroline Ferriday at France
       Forever, n.d. See F°delta rés 797/I: Archives de Caroline Ferriday et des
       amis américains de l'ADIR (1940–1983), BDIC.

303   'She became a sister': Péry-d'Alincourt's memorial address, 24 April 1990.

303   'keep up the pretence of wealth': Picardie, *Coco Chanel*, p. 278.

303   'shaped her life and bore her name': ibid., p. 281.

305   'unassailably rich': ibid., p. 278.

305   which saved it: French National Archives at Pierrefitte-sur-Seine, Dossier
       FreCaran AJ/38/2.

305   returned to her beloved Paris with a new name: information from Sally
       Gordon Mark, letter to author, 28 August 2014.

306   'in a hat shop with a friend': Allanah Harper to Sybille Bedford, 19
       September 1946, thanks to Harry Ransom Center, The University of
       Texas at Austin.

307   'end of the proceedings': Mary Wallington, letters to her family, private
       collection, 16 August 1946.

307   'dared buy 3 pairs of stockings!': ibid., August 1946.

307   'but Naafi don't rise to Turkish': ibid., 24 August 1946.

307   'country butter and a roast of veal': Janet Flanner, *Paris Journal, 1944–55*,
       New York, Harcourt Brace Jovanovich, 1965, p. 48.

308   'the demi-god Gide': ibid., p. 72.

308   'at the end of the evening': Mary Wallington to family, 21 October 1946.

309   'above any differences of political opinion': Gilot, *Life with Picasso*,
       p. 133.

309   'So I'll stay, whatever the cost': ibid., p. 38.

310   'stop being aggressively punctual': quoted in Le Bourhis, 'Vive la
       Différence'.

311   '[the Germans] were here': Fabienne Jamet, *Palace of Sweet Sin*, W. H.
       Allen, 1977, pp. 93–97.

312   'bad language, and lesbian sex : Mary Louise Roberts, 'The Price of
       Discretion: Prostitution, Venereal Disease, and the American Military in
       France, 1944–1946', *American Historical Review* vol. 115, no. 4 (October
       2010), pp. 1002–1030.

312   'eat raw carrots in a steakhouse': *What Soldiers Do: Sex and the American
       GI in World War II France*, Chicago, University of Chicago Press, 2013, p.
       176.

312   'represent "Frenchness" itself': ibid., p. 176.

312   'at a more symbolic level as well': ibid., p. 179.

313   'difficult for a foreigner to find': Nancy Mitford, *The Blessing*, Hamish Hamilton, 1951, p. 113.

1947: Paris Looks Newish

320   'countless SOE lives': Sarah Helm, *A life in Secrets*, pp. 295–6.

320   'as they struggled along': Noreen Riols, *The Secret Ministry of Ag. & Fish*, pp. 80–81, and conversation with the author, 29 May 2014.

320   'there was no one else to send': quoted in Basu, *Indian Princess*, p. 237.

321   'one of my own not to accept the truth': Marks, *Between Silk and Cyanide*, p. 406; see also The National Archives, Kew, HS 9/836/5.

322   'she was shot in her cell': Basu, *Spy Princess*, p. 221.

323   'cold and distant', 'cold blooded', 'to be clear about things': Helm, *A Life in Secrets*, pp. 411, 422.

323   'why she was a little wary of me': ibid., p. 99; The National Archives, Kew, HS 9/59/2.

326   'What New Look?': Marie-France Pochna, *Christian Dior: The Man Who Made the World Look New*, Aurum Press, 1998, p. 195.

326   'in a way no sables could': quoted in Antony Beevor and Artemis Cooper, *Paris after the Liberation, 1944–1949*, Hamish Hamilton, 1994, p. 315.

327   'had been killed by the Gestapo': Gitta Sereny, *The Healing Wound: Experiences and Reflections on Germany, 1938–2001*, New York, W. W. Norton, 2002, pp. 15–16.

327   'adoptive Parisians could ever emulate': ibid., p. 15.

328   she had declared to Ballard: Picardie, *Coco Chanel*, p. 283.

328   'I can't walk, eat or even sit down': Pochna, *Christian Dior*, p. 167.

329   'taught me to mistrust possessions': Ginette Spanier, *It Isn't All Mink*, Collins, 1959, p. 164.

332   'tragic destinies or restrained suffering': quoted in Sandy Flitterman-Lewis, 'Anouk Aimée', *Jewish Women: A Comprehensive Historical Encyclopedia*, Jewish Women's Archive, 2009 (http://jwa.org/encyclopedia/article/aimee-anouk).

332   'unclouded blue skies and sunshine: timeless': Emma Smith, *As Green as Grass: Growing Up before, during and after the Second World War*, Bloomsbury, 2013, p. 259.

333   'to adore them both': ibid., p. 261.

334   'never quite enough to eat,' said Emma: Emma Smith, conversation with the author, 17 September 2014.

336   'Europe lay rotting in the sun': quoted in Greg Behrmann, *The Most Noble Adventure: The Marshall Plan and How America Helped Rebuild Europe*, New York, Free Press, 2008, p. 27.

336   'except for leaving the library': *The Duff Cooper Diaries, 1915–1951*, ed. John Julius Norwich, Phoenix, 2014, 28 April 1946.

336   'tight, tight against your heart': quoted in Susan Braudy, 'Camelot's Second Lady', *Vanity Fair*, February 2006.

336   this was her first child: Caroline de Margerie, *American Lady: The Life of Susan Mary Alsop*, Viking, 2011, p. 59.

1948–1949: Paris Americanized

341   'a vague sense of being suffocated': Julia Child, *My Life in France*, New York, Alfred A. Knopf, 2006, p. 24.

342   'take a pill and say goodbye': Beevor and Cooper, *Paris after the Liberation*, p. 388.

342   'Combatants without Weapons': Ludi, *Reparations for Nazi Victims in Postwar Europe*, p. 52.

342   entitle them to use the word 'combatant': Louise Alcan, *Sans armes et sans bagages*, Limoges, Imprimerie d'Art, 1946.

343   'or the Coca-Cola Corporation': Quoted Thierry Coudert, *Café Society: Socialites, Patrons and Artists 1920–1960*, Flammarion, 2010, p. 7.

343   'the banality of France becoming Americanized': Gold and Fizdale, *Misia*, p. 296.

343   'will we be coca-colonized?': William I. Hitchcock, *The Struggle for Europe: The Turbulent History of a Divided Continent, 1945–Present*, New York, Anchor Books, 2004, p. 160.

343   'and the brain of a pea hen': ibid., p. 157.

344   'after the war': Correspondence with the author, 8 July 2015.

344   'knew from catalogues': ibid.

347   'That's why I couldn't refuse': Barbara Probst Solomon, conversation with the author, 19 May 2014.

348   their own 'personal Marshall Plan': Caroline Ferriday to Mr Viret, 1 March 1948, American Aid to France, Ferriday archives.

348   'rapacious Russia was not to be trusted': Child, *My Life in France*, p. 22.

349   'get a watchband fixed': Child, *My Life in France*, p. 41.

351   'singing defiantly, triumphantly': Smith, *Green as Grass*, p. 274.

351   'we are going to do new things': Emma Smith, conversation with the author, 17 September 2014.

351   'There wasn't!': ibid.

352   'pleasure and easy life': Martine Guyot-Bender, 'Seducing Corinne: The Official Popular Press during the Occupation', in Melanie Hawthorne and Richard J. Golsan (eds), *Gender and Fascism in Modern France*, Hanover, NH/London, University Press of New England, 1997, p. 74.

352   'ingrained attitudes to perpetuate its power': ibid., p. 82.

353   'no one had worn since 1900,' wrote Nizan: Alice Kaplan, *Dreaming in French: The Paris Years of Jacqueline Bouvier Kennedy, Susan Sontag and Angela Davis*, Chicago, University of Chicago Press, 2012, p. 43.

353   'being a terrible snob': Claude du Granrut, conversation with the author, 8 September 2014.

354   'The teeth were gritted': Edmonde Charles-Roux in interview with
        Michel Enrici for *Culture 13*, http://www.culture-13.fr/agenda/edmonde-
        charles-roux-parle-de-la-comtesse-lily-pastre.html.

355   'a different story', ibid.

355   as his memoirs later revealed: Gabriel Dussurget, *Le Magicien d'Aix:
        mémoires intimes*, Arles, Actes Sud, 2011.

355   'three generations of *Tout Paris*,' wrote Janet Flanner: Flanner, *Paris
        Journal*, p. 110.

356   'here is one that has no need of it': *Les Nouvelles de Bordeaux et du
        Sud-Ouest*, 23 September 1949, quoted in Sherwood, *Georges Mandel and
        the Third Republic*, p. 358, with the additional comment that although the
        local newspaper was the only one to print the letter in full, a copy of it is
        in the archives of *Le Monde*.

356   she had not been in danger: Nicolas Sarkozy, *Georges Mandel: le moine de
        la politique*, Paris, Grasset, 1994, p. 303.

357   'a miracle of recovery has been performed': quoted in address by Paul Gray
        Hoffman to Association of American Colleges, 10 January 1950, p. 295. Paul
        G. Hoffman Papers, Harry S. Truman Library, Independence, Missouri.

357   'their favourite topic of conversation': Joseph Wechsberg, 'A Reporter
        in France: The Finest Butter and Lots of Time', *New Yorker*, 3
        September 1949 (http://www.newyorker.com/magazine/1949/09/03/
        the-finest-butter-and-lots-of-time).

358   'une poignée de misérables et d'indignes': Speech given by de Gaulle in
        Paris, 14 October. *Vers une France unie, discours prononcé à Paris le 14
        Octobre 1944*, Paris, Plon, 1970.

359   aroused by stories such as theirs: Caroline Moorehead, 'Sleeping with the
        Enemy', *Intelligent Life*, September–October 2013, pp. 80-87.

359   the Second World War: Deutsche Welle, http://www.dw.com/en/
        french-children-of-wehrmacht-soldiers-seek-german-nationality/a-5382826.

359   'with the Liberation': Fabrice Virgili, *Naître ennemi: les enfants de couples
        franco-allemands nés pendant la Seconde Guerre mondiale*, Paris, Payot,
        2009, p. 203.

360   'there were German women who suffered': Claude du Granrut,
        conversation with the author, 8 September 2014.

Epilogue: Peacetime Paris – Some Beginnings and Some Endings

365   'with new materials as a necessity': Lee Miller, 'letter to Miss Crockett'
        (*Life* Magazine), 'Paris, its Joy. . . its Spirit. . . its Privations', in *Lee
        Miller's War*, pp. 67-87.

365   'all of them, except for Gilot, would share': John Richardson, 'Picasso's
        Broken Vow', *New York Review of Books*, 25 June 2015.

367   'pieces kept by the national museums': Robert M. Edsel, *The Monuments
        Men: Allied Heroes, Nazi Thieves and the Greatest Treasure Hunt in
        History*, 2009, Preface, 'In the Footsteps of Rose Valland', p. 11.

368 'anyone at any time': *The Monuments Men: Allied Heroes, Nazi Thieves and the Greatest Treasure Hunt in History*, Preface, 2009, p. 412–13.

369 directed in Africa, Taiwan and China: Denise Grady, 'Florence Waren, Jewish Dancer Who Resisted Nazis, Dies at 95', *New York Times*, 4 August 2012 (http://www.nytimes.com/2012/08/05/world/europe/florence-waren-dancer-who-resisted-nazis-dies-at-95.ht).

369 'It was simply what one did': ibid.

369 'as if she did not hear it': Flanner, *Paris Journal, 1956–1964* p. 170.

373 'combat misery and exclusion': Geneviève de Gaulle, conversation with the author, December 1999.

374 'not the higher brain': David Ignatius, 'After Five Decades, a Spy Tells her Tale', *Washington Post*, 28 December 1998 (http://www.tournemire.net/jeannie.htm).

374 based on her instinctive moral values: Marie-Odile Tuloup, Paris Conference, 'Hommage à Geneviève de Gaulle-Anthonioz et Germaine Tillion', 24 January 2015.

375 'what mankind was capable of doing to women': Helm, *If This Is a Woman*, p. 650.

376 'I ever had on this earth': Fabius, *Un Lever de soleil*, p. 231.

376 suicide became the ultimate correction: Ruth Franklin, 'The Art of Extinction: The Bleak Laughter of Thomas Bernhard', *New Yorker*, 25 December 2006 (http://www.newyorker.com/magazine/2006/12/25/the-art-of-extinction).

377 'we were hidden': interview with Elisabeth Gille (née Epstein) in *The Mirador*, p. 238.

377 'precious to mother': Flitterman-Lewis 'Irène Némirovsky.' *Jewish Women: A Comprehensive Historical Encyclopedia*, Jewish Women's Archive, 1 March 2009.

377 suggested publication: Thomas Nolden, 'Myriam Anissimov.' *Jewish Women: A Comprehensive Historical Encyclopedia*, Jewish Women's Archive, 1 March 2009.

378 an innate 'precarious duality' at its core: Richard Cohen, *The Burden of Conscience: French Jewish Leadership during the Holocaust*, Bloomington, Indiana University Press, 1987, p. 141.

379 'for him to bear,' Mariette explained: Elizabeth Grice, 'How the Diaries of Hélène Berr, the "Anne Frank of France", Came to be Published', *Daily Telegraph*, 30 October 2008 (http://www.telegraph.co.uk/culture/books/3562700/How-the-diaries-of-Helene-Berr-the-Anne-Frank-of-France-came-to-be-published.html).

379 'whose words were annihilated': Berr, *Journal*, p. 272.

379 'is it a betrayal to be alive?': Mesnil-Amar, *Maman, What Are We Called Now?*, p. 90

379 'When you lost faith, everything collapsed': quoted in obituary of Lise London, *El País*, 9 April 2012.

380   'the most natural thing in the world': Rodríguez, 'The Last Female Veteran', *El País*, 20 December 2011.

380   'and who died for freedom': Lise London, interview with *El País*.

381   'that we did run massive risks': Caroline McAdam Clark, conversation with the author, 1 October 2014.

382   'I decided to stay': Samuel, *Rescuing the Children*, p. 141.

382   'associations of former resisters': Regula Ludi, *Reparations for Nazi Victims in Postwar Europe*, p. 74.

383   'Nobody came . . .': Vaughan, *Doctor to the Resistance*, p. 166.

385   'a degree above what I would have liked': quoted in Jonathan Fenby, *The General: Charles de Gaulle and the France He Saved*, Simon & Schuster, 2010, p. 265.

387   'we women were capable of resisting': quoted in Humbert, *Résistance*, p. 309.

BIBLIOGRAPHY

Books are published in London unless otherwise stated.

Books
Alcan, Louise, *Sans armes et sans bagages*, Limoges, Imprimerie d'Art, 1946
Assouline, Pierre, *Le Dernier des Camondo*, Paris, Editions Gallimard, 1997
Bade, Patrick, *Music Wars, 1937–1945*, Bishop's Stortford, East & West
    Publishing, 2012
Bailey, Roderick, *Forgotten Voices of the Secret War, An Inside History of Special
    Operations during the Second World War*, Ebury Press, 2008
Ballard, Bettina, *In my Fashion*, Secker & Warburg, 1960
Barber, Noel, *The Week France Fell: June 10–June 16 1940*, Stein & Day, 1976
Basu, Shrabani, *Spy Princess: The Life of Noor Inayat Khan*, Stroud, The History
    Press, 2008
Beevor, Antony and Cooper, Artemis, *Paris after the Liberation, 1944–1949*,
    Hamish Hamilton, 1994
Behrman, Greg, *The Most Noble Adventure: The Marshall Plan and How America
    Helped Rebuild Europe*, New York, Free Press, 2008
Berr, Hélène, *Journal*, trans. David Bellos, MacLehose Press, 2008
Bertin, Célia, *Femmes sous l'Occupation*, Paris, Stock, 1993
Blum, Suzanne, *Vivre sans la Patrie, 1940–1945*, Paris, Plon, 1975
Bonney, Mabel Thérèse, *Europe's Children, 1939–1943*, New York, Rhode
    Publishing, 1943
Bood, Micheline, *Les Années doubles: journal d'une lycéenne sous l'occupation*,
    Paris, Robert Laffont, 1974
Bourderon, Roger, *Rol-Tanguy: des brigades internationales à la libération de
    Paris*, Paris, Tallandier, 2004
Brandon, Ruth, *Ugly Beauty: Helena Rubinstein, L'Oréal, and the Blemished
    History of Looking Good*, New York, HarperCollins, 2011
Bray, Elizabeth Irvine, *Paul Flato: Jeweller to the Stars*, Woodbridge, Suffolk,
    Antique Collectors' Club, 2010
Bretty, Béatrice, *La Comédie-Française à l'envers*, Paris, Fayard, 1957
Brody, J. Kenneth, *The Trial of Pierre Laval: Defining Treason, Collaboration and
    Patriotism in World War II France*, Piscataway, NJ, Transaction, 2010
Buisson, Patrick, *1940–1945: Années érotiques*, Paris, Albin Michel, 2008

Burch, Noël, *The Battle of the Sexes in French Cinema, 1930–1956*, trans. Peter Graham, Durham, NC, Duke University Press, 2014

Burke, Carolyn, *Lee Miller on Both Sides of the Camera*, Bloomsbury, 2006

Burrin, Philippe, *Living with Defeat: France under the German Occupation, 1940–1944*, Hodder Headline, 1996

Buruma, Ian, *Year Zero: A History of 1945*, Atlantic Books, 2013

Callil, Carmen, *Bad Faith: A Forgotten History of Family and Fatherland*, Jonathan Cape, 2006

Carrard, Philippe, *The French Who Fought for Hitler: Memories from the Outcasts*, Cambridge, Cambridge University Press, 2010

Chadwyck-Healey, Charles, *Literature of the Liberation: The French Experience in Print, 1944–1946*, Cambridge, Cambridge University Library, 2014

Les Chambres à gaz, secret d'Etat, Paris, Editions de Minuit, 1984

Chevrillon, Claire, *Code Name Christiane Clouet: A Woman in the French Resistance*, trans. Jane Kielty Stott, College Station, Tex., Texas A & M University Press, 1995

Child, Julia, *My Life in France*, New York, Alfred A. Knopf, 2006

Cobb, Matthew, *Eleven Days in August: The Liberation of Paris in 1944*, Simon & Schuster, 2013

Cohen, Richard, *The Burden of Conscience: French Jewish Leadership during the Holocaust*, Bloomington, Indiana University Press, 1987

Collins Weitz, Margaret, *Sisters in the Resistance: How Women Fought to Free France, 1940–45*, New York, John Wiley, 1995

Cone, Michèle, *Artists under Vichy: A Case of Prejudice and Persecution*, Princeton, Princeton University Press, 1992

Conrad, Doda, *Dodascalies: ma chronique du XXe siècle*, Arles, Actes Sud, 1997

Coudert, Thierry, *Café Society: Socialites, Patrons, and Artists: 1920 to 1960*, Paris, Flammarion, 2010

d'Albert-Lake, Virginia, *An American in the French Resistance; the Diary and Memoir of Virginia d'Albert-Lake*, ed. Judy Barrett Litoff, New York, Fordham University Press, 2006

Dali, Salvador, *Hidden Faces*, Peter Owen, 1973

Day, Barry (ed.), *The Letters of Noël Coward*, Methuen, 2007.

de Gaulle Anthonioz, Geneviève, *God Remained Outside: An Echo of Ravensbrück*, Souvenir Press, 1999

de Gaulle, Charles, *Vers une France unie*, discours prononcé à Paris le 14 octobre 1944, Paris, Plon, 1970

de Margerie, Caroline, *American Lady: The Life of Susan Mary Alsop*, Viking, 2011

de Réthy, Esmeralda and Perreau, Jean-Louis, *Christian Dior: The Early Years, 1947–1957*, New York, Vendome Press, 2001

de Waal, Edmund, *The Hare with Amber Eyes: A Hidden Inheritance*, Vintage, 2011

Diamond, Hanna, *Fleeing Hitler: France 1940*, Oxford, Oxford University Press, 2007

Diamond, Hanna, *Women and the Second World War in France, 1939–48: Choices and Constraints*, Routledge, 1999

Doré-Rivé, Isabelle and others, *Pour vous, Mesdames! La mode en temps de guerre*, Lyons, Libel, 2013

Dorléac, Laurence Bertrand, *Art of the Defeat: France, 1940–1944*, trans. Jane Marie Todd, Los Angeles, Getty Publications, 2008

Doucet, Andrée, *Paroles de femmes d'artistes*, Paris, Somogy Editions, 2006

Drake, Alicia, *The Beautiful Fall: Fashion, Genius and Glorious Excess in 1970s Paris*, Bloomsbury, 2007

Dreyfus, Jean-Marc and Gensberger, Sarah, trans. Jonathan Hensher, *Nazi Labour Camps in Paris: Austerlitz, Lévitan, Bassano, July 1943–August 1944*, Oxford, Berghahn Books, 2011

Duchen, Claire, *Women's Rights and Women's Lives in France, 1944–1968*, Routledge, 1994

The Duff Cooper Diaries, 1915–1951, ed. John Julius Norwich, Phoenix, 2014

Dufournier, Denise, *La Maison des mortes: Ravensbrück*, Paris, Julliard, 1992

Duras, Marguerite, *The War: A Memoir*, The New Press, 1994

Duras, Marguerite, *Wartime Notebooks and Other Texts*, trans. Linda Coverdale, MacLehose Press, 2011

Dussurget, Gabriel, *Le Magicien d'Aix: mémoires intimes*, Arles, Actes Sud, 2011

Eder, Cyril, *Les Comtesses de la Gestapo*, Paris, Grasset, 2006

Edsel, Robert M., *The Monuments Men: Allied Heroes, Nazi Thieves and the Greatest Treasure Hunt in History*, Preface, 2009

Ehrlich, Evelyn, *Cinema of Paradox: French Filmmaking under the German Occupation*, New York, Columbia University Press, 1985

Eluard, Paul, *Au Rendez-vous allemand*, Paris, Editions de Minuit, 1945

Eparvier, Jean (ed.), *A Paris: sous la botte des Nazis*, Paris, Editions Raymond Schall, 1944

Escott, Beryl E., *The Heroines of SOE: Britain's Secret Women in France*, Stroud, The History Press, 2010

Fabius, Odette, *Un Lever de soleil sur le Mecklembourg: mémoires*, Paris, Albin Michel, 1986

Farago, Ladislas, *The Game of the Foxes: British and German Intelligence Operations and Personalities Which Changed the Course of the Second World War*, Hodder & Stoughton, 1972

Feldman, Gerald and Seibel, Wofgang (eds), *Networks of Nazi Persecution: Bureaucracy, Business and the Organization of the Holocaust*, Oxford, Berghahn Books, 2004

Fenby, Jonathan, *France on the Brink: A Great Civilisation Faces the New Century*, New York, Arcade Publishing, 1998

Fenby, Jonathan, *The General: Charles de Gaulle and the France He Saved*, Simon & Schuster, 2010

Fishman, Sarah, *We Will Wait: Wives of French Prisoners of War, 1940–1945*, New Haven/London, Yale University Press, 1991

Flanner, Janet, *Paris Journal, 1944–55*, New York, Harcourt Brace Jovanovich, 1965

Flanner, Janet, *Paris Journal, 1956–1964*, New York, Harcourt Brace Jovanovich, 1965

Flanner, Janet, *Paris Was Yesterday, 1925–1939*, New York, Viking, 1972

Fogg, Shannon L., *The Politics of Everyday Life in Vichy France*, Cambridge, Cambridge University Press, 2009

Foot, M. R. D., *SOE in France*, Her Majesty's Stationery Office, 1996

Fredj, Jacques, *The Jews of France during the Holocaust*, Paris, Gallimard/Mémorial de la Shoah, 2011

Galtier-Boissière, Jean, *Mon journal pendant l'occupation*, Paris, La Jeune Parque, 1944

Gensburger, Sarah, *Witnessing the Robbing of the Jews: A Photographic Album, Paris, 1940–1944*, trans. Jonathan Hensher with Elisabeth Fourmont, Bloomington, Indiana University Press, 2015

Gildea, Robert, *Fighters in the Shadows: A New History of the French Resistance*, Faber & Faber, 2015

Gildea, Robert, *Marianne in Chains: Everyday Life in the French Heartland under the German Occupation*, New York, Henry Hood, 2002

Gille, Elisabeth, *The Mirador: Dreamed Memories of Irène Némirovsky by her Daughter*, New York, New York Review Books, 2000

Gilles, Cornut-Gentille, *Florence Gould: une Américaine à Paris*, Paris, Mercure de France, 1989

Gilot, Françoise, *Life with Picasso*, New York, McGraw-Hill, 1964

Glass, Charles, *Americans in Paris: Life and Death under Nazi Occupation, 1940–44*, HarperCollins, 2009

Goering, Emmy, *My Life with Goering*, David Bruce & Watson, 1972

Gold, Arthur and Fizdale, Robert, *Misia: The Life of Misia Sert*, Vintage Books, 2002

Goldfarb, Michael, *Emancipation: How Liberating Europe's Jews from the Ghetto Led to Revolution and Renaissance*, Victoria, Australia, Scribe Publications, 2009

Granrut, Claude du, *Le Piano et le violoncelle*, Paris, Editions du Rocher, 2013

Grumberg, Jean-Claude, *Zone Libre*, Paris, Flammarion, 2010

Grunberg, Albert, *Journal d'un coiffeur juif à Paris sous l'Occupation*, Paris, Editions de l'Atelier, 2001

Guéhenno, Jean, *Diary of the Dark Years, 1940–1944: Collaboration, Resistance and Daily Life in Occupied Paris*, trans. David Ball, Oxford, Oxford University Press, 2014

Guéno, Jean-Pierre and Pecnard, Jérôme, *Paroles de l'ombre: lettres et carnets des Français sous l'Occupation (1939–1945)*, Paris, Les Arènes, 2009

Guenther, Irene, *Nazi Chic?: Fashioning Women in the Third Reich*, Oxford, Berg, 2004

Guillemot, Gisèle, *Elles . . . Revenir*, Paris, Editions Tirésias–AERI, 2006

Guyot-Bender, Martine, 'Seducing Corinne: The Official Popular Press during the Occupation', in Melanie Hawthorne and Richard J. Golsan (eds), *Gender and Fascism in Modern France*, Hanover, NH/London, University Press of New England, 1997, pp. 69–82

Halimi, André, *La Délation sous l'Occupation*, Paris, Editions Alain Moreau, 1998

Hardy, Françoise, *Le Désespoir des singes . . . et autres bagatelles*, Paris, Editions Robert Laffont, 2008

Hawthorne, Melanie and Golsan, Richard J. (eds), *Gender and Fascism in Modern France*, Hanover, NJ/London, University Press of New England, 1997

Hazan, Katy and Weill, Georges, *Andrée Salomon: une femme de lumière*, Paris, Collection Témoignages de la Shoah/Editions Le Manuscrit, 2011

Helm, Sarah, *If This Is a Woman: Inside Ravensbrück: Hitler's Concentration Camp for Women*, Little, Brown, 2014

Helm, Sarah, *A Life in Secrets: The Story of Vera Atkins and the Lost Agents of SOE*, Abacus, 2006

Hitchcock, William I., *Liberation: The Bitter Road to Freedom, Europe 1944–1945*, New York, Free Press/Simon & Schuster, 2008

Hitchcock, William I., *The Struggle for Europe: The Turbulent History of a Divided Continent, 1945–Present*, New York, Anchor Books, 2004

Humbert, Agnès, *Résistance: Memoirs of Occupied France*, Bloomsbury, 2008

Jackson, Julian, *France: The Dark Years, 1940–1944*, Oxford, Oxford University Press, 2001

Jamet, Fabienne, *Palace of Sweet Sin*, W. H. Allen, 1977

Janin, Geneviève, *Mémoires de jeunesse, 1934–1945*, Paris, Editions Pays et Terroirs, 2006

Jones, Colin, *Paris: Biography of a City*, Allen Lane, 2004

Jones, R. V., *The Wizard War: British Scientific Intelligence, 1939–1945*, Coronet Books, 1990

Josipovici, Gabriel, *A Life*, London Magazine Editions, 2001

Kaplan, Alice, *The Collaborator: The Trial and Execution of Robert Brasillach*, University of Chicago Press, 2000

Kaplan, Alice, *Dreaming in French: The Paris Years of Jacqueline Bouvier Kennedy, Susan Sontag and Angela Davis*, Chicago, University of Chicago Press, 2012

Kedward, Rod, *Occupied France: Collaboration and Resistance, 1940–44*, Oxford, Wiley-Blackwell, 1991

Killius, Rosemarie, *Frauen für die Front: Gespräche mit Wehrmachtshelferinnen*, trans. Turlach O'Broin, Leipzig, Militzke Verlag, 2003

Kladstrup, Don and Petie, *Wine & War: The French, the Nazis and France's Greatest Treasure*, Coronet Books, 2001

Knoller, Freddie and Landaw, John: *Desperate Journey, Vienna – Paris – Auschwitz*, Metro Books 2002

Koreman, Megan, *The Expectation of Justice: France, 1944–1946*, Durham, NC, Duke University Press, 1999

Kramer, Rita, *Flames in the Field: The Story of Four SOE Agents in Occupied France*, Michael Joseph, 1995

Kruks, Sonia, *Simone de Beauvoir and the Politics of Ambiguity*, Oxford, Oxford University Press, 2012

Laski, Marghanita, *Little Boy Lost*, Persephone Classics, 2008

Lawrence, Marjorie, *Interrupted Melody: An Autobiography*, Sydney, Invincible Press, 1949

Le Boterf, Hervé, *La Vie parisienne sous l'occupation, 1940–1944*, Paris, Editions France-Empire, 1974

Leduc, Violette, *La Bâtarde*, Peter Owen, 1965

London, Lise, *La Ménagère de la Rue Daguerre*, Souvenirs de Résistance, Paris, Seuil 1995

Loridan-Ivens, Marceline, *Et tu n'es pas revenu*, Paris, Grasset, 2015

Lowe, Keith, *Savage Continent: Europe in the Aftermath of World War II*, Viking, 2012

Luchaire, Corinne, *Ma drôle de vie*, repr. Paris, Dualpha Editions, 2003

Ludi, Regula, *Reparations for Nazi Victims in Postwar Europe*, Cambridge, Cambridge University Press, 2012

Malcolm, Janet, *Two Lives: Gertrude and Alice*, New Haven/London, Yale University Press, 2007

Marks, Leo, *Between Silk and Cyanide: A Code Maker's War, 1941–45*, Stroud, The History Press, 2008

Maurel, Micheline, *Ravensbrück*, Anthony Blond, 1958

Maxwell, Betty, *A Mind of my Own: My Life with Robert Maxwell*, Sidgwick & Jackson, 1994

Mesnil-Amar, Jacqueline, *Maman, What Are We Called Now?*, trans. Francine Yorke, Persephone Books, 2015

Mitford, Nancy, *The Blessing*, Penguin Books, 2010

Modiano, Patrick, *Dora Bruder*, Paris, Editions Gallimard, 1997

Modiano, Patrick, *The Search Warrant*, Harvill Secker, 2014

Moltke, Helmuth James von, *Letters to Freya, 1939–1945*, New York, Alfred A. Knopf, 1990

Moorehead, Caroline, *Dunant's Dream: War, Switzerland, and the History of the Red Cross*, New York, Carroll & Graf, 1999

Moorehead, Caroline, *A Train in Winter: An Extraordinary Story of Women, Friendship and Resistance in Occupied France*, HarperCollins, 2011

Moorehead, Caroline, *Village of Secrets: Defying the Nazis in Vichy France*, Chatto & Windus, 2014

Muel-Dreyfus, Francine, *Vichy and the Eternal Feminine: A Contribution to a Political Sociology of Gender*, trans. Kathleen A. Johnson, Durham, NC, Duke University Press, 2001

Muggeridge, Malcolm, *Chronicles of Wasted Time*, vol. 2: *The Infernal Grove*, Fontana, 1975

Némirovsky, Irène, *Suite Française*, trans. Sandra Smith, Chatto & Windus, 2006

Nicholas, Elizabeth, *Death Be Not Proud*, Cresset Press, 1958

Nicholas, Lynn H., *The Rape of Europa: The Fate of Europe's Treasures in the Third Reich and the Second World War*, New York, Vintage, 1995

Ousby, Ian, *Occupation: The Ordeal of France, 1940–1944*, John Murray, 1997

Paxton, Robert, *Vichy France: Old Guard and New Order, 1940–1944*, New York, Alfred A. Knopf, 1972

Paxton, Robert and Marrus, Michael, *Vichy France and the Jews*, New York, Basic Books, 1981

Penrose, Antony (ed.), *Lee Miller's War Beyond D-Day*, Thames & Hudson, 2005

Perrault, Gilles, *Paris under the Occupation*, André Deutsch, 1989

Perry, George, *Bluebell: The Authorized Biography of Margaret Kelly, Founder of the Legendary Bluebell Girls*, Pavilion Books, 1986

Philipponnat, Olivier and Lienhardt, Patrick, *The Life of Irène Némirovsky, 1903–1942*, trans. Euan Cameron, Chatto & Windus, 2010

Picardie, Justine, *Coco Chanel: The Legend and the Life*, HarperCollins, 2010

Pochna, Marie-France, *Christian Dior: The Man Who Made the World Look New*, Aurum Press, 1998

Poznanski, Renée, *Etre juif en France pendant la Seconde Guerre Mondiale*, Paris, Hachette, 1994

Pryce-Jones, David, *Paris in the Third Reich*, New York, Holt, Rinehart & Winston, 1981

Raulet, Sylvie and Baroin, Olivier, *Suzanne Belperron*, Woodbridge, Suffolk, Antique Collectors' Club, 2011

Rémy, Colonel, *La Maison d'Alphonse*, Paris, Librairie Académique Perrin, 1968

Renault, Maisie, *La Grande Misère/Great Misery*, trans. Jeanne Armstrong, Lincoln, Nebr., Zea Books, 2013 (http://digitalcommons.unl.edu/zeabook/19/)

Richard, Jean-Jacques, *L'Histoire des Van Cleef et des Arpels*, Books on Demand, 2010

Richard, Jean-Jacques, *Renée Rachel Van Cleef: l'oubliée de la place Vendôme*, Books on Demand, 2015

Riding, Alan, *And the Show Went On: Cultural Life in Nazi-Occupied Paris*, Duckworth Overlook, 2012

Riffaud, Madeleine, *On l'appelait Rainer (1939–1945)*, Paris, Julliard, 1994

Riols, Noreen, *The Secret Ministry of Ag. & Fish: My Life in Churchill's School for Spies*, Macmillan, 2013

Roberts, Mary Louise, *What Soldiers Do: Sex and the American GI in World War II France*, Chicago, University of Chicago Press, 2013

Rothschild, Philippe de, *Milady Vine: The Autobiography of Philippe de Rothschild*, ed. Joan Littlewood, Century Hutchinson, 1985

Rousset, David, *Le Pitre ne rit pas*, Paris, Christian Bourgois Editeur, 1979

Rousso, Henry, *The Vichy Syndrome: History and Memory in France since 1944*, Boston, Mass., Harvard University Press, 1994

Sabbagh, Antoine, *Lettres de Drancy*, Paris, Editions du Seuil, 2004

Samuel, Vivette, *Rescuing the Children: A Holocaust Memoir*, Madison, University of Wisconsin Press, 2002

Sarkozy, Nicolas, *Georges Mandel: le moine de la politique*, Paris, Grasset, 1994

Say, Rosemary and Holland, Noel, *Rosie's War: An Englishwoman's Escape from Occupied France*, Michael O'Mara Books, 2011

Scali, Arlette, *Une Vie pas comme une autre*, Neuilly-sur-Seine, Michel Lafon, 2003

Schiaparelli, Elsa, *Shocking Life: The Autobiography of Elsa Schiaparelli*, Dent, 1954

Seidel, Ina and Grosser, Hanns, *Dienende Herzen: Kriegsbriefe von Nachrichtenhelferinnen des Heeres*, Berlin, Wilhelm Limpert-Verlag, 1942

Sereny, Gitta, *The Healing Wound: Experiences and Reflections on Germany, 1938–2001*, New York, W. W. Norton, 2002

Seymour-Jones, Carole, *A Dangerous Liaison*, Century, 2008

Shakespeare, Nicholas, *Priscilla: The Hidden Life of an Englishwoman in Wartime France*, Harvill Secker, 2013

Sherwood, John, *Georges Mandel and the Third Republic*, Palo Alto, Calif., Stanford University Press, 1970

Shirer, William L., *The Collapse of the Third Republic: An Inquiry into the Fall of France in 1940*, New York, Simon & Schuster, 1969

Sigmund, Anna Maria, *Women of the Third Reich*, Richmond Hill, Ontario, NDE Publishing, 2000

Signoret, Simone, *Adieu, Volodya*, Random House, 1986

Signoret, Simone, *Nostalgia Isn't What It Used to Be*, Grafton Books, 1979

Sinclair, Anne, *My Grandfather's Gallery: A Legendary Art Dealer's Escape from Vichy France*, trans. Shaun Whiteside, Profile Books, 2014 (first published in France as *21 Rue La Boétie*, Grasset, 2012)

Smith, Emma, *As Green as Grass: Growing Up before, during and after the Second World War*, Bloomsbury, 2013

Spanier, Ginette, *It Isn't All Mink*, Collins, 1959

Spears, Edward, *Assignment to Catastrophe*, vol. 1: *Prelude to Dunkirk, July 1939–May 1940*; vol. 2: *The Fall of France, June 1940*, William Heinemann, 1954

Spotts, Frederic, *The Shameful Peace: How French Artists and Intellectuals Survived the Nazi Occupation*, New Haven/London, Yale University Press, 2010

Stevenson, William, *A Man Called Intrepid: The Incredible WWII Narrative of the Hero Whose Spy Network and Secret Diplomacy Changed the Course of History*, Sphere, 1977

Stourton, Edward, *Cruel Crossing: Escaping Hitler across the Pyrenees*, Black Swan, 2014

Tartière, Drue, *The House near Paris: An American Woman's Story of Traffic in Patriots*, New York, Simon & Schuster, 1946

Teissier du Cros, Janet, *Divided Loyalties: A Scotswoman in Occupied France*, Hamish Hamilton, 1962

Testyler, Arlette and Charles, *Les Enfants aussi!*, Paris, Editions Delattre, 2009

Thurman, Judith, *A Life of Colette: Secrets of the Flesh*, Bloomsbury, 1999

Tillion, Germaine, *Ravensbrück*, Paris, Editions du Seuil, 1973 (1st edn 1946)

Todorov, Tzvetan, *A French Tragedy: Scenes of Civil War, Summer 1944*, Hanover, NH, University Press of New England, 1996

Tooze, Adam, *The Wages of Destruction*, Allen Lane, 2006

Ullmann, Bernard, *Lisette de Brinon, ma mère: une juive dans la tourmente de la collaboration*, Paris, Editions Complexe, 2004

Valland, Rose, *Le Front de l'art: défense des collections françaises, 1939–41*, Paris, Plon, 1961

Vaughan, Hal, *Doctor to the Resistance: The Heroic True Story of an American Surgeon and his Family in Occupied Paris*, Washington, DC, Brassey's, 2004

Veillon, Dominique, *Fashion under the Occupation*, Oxford/New York, Berg, 2002

Verity, Hugh, *We Landed by Moonlight*, Ian Allan, 1978

Villiers, José, *Granny Was a Spy*, Quartet Books, 1988

Virgili, Fabrice, *La France 'virile': des femmes tondues à la Libération*, Paris, Editions Payot & Rivages, 2004

Virgili, Fabrice, *Naître ennemi: les enfants de couples franco-allemands nés pendant la Seconde Guerre mondiale*, Paris, Payot, 2009

Weiss, Jonathan, *Irène Némirovsky: Her Life and Works*, Palo Alto, Calif., Stanford University Press, 2006

Weiss, Stephen J., *Second Chance: In Combat with the US Texas Infantry, the OSS, and the French Resistance during the Liberation of France, 1943–1946*, Saffron Walden, Military History Publishing, 2011

Welsh Hemingway, Mary, *How It Was*, New York, Alfred A. Knopf, 1976

Wieviorka, Annette, *Déportation et Génocide: Entre la mémoire et l'oubli*, Plon, 1992

Wrona, Carole, *Corinne Luchaire: un colibri dans la tempête*, Paris, La Tour Verte, 2011

Zuccotti, Susan, *The Holocaust, the French, and the Jews*, New York, Basic Books, 1993

Zuccotti, Susan, *Père Marie-Benoît and Jewish Rescue: How a French Priest Together with Jewish Friends Saved Thousands during the Holocaust*, Bloomington, Indiana University Press, 2013

Articles etc

A qui appartenaient ces tableaux?, exhibition catalogue published jointly by the
    Israel Museum, Jerusalem, and the Musée d'art et d'histoire du Judaïsme,
    Paris, 2008

Auslander, Leora, 'Coming Home? Jews in Postwar Paris', *Journal of
    Contemporary History*, vol. 40, 2005, pp. 237–59

Bradshaw, Peter, '*Violette* Review – Fine Biopic of Simone de Beauvoir's
    Protégée', *Guardian*, 2 October 2014 (http://www.theguardian.com/
    film/2014/oct/02/violette-review-biopic-simone-de-beauvoir)

Childs, Martin, 'Co-conspirator in the plot to assassinate Hitler', *Independent*,
    11 January 2010

Clarens, Jeannie, Vicomtesse de (née Rousseau), video interview with David
    Ignatius, International Spy Museum, Washington, DC

Enrici, Michel, 'Edmonde Charles-Roux parle de la Comtesse Lily Pastré',
    Culture 13, http://www.culture-13.fr/agenda/edmonde-charles-roux-parle-de-
    la-comtesse-lily-pastre.html

Fenby, Jonathan, 'Charles de Gaulle and the French Resistance', http://
    fivebooks.com/interview/jonathan-fenby-on-charles-de-gaulle-and-the-
    french-resistance/

Fleury, Jacqueline, 'Témoignage de Jacqueline Fleury (née Marié)', http://
    lesamitiesdelaresistance.fr/lien17-fleury.pdf

Flitterman-Lewis, Sandy, 'Anouk Aimée', *Jewish Women: A Comprehensive
    Historical Encyclopedia*, Jewish Women's Archive, 2009 (http://jwa.org/
    encyclopedia/article/aimee-anouk)

Fontaine, Thomas, 'Chronology of Repression and Persecution in Occupied
    France, 1940–44', *Online Encyclopedia of Mass Violence*, 2007, http://www.
    massviolence.org/chronology-of-repression-and-persecution-in-occupied-
    france

Fort, José, interview with Lise London: 'Lise London, Combattante depuis son
    enfance', *L'Humanité*, republished 1 April 2012

Franklin, Ruth, 'The Art of Extinction: The Bleak Laughter of Thomas
    Bernhard', *New Yorker*, 25 December 2006 (http://www.newyorker.com/
    magazine/2006/12/25/the-art-of-extinction)

Franklin, Ruth, 'A Life in Good Taste: The Fashions and Follies of Elsie de
    Wolfe', *New Yorker*, 27 September 2004 (http://www.newyorker.com/
    magazine/2004/09/27/a-life-in-good-taste)

Goetz, Henri, 'My Life, my Friends', http://henrigoetz.com/index.php?/
    tests-goetz/my-life/

Grady, Denise, 'Florence Waren, Jewish Dancer Who Resisted Nazis, Dies at
    95', *New York Times*, 4 August 2012 (http://www.nytimes.com/2012/08/05/
    world/europe/florence-waren-dancer-who-resisted-nazis-dies-at-95.ht)

Grice, Elizabeth, 'How the Diaries of Hélène Berr, the "Anne Frank
    of France", Came to be Published', *Daily Telegraph*, 30 October
    2008 (http://www.telegraph.co.uk/culture/books/3562700/)

How-the-diaries-of-Helene-Berr-the-Anne-Frank-of-France-came-to-be-published.html)

Heminway, John, 'A Legendary Flying Doctor's Dark Secret', *Financial Times*, 21 May 2010

Ignatius, David, 'After Five Decades, a Spy Tells her Tale', *Washington Post*, 28 December 1998 (http://www.tournemire.net/jeannie.htm)

Ivry, Benjamin, 'Confronting Father's Mountain of Exaggerations', *Forward*, 13 October 2012

Lavigue, Robert, 'Panthéonisations résistantes . . . On l'a échappé belle!', 20 February 2014, http://lavigue.blogspot.gr/2014/02/pantheonisations-resistantes-on-la.html

Mania Stanton, Miriam, 'Escape from the Inferno of Europe', ed. Ben Stanton, unpublished ms

Melanson, Elizabeth, 'The Influence of Jewish Society Patrons on Renoir's Stylistic Transformation in the Mid-1880s', *Nineteenth-Century Art Worldwide*, vol. 12, issue 2, Autumn 2013 (http://www.19thc-artworldwide.org/autumn13/melanson-on-renoir-and-the-influence-of-jewish-patrons)

Modiano, Patrick, 'Lettre à Thierry Laurent', http://lereseaumodiano.blogspot.co.uk/2011/11/lettre-thierry-laurent.html

Moorehead, Caroline, 'Sleeping with the Enemy', *Intelligent Life*, September/October 2013 (http://www.intelligentlifemagazine.com/content/features/anonymous/sleeping-enemy)

Péry d'Alincourt, Jacqueline, 'Surviving Ravensbrück: "Forgive, Don't Forget"', https://www.utexas.edu/cola/insts/france-ut/_files/pdf/resources/Pery.pdf

Richardson, John, 'Picasso's Broken Vow', *New York Review of Books*, 25 June 2015

Roberts, Mary Louise, 'The Price of Discretion: Prostitution, Venereal Disease, and the American Military in France, 1944–1946', *American Historical Review*, October 2010, pp. 1002–30

Roden, Franz, 'Paris 1943: Eindrücke dieses Sommers', *Das Reich*, no. 31, 1 August 1943

Rodríguez, Jesús, 'The Last Female Veteran', *El País*, 20 December 2011

Rogister, John, review of Yves Pourcher, *Pierre Laval vu par sa fille, d'après ses carnets intimes* (Paris, Cherche Midi, 2002), *Parliaments, Estates and Representations*, vol. 25, issue 1, 2005, p. 251

Sabbagh, Antoine, 'Sir, you will no longer consider yourself my son', *Guardian*, 11 July 2009 (http://www.theguardian.com/lifeandstyle/2009/jul/11/antoine-sabbagh-family-nazis-resistance)

Sapiro, Gisèle, 'Portrait of the Writer as a Traitor: The French Purge Trials (1944–1953)', trans. Jennifer Birkett, 2006, https://erea.revues.org/257

Taylor, Alexandra, 'Part IV: France <3 Food – Adapting to the Ration System', https://tayloralexandra.wordpress.com/2012/02/18/part-iv-france-3-food-adapting-to-the-ration-system/

Thatcher, Nicole and Tolansky, Ethel (eds), 'Six Authors in Captivity: Literary

Responses to the Occupation of France', *New Zealand Journal of French Studies*, vol. 28, 2007, chapter on Madeleine Riffaud, pages 111–141

Thibaudat, Jean-Pierre, 'Le Jour où Copeau a exclu les acteurs juifs du Français', *Libération*, 2 January 1995 (http://www.liberation.fr/culture/1995/01/02/le-jour-ou-copeau-a-exclu-les-acteurs-juifs-du-francais_117860)

Wassem, Violette, 'Violette's Story: Paris – Life during the Occupation', July 1997, http://timewitnesses.org/english/~viol2.html

Wechsberg, Joseph, 'A Reporter in France: The Finest Butter and Lots of Time', *New Yorker*, 3 September 1949 (http://www.newyorker.com/magazine/1949/09/03/the-finest-butter-and-lots-of-time)

Workman, Debra, 'Engendering the Repatriation: The Return of Female Political Deportees to France Following the Second World War', http://quod.lib.umich.edu/w/wsfh/0642292.0035.017/--engendering-the-repatriation-the-return-of-female-political?rgn=main;view=fulltext

CAST

Abetz, Suzanne (died 1958) French-born wife of Otto Abetz, German Ambassador to Vichy government

Alsop, Susan Mary (1918–2004) American, born in Rome, came to Paris in 1945 with her diplomat husband and fell in love with Duff Cooper, British Ambassador, whose child she secretly bore

Arletty (1898–1992) Popular French actress and singer known for her wisecracks, imprisoned briefly in 1945 for wartime liaison with a Luftwaffe officer, Hans-Jürgen Soehring

Arpels, Hélène (née Ostrowska) (1907–2006) Model born in Monte Carlo to Russian parents, married Louis Arpels in 1933 and moved to New York

Atkins, Vera (1908–2000) Romanian-born head of SOE's French Section based in London, never married

Aubrac, Lucie (1912–2007) Catholic teacher and resister, married Jewish resister Raymond Samuel and helped organize a daring escape for him, later a government minister

Belperron, Suzanne (1900–83) Influential and original jewellery designer based in Paris who took over the business from Bernard Herz, the Jewish owner, under compulsory aryanization

Berr, Hélène (1921–45) Gifted Sorbonne student who refused to escape but wrote a diary of her daily travails, helping her parents and abandoned children

Bretty, Béatrice (1893–1982) Comédie-Française actress who left the company to support her lover, politician Georges Mandel, and his daughter Claude

Brinon, Lisette de (née Jeanne Louise Rachel Franck) (1896–1982) Married, first, Jewish banker Claude Ullmann; second, Fernand, Marquis de Brinon, Catholic aristocrat and Vichy activist who made her an honorary Aryan

Bucher, Jeanne (1872–1946) Avant-garde gallery-owner who supported many banned artists; divorcee

Camondo, Béatrice de (later Reinach) (1894–1944) Born into prominent Jewish banking family, converted to Catholicism, went riding with Germans but was arrested with her two children and killed at Auschwitz

Carven, Marie-Louise (née Carmen de Tommaso) (1909–2015) French fashion designer who founded the house of Carven in 1945 for petite women

Casadesus, Gisèle (1915–) Comédie-Française actress who joined as a *pensionnaire* in 1934, worked throughout the war and left in 1962. She continued to act in films and had a second career in her 90s

Casanova, Danielle (1909–43) Communist women's organizer and resister

Chanel, Gabrielle 'Coco' (1883–1971) Influential French fashion designer who closed her shop at the beginning of the war and lived at the Ritz with a German lover

Chevrillon, Claire (1907–2011) Teacher, resister, spent four months in prison in Paris

Chevrillon, Vivou (later de Boysson) Musician cousin of Claire, worked on forged identity cards

Child, Julia (1912–2004) American-born cook and educator who discovered French cooking when she came to live in Paris with her husband in 1948

Churchill, Odette (formerly Sansom) (1912–1995) British SOE agent, mother of three children, captured in France in 1943. She maintained she was married to Peter Churchill, nephew of the Prime Minister. Eventually released in 1945 after almost a year in Ravensbrück and was one of the first women to win the George Cross

Colette, Sidonie Gabrielle (1873–1954) French novelist who remained anxiously in Paris during the Occupation even though her Jewish husband Maurice Goudeket had once been arrested by the Gestapo

d'Albert-Lake, Virginia (1910–97) American resister with Comet line, imprisoned in Ravensbrück

de Beauvoir, Simone (1908–86) Feminist writer and long-term lover of Jean-Paul Sartre

de Gaulle Anthonioz, Geneviève (1920–2002) Resister with Défense de la France, imprisoned in Ravensbrück, niece of General de Gaulle

de Gaulle, Sylvie (1925–2012) Resister and daughter of the Anglophile painter Charles Geoffroy-Dechaume, married Bernard de Gaulle, nephew of the General

de Gaulle, Yvonne (1900–79) Wife of General Charles de Gaulle, widely known as Tante Yvonne to French public

de Wolfe, Elsie (later Mendl) (1859–1950) American-born interior decorator and influential Parisian hostess

Desnos, Youki (formerly Lucie Badoul) (1903–66) Daring model and muse married to surrealist poet and resister Robert Desnos who died at Theresienstadt

Dior, Catherine (1917–2008) Resister and sister of designer Christian Dior, she was a member of the Polish intelligence unit based in France but was arrested in July 1944 and deported to Ravensbrück

Dufournier, Denise (later McAdam Clark) (1915–94) French novelist, barrister and resister who wrote an early account of Ravensbrück, called *La maison des mortes*, after she was imprisoned there in 1943

Fabius, Odette (née Schmoll) (1910–90) French Jewish resister, one of the few women who tried to escape from Ravensbrück, fell in love with Marseilles trade union leader and fellow resistant Pierre Ferri-Pisani

Ferriday, Caroline (1902–90) American philanthropist and Francophile who devoted her life to helping Polish women experimented on by Nazis in Ravensbrück

Flanner, Janet (1892–1978) American writer and journalist who worked as Paris correspondent of the *New Yorker* from 1925

Fleury, Jacqueline (née Marié) (1923–) Teenage resister imprisoned in Ravensbrück with her mother, survived the death march with her and became active member of ADIR and speaker

Gilot, Françoise (1921–) Young painter in Paris, lover and muse of Pablo Picasso 1944–53 and mother of two of his children, Claude and Paloma

Gould, Florence (née Lacaze) (1895–1983) American beauty married to wealthy older philanthropist Frank Jay Gould, became Paris hostess during the war entertaining many Germans

Haag, Inga (née Abshagen) (1918–2009) German socialite, journalist and spy, worked for Admiral Wilhelm Canaris in Paris, opposed Nazis

Hardy, Françoise (1944–) French singer and actress who won huge fame with her first recording in 1962, 'Tous les Garçons et les Filles'

Humbert, Agnès (1894–1963) Resister with the Musée de l'Homme group, divorced mother, author of diary called *Résistance*

Inayat Khan, Noor (Nora Baker) (1914–44) Russian-born Indian princess, part American, Paris-educated musician and writer, became an SOE agent, murdered at Dachau

Jackson, Charlotte 'Toquette' (1889–1968) French nurse who married Sumner Jackson and helped run the American Hospital in Paris, a resister and Ravensbrück survivor

Jamet, Fabienne (née Georgette Plagie ?) Nightclub- and brothel-owner who wrote racy memoirs called *Palace of Sweet Sin* about her time running the infamous One Two Two

Kaminker, Simone (later Signoret) (1921–95) French Jewish cinema actress who started working for collaborationist journal of Jean Luchaire, wrote autobiographical novel *Adieu Volodya*

Kelly, Margaret (later Leibovici) (1910–2004) Irish-born dancer who founded the Bluebell Girls in Paris and sheltered Jewish pianist husband Marcel Leibovici

Lanvin, Jeanne (1867–1946) Former milliner and founder of French couture house Lanvin, whose daughter became the Comtesse de Polignac

Laval, Josée (later Comtesse de Chambrun) (1911–92) Only daughter of Vichy politician Pierre Laval, married lawyer Count René de Chambrun and never gave up fight to defend her father's innocence

Lawrence, Marjorie (1907–79) Australian soprano and noted Wagnerian, rival of Germaine Lubin

Leduc, Violette (1907–72) Bisexual novelist befriended and nurtured by Simone de Beauvoir, whose frank autobiography has been adapted as a film, *Violette* (2014)

Leigh, Vera (1903–44) Leeds-born Paris-educated milliner and resister, became British SOE agent parachuted into France, captured in 1944 and executed at Natzweiler-Struthof camp

Liwarrak, Rosa (later Lady Lipworth) (1933–) Child victim hidden during war, later a state orphan, now a London-based philanthropist

London, Lise (née Ricol) (1916–2012) Member of communist women's resistance, wife of Spanish Civil War veteran Artur London

Lubin, Germaine (1890–1979) French dramatic soprano and Wagnerian praised by Hitler and other Nazis, later punished for alleged Nazi sympathies

Luchaire, Corinne (1921–50) Actress daughter of Vichy newspaper editor Jean Luchaire, married twice, died of TB, leaving orphan child

Luchaire, Ghita (1904–?) Sister of Jean Luchaire, married to Théodore Fraenkel, a Jewish doctor and writer

Maar, Dora (née Henriette Theodora Marković) (1907–97) Part Argentinian, part Croatian Jewish and French Catholic, photographer, poet, artist and Picasso's lover and muse for nearly a decade from 1936

MacCarthy, Marie-France (1919–2011) Resister and daughter of the Anglophile painter Charles Geoffroy-Dechaume, married British paediatrician Dermod MacCarthy

Maurel, Micheline (1916–2009) Communist resister and teacher imprisoned in Ravensbrück, wrote one of the first books about the camp

Mesnil-Amar, Jacqueline (1909–87) Assimilated Jewish mother and writer, author of *Maman, What Are We Called Now?*, became Jewish activist for deportees

Meynard, Elisabeth (later Dr Betty Maxwell) (1921–2013) Worked as interpreter for the Welcome Committee in Paris where she met her husband Robert Maxwell

Miller, Lee (later Lady Penrose) (1907–77) American fashion model and photographer, lived in Paris with Man Ray and later became accredited war photographer for *Vogue*

Mitford, Nancy (1904–73) English novelist, eldest of the renowned Mitford sisters, involved in long-term relationship with French politician Gaston Palewski, moved to Paris in 1945

Morris, Violette (1893–1944) French lesbian athlete who won gold and silver medals at Women's World Games in 1921–2 but collaborated with Gestapo in Paris after French officials disqualified her

Némirovsky, Irène (1903–42) Russian-born French writer, died in Auschwitz, whose unfinished novel *Suite Française* became a bestseller when it was published in 2004

Oddon, Yvonne (1902–82) Resister with Musée de l'Homme group

Pastré, Comtesse Lily (1891–1974) French liquor heiress who sheltered many Jewish artists and musicians in her chateau near Marseilles and after the war helped establish the Aix-en-Provence opera festival

Péry d'Alincourt, Jacqueline (1919–2009) Resister friend of Geneviève de Gaulle in Ravensbrück and of Caroline Ferriday in post-war America

Piaf, Edith (1915–1963) French singer and actress who controversially visited Germany and entertained prisoners of war

Portes, Comtesse Hélène des (1902–40) Fascist sympathizer, mistress of Prime Minister Paul Reynaud

Puissant, Renée (née Rachel Van Cleef) (1896–1942) Heiress of the jewellery firm Van Cleef & Arpels who committed suicide in Vichy

Renty, Comtesse Germaine de (1899–1994) Resister with Alliance network, imprisoned in Ravensbrück, later hosted Jacqueline Bouvier in Paris

Riffaud, Madeleine (1924–) Journalist, poet and teenage resister who took a man's name, Rainer, killed a German soldier in the final days of the Occupation and was threatened with execution

Rigal, Sadie (aka Florence, later Waren) (1917–2012) South African-born Jewish dancer who worked at Bal Tabarin music hall and helped refugees and resisters

Riols, Noreen (1925–) Born in Malta to British parents, became F Section (SOE) operative in London

Rol-Tanguy, Cécile (1919–) Liaison agent of Henri Rol-Tanguy, her husband, and communist resister

Rothschild, Elisabeth de (née Pelletier de Chambure) (1902–45) Wife of Philippe de Rothschild, mother of Philippine, killed in Ravensbrück

Rousseau, Jeannie (later Vicomtesse de Clarens) (1919–) Early resister in the Druids network who evaded Gestapo agents while gathering crucial information on the Germans' emerging flying-bomb and rocket programmes. Eventually sent to Ravensbrück where she organized a protest in the Torgau munitions factory

Rozenberg, Marceline (later Loridan Ivens) (1928–) Writer and film director whose prize-winning memoir *But You Did Not Come Back* details her time in Auschwitz-Birkenau

Salomon, Andrée (1908–1985) Worked with OSE to save Jewish children

Sandzer (later Stantun), **Miriam** (1914–2005) Polish-born daughter of lingerie manufacturer, who with English fiancé was trapped in France for months

Say, Rosemary (1919–1996) English girl working as nanny trapped in Paris after fall of France, later worked for SOE in London

Scali, Arlette (1911–2011) Jewish socialite who escaped Paris and survived in south of France, close friend of Vichy functionary Colonel Marty and Renée Puissant (née Rachel Van Cleef)

Schiaparelli, Elsa (1890–1973) Italian fashion designer, influential in Paris between the wars

Schoenebeck, Maximiliane 'Catsy' von (1899–1978) Half-sister of British writer Sybille Bedford, once married to Hans Günther von Dincklage, Chanel's lover, imprisoned during war and after

Sinclair, Anne (1948–) French television journalist and granddaughter of Paul Rosenberg, Picasso's art dealer, still fighting for her family's looted art

Smith, Emma (1923–) British writer who went to stay with the Geoffroy-Dechaume family after the war and wrote a successful novel in 1948 while staying in a Paris hotel

Spanier, Ginette (1904–1988) Paris-born, English-educated, married to French Jewish doctor when war broke out. They fled the capital and helped refugees. She became Directrice for Balmain

Szabo, Violette (1921–1945) Joined SOE after her Hungarian husband, with whom she had a daughter Tania, was killed, but was captured in France in 1944 and sent to Ravensbrück, where she was executed. Posthumously awarded George Cross

Tartière, Drue (née Leyton) (1903–97) American actress and resister who married Frenchman Jacques Tartière

Teissier du Cros, Janet (née Grierson) (1905–90) Born in Scotland, married to François Teissier du Cros, scion of an old French Protestant family

Testyler, Arlette (1933–) Survivor of the Vél d'Hiv round-up of 1942 and other camps, who has devoted adult life to testifying

Tillion, Germaine (1907–2008) Ethnographer and resister with Musée de l'Homme group, wrote operetta while imprisoned in Ravensbrück alongside her mother, art historian, Emilie Tillion

Toussaint, Jeanne (1887–1976) Cartier's creative director 1933–70, Louis Cartier's lover and the woman who inspired panther jewellery beloved of the Duchess of Windsor

Valland, Rose Antonia (1898–1980) Blacksmith's daughter who became a volunteer assistant curator at the Jeu de Paume Museum and later directed the commission working in Germany to recover looted art

Wiborg, Mary 'Hoytie' Hoyt (1888–1964) American heiress active in expatriate circles in Paris, also art patron, collector, critic and amateur playwright

Witherington, Pearl (later Cornioley) (1914–2008) Born in Paris to British parents, SOE agent parachuted into France, became leader of Wrestler network

ACKNOWLEDGEMENTS

My first thanks must go to all those who experienced the events described in this book. I have been lucky enough to meet several women who, perhaps as children or teenagers during the war years, were forced to act the part of adults and have often retained vivid memories. These are extraordinarily valuable for anyone trying to recreate what it felt like to live through years that are often beyond imagining. Talking to these women has, without exception, been a privilege. In addition to these few survivors, many wrote about their experiences at the time and I have also been fortunate to meet the children and grandchildren of survivors.

I would also like to thank numerous institutions and the individuals who work there, for their help both in France and in England. In Paris, the Mémorial de la Shoah is where my research started as I stared at a wall with the name Anna Rubinstein, my own childhood name, and one of France's many victims carved on it. I have also consulted in Paris the Archives Nationales at Pierrefitte-sur-Seine, the Bibliothèque Nationale, the Musée des Arts Decoratifs, the Musée de la Résistance Nationale at Champigny-sur-Marne, the Musée d'Art et d'Histoire du Judaïsme. Christine Levisse-Touzé, Directrice du Mémorial du Maréchal Leclerc et de la Libération de Paris and of the Musée Jean Moulin Camille Guédon, and Anne-Marie Pavillard at the Bibliothèque de Documentation Internationale Contemporaine (BDIC) deserve a special mention, as does Sophie le Tarnec at the Musée Nissim de Camondo. In Lyons, the Centre d'Histoire de la Résistance et de la Déportation was chillingly fascinating and in England the National Archives at Kew, the Imperial War Museum, the British Library, the Library and Cinema of the Institut Français as well as the Churchill Archives Centre in Cambridge have all helped me with finding particular documentation. In particular, the staff of the London Library have gone out of their way, as ever, to find at short notice articles and books for me to take home and consult at leisure and I cannot imagine undertaking this task without their help.

I have a special debt of gratitude to Natasha Lehrer in Paris, who explored with me, researched, translated, debriefed and made valuable suggestions of avenues to examine; to Nicola and Christopher Beauman, who encouraged me to pursue this idea from the first, as did Jennie McCahey, who remembered hearing about her mother's adventures in Paris in the 1940s with dollar bills sewn into her coat lining for emergencies.

I would also like to thank the following for their help and contributions: Nicole Alby, Michel Aliaga (Cartier), Vicki Anstey, Melanie Aspey (Rothschild Archives), David Barrie, Patrick Bade, Sally Bedell Smith, Roderick Bailey, Her Excellency Sylvie Bermann (French Ambassador), Vivou de Boysson, Ruth Brandon, Tom Bower, Lorna Bown, Tim Buckmaster, Caroline Brothers, William Banks-Blaney, Katell le Bourhis, Georges Bensoussan (Mémorial de la Shoah), Robert Bensoussan, Euan Cameron, Catherine Cariou (Van Cleef & Arpels), Gisèle Casadesus, Sir Charles Chadwyck-Healey and the Chadwyck-Healey Liberation Collection at Cambridge University Library, Joan Chapman, Hilary Cartmel, Karin Demorest, Andrée Doucet, Davina Eastwood, Dorothea Elkon (on behalf of Françoise Gilot), Rachel Erlbaum, Jamie Fontaine (Connecticut Landmark Trust), Henrietta Foster, James Fox, Moris Farhi, Nicole Farhi, Jonathan and Renée Fenby, Sophie Faudel, Jonathan Fryer, Claude Fillet, Andrew Franklin, Professor Lawrence Goldman, Sally Gordon Mark, Claude du Granrut, Bernard de Gaulle, the late Geneviève de Gaulle Anthonioz, Lucienne Hamon, Emmanuel Hamon, Janie Hampton, Kristin Havill, Lady Selina Hastings, Georgina Hayman, Marie-Claude Hayman, Sarah Helm, Lisa Hilton, Vincent Houghton (Washington Spy Museum), David Ignatius, Julian Jackson, Philip Jackson, Véronique Jaeger (Galerie Jeanne Bucher Jaeger), John Jammes, Sylvie Jessua-Amar, Gabriel Josipovici, Mark Kidel, Claude-Catherine Kiejman, Freddy Knoller, Sarah Lawson, Katell Le Bourhis, Lawrence Lever, Jeremy Lewison, Lady (Rosa) Lipworth, Caroline McAdam Clark, Giles MacDonogh, Jennie McCahey,

Sophie MacCarthy, Aliette Martin, Hedwige Morris-Gillet, Caroline Moorehead, Anne-Elisabeth Moutet, Anne-Solange Noble, Julian Nundy, Turlach O'Broin, Laurent Papillault, Antony Penrose, Justine Picardie, Diana Pinto, Munro Price, David Pryce-Jones Evelyne Possémé, Pierre Rainero, Jean-Jacques Richard, Alan Riding, Madeleine Riffaud, Noreen Riols, John Rogister, Dr Martin Roth, Cécile Rol-Tanguy, Tatiana de Rosnay, Baron Eric de Rothschild, Nicola Russell, Beatrice Saalburg, Claudine Sablier (Boucheron), Agathe Sanjuan, Claudine Seroussi, Nicholas Shakespeare, Anne Sinclair, Zhivka Slavova, Emma Smith, Barbara Probst Solomon, Nicola Solomon, Andy Smith, Sarah Sheridan, Mica Schlosser, Mark Sullivan, Carolyn Sumberg, Arlette and Charles Testyler, Phil Tomaselli, Robert Tombs, Olav Van Cleef, Marc Vellay, Ginette Vincendeau, Edmund de Waal, Jeanne Wilkins, Sarah Wilson, Stanislas de Quercize and Françoise Xenakis. I am grateful to the Harry Ransom Center, The University of Texas at Austin, for permission to quote from a letter written by Allanah Harper to Sybille Bedford.

Many people have improved the book and I am enormously grateful to them. I would like to thank Peter James, my incomparable copy editor, Christopher Phipps for an exemplary index, Dr Jean-Marc Dreyfus, who read the manuscript and corrected many mistakes, Lucinda McNeile, Simon Wright and Elizabeth Allen and the team at Orion who have all worked hard on various aspects of the book. But in addition, before they set to work, I have enjoyed the stimulating and unwavering support and advice of three people: Alan Samson in London, Charlie Spicer in New York and my agent, Clare Alexander, and I thank them all most warmly.

Finally – to my family a verbal bouquet. Adam, Amy and Imogen have given me technical advice and offered support in numerous ways during the research for and writing of this book and I thank them all, especially my daughter Imogen for providing several stimulating suggestions as well as practical help with proof reading and other tasks, and my beloved husband Mark for listening as well as sharing many journeys, metaphorical and real – in anguish to Ravensbrück, with incomprehension to Vichy; as well as occasionally, with pleasure, to Paris, the city where he lived before he knew me. As ever, all mistakes are my own.

LIST OF ILLUSTRATIONS

Notice in a shoe shop indicating a shelter for customers (Roger-Violett / Topfoto)

Jeanne Lanvin's cylindrical bag for a gas mask (Diktats Bookstore)

Gabrielle 'Coco' Chanel in her suite at the Ritz Hotel (Roger-Viollet / Topfoto)

Irène Némirovsky (Roger-Viollet / Topfoto)

Corinne Luchaire publicity shot (Photos 12 / Alamy)

Bernard Herz (Mémorial de la Shoah)

Refugee women and children fleeing Paris, 1940 (FPG / Hulton Archive / Getty)

Women scrutinize the first official lists of the wounded and captured (Print Collector / Alamy)

German Occupation propaganda poster (Photos 12 / Alamy)

German soldiers outside the Moulin Rouge, summer 1940 (Art Media / Print Collector / Getty)

German auxiliaries ('Grey Mice') at Printemps department store (Roger-Viollet / Topfoto)

Dancers at the Moulin de la Galette (Roger Schall)
   Queuing for bread during rationing (Keystone-France / Getty)

Workshop to mend mesh stockings (LAPI / Roger-Violett / Getty)

Shopping for underwear with coupons (Roger-Viollet / Topfoto)

Béatrice Bretty as Dorine in *Tartuffe* (Coll. Comédie-Française)

Looting of the Paris home of former minister Georges Mandel (Roger-Viollet / Topfoto)

Rose Valland (Everett Collection Historical / Alamy)

Jeanne Bucher (Jeanne Bucher Jaeger, Paris)

French Jews and foreigners arrested, 14 May 1941 (AFP / Getty)

Le Juif et la France exhibition at the Palais Berlitz, 1941 (RDA / TAL / Getty)

SECOND PLATE SECTION

Fashion show of the milliner Madame Agnès's 1941 collection (Private collection)

Day of Elegance on Bicycles, June 1942 (LAPI / Roger-Viollet / Getty)

Open-air hairdresser (Robert Doisneau / Gamma-Rapho / Getty)

1942 evening clutch bag made by Boucheron (Boucheron)

Women and children shelter in a metro station (Robert Doisneau / Gamma-Rapho / Getty)

Two girls with yellow stars, 1942 (Fratelli Alinari Museum Collections-Favrod Collection, Florence / Bridgeman)

Buses used in the Vél d'Hiv round-up on 16 and 17 July 1942 (Roger-Viollet / Topfoto)

Washing clothes in the courtyard at Drancy (Roger-Viollet / Getty)

Renée Puissant, 1942 (Private collection)

Béatrice de Camondo Reinach (Photo Les Arts Décoratifs, Paris)

THIRD PLATE SECTION

Milliners on strike (AGIP / Bridgeman)
Emma Smith, July 1948 (Robert Doisneau / Gamma-Rapho / Getty)
Julia Child (Paul Child / Schlesinger Library, Harvard University)
Princess Elizabeth in Paris, 15 May 1948 (Keystone / Getty)
The Murphy sisters on the *Queen Elizabeth* (Private collection)
Germaine de Renty (Claude du Granrut)
Gisèle Casadesus (Author's collection)
Rachel Erlbaum (Author's collection)
Renée Fenby
Jacqueline Fleury (Author's collection)
Rosa Lipworth
Madeleine Riffaud (Author's collection)
Noreen Riols (Philipppe Petit / Getty)
Cécile Rol-Tanguy (Author's collection)
Marceline Rosenberg (Dominique Faget / AFP / Getty)
Emma Smith (Suki Dhanda)
Barbara Probst Solomon (Author's collection)
Arlette (with Charles) Testyler

INDEX

Italic page numbers refer to illustrations.